INSIGHT GUIDES
SOUTH KOREA

APA PUBLICATIONS
Part of the Langenscheidt Publishing Group

✠ INSIGHT GUIDE
SOUTH KOREA

Editorial

Project Editor
Tom Le Bas
Art Director
Ian Spick
Picture Manager
Steven Lawrence
Series Manager
Rachel Fox

Distribution

UK & Ireland
GeoCenter International Ltd
Meridian House, Churchill Way West
Basingstoke, Hampshire RG21 6YR
sales@geocenter.co.uk

United States
Langenscheidt Publishers, Inc.
36–36 33rd Street 4th Floor
Long Island City, NY 11106
orders@langenscheidt.com

Australia
Universal Publishers
1 Waterloo Road
Macquarie Park, NSW 2113
sales@universalpublishers.com.au

New Zealand
Hema Maps New Zealand Ltd (HNZ)
Unit 2, 10 Cryers Road
East Tamaki, Auckland 2013
sales.hema@clear.net.nz

Worldwide
**Apa Publications GmbH & Co.
Verlag KG (Singapore branch)**
7030 Ang Mo Kio Avenue 5
08-65 Northstar @ AMK
Singapore 569880
apasin@singnet.com.sg

Printing

CTPS - China

©2010 Apa Publications GmbH & Co.
Verlag KG (Singapore branch)
All Rights Reserved

First Edition 1981
Ninth Edition 2010

ABOUT THIS BOOK

The first Insight Guide pioneered
the use of creative full-color
photography in travel guides in
1970. Since then, we have
expanded our range to cater for
our readers' need not only for
reliable information about their
chosen destination but also for a
real understanding of the culture
and workings of that destination.
Now, when the internet can supply
inexhaustible (but not always reliable) facts, our books marry
text and pictures to provide
those much more elusive
qualities: knowledge
and discernment.
To achieve this,
they rely heavily on
the authority and experi-
ence of locally based writers
and photographers.

This fully updated edition of
Insight Guide: South Korea is

structured to convey an understanding of this fascinating country and its
culture, and to guide readers through
its major sights and activities:

◆ The **Features** section, indicated
by a pink bar at the top of each page,
covers the history and culture of
South Korea in a series of informative essays.

◆ The main **Places** section, indicated by a blue bar, is a guide to the
sights and areas worth visiting.
Places of special interest are
coordinated by number with
the maps.

◆ The **Travel Tips**
listings section,
with a yellow bar,
provides a handy point of reference for information on
travel, hotels, shops, restaurants and more. An index to
the section is on the back
flap of the book.

LEFT: tradi... music at the Centre for Traditional Performing Arts

Architecture were comprehensively revised by **Ed Peters**, a travel writer, journalist and long-standing Insight contributor who has been based in Hong Kong for the past 20 years and makes frequent trips to South Korea.

The current edition builds on the work of previous authors, including **Beth McKillop**, curator of the Chinese and Korean section of the British Library in London, and **Keith Howard**, a leading authority on Korean culture and head of the Department of Korean Studies at London's prestigious School of Oriental and African Studies (SOAS), and **James Grayson**, who served as a missionary in South Korea for 16 years and went on to head the School of East Asian Studies at the University of Sheffield. Other previous contributors include **Craig Brown, Linda Grove, Professor An Sonjae, James Grayson, Leonard Lueras, Nedra Chung, Michael Breen, John Gustaveson, Barbara Mintz, Norman Thorpe, James Wade, Jon Carter Covell, Gary Clay Rector, Laurel Kendall, Norman Sibley, Gertrude Ferrar, Michael E. Macmillan, Tom Coyner and Ken Kaliher**.

The principal photographer for this new edition of the book was **Chris Stowers** . Former contributing photographers have included **Blaine Harrington, Leonard Lueras, Bill Wassman, Andreas M. Gross** and **Catherine Karnow**.

Thanks go to the **Korean National Tourism Organization** and to **Malcolm Grove** for their valuable help. The book was copy edited by **Mick Meikleham** and proofread by JanMcCann. The index was compiled by **Helen Peters**.

The contributors

This ninth edition of Insight Guide: South Korea was co-ordinated and edited by Managing Editor **Tom Le Bas** at Insight Guides' London office. The book has been fully updated with the invaluable help of a team of specialists.

The Places section and the Travel Tips were updated by **Ray Bartlett**, an American travel writer, filmmaker, and photographer (www.Kaisora.com) who has written about South Korea numerous times and has traveled extensively throughout the peninsula covering a range of subjects. Ray contributed the new Best Of South Korea recommendations, the new feature on the Korean diaspora, and the new photo features on Korean Street Food, Gyeongju Treasures, and Hiking.

The chapters on Korean History, The Koreans, Performing Arts, and

Map Legend

▬▬ --	International Boundary
▬ ▬ ▬	Province Boundary
⊖	Border Crossing
▬•▬	National Park/Reserve
▬ ▬ ▬	Marine Park
▬ ▬ ▬	Ferry Route
Ⓜ	Subway
✈ ✈	Airport: International/Regional
🚌	Bus Station
❶	Tourist Information
⛪ ✝ ✟	Church/Ruins
✝	Monastery
▪🏰	Castle/Ruins
☪	Mosque
✡	Synagogue
∴	Archaeological Site
⋂	Cave
𝗜	Statue/Monument
★	Place of Interest
✉	Post Office
⌁	Lighthouse

The main places of interest in the Places section are coordinated by number with a full-colour map (eg ❶), and a symbol at the top of every right-hand page tells you where to find the map.

Contents

LEFT: peaceful Songgwang-sa temple in southern Jeollanam-do.

Maps

Travel Tips

THE BEST OF SOUTH KOREA: TOP ATTRACTIONS

Our guide to the best of South Korea's many sights, from the megalopolis of Seoul to the forested mountains of Seoraksan, the Ten Thousand Islands off the southwest coast, atmospheric temples, folk villages and more

▷ **Gyeongju** The giant tumuli mounds are just one of the captivating sights in and around Korea's magnificent Silla-era capital, the "museum without walls". *See page 223*

△ **Changdeokgung Palace (Seoul)** Splendid Korean palace buildings and serene, Zen-inspired grounds highlight the grandeur of Korean royalty. Be sure to see the Secret Garden (Biwon), the gem within a gem here. *See page 120*

▽ **Demilitarized Zone (DMZ)** The world's most heavily fortified border almost seems part of an absurdist play, but there's no denying the barbed wire or the grim skirmishes that have occurred here. The Third Tunnel of Aggression is a must-see. *See page 160*

△ **Seoraksan National Park (Gangwon)** South Korea's most popular national park, Seoraksan's natural beauty consists of towering rock pinnacles, dense alpine forests, wildflowers at every turn, and wonderfully remote temples to Buddhist gods. *See page 178*

◁ **King Munmu's Underwater Tomb (Gyeongju)** This revered underwater tomb lies just off the east coast. Come here for peeks at modern shamanist rituals, delectable seafood, and the tomb of a king said to have returned as a fearsome dragon. *See page 218*

△ **Haein-sa Temple (Gyeongsangnam)** Perhaps South Korea's most venerated temple, this Unesco World Heritage Site houses one of the world's oldest copies of Buddhist scripture, carved into wooden plates that have been preserved for centuries. *See page 242*

△ **Dadohae Haesang Maritime National Park (Jeollanam)** Looking like a thousand scattered jigsaw pieces, the "ten thousand" islands off the southwest coast offer a wealth of unmatched maritime vistas. *See page 262*

◁ **Insadong Shopping Street (Seoul)** A maze of streets and alleys harbors a copious quantity of galleries and antique stores, souvenir stands, and tea houses. Hawkers, street performers, and throngs of tourists all add to the fun. *See page 123*

△ **Manjang cavern (Jeju)** One of the world's largest lava tubes and part of an even larger cave system, Manjanggul offers unique glimpses of geologic wonders. Highlights include the tube itself and various features, such as a massive lava column. *See page 271*

◁▷ **Hahoe Folk Village (Gyeong-sangbuk)** The best place to come to gain an understanding of traditional Korean life. *See page 214*

THE BEST OF SOUTH KOREA: EDITOR'S CHOICE

Fabulous mountain hikes, otherwordly temples, mega-markets and larger-than-life festivities... here at a glance are our recommendations on what to prioritize

BEST FESTIVALS AND EVENTS

- **Lunar New Year:** Koreans ring in the New Year with an exuberant combination of fireworks, drums, festive costumes, and music. *See page 293*
- **Dano Festival:** The Dano Festival is Korean "May Day" and offers masked dancers and staged performances. *See page 293*
- **Boryeong Mud Festival:** A relatively new tradition that celebrates the art of getting dirty. Wear a swimsuit or old clothes and take part in this exuberant mudfest. *See page 194*

- **Cherry Blossom viewing:** After the cold winter months, Koreans enjoy the coming of spring just as much as anyone. Picnic, drink, and socialize beneath the pink snow of the petals. *See page 293*

ABOVE: relic in the National Museum of Korea.
BELOW: night shopping in Seoul's Myeongdong district.

BEST MUSEUMS AND GALLERIES

- **Gyeongju National Museum:** Countless treasures from the country's most spectacular ancient site. *See page 225*
- **National Museum of Korea (Seoul):** An outstanding collections of ancient Korean treasures, archeological finds, modern art, and much more in permanent and rotating exhibitions. *See page 132*
- **Samsung Museum of Art LEEUM (Seoul):** Divided into two sections of traditional and modern art, with a stunning permanent collection and exhibits from around the globe. *See page 133*
- **Hahoe Mask Museum (Gyeongsangbuk):** Come to the country's premier folk museum to delve into the fascinating world of Korean mask-making, as well as see a variety of masks from around the world. *See page 216*
- **Gansong Museum (Seoul):** Local hero Jeon Hyeongpil used his own fortune to keep these Korean treasures from being taken abroad. Only open twice a year, in spring and fall. *See page 122*

BEST TEMPLES AND SHRINES

See also Haien-sa, Top Attractions page 7

- **Bulguk-sa (Gyeongju):** Buddhist architectural masterpiece with stunning stone pagodas, bridges, and the Seokguram Grotto nearby. *See page 228*
- **Jikji-sa (Gyeongsang-buk):** Expansive temple set in lush, forested grounds. One of South Korea's oldest temples,

it was rebuilt after the Japanese invasion in the 1500s. *See page 211*
- **Dosan Seowan (Gyeongsangbuk):** A beautiful Confucian academy situated in a peaceful rural area near Andong in the east of the country. *See page 213*
- **Yakcheon-sa (Jeju):** One of South Korea's largest and busiest temples. Highlights include monks who will read your face for inner illnesses and recommend appropriate prayers for healing. *See page 272*
- **Beomeo-sa (Busan):** This "Temple of the Nirvana Fish" contains a holy well which never dries in drought, and is Busan's largest and most popular temple. *See page 237*

ABOVE: Boryeong mud festival. **LEFT:** bronze bell at Jikji-sa. **BELOW:** hiking amid fall foliage, Seoraksan.

BEST HIKES AND TRAILS

See also Seoraksan, Top Attractions page 6

- **Bukhansan (Gyeonggi):** One of Seoul's best day trips, and while often crowded, it's still a beautiful escape from the big city. *See page 153*
- **Hallasan (Jeju):** All four seasons are stunning at Hallasan, be it snow in winter, changing leaves in fall, mountain wildflowers in spring, or lush green in summer. *See page 272*
- **Ilchulbong Sunrise Peak (Jeju):** Sunrise in Korea doesn't get any better than when viewed from Ilchulbong Peak. This extinct

volcano is a top spot with honeymooners. *See page 271*
- **Chiaksan (Gangwon):** Quiet and mystical and often missed by tourists, Chiaksan is Wonju city's gemstone. Ancient temples are perched atop its verdant peaks. *See page 168*
- **Jirisan (Jeolla and Gyeongsangnam):** The highest peak on the South Korean mainland. If you're a hiker, add this to your list. *See page 260*
- **Ulleung-do:** Island outpost in the East Sea with dramatic cliffs and high mountains. *See page 219*

BEST CULTURAL EXPERIENCES

- **Myeongdong (Seoul):** This multi-block shopping hub has 24-hour stores that never shut their doors. Trends that rock the world start on these streets. *See page 127*
- **Yongsan (Seoul):** Technogeeks will find everything from cameras to computers to memory cards. It's all here. Bargains aplenty, but buyer beware. *See page 133*

- **Gyeongdong Medicine Market (Seoul):** Giant jars of ginseng and powdered roots for all that ails make this a fascinating meander. *See page 128*
- **Jagalchi Fish Market (Busan):** Just about everything that swims, creeps, crawls, or slithers is waiting for you, often in glistening rows or, in many cases, still very much alive. *See page 235*

THE SHRIMP BETWEEN WHALES

Ancient and modern casually co-exist in this little-known East Asian land. South Korea is full of interest, yet remains happily removed from the tourist trail

Surrounded by the less-than-gentle giants of Japan, China, and the former Soviet Union, the Korean peninsula has long been the "shrimp between whales," as it is described in a Korean proverb. The situation is exacerbated by the long-standing schism between North and South, a Cold War fault line that continues to divide the Korean people into rich and poor, free and oppressed.

Still fiercely independent after centuries of invasions and wars, South Korea combines Confucian and Buddhist traditions with the modernity that makes it one of the world's most technologically advanced nations.

The teeming, high-rise, high-energy conurbation of the capital, Seoul, is home to over 11 million people and a global leader in cutting-edge computer technology, yet is also a 600-year-old city with a rich history, with the traditions of the old Joseon dynasties surviving amid the clamor. Monks and fortune-tellers wander among the fashionable young, shrines and temples sit quietly beneath towering office blocks.

You can expect a friendly, humorous reception from the proud, spontaneous people: even in the main cities you will be regarded with a certain curiosity and hospitality. With a penchant for entertainment, including drinking, song, dance, and theater, the Koreans are boisterous and joyous hosts. The food is fantastic, too.

Yet South Korea remains firmly off the tourist trail, and the staggering economic achievements of the past 50 years sometimes overshadow its rich cultural heritage and haunting natural beauty. The fact that there are few tourists makes for a more authentic and rewarding experience for those who do travel here to explore the mountains and their lost-in-the-clouds temples, the timeless rural landscapes, ancient villages and imperial ruins. ❑

PRECEDING PAGES: guardian figure on a doorway at Woljeong-sa temple, Odaesan; in the heart of Seoraksan National Park; glorious fall foliage near Buyeo.
LEFT: the Silla tombs at Gyeongju. **ABOVE LEFT:** posing for the camera at Jikji-sa temple. **ABOVE RIGHT:** shopping at Seoul's Namdaemun market.

GEOGRAPHY

Many parts of the compact, mountainous peninsula of South Korea are urbanized, industrialized, and overpopulated, yet substantial areas of natural beauty remain

Wherever the traveler walks, drives, or flies in South Korea, he or she will see hills and mountains, poetically rendered as "…the distant peaks." Whether in the joyous lyricism of the great classical *(sijo)* poet Yun, or in the many paintings of South Korea's Geumgangsan (Diamond Mountains), the majestic peaks of this lovely country are depicted time and again.

From Manchuria south to Jeju Island in the East China Sea, the entire Korean landscape is ribbed by forested, rocky mountain ridges. In fact only about 20 percent of the peninsula's total land area is flatland. Yet the mountains do not reach any great elevation; the highest point on the peninsula, Baekdusan on the North Korean border with China, reaches 2,744 meters (9,002ft). Mainland South Korea's loftiest peak is Jirisan, in Jeollanam Province, at 1,915 meters (6,283ft); the summit of volcanic Hallasan, on Jeju Island, reaches 1,950 meters (6,400ft).

The Korean peninsula is relatively small – approximately 1,000km (620 miles) long and 215km (135 miles) wide at its narrowest points. Seoul is, as the crow flies, approximately 1,100km (680 miles) east of Beijing and approximately 1,400km (870 miles) west of Tokyo.

Ancient land bridge

This small offshoot from the Asian landmass is one of the world's oldest land areas, dating back to the pre-Cambrian period (1,600 to 2,700 million years ago). The basic foundation of granite and limestone is old and tough. As you travel up and down the peninsula, take note that you

LEFT: scenery at Bisondae, one of the highlights of Seoraksan National Park. **RIGHT:** squid drying in the sun, Sokcho.

are crossing an ancient land bridge that is tilted toward the west and into the Yellow Sea. This tipping, caused by volcanic pressure on the peninsula in ancient times, has left the offshore area of Korea's west coast dotted with hundreds of islands. Also, in concert with the Yellow Sea's wide tide changes, this west-side sinking produced far-reaching, shallow inlets which look like huge, placid, sky-blue lakes at high tide.

On the east coast fronting the East Sea (the Japan Sea to non-Koreans), the mountains march right down to a coastline marked by tiny coves. These eastern waters, cooled by the Japan current which flows south from the Siberian coast, nurture an abundance of cuttlefish and salmon, while the warmer, shallower Yellow Sea is populated by clams, oysters, shrimp, sea snails, and abalone.

Birds' migratory pit stop

Along the shallow inlets that characterize the west coast, great expanses of sedge play host to a variety of water birds – the most notable of which is the Manchurian crane (also known as the red-crowned crane). This bird was assumed to be virtually extinct, but in 1977 Dr George Archibald, head of the International Crane Foundation, found a large colony thriving in Korea's Demilitarized Zone (DMZ) – the

for a limited period every fall, and, where only a decade or so ago the pheasant seemed on its way to extermination, it is now common.

Mammals and snakes

Mammals have not fared as well as birds, for two reasons. Firstly, the wholesale deforestation that occurred during the Japanese occupation destroyed a range of habitats that were already under stress. Secondly, and this is still a problem today, the common perception persists that wild animals are considered to have medicinal properties – few of the larger mammals and reptiles have managed to escape the Korean stew pot.

heavily guarded strip between North and South which has become an unlikely refuge for wildlife *(see below)*.

These shallow waters are also home to the white-naped crane and many different species of ducks, geese, and swans. Korea has a large population of oriental storks, their huge unwieldy nests capping many trees the length and breadth of the land. The peninsula also acts as a part-time home for many birds that follow migration routes cutting across the country.

The avian population has been rising in recent years as government regulations crack down on shooting. As the result of a bird-killing ban, the sparrow population has increased so much that sparrow netting is now permitted

The tiger is still celebrated in art, but disappeared from South Korea in the 1920s; a small population may remain in the remote mountains of North Korea. Local leopards are another popular subject, but all that remains of them is speculation that they may still be roaming in the remote forests of the North.

One of life's ironies is that the DMZ between North and South Korea has provided a peaceful place where wildlife can proliferate. One creature which has benefitted from this DMZ refuge is a small wildcat, which has all but completely disappeared in mountains south of the 38th parallel.

Some of the small native Korean bears, which are now protected, have been found on Jirisan in the southwest. They had almost disappeared, as the consumption of bear meat has long been considered good for the health. Also, an entire community of otters – about 100 of them – was found along the Nakdong River at about the same time the bears were discovered. The wild boar population is thriving, and there are several indigenous species of deer, including the roe deer and the Siberian musk deer.

Korea used to have a large indigenous snake population, but they are now rarely seen. You are more likely to see snakes in the Oriental medicine market than slithering across the trails of Seoraksan.

indigenous plants are most likely to be preserved in temple gardens where, for centuries,

> *City streets in South Korea are often edged with ginkgos, ailanthus, plane trees, sumac, and paulownia, and most villages have an ancient zelkova or persimmon tree.*

Buddhist monks tended Korea's flora and fauna with loving care. It is here that the finest specimens of the ginkgo tree, a variety of maple, and herbaceous plants thrive.

Jeju Island is famous for its horses, which are allowed to roam freely. The island's subtropical climate provides ample forage for grazing throughout the year. South Korea also boasts a unique breed of dog, the *Jindotgae*. This is a medium-sized, short-haired canine with a moderately pointed snout, heavy shoulders, and a coloring that varies from cream to off-brown.

Fruits of the forest

Korea's forest flora is closely related to that of neighboring China and Japan. The peninsula's

Korea has such a large population of azaleas that it is quite often impossible to cross forest clearings without trampling them. Wild weigela, spiraea, viburnums, holly, hydrangeas, boxwood, daphne, and a host of other plants are all viewed as "weeds," but it is now against the law to dig up such plants in the wild or cut down a tree without government permission (at least in theory). The woody plants have become common as a result of reforestation programs.

Oddly enough, the azalea that covers almost every mountainside and fills every untilled field is not the national flower. That official honor has been bestowed on the Rose of Sharon (Mugunghwa), which supposedly symbolizes the resilient spirit of the Korean people.

LEFT: tea-picking in Jeollanam-do. **ABOVE:** Korean fir cones. **RIGHT:** Eurasian magpies, one of almost 500 recorded bird species in South Korea.

Korean roadsides in the fall are adorned with a beautiful floral froth of lavender, pink, white, and deep-red cosmos.

The rural landscape

Until a few generations ago, South Korea was a land of farmers. While the vast majority of young people have abandoned the countryside, they dutifully pack into their new cars and head back to their rural homes whenever an opportunity arises. Farms and country villages still have strong sentimental appeal for Koreans, even though they avoid physically demanding, poorly paid farm jobs as they would the plague.

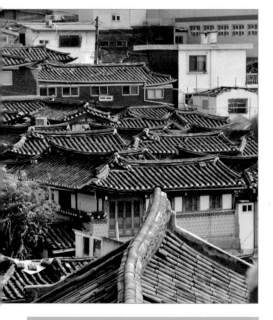

SATELLITE CITIES

South Korea faces a major problem in that only 20–30 percent of its land area is habitable. There are simply too many people living in such a small, mountainous country, especially in the main urban areas. Concerned with the rapid urban growth, particularly in the Seoul area, the Korean government came up with the idea of building satellite cities to encourage decentralization. The new cities (and they are called "new cities") of Gwacheon, Ilsan, Bucheon, and Bundang were built in record time. These planned communities are graced with wide avenues, pleasant parks, and mile after mile of high-rise apartments.

Drive through the countryside and you will notice that a large proportion of those working the fields are elderly. While the rest of the economy has modernized, agriculture has largely been left behind, stuck with farming methods from a bygone era. In some of the more remote rural areas you can still see farmers harvesting rice by hand (though this is becoming rare).

Mostly because of their older populations, Korean villages are bastions of tradition and conservatism, where change comes slowly. Many village homes are traditional in style, with sliding *hanji* doors (made of mulberry tree paper), surrounded by a clay and rock wall. These dwellings huddle together in tight hillside clusters, their roofs tiled in matching colors. It is ironic that there are so many tourist-targeted "folk villages," when all you have to do is drive a half-hour out of the city and walk around almost any rural village to get a glimpse of traditional Korean life.

Yet changes are coming to the countryside. The hillier regions are not well suited to efficient farming, but are attractive areas for recreational activities. And these days new roads, building projects, leisure complexes, and second homes are much more common in the areas around major cities.

The urban landscape

The contrasts between urban and rural life are extremely pronounced in South Korea. Most of the large urban areas have experienced phenomenal rates of growth in the past few decades, a fact which lends them a slightly rough and ready appearance. As befits such a technologically advanced country, the streets are full of energy. The sidewalks are crowded, there are neon lights plastered on every wall, and youths on scooters swerve in and out of pedestrian traffic. On the outskirts, islands of apartment complexes are gobbling up green space, extending the cities inexorably outward.

Urbanization has, as ever, come at a price. There are far too few green spaces among the honking horns and blaring loudspeakers, and the ever-increasing number of cars has given South Korea one of the worst air pollution problems in the world.

There is some good news for the human landscape, though. Rapid economic development has curtailed population growth, and increased affluence has allowed the government to turn its attention to the worst environmental problems. It has done a good job of limiting development in mountain regions – South Korea has one of the best National Park systems in Asia, providing temporary escape from the hustle and bustle of urban life.

> Out of the 25 highest accessible peaks in South Korea, 21 can be found in just 4 national parks – Jirisan, Seoraksan, Deogyusan, and Taebaeksan – 14 of these are in Jirisan alone.

Parks Service, which was set up in 1987, and operates its own police force to ensure that regulations are adhered to.

Few weekends pass when Koreans don't take to the trails that crisscross the parks. Spring and fall are especially popular trekking times, as either blossoming trees or fading leaves make for particularly photogenic outings. *For more on hiking, see pages 184–5.*

South Korea's affection for the great outdoors has taken a new turn in recent years, with the advent of a beach culture – especially in the south, where warmer temperatures make swimming possible through much of the year.

The great outdoors

South Korea's national parks protect many of the country's most picturesque mountain and coastal regions, and have grown steadily in size, and in popularity, since they were first established in 1967. Jirisan, in the southwest of the country, was the first, and remains the third largest at 471 sq km (182 sq miles). There are now a total of 20 parks, including three marine parks, covering roughly 6 percent of the nation's area. Apart from Hallasan on Jeju Island, the parks are nowadays overseen by the Korea National

LEFT: traditional housing *(hanok)* in the Bukchan-dong area of Seoul. **ABOVE:** hiking is a popular pastime, particularly in the fall.

Environmental issues

The main environmental problem facing South Korea is city air pollution, as approximately 80 percent of the population lives in urban areas. One of the world's major consumers of ozone-depleting CFCs, there are also issues with water pollution, acid rain, destructive fishing techniques, and other challenges. In response, the government has boosted investment in renewable energy to reduce its reliance on foreign oil imports, and is looking at the possibilities of solar power, as well as wind energy and biofuels. The problem of deforestation has been offset by the decline in the use of firewood as a source of energy, together with an aggressive tree-planting program. ❑

DECISIVE DATES

PREHISTORIC PERIOD
c.30,000 BC
Earliest known settlement of the peninsula.

GOJOSEON PERIOD
800–400 BC
Korea's Bronze Age.

UNITED SILLA DYNASTY
668
The Silla Kingdom unifies the peninsula, starting a cultural, artistic, and religious golden age centered in Gyeongju.

mid-700s
Buddhist texts are printed.

751
Construction of Seokguram and Bulguk-sa temple begins.

GORYEO KINGDOM
918
The Kingdom of Goryeo is founded by Wang Geon.

958
A competitive civil examination system is created.

1018
Invasions of the Khitans.

1231
Mongols overrun most of northern Korea and force the government to surrender.

1271
The Mongols adopt the dynastic name Yuan, and take over the rest of China, making Korea a tributary state.

JOSEON DYNASTY
1392
Yi Seonggye ousts the Goryeo king and founds own dynasty.

1446
King Sejong inaugurates the Korean alphabet (Hangeul).

1592–98
The Imjin War: Japan invades Korea and lays waste to the peninsula.

1598
Yi Sun-sin, Admiral of the Korean Navy, dies heroically, having outwitted the Japanese, who withdraw under Chinese pressure.

1627
First Manchu invasion.

THE WESTERNERS ARRIVE
1780s
Catholicism introduced.

1811, 1862
Rebellions follow decades of social unrest.

1839
130 Christians killed in religious persecution.

1860
The Donghak ("Eastern learning") movement is founded as a religious society.

1866
Nine French Catholic priests and 8,000 Korean converts executed.

1871
Americans try to establish trade links.

1876
Confrontations take place as Japan and China jockey for power.

1894
Donghak uprising, followed by Sino-Japanese War.

RUSSO-JAPANESE WAR
1895
Korea's Queen Min murdered.

JAPANESE CONTROL
1905
Japan's control of Korea is officially recognized.

1919
The March 1 Independence Movement, with provisional governments formed outside of Korea.

1937
Colonial policy turns toward a complete "Japanization" of Korea.

1939–42
Thousands of Korean workers are conscripted into the Japanese army.

INDEPENDENCE AND THE KOREAN WAR

1945
Despite bitter opposition from Koreans, the Allies agree to direct Korean affairs through a provisional government, staffed by Koreans, for at least five years.

1946
Communists begin to dominate politics under leadership of Soviet-backed Kim II Sung.

1948
UN recognizes Republic of Korea; Syngman Rhee becomes president.

1950
June 25, North Korean troops attack, to be met by UN forces.

FAR LEFT: Koryo-period ceramic vase. LEFT: Korean rioters in conflict with the Japanese, 1907. ABOVE: a US Marine searches a captured Chinese Communist soldier in the Korean War. RIGHT: the late Roh Moo-hyun.

1953
Armistice agreed.

MODERN HISTORY

1948–60
Military rule under President Rhee; economic stagnation.

1960
Yun Po-son is elected.

1962
Yun's government falls. Major General Park Chung-hee heads military government until assassination in 1979.

1980
Major General Chun Doo-hwan becomes president. Military crushes citizens' democratic movement in Gwangju.

1987
Roh Tae-woo becomes South Korea's first "democratically" elected president, merging his party with Kim Young-sam's ("YS").

1988
South Korea hosts the Olympic Games.

1993
"YS" takes office as the first civilian president in more than 30 years, promising real democratic reform.

1996
Former presidents Roh and Chun go on trial for corruption, sedition, and treason.

1997
Korea battered by Asian economic crisis.

1998
Opposition leader Kim Dae-jung elected president.

2000
On June 13, Kim Dae-jung visits Kim Jong-il in Pyongyang – an unprecedented thaw in relations.

2002
South Korea co-hosts soccer World Cup with Japan.

2003
Roh Moo-hyun becomes president, amid rising tension between North Korea and the United States.

2003–06
Six-party talks with North Korea over the nuclear issue fail to make significant progress.

2007
North Korea provisionally agrees to abandon its nuclear energy program.

2008
Economy seriously damaged by global downturn.

2009
North Korea pulls out of nuclear talks. Roh Moo-hyun commits suicide.

2010
North–South relations are plunged into crisis following the sinking of a South Korean naval ship with the death of 46 sailors.

EARLY KINGDOMS AND DYNASTIES

Koreans are proud of their five millennia of history.
Despite foreign incursions, they have developed
and preserved a unique identity

Located at a strategic crossroads in northeast Asia, the Korean peninsula has been overrun by armies of Chinese and Japanese, Mongols and Manchus, and, more recently, Russians and Americans. Yet, although often overshadowed by the political might of China, and the economic power of Japan, the Koreans have managed to maintain a distinct political and cultural identity. They have borrowed much from Chinese civilization and then, in turn, transmitted elements of this to Japan. The ability of Koreans to assimilate yet preserve a unique identity while enduring the depredations of intruders is a striking theme in modern history. Koreans proudly contest that, among other inventions, they designed movable type in 1234 (some 200 years before the Germans), and iron-clad ships in the 1590s (centuries before the Americans).

Archeological finds of Paleolithic stone tools indicate the Korean peninsula was first settled some 30,000 years ago by wandering tribes from Central and Northern Asia. Waves of migration followed, pushing earlier settlers deeper into the mountains, and creating rival states and tribal federations. The oldest evidence of a Neolithic society has been estimated at 4270 BC.

By around 300 BC, Chinese records suggest various tribes had established loosely affiliated organized states in the peninsula. The most powerful was the Gojoseon, in the north. Skirmishes with the Chinese Han dynasty (206 BC to AD

220) resulted in invasion by the Han in 108 BC, who established four military command posts, one of which, at Nangnang near present-day Pyongyang, survived as a military and trading post until AD 313. A variety of minor kingdoms and principalities eventually gave way to the Silla dynasty by 676. In one form or another, this unified Korea was to last until 1945.

Scholars and monks

Buddhism, Confucianism, art, architecture, a written language, and bureaucratic organizational principles were all introduced from China during the Three Kingdoms Period. Under Unified Silla, Buddhism flourished as

LEFT: the now-extinct Korean tiger, once worshipped as a messenger of the mountain gods.
RIGHT: dating from the 1st century AD, this lacquered basket was discovered at the Han military post of Nangnang, near present-day Pyongyang.

rulers lavished funds on temples and images, and dispatched monks to China and India to study. The epitome of Silla Buddhist art can still be seen in the Seokguram stone grotto near the former capital of Gyeongju *(see page 231)*, which was begun, along with the nearby temple of Bulguk-sa, in 751.

> Koreans became the tutors of Japan's Prince Shotoku, and nearly one-third of the nobles in the 815 Japanese family register were of Korean descent.

Silla maintained a tributary relationship with the Tang, preventing Chinese domination, but adopting its administrative system.

By the late 8th century, the growth of the royal clan led to intense internal rivalries, as the aristocracy came under increasing attack from lower echelons who felt that they were excluded from power. Major revolts broke out as early as 768, and in 780 King Hyegong was assassinated. From this chaos, rebel chieftains rose up and struggled for position until the appearance of Wang Geon. Supported by the landlord and merchant class from which he sprang, Wang Geon's power grew until 935 when the ruler Gyonhwon sent him to the northern border to face Song Chinese forces. He turned around, reunited the peninsula, and

founded his own dynasty, Goryeo, which lasted for more than 450 years.

Wang Geon's mandate of Heaven

Wang Geon moved his capital to Gaeseong, just north of today's demilitarized zone. The power base of the Goryeo dynasty (which is the origin of the Western name for the country) was a partially non-aristocratic élite of literati who gained office through a state examination system set up in 958.

To prepare candidates, a national university was created in 992, and by the 12th century a network of schools was training boys in the

Chinese classics required for the top exam. However, Wang Geon invoked the Chinese notion of the "mandate of Heaven" as his justification for assuming the throne. He claimed moral superiority, and he and his successors developed a centralized system of government that outwardly resembled Chinese practice.

There was an abrupt change in August 1170, when a military escort conveying the king, Uijong, and his party revolted and killed every man except the king himself. The king was banished to Geoje Island, where he was murdered. The coup is normally interpreted as a revolt against discrimination by civilian officials and against the debauchery of the royal court. After a confused period, a soldier, Choe Chungheon, managed to seize power in 1196. He suppressed all opposition and, in a gesture that marked the beginning of the end of Buddhist dominance, banished monks and clergy from the capital. He soon induced scholar-officials to join him in reviving the dynasty, but other powers were looking to expand into Korea.

The Khitan, ruling around the Yalu River basin as the Liao, had launched three attacks against Goryeo between 993 and 1018; in the last attack they were heavily defeated. The Jurchen, who set themselves up as the Jin dynasty in northern China, then came into conflict with Goryeo.

A century later, in 1231, Goryeo faced an invasion by a Mongol army. Initially, Goryeo assistance was sought to overrun the Song Chinese, and the Koreans agreed in order to subvert other border threats. From 1219 until 1224, Goryeo reluctantly met demands for large tribute payments in return for Mongol help. Relations were broken off after the murder of a Mongol envoy to Korea, and the reckoning came in 1231, when the Mongols quickly overran most of northern Korea, laid siege to Gaeseong and forced the government to surrender.

As the Mongols relaxed their grip a year later, the Goryeo government fled from Gaeseong with most of its people, and took refuge on Ganghwa Island at the mouth of the Han River. This led to a full invasion, in which all major towns were sacked, yet the Mongols failed to cross the narrow channel separating Ganghwa from the mainland. In 1259 a truce was brokered, but military officials who dominated the government refused to capitulate, and the government remained on Ganghwa.

A match made in Mongolia

The situation worsened under King Wonjong, who ruled from 1259 to 1274. He went in person to the Mongols and offered submission in return for aid against the military clique in his court. He even agreed to marry the crown prince to a Mongol princess to seal the bargain. When he returned to Goryeo with a Mongol army, many among the military faction still refused to capitulate. As the *Sambyeolcho*, they boarded boats and set up a rival government

on islands off the southwest coast. It took four years to restore the civilian bureaucracy.

The Mongols, who from 1279 ruled as the Yuan dynasty in China, then allowed the Goryeo government to retain control, but required Goryeo princes to marry Mongol princesses, thus effectively subjugating the peninsula. In addition, Korea had to build hundreds of ships and furnish soldiers for ill-fated Mongol expeditions to Japan in 1274 and 1281. On the positive side, Koreans gained Mongol knowledge of astrology, medicine, artistic skills, and cotton cultivation.

By the mid-14th century, rebellions in China

were undermining the Mongol regime, culminating in the founding of the Ming dynasty in 1368. Korean independence revived after the enthronement of King Gongmin in 1351. Gongmin reorganized his government and army. Landholders proved so powerful, however, that he was forced to compromise when he tried to return appropriated slaves to their rightful owners. In 1374, he was assassinated, and his 10-year-old son was made king.

> In the 13th century, the Mongols extracted a large annual tribute from Korea – including gold, silver, horses, ginseng, artisans, eunuchs, and women.

FAR LEFT: Confucius is *Gongja* to Koreans.
LEFT: Silla crown from the 6th century AD.
RIGHT: an 8th-century Buddha at Gyeongju.

Chinese brigands and Japanese pirates had by this time increased their attacks on the country, and disagreement on how to control Goryeo raged among military leaders, until one of them, Yi Seonggye (Taejo), seized power in 1388. Yi proclaimed the Joseon dynasty four years later, which was fated to be Korea's last, retaining power until 1910.

The Joseon dynasty

The new kingdom moved its capital to Han-yang, today's Seoul, and promptly resumed tributary relations with Ming China. The third king of the dynasty, Taejong, who came to power in

1401 after killing his brother, the heir-apparent, reorganized the government to strengthen the throne. He was succeeded by King Sejong (r. 1418–50) – intelligent and scholarly, he presided over the creation of the Korean alphabet, Hangeul, and a widespread cultural renaissance. He was succeeded by men of lesser capacity, Munjong (r. 1450–52) and the ill-fated boy-king Danjong (r. 1452–55). This unfortunate youth was forced to abdicate by his uncle, imprisoned, then strangled. His uncle took the throne as the tyrannical King Sejo (r. 1456–68). He banished or executed critics and seized property, so when his reign ended, a backlash diminished the power of the monarchy and initiated a long period of decline.

Admiral Yi and the turtle ships

The threat of foreign invasion was never far away, and in April 1592 a newly reunified Japan under Toyotomi Hideyoshi launched an invasion fleet. The Koreans had little military expertise on land, but their navy presented a very different proposition. Korea's naval hero, Admiral Yi Sun-sin, commanded a force based at Yeosu on the south coast. Among his fleet were several "turtle ships," which were used to foil the Japanese invasion by cutting supply lines and disrupting reinforcements. The "turtle ships" averaged 30 meters (100ft) in length, and were powered by oars that made them faster and more maneuverable than the Japanese vessels. Iron jackets studded with pointed rivets made them invulnerable to projectiles, and each vessel was heavily armed. The bow of each ship was adorned with a large turtle's head.

From May to July 1592, the Korean fleet sank more than 250 Japanese vessels in eight major engagements. Negotiations led to the withdrawal of the bulk of Japan's troops, but in January 1597 the Japanese renewed their attack, sending 100,000 men to Korea. This time, they met stiff resistance in land battles, and the invasion was confined to the southern provinces. According to Japanese history, Hideyoshi's death in September 1598 prompted a final withdrawal. Local Korean belief differs, however, and recalls how Yi Sun-sin led the pursuing Japanese fleet into a strait between the mainland and the island of Jindo. There, Yi had assembled women on local hilltops to give the illusion of a massive force waiting to engage the enemy and, not knowing the tides, the Japanese were caught and fled in disarray. Fate, though, failed to smile on the admiral: in the final battle of the war, in 1598, he was killed by a bullet on the deck of his flagship.

The "Hermit Kingdom"

Threats also came from the north, where Jurchen tribes had united in the Manchurian mountains. Following attacks in 1583, by the 1590s Ming Chinese outposts in Manchuria were under pressure. Joseon, under King Injo (r. 1623–49), sided with the Ming, which led to invasions in 1627 and 1636. In the first, Pyongyang fell, and the court fled once more to Ganghwa Island. The king signed a peace treaty that committed Joseon to a Confucian-style, elder-younger brother relationship with the Manchus. Dissatisfied, in 1632 the Manchus demanded annual tribute, and the

Koreans responded by declaring war. This time the capital, Hanyang, was taken, before the Manchus captured Ganghwa and took 200 hostages, including the queen. They extracted a heavy price: tributes, severance of ties with the Ming court, and the submission of two princes as hostages. Soon, the Manchus established themselves in Beijing, ruling from 1644 as the Qing dynasty. The suzerain relationship allowed the Joseon court to retain control, but from this point on Joseon controlled all border access, treating China as a superior state and keeping its distance from Japan as a trading neighbor. In this way, Korea became the "Hermit Kingdom."

as the first Christian convert. Others converted, and in 1791, when Yun Jichung failed to perform a Confucian service for his dead mother, he was sentenced to death. He became Korea's first Christian martyr; many more persecutions followed. In 1839, 130 Christians were killed, and some 8,000 perished between 1866 and 1873.

The 19th century was marked by widespread social unrest, including major rebellions in 1811 and 1862, and this rendered the conservative ruling class even more inward-looking and isolationist. By the second half of the century, Korea was ill prepared to open its doors to an expansion-hungry and technologically superior West. ❑

In the 18th century, Joseon recovered some vitality. The reigns of Yeongjo (1724–76) and Jeongjo (1776–1800) are remembered as periods of relative stability, but these were also times when new intellectual currents stimulated Korean thinkers, starting a process that would lead to dismissing the speculative metaphysics of the orthodox neo-Confucian tradition.

Western ideas flowing into China reached Korea through traders and envoys. In 1783, a young Korean, Yi Seunghun, was baptized in Beijing by a Catholic priest; he returned to Korea

LEFT: the "Floating Rock" at Buseok-sa.
ABOVE: *Korean Chief and Attendants*, a lithograph sketched in 1817.

CONFUCIANISM CHANGES KOREAN LIFE

In the late 14th century, reformers embraced the ideas of Chinese neo-Confucianism, bringing about many changes in Korean society. Koreans had long practiced burial rituals that were an amalgam of local and Buddhist traditions. Now these customs, including cremation, were thrust aside in favor of Confucian ancestor worship and its related rituals. Until the end of Goryeo times, endogamy, polygamy and remarriage of widows had been allowed. The Joseon court, however, broadened the circle of kin with whom marriage was prohibited. They also forbade the practice of giving equal social status to multiple wives, as well as discouraging remarriage.

A CENTURY OF CONFLICT

The hundred years from 1850 saw the Koreans forced
to abandon their policy of seclusion, as both Western
and Oriental powers sought to gain influence

In 1860, Korean officials were shaken by the news that British and French forces had occupied Beijing. The Koreans had looked to China for many centuries, offering tribute to its leaders, and absorbing Chinese culture and civilization. Determined that the same fate should not befall Korea, the exclusionist foreign policy was reinforced when the 12-year-old Gojong (r. 1864–1907) ascended the throne. The dowager queen was his nominal regent, but actual power was in the hands of his father, Yi Hang. For a decade, Yi effectively ruled as the Daewongun ("Great Prince of the Court").

The Daewongun confronted a second peril, for domestic disputes also threatened the survival of the dynasty. To break up the factions jockeying for power, he began a program of Confucianist reform, banishing officials, and appointing on merit rather than lineage. Yi chose a queen for Gojong from a minor aristocratic family, the Min from Yeoheung. He also rebuilt the royal palace – which had been in ruins since the Japanese invasion in the 1590s – and reformed the tax system.

Western pressure

The outside pressures on Korea continued. Russia demanded coaling rights, trade, and diplomatic relations, but was turned down in 1866. In the same year, nine French Catholic priests and thousands of Korean Christian converts were executed. One priest escaped, and persuaded the French Asiatic Squadron to send seven warships to seize Ganghwa Island. In August, the US *General Sherman* ran aground in the Daedong River; the Koreans set her on fire, killing her crew. In 1871, the American minister to China, Frederick Low, accompanied five warships to Korea to try to open trade links. After a clash, the Americans occupied Ganghwa, where 350 Koreans and three Americans were killed before the mission withdrew.

In 1875, the Japanese determined to force Korea to abandon its policy of seclusion. For several centuries, the Koreans had insisted that trade with Japan should be limited, carried out through a closed quarter in Busan port. Now, after a clash between Korean shore batteries and a Japanese ship, Japan pressed upon Korea a treaty of friendship and commerce, opening three ports and permanent diplomatic offices.

Military coups

Japan itself was modernizing rapidly, and its increased presence in Korea spurred the Chinese to redouble their efforts to preserve their influence. Korea was forced, often unsuccessfully, to balance the desires of its two neighbors. In 1882, China despatched troops to quell a Korean army mutiny, and following a stand-off, Japan won indemnity, and was granted permission to station a legation guard in Korea.

In December 1884, a faction of Koreans sympathetic to Japan launched a further revolt. Known as the Gapshin coup, and beginning on the night when the opening of the first Korean post office was being celebrated, it eventually led to the temporary withdrawal of both Chinese and Japanese troops.

ening economic problems and the activities of foreign merchants. A peasant force marched northwards from Jeolla province, twice defeating government troops. The king appealed to China for assistance. China responded, but the Japanese, feeling their presence in Korea threatened, sent 7,000 men and warships.

The rebellion was quashed, but Japan refused to withdraw its forces, using them to press the Korean government for a program of reform and modernization. In July, the Japanese occupied the royal palace and ousted the administration. They installed a progressive, pro-Japanese cabinet. This, through a deliberative council,

The Donghak uprising

The Donghak ("Eastern learning") movement began around 1860 as a mix of Confucian, Buddhist and shamanist ideas, opposing the new philosophies coming from the West. Its founder, Choe Jewoo, had been born into a disenfranchised aristocratic family. He was eventually executed for challenging orthodoxy, but his movement developed both religious and social dimensions, challenging external influences on Korea, and embracing both peasants and discontented upper-class elements. In early 1894, a rebellion broke out, caused in part by deep-

LEFT: a courtesan in the 1880s. **ABOVE:** lithograph of Japanese troops on the attack in Korea, 1904.

began to put in place a series of reforms. Japan now planned to match the European powers by creating her own East Asian empire. This was to pit the fading Qing empire against the rising imperial power of Meiji Japan in the Sino-Japanese War. In the brief conflict, the Chinese were defeated, and in a treaty signed at Shimonoseki they formally ended the many centuries of the Korean suzerain-vassal relationship.

Koreans, opposed to Japanese dominance, needed a new counterforce, and they found one in Russia. In 1895, Russia forced Japan to restore to China the Liaotung peninsula, which she had seized during the war. In Korea, a pro-Russian faction associated with Queen Min obtained the dismissal of pro-Japanese ministers. Soon, though, Queen Min was murdered, officially by disaffected Korean troops, but clearly in an action planned by Japan. In fear for his life, Gojong took refuge in the Russian legation. He dismissed his cabinet and replaced it with pro-Russian ministers.

Gojong reigned for a year from the legation, his decrees passed through a small group of trusted officials. He returned to the palace only in February 1897, once he was convinced he need not fear Japanese reprisals. Seeking to reassert Korea's independence, he took the title of "emperor", by so doing claiming equality with the rulers of both China and Japan; he

announced that the name of Korea would be changed, from Joseon to Daehan Jeguk, "Empire of the Great Han".

Gojong's efforts were initially aided by the emergence of the Independence Club, formed by nationalists and by participants in the unsuccessful 1884 coup (see panel, below).

The Russo-Japanese War

Japan and Russia maintained an uneasy truce in Korea. Russian interests were balanced by other Western powers, notably when Britain occupied the southern island of Geomun-do to prevent expansionism, and as American mis-

THE INDEPENDENCE CLUB

Using public subscriptions, the so-called Independence Club (founded by nationalists and those involved in the failed 1884 coup) built a gate known as the Independence Arch at the entrance to Seoul on the road from Beijing. They founded a newspaper, *The Independent*, published in Korean script, Hangeul (rather than Chinese characters), and in English. The paper proved an important means of popularizing reformist ideas. The club quickly grew, and was recast two years later as a political party, criticizing foreign encroachment and the influence of Russia, and attacking government policies; in November 1898, the government dissolved it, jailing prominent leaders.

sionaries and traders increased their presence. In February 1904, Japan launched an attack on the Russian fleet at Port Arthur. Korea declared its neutrality, but Japan moved into the peninsula in force, and compelled the Korean government to authorize military occupation. By the end of 1905, Japan's control over Korea was recognized, ending the conflict.

Next, the Japanese moved to gain Korea's formal acceptance of Japan as her protector. Ito Hirobumi arrived in Seoul in November 1905 to persuade Gojong to approve a treaty transferring partial sovereignty to Japan. Gojong and his ministers resisted, but pressure was applied by isolating the emperor from his advisers, and within two weeks a majority of the cabinet had agreed to accept the arrangement. A treaty was signed on November 18 that gave Japan control of Korea's foreign relations and the right to station in Korea a resident-general to manage her external affairs. The treaty was greeted with public protests and demands for the punishment of the "Five Traitors" who had approved it. Japanese gendarmes were called out to suppress the demonstrations, and both the emperor's aide, Min Yonghwan, and his former prime minister, Jo Byeongse, committed suicide.

In June 1907, Gojong sent an envoy to the International Peace Conference at The Hague to generate international pressure for Japan's withdrawal. The Japanese delegation argued that Korea had ceded control of external affairs, and the envoy was refused admission. Japanese retaliation for this was channeled through Gojong's cabinet; announcing he had lost the trust of his people, Gojong was forced to abdicate in favor of his son, Sunjong (reigned 1907–10). Sunjong is widely remembered as being feeble-minded and, to further undermine Korean royalty, he was given a Japanese consort.

In fact, the 1905 treaty was extremely wide-ranging. It claimed the right to maintain law and order, the right to intervene in Korea's internal administration, the authority to supervise Japanese officials in Korea, including those employed by the Korean government, and the power to issue ordinances. In December 1907, the treaty was revised to give the resident-general a veto over administrative acts, internal reforms, and the appointment and dismissal of high officials. By mid-1909, the administration of justice was in Japanese hands, and a year later the Japanese had complete police power.

Korean resistance to the treaty erupted in a series of guerrilla actions mounted by the so-called "righteous armies". In October 1909, Ito was assassinated by a Korean patriot. Reprisals were severe. On August 22, 1910, a further treaty finally annexed Korea to Japan, extinguishing hopes for independence. Resistance waned under the iron-fisted rule of General Terauchi Masatake, the new governor-general. Suppression reflected Japanese confidence, and a belief that they had a divine mission to control Korea.

LEFT: 1880s Presbyterian missionary Reverend Samuel Moffett with new Korean Christians.
RIGHT: Prince Yi Un, seventh son of Gojong, became a "puppet" figurehead for the Japanese regime in Korea.

The March 1 Movement

Early 1919 marked one of the most significant events in Korean history. A coalition of nationalists, inspired by the call for the self-determination of subject peoples at the Versailles Conference following World War I, planned a non-violent protest. Korean students in Japan

> In an attempt to refute Japanese cultural domination following the March 1 Movement, Koreans promoted cultural links with Siberia, suggesting that this was where their people originated.

JAPANESE COLONIZATION

The process of Japanese colonization was a painful one for the independently minded Koreans. In 1937, the Japanese language was made mandatory in schools and public places, and Korean history was dropped from the curriculum. Koreans were compelled to adopt Japanese names and were required to participate in Shinto rituals. The colonial period did, however, prepare Korea for modernization, developing agriculture and industry, installing highways, railroads, ports, and communications facilities. Yet all this took place along lines dictated by the needs of Japan's domestic economy, and profits, together with agricultural surplus, went primarily to the Japanese.

produced a draft declaration of independence, and in Korea it was distributed by Christians, Buddhists, and members of the Cheondogyo (Heavenly Way) religion, which had emerged from the Donghak movement. Gojong had died, and his funeral was slated for March 3; thousands of people would be in Seoul. It was decided that the declaration should be read on March 1, in Seoul's Pagoda (Tapgol) Park. Along the streets near the park shouts of *"Dongnip manse!"* ("Long live independence!") rang out.

The declaration, and the size and ferocity of the protests that followed it, caught the Japanese by surprise. By the end of May, more than

standardized Korean alphabet, and fought for a Korean university. In an attempt to refute Japanese cultural domination, they popularized the legend of Korea's mythical founder, Dangun *(see panel, page 50)*. But they argued for gradual reform, and their tolerance for Japanese rule left them out-maneuvered by left-wing groups.

In September 1931, the Japanese army attacked Chinese troops in Manchuria. Korea was the land bridge for this operation, and industrial plants were built to link Japan to Manchuria. Korean workers were drafted to staff Japanese factories, and to work in Manchurian mines. At the same time, students were com-

2 million had protested. Predictably, the Japanese brutally suppressed the movement, with the result that 7,500 Koreans lost their lives and 50,000 were arrested.

Yet despite the bloodshed, the uprising eventually resulted in a new, softer Japanese administration promoting what became known as "cultural rule." Officials and school teachers stopped carrying swords, and the number of military police was temporarily reduced. Korean publications were permitted, including two newspapers that still survive, the *Donga ilbo* and the *Chosun ilbo*. Youth, religious, social, and labor organizations launched journals, which encouraged a loose grouping of moderate ideologues to emerge. They established an indigenous style of literature, promoted a

pelled to join patriotic "volunteer" forces, and women were enlisted to repair roads and maintain transport infrastructure. Many thousands of women were forced into frontline brothels to service Japanese soldiers (Japan is still under pressure from the international community to compensate survivors). By 1945, several million Koreans had been conscripted.

Liberation

Many Koreans took it for granted that Japan's surrender at the end of the Pacific War in August 1945 would mean immediate independence. But international politics had other plans. In 1943, at meetings of the Allies in Cairo and Tehran, the US advanced the idea of a four-power trusteeship for the peninsula. In Cairo, President Roosevelt, conscious that Russian territory touched the Korean border, talked of independence "in due course." The British, French, and Russians were not enthusiastic, but nobody rejected the plan.

When Roosevelt died in April 1945, the Grand Alliance was already being split by tensions that would give rise to the Cold War. US planners were concerned that a Soviet occupation of Korea would harm their security interests in the region. When the Russians entered the Pacific War on August 9, Washington officials hurriedly proposed that a demarcation line be drawn across the peninsula, along the 38th par-

but these were undermined less by the Soviets than by American attempts to practice an early "containment" doctrine. This interpreted the

> The choice of the 38th parallel as the dividing line placed the Korean capital, Seoul, in the American zone but left most raw materials and energy sources in the Russian zone.

initial resistance to US policy among Koreans in the South as radical and pro-Soviet.

The two armies of occupation began to create

allel. The Russians were to accept the Japanese surrender north of the line and the Americans south of it. The division was not conceived of as permanent, but with world affairs competing for attention, little progress was made towards reunification. Allied foreign ministers met in Moscow in December 1945 and agreed a modified multilateral trusteeship to direct Korean affairs. This envisaged a provisional government, staffed by Koreans, for a minimum of five years. Protracted attempts were made in 1946 and 1947 to implement this agreement,

LEFT: bronze mural at Seoul's Pagoda Park to commemorate the March 1 Movement. **ABOVE:** Korean refugees fleeing to the south from advancing armies.

the beginnings of two separate Korean states. North of the demarcation line, the Russians moved to establish a regime that would be friendly to them. They recognized the populist people's committees that sprang up immediately after Japanese capitulation, and worked through them. Korean Communists, some of whom had been with Mao Zedong in Yan'an, and others who had been in Siberia, returned, jostling for position with those who had stayed in Korea. Pak Heon Yeong, who had established the Korean Communist Party, was the best known within Korea. In December 1945, however, Kim Il Sung became leader of the North Korean Communist Party. In July 1946, he merged his party with the group of Koreans who had returned from China, to create the North Korean Workers Party. Later, as this was merged with equivalent South Korean organizations in 1949, Kim wrested control from Pak.

South of the demarcation line, the US occupation force distrusted local people's committees. General Hodge decided to retain many of the authority structures left by the Japanese, and in this way failed to remove collaborators. In September 1945, the Korean People's Republic was formed, with a cabinet joining the nationalist Kim Ku and the right-wing Syngman Rhee. Hodge refused to recognize it, so Kim organized strikes, which Hodge interpreted as a threat to

stability. After February 1946, when a right-wing Representative Democratic Council was set up, Hodge sided increasingly with Rhee, particularly as he struggled to cope with refugees from the Russian zone and with returnees from Japan. When in October Rhee announced an Interim Legislature, his supporters stirred up demonstrations, further undermining the Americans. It was from this weak position that the US began to look for ways to reduce its involvement.

The Republic of Korea

Elections were proposed for a Korean government, with US and Soviet troops to be withdrawn three months later. By the start of 1948, the Russians considered that Communist rule

> To reduce their involvement in Korea in 1947, the US turned to the fledgling UN, and the United Nations' Temporary Commission on Korea (UNTCOK) was set up.

was sufficiently secure in the north to begin a withdrawal. The United Nations representative body, UNTCOK, now found itself faced with an impossible task; unable to observe anything north of the demarcation line, it agreed in February 1948 to supervise elections only in the south. In this way, on May 10, just half of Korea chose a constituent assembly to draft a constitution and elect a chief executive.

The assembly picked as chairman, and, on July 15 as president, Syngman Rhee. A new constitution, approved on July 12, enshrined the claim that the assembly represented "all Korea." In reaction, a constitution was approved in the north in September 1948, partly modeled on the Soviet constitution. This thereby created a separate state, the Democratic People's Republic of Korea. To assist the state to develop, the Soviets supplied arms, creating a formidable army.

The Americans, for their part concerned more with Taiwan and the Communist takeover of mainland China, established a Korean Military Advisory Group. Military manpower was enhanced, to leave a standing force that in May 1950 numbered 100,000, but the Senate refused to pay for arms, on the grounds that South Korea should develop a policy of self-defense. As a result, weapon stocks were low: South Korea had just 14 obsolete military aircraft.

The Korean War

The stage was set for war. North Korean troops poured across the 38th parallel early on June 25, 1950. Seoul fell in three days. What began as a civil conflagration soon took on international dimensions. The US was concerned that global communism, directed from Moscow, would spread. President Truman ordered American forces into battle. The first troops arrived on July 5, but by the middle of the month the joint South Korean and US forces had been pushed back to a small pocket around Busan.

The US asked the UN for backing, and got it, since the Soviets were boycotting the assembly in protest at the failure to seat the People's Republic of China. Support for Korea was placed under the flag of the UN, and forces from 16 other states followed the US to the peninsula. Overall command was given to Truman, who appointed General MacArthur, the Commander in Chief in Japan, as Supreme Commander. MacArthur, to relieve the pressure on Busan, planned an amphibious landing at Incheon to the west of Seoul, well behind enemy lines. This took place in September and, meeting little resistance, quickly created a pincer movement. The forces in Busan broke out of the perimeter and fought their way north, crossing the 38th parallel by the end of the month. On October 19, the North Korean capital, Pyongyang, fell, and on October 26, US and South Korean

Rhee. The armistice was finally signed, near the village of Panmunjeom, on July 27, 1953, by the Chinese, the North Koreans, and the UN Command; Rhee refused to sign. The armistice created a demilitarized zone (DMZ) to replace the 38th parallel, stretching from coast to coast. A Military Armistice Commission was set up to supervise the implementation of the agreement. Although the signatories were charged with recommending to their governments that a conference be held within three months to settle the issue of Korean reunification, the Commission, never making much progress, has continued to meet periodically at Panmunjeom ever since. ❏

troops reached the Yalu River, the border with China. MacArthur proposed using nuclear weapons. China reacted by sending troops across the border, driving the UN back. The Chinese pushed south, across the 38th parallel, and on January 4, 1951, they took Seoul.

Seoul was recaptured on March 15, and the battlefront gradually stabilized in an area just north of the 38th parallel. A stalemate prompted the start of truce negotiations in July. These dragged on for two years, opposed by Syngman

LEFT: US General Douglas MacArthur makes an inspection tour of the front line. **ABOVE:** American GIs watch as British troops arrive in South Korea, September 1950.

SYNGMAN RHEE

In 1948, Syngman Rhee (1875–1965) was elected as president of the assembly for the new Republic of Korea. A conservative anti-Communist, he had played a minor role in the Independence Club, and had been jailed for his activities. Rhee spent the 36 years prior to 1945 abroad, earning a PhD from Princeton University in 1919. He served briefly as premier of the Korean Provisional Government in Shanghai, but then chose to agitate for Korean independence from the United States. As an aristocrat, he was authoritarian and had scant regard for liberal democracy. Riots eventually forced him to resign and flee the country in 1960.

RECOVERY AND PROSPERITY

In East Asian mythology, the phoenix rises from the ashes.
After the devastation of the 1950–53 war, this is what has
happened in South Korea

The Korean War reduced Seoul and Pyongyang to rubble. Millions were homeless, more were displaced, and untold millions had died. The war left the DMZ as a 4km (2½-mile)-wide scar etched across the peninsula that neither side would allow to heal: even after both sides simultaneously joined the UN in 1991, there was no peace treaty.

Personality cult

North Korea quickly rebuilt its shattered economy with Soviet aid, skillfully avoiding total dependence on either China or the Soviet Union itself. Kim Il Sung encouraged a personality cult to grow that allowed him to purge all domestic opposition. He developed his own socialist ideology based on the principles of self-reliance and non-alignment. Inspiration often came from China – Beijing's Great Leap Forward became North Korea's Cheollima (Galloping Horse) Movement, and the Cultural Revolution was reflected in Kim's *juche* philosophy.

As aid declined, barter trade propped up an economy that during the 1960s and 70s became over-reliant on outdated heavy industry and unmodernized farming methods.

Kim's personality cult was such that after a traditional mourning period following his death in 1994 he was elected "Eternal President." The state he founded has found it difficult to change, and his son and successor, Kim Jong-il, formerly the "Dear Leader," continues with the

same "on-the-spot guidance" to encourage interminable "revolutionary speed campaigns."

In the 1950s, South Korea stagnated. Despite massive American aid, recovery was slow. Favoritism and corruption within the administration were widespread.

Syngman Rhee clung to power, but by 1960 his Liberal Party was deeply unpopular and, even after the execution of his main rival, Cho Pongam, for alleged Communist connections, the election was marred by such blatant fraud that popular demonstrations broke out. On April 19, police fired on a crowd in Seoul, killing 115 people. He resigned on April 27, and left for exile in Hawaii.

LEFT: General Park Chung-hee, South Korean president from 1961 to 1979.
RIGHT: a visit to the War Memorial in Seoul's Itaewon district is a sobering experience.

A fledgling democracy

In 1960, the constitution was changed to form a government with a cabinet responsible to the legislature. Yun Poson, from the Democratic Party, was elected to the largely ceremonial role of president to the new Second Republic. Chang Myon, who had served as prime minister and vice-president under, Rhee Syngman was chosen as prime minister. Rivalry between the two compromised the government. In 1961, after Chang announced he would cut 30,000 military posts, a junta led by General Park Chung-hee took control. The architect of the coup was Park's nephew by marriage, Kim Jongpil. The junta promised

A year later he declared martial law, bringing to a close the Third Republic. This allowed him to redraw the constitution in a way that allowed him presidential power for life. The new constitution, named Yusin to indicate that it was to revitalize Korea, came with a glimmer of hope for détente with North Korea, but this was shattered after infiltrators assassinated Park's wife.

Park's harsh rule is today measured against his remarkable success at developing an export-led economy that laid the foundations for prosperity. Park forged a partnership with industry, effectively encouraging the emergence of today's conglomerates, the *jaebeol*. Tax concessions and

to stamp out corruption, build a self-supporting economy, and work for reunification. With a nod to the international community, it announced it would respect the UN charter and seek closer relations with the free world.

Military rule – economic success

Park was a career officer from rural Gyeongsangbuk province, who would now rule until assassinated in 1979 as he moved to quell popular demonstrations. In 1963, Park retired from the army and ran as presidential candidate for a new civilian government. He narrowly beat Yun Poson, was re-elected in 1967, and two years later secured a constitutional amendment to permit him a third term, which he duly won in 1971.

favorable loans were provided through state banks. In the first five years, the average annual GNP growth was 8.5 percent and exports increased at an annual 40 percent. The state developed a transport and communications network. His administration built domestic car- and ship-building industries, then gradually moved from labor-intensive heavy industry to skill-intensive electronics and high-technology production.

In 1979, Park was assassinated by his own head of intelligence, Kim Jae Kyu. Kim was later executed, along with six accomplices. The Defense Security Command, the agency investigating the assassination, was led by Major General Chun Doo-hwan. On December 12, 1979, Chun called on the Ninth Army, under General

Roh Tae-woo, to enter Seoul and, after arresting a number of senior military officers, it became clear that a bid for power was under way.

In May 1980, Chun declared martial law and ruthlessly put down a revolt in the south-western city of Gwangju. Local residents claim that more than 2,000 died. In August, Chun

> North Korea's leader, held up as a paragon to his subjects, miraculously hit 11 holes in one the very first time he played golf, according to state media.

resigned from the army and an electoral college declared him president. Chun recycled Park's government style, depriving people of civil and political rights and, through a new economic plan, forcing conglomerates to swap interests.

While GNP figures increased rapidly, so did Korea's international debt. In early 1987, Chun announced that Roh Tae-woo would be his favored successor as president. The public became restless, and when a student was tortured to death by police early in January, demonstrators took to the streets.

Democracy reborn

On June 29, 1987, after months of demonstrations, Roh announced an unexpected liberalization of politics and the release of political prisoners, effectively separating himself from Chun. In the elections that autumn, the opposition, led by Kim Young-sam, Kim Dae-jung, and Kim Jongpil, was split by internal rivalry, and Roh became the first democratically elected president. Roh lifted restrictions on media and unions, allowing bitter labor disputes to erupt. However, his five-year tenure began as South Korea emerged from under the wing of the US, and as the 1988 Olympics brought the world's media to Seoul. As a partner on the world stage, and keen to find new markets for its exports, South Korea embarked on a diplomatic initiative it called *Nordpolitik*. In part, this would further isolate North Korea, as was apparent when full relations were established with the Soviet Union in 1990 and with China in 1992.

LEFT: Syngman Rhee and his wife are greeted at LaGuardia airport, New York, in July 1954.
RIGHT: a police SWAT unit, Korea's anti-terrorism force.

In 1990, to overcome a political stalemate Roh merged his party with two opposition parties led by Kim Young-sam and Kim Jongpil. After much wrangling, Kim Young-sam became Roh's presidential candidate. In 1992, he took office as the first civilian president in over 30 years.

Kim Young-sam promised democratic reform. Within days of taking power he launched a sweeping anti-corruption drive, which toppled prominent figures in the military, government, and business – including some of his own allies. Although he initially released many prisoners, including some held for decades under the archaic National Security Law, he was intolerant

of dissidence. In 1995, he sent police to the Buddhist Jogye sect's HQ to evict squatting monks.

By the early 1990s, the major conglomerates were responsible for around 75 percent of Korean exports, but Kim Young-sam alienated them, forcing them to sell off land, and accusing the head of Hyundai of tax evasion. He soon incurred the wrath of farmers when he agreed in GATT talks to open the local market to rice imports, and his campaign for "globalization" was seen as a sell-out of local industry. The protected local market had been threatened by anti-dumping legislation in the US and elsewhere, and the administration now saw it as inevitable that import tariffs be reduced. However, per capita income continued to rise.

But the policies gradually unraveled due to incompetence and corruption. Pressure increased to bring ex-presidents Roh Tae-woo and Chun Doo-hwan to trial. In 1995, Roh made a televised apology for having amassed a fortune of US$650 million during his term in office. In 1996 Roh and Chun, along with other former military leaders, went on trial for corruption and treason.

Kim Young-sam distanced himself from his former allies before the 1996 National Assembly elections and managed a slim majority, but some of those who opposed Kim boycotted the Assembly, creating legislative turmoil. The final blow came when the Asian economic turmoil

of summer 1997 spread to South Korea, and the currency collapsed.

Enter Kim Dae-jung, who had stood against Park Chung-hee in the 1971 presidential elections. In August 1973, he was kidnapped in Tokyo, repatriated to Seoul and placed under house arrest. Kim was arrested again in 1980, when Chun Doo-hwan declared martial law. When Chun moved against the revolt in Gwangju, Kim was charged with inciting the revolt and sentenced to death. He was allowed to go to America for medical treatment, but was returned to house arrest when he arrived back in Seoul in 1984. Having been defeated by Roh and Kim Young-sam, Kim stood for president once more in the 1995 elections. This time he was successful.

The first opposition candidate to take power, uniquely able to isolate himself from past regimes and present himself as the people's

> In the economic turmoil of 1997, the Korean currency collapsed, leading to an appeal to the IMF for loans totaling US$57 billion. South Korea took another hit in the 2008 crisis, but managed to recover quickly.

choice, Kim Dae-jung proved himself an able administrator. Within two years, South Korea had re-emerged from economic collapse; state support for banks and loss-making companies had been withdrawn, allowing them to be sold off, amalgamated, or to fail. Foreign capital was flowing in, and foreign reserves were healthy.

The "Sunshine Policy"

At the same time, Kim set about *rapprochement* with North Korea. This was the "Sunshine Policy." North–South relations had ground to a halt after the death of Kim Il Sung in 1994, but the deepening food shortage in the North – mass starvation, with the loss of perhaps 10 percent of the people, occurred between 1995 and 1999 – and an international effort to stop the North's nuclear program presented opportunities for renewed relations. In 1995, Seoul donated 150,000 tonnes of rice, but several incidents, including forcing South Korean vessels to raise North Korean flags when in port, led to a suspension of aid. Rice and fertilizer were sent in subsequent years, while Hyundai was allowed to start a tourist operation from the South to the North in late 1998 *(see page 164)*.

The summer of 2000 saw a sensational breakthrough in North–South relations, when Kim Dae-jung became the first South Korean leader to visit Pyongyang. This historic meeting was hailed as a definite step towards reunification, and as a result Kim was awarded the Nobel Peace Prize. The most high-profile result of the thaw saw the first reunions between family members who had been separated by the war.

But five decades of stand-off could not be solved with a handshake. The deep divide was emphasized in early 2003 with US/North Korea relations deteriorating rapidly over the issue of the North's refusal to abandon its nuclear weapons program.

After tense negotiations at the six-party talks in Beijing in February 2007, North Korea agreed to dismantle its nuclear programs in return for economic aid and normalization of relations between itself and other states, including the United States.

Meanwhile, in the South, the administration of the new pro-reform president, Roh Moo-hyun, proved erratic, and the president was unsuccessfully impeached. However, his popularity increased dramatically after the signing of the Free Trade Agreement between the US and South Korea in April 2007. Roh left office in February 2008, and a year later became involved

mounted, while North Korea has accused the South of preparing to invade in concert with US troops. Behind the diplomatic squabbling lies the very real question of who will succeed Kim Jong-il, who is now in his 60s and suffering from ill health. One of his sons, or a military or political figure, has been mooted as the next leader.

In early 2010, relations nose-dived when a South Korean naval ship sank off the coast following an explosion that killed 46 sailors. Later in the year, two North Koreans were arrested in Seoul and charged with conspiring to assassinate a high-ranking defector, Hwang Jang-yop. ❑

in a bribery scandal. In May 2009 he committed suicide by jumping from a cliff.

New challenges and the North

Roh's replacement, Lee Myung-bak, was no stranger to power, having formerly been CEO of Hyundai Engineering and Construction and mayor of Seoul. He has pursued a more confrontational stance with North Korea, which has provoked a chorus of saber rattling from Pyongyang. Continued international pressure to defuse its nuclear program fully has

LEFT: Kim Jong-Il and Kim Dae-Jung at the historic Pyongyang summit, 2000. **ABOVE:** a train crosses the border for the first time in 50 years, 2007.

GREAT SOUTH GATE FIRE

To South Koreans, the fire that destroyed historic Namdaemun in Seoul on the evening of February 10, 2008 was not so much an act of arson as attempted national assassination. The gate, built of wood and stone with a two-tiered, pagoda-shaped tiled roof, dated from 1398 and was the oldest wooden structure in the country, and an icon of its resilience. That the culprit, Chae Jong-gi – who was protesting a land dispute – confessed swiftly after his arrest was of little consolation. The Cultural Heritage Administration has estimated it will cost US$14 million to rebuild the gate in its entirety, and the project is expected to take three years to complete.

THE KOREANS

To understand the Koreans and their intriguing society, you need to consider the peninsula's long and turbulent history

Koreans have long memories. They have learned to survive in a dangerous neighborhood, surrounded by China, Japan, and Russia (with which North Korea today shares a 16km/10-mile border) and, from the 19th century, threatened by Occidental powers. To survive, the Korean people have had to develop patience, flexibility, stubbornness and a robust, satirical, and unabashed sense of humor.

Korean patience does not mean passivity, nor does flexibility imply lack of individuality. Complementing and contrasting these, stubbornness – which might better be referred to as perseverance – has produce a time-tested resilience. These counterpointed national traits can be traced back many centuries. They also echo influences absorbed from outside Korea's borders, namely the patience of the Chinese, Japanese adaptability, and American determination.

The long-standing close relationship with China, and a willingness to accept Chinese notions of governance, ethics, and morality, has left indelible marks on the Korean psyche. Japanese colonialism represented a more recent threat to Korean uniqueness, and memories of exploitation and brutality, of being forced to speak Japanese and to take Japanese names, remain painful. More recent still, the devastation of the Korean War, and the influence of America thereafter, forced Koreans to confront the outside world in a new way.

Today, Seoul looks and feels much like any other sophisticated international city. When a traveler first meets a Korean man, there may

PRECEDING PAGES: the "thousand Buddhas" at Jikji-sa temple. **LEFT:** traditional dress at Suwon Folk Village. **RIGHT:** a family outing to a Busan park.

seem to be little mystery in his character. With his tailored suit and silk tie, a Korean businessman would not be out of place in Tokyo, London, or New York. Seoul's subway system would put many other capitals to shame, and Korean excellence in technology has ensured Samsung and similar brands have entered the international lexicon. There are small cafés on the busy streets, as well as the more traditional restaurants, and the inevitable and interchangeable global coffee chains. Scratch the surface, however, and things are still very different. Old ways of thinking and behavior remain remarkably strong in the minds of Korean people, almost regardless of their education and rank.

Etiquette

Korean codes of etiquette remain strong, an elaborate system of formalized gestures designed to foster smooth relations. The maintenance of proper *gibun*, by avoiding arguments or any overt display of emotion, is paramount. *Gibun* signifies mood or aura, and literally translates as "personal energy." Koreans also employ a strategy known as *nunchi* to observe and imitate the feelings of others. *Nunchi* means that Koreans will avoid saying anything that could be construed as negative; stating the truth, being scrupulously fair, or quickly settling any contractual agreement are all alien to the face-saving that *nunchi* usually requires.

Nunchi means that visitors tend to find the Koreans warm, friendly, and sympathetic. Foreigners are considered classless and they are not expected to know how to behave in an appropriate manner (once they were "non-persons," little different to outcasts).

Social hierarchy and Confucian influence

Until reforms in the 1890s, Korean society was rigidly hierarchical, from royalty and aristocracy (the *yangban*) down to farmers (*nongmin*) and below (*cheonmin*). Yet although a great deal has changed, strong echoes of the past remain. For

THE LEGEND OF DANGUN

It is believed that the Korean peninsula was first settled some 30,000 years ago by wandering tribes from Central and Northern Asia, who brought with them elements of their own cultures, shamanist rituals, and a language. The Korean language is part of the Altaic linguistic group, related to such widely separated tongues as Mongolian, Finnish, and Hungarian.

The founder of Korea, according to legend, was Dangun, born on Baekdusan (Changbaishan in Chinese), on the border between present-day North Korea and China, close to where the earliest migrants would have entered the Korean peninsula. The story begins when Hwanung, the son of the Divine Creator, heard the prayers of a bear

and a tiger who wished to become human. He gave them each 20 pieces of garlic and a piece of artemisia, and told them they would be transformed if they ate the plants and avoided sunlight for 100 days. The tiger failed, but the bear remained in a cave for the prescribed period and emerged as a woman. Her wish was to have a son; soon her prayers were answered, and Dangun was born. He ruled from 2333 BC to 1122 BC, then resumed his spirit form and disappeared.

The legend was revived in the early 20th century to reassert Korean national identity. In the 1990s the North Koreans claimed to have uncovered his bones: these are now displayed in a mausoleum near Pyongyang.

instance, the Korean language still preserves the hierarchy, offering a mass of honorifics that are used to reflect status, education, and age. When Koreans first meet, apart from exchanging namecards, they quickly size up a new friend, deciding within a few brief seconds whether to talk up, down, or as an equal.

Within families, as within all social groups, a hierarchy based on age is still the norm. A child is taught to respect parents and elders; in all things, he or she should behave properly, so as not to bring shame on the family. Koreans routinely call each other older brother (*chyeong-nim, oppa*) or older sister (*nuna, eonni*). Within schools, and later in life within the workplace, seniors are *seonbae* and juniors are *hubae; seonbae* have a responsibility to guide *hubae*.

Yet while the dictates of their parents remain strong, young Koreans today are gradually reshaping their society, taking their cue from the outside world. Traditional mores may still dictate bowing and similar lengthy courtesies to seniors in the office, but having glimpsed pastures new, young Koreans have ideas of their own which they are determined to implement.

Much of the Korean psyche stems from deeply rooted Confucian values. Chinese emperors called the Koreans "the ceremonious people of the East," in effect an admission that the Koreans had outdone Confucius' own people, the Chinese. Confucianism *(see page 62)* stresses the importance of a strong family structure, the ethic of frugality, hard work (not just for oneself but for the common good), and respect for education. A Korean child is given a two syllable name chosen by a wise elder, one syllable indicating his or her generation, and one predicting his or her character. This name is added to the *jokbo*, a book that links families into lineages and clans traced back to founder figures.

Life begins at 100 days

It is hard to overemphasize the importance of children in Korea. In every district of Seoul there is a photography shop that proudly displays pictures of small children. In villages, one still finds strings of dried red peppers hung across the gateway to a home; void of all culinary connotations, the peppers proclaim the birth of a baby boy a week or less before. Girls are announced by strings of charcoal and pine needles, the significance of which is rather less apparent. Once, the strings conveyed a message: it was taboo for visitors to enter, since it was believed that during the first week the newborn child was vulnerable to bad luck or evil spirits brought by visitors.

After 100 days, it is time to name the child. In the past, when the death of newborn children was common, this was the time to publicly celebrate in a ceremony known as the *baegil janchi;*

today, this is when the photographer is called. Next, the first birthday is celebrated with a special rice cake flavored with mugwort. This is the time to predict a child's future. Everyone is invited, and pencils, thread, and other gifts are placed before the child. If the child takes the pencils, then they are destined to become a scholar, while the thread indicates a long and full life.

Willingly to school

At the age of three, most Korean children start kindergarten, the first step up a highly competitive educational ladder in a country where memories of the poverty that followed the war are enhanced by Confucian respect for learning per se.

LEFT: respectful progeny gathers round at a *hwangap*, or 60th birthday party, in 1933. **RIGHT:** South Korean children benefit from an excellent education.

The Korean Diaspora

Korea's industrious people have spread far and wide in search of work and better conditions, many settling in the US, China, and Russia

Some 7 million Koreans live abroad, the result of a long-sustained diaspora to the West, with the majority heading across the Pacific to the US. Migration to America began in earnest when 7,000 Koreans were sent to work on sugar

plantations in Hawaii, between 1903 and 1905; many later moved to the mainland, particularly to California. Early exiles from Korea included some who had argued for modernization and change during the late Joseon period. Following the Korean War, emigration began to accelerate, and by 1980 there were some 357,000 Korean-Americans. Almost 56,000 Korean women had married US servicemen, and many Korean children had been adopted into American families.

A second community of fugitive Koreans traces its roots back further. Korean peasant farmers, escaping poverty, began to cross into Manchuria in the 1860s; they were granted land tenancy in the provinces of Liaoning, Jilin, and Heilongjiang during the 1880s. Some moved eastwards to what later

became the Soviet Far East, and in 1884 were offered Russian citizenship. Korean guerrillas based in China and Russia harried the Japanese during the early colonial period.

During the 1930s, when Japan established its puppet state in Manchuria, it began to draft in Korean labor, and the Korean population peaked at 2,163,000 in 1945. The 1985 Chinese census reported 1,765,000 citizens of Korean descent.

The Koreans in the Soviet Far East fared less well. 168,000 Koreans are recorded in the region in the 1926 census, and Vladivostok had its own Korean quarter. The population came under suspicion as Stalin sought to liquidate his opponents during the next decade, and in 1937 the entire community was relocated to Central Asia. Around 180,000 resettled in Kazakhstan and Uzbekistan. Increasingly, Koreans have utilized their high levels of education to emerge as a distinct urban professional class in the region. Beyond Central Asia, 40,000 Korean laborers were isolated on Sakhalin at the end of the Pacific War, when the island was transferred from Japanese to Soviet control.

The Japan population dates back to the 16th century, when Korean potters and other artisans were moved across the East Sea; earlier still, there is evidence of Korean royalty living around Nara near Kyoto. Some 900,000 Koreans still live in Japan, forming around 40 percent of Japan's officially recognized "foreigners" and living primarily around Osaka and Fukuoka. Migration, though, is largely a result of the colonial period. By 1940, some 1,250,000 Koreans, mostly from the south, had been drafted to work in Japan. Repatriation of around 60 percent to South Korea took place after 1945, and a Red Cross agreement allowed 100,000 more to return to North Korea.

There are other significant communities of Koreans scattered around the globe, including 125,000 in Australia, 50,000 in Brazil, 46,000 in the United Kingdom and smaller populations in Argentina, Germany, New Zealand and across Southeast Asia. ❑

LEFT: Korean migration to the US began in the early 20th century. **ABOVE:** becoming a US citizen.

The state education system is extremely good, yet parents who are able to afford it often choose to send their children to private academies. Alternatively, *hagwon* (crammers) provide extra tuition – at a cost – to boost the state system. By the age of seven, children will move into elementary school, and get to grips with such core subjects as maths, science, Korean, social studies, and foreign languages. The school year is divided into two terms, from March to July, and August to February. Sports take second place to academic subjects, and homework is in most cases plentiful. South Korea was the first country in the world to provide all its schools with high-speed internet access.

Middle school ends at 15, with most students going on to complete high school. The vocational school system is popular, offering programs in agriculture, technology and engineering, commerce, fishery, and home economics. The final hurdle is university, and winning a place at one of the top institutions can set students on course for a successful life in business.

> Loyalty is prized in alumni groups for students and young soldiers. Both Chun Doo-hwan and Roh Tae-woo, presidents in the 1980s, were members of secretive military alumni group Hanahoe.

It's not unknown for a mother to take up residence abroad with her children so they can improve their English (or, increasingly, Chinese), leaving the father behind to carry on at work.

A world away from the small, isolated villages of old Korea, urban children develop alliances beyond the family. Alumni groups feature in most Korean schools and universities, and also play an important part in young men's lives during their compulsory military service. This is a rite of passage that plays an important part in the national psyche, imparting a lifelong set of loyalties with fellow conscripts as well as a variety of disciplines and re-emphasizing the ever-present threat from the North.

A healthy health system

From their earliest days to the end of their lives, South Koreans benefit from a highly advanced

RIGHT: Koreans venerate their ancestors and tend their graves with great care.

health system that is inexpensive, accessible, and efficient – in short, the envy of many so-called developed countries. Apart from a number of community hospitals, most of the health-care system is in private hands. A compulsory national health insurance scheme finances the system, with worker and employer each paying half. If a Korean falls ill, he or she pays a token amount for a doctor's advice and the prescription for medicine. The balance is picked up by the national scheme.

Most Koreans agree that there are plusses and minuses to this system. On the positive side, healthcare is affordable, devoid of red tape, and

queues at doctors' surgeries are minimal. On the negative side, doctors get a set fee for every consultation, so there is a temptation to accept as many appointments as will fit in a day. Korean surgeons perform a large number of Caesarean sections, partly, it is believed, because their fee for doing so is higher than for a regular delivery. Such issues aside, the sophistication and efficiency of the country's healthcare system ensures that South Koreans are well protected throughout their lives.

Good matches and marriage

In the past, marriage was a contract between families, and spouses were chosen by parents. Many Koreans now want more say in selecting their own partners. Nightclubs and discos are often where the search begins, but a more popular method among university students is the "line-up," where an equal number of men and women meet in a coffee shop and, through games or ballots, pair off. Still, roughly half of all Korean marriages begin with a matchmaker. Meetings are arranged, most commonly in the coffee shop of a hotel on a weekend afternoon. Sometimes the matchmaker will be present to smooth the introduction. Before this, though, the mothers will most likely have visited a fortune-teller to check the prospective couple's compatibility (*gunghap*) based on their birth date and time (their *saju*).

Koreans are marrying later. According to a survey in 2007, women are considered "old maids" (*nocheonyeo*) only if they are unmarried after the age of 32. Men are considered bachelors (*nochonggak*) if they are still single at 35.

Today, most South Korean weddings take place in gaudy *yesikjang* (wedding halls). These are like factories, and they provide everything from flowers and dress hire to piped organ music. The ceremony is captured on video; friends and relatives gathered in the pew-like seats struggle to see the couple through lines of photographers. After the ceremony, guests are issued with a meal ticket leading them to a restaurant,

THE SOUTH KOREAN FLAG

One of the most distinctive flags among the world's nations, the Taegeukgi is endowed with symbolism and embodies a number of significant Korean values. Its design was inspired principally by the Chinese yin and yang symbol, and the flag comprises three distinct parts: a white background; a red and blue *taegeuk* in the center; and four black trigrams, one in each corner of the flag.

The four trigrams were taken from the Chinese book of I Ching, and represent the four Taoist philosophical ideas about the universe: harmony, symmetry, balance, circulation. The overall design of the flag also derives from Koreans' traditional use of the tricolor symbol – red, blue, and yellow – from early in the peninsula's history. The white

background is taken to mean spiritual cleanliness of the people, while the *taegeuk* represents the origin of all things in the universe. The complementary principles of Yin, the negative aspect rendered in blue, and Yang, the positive aspect rendered in red, are held in perfect balance. Together, they represent a continuous movement within infinity, the two merging as one.

The trigrams are related to the five elements – fire, water, earth, wood, and metal – and each signifies one of the seasons, a point of the compass, one of the four virtues, a family member (father, mother, son, and daughter), and an aspect of nature. Each has an overall meaning: justice, wisdom, fertility, and vitality.

usually within the wedding hall building.

Finally, today as in the past, the new couple is expected to produce a child – preferably a son

> Professional matchmakers often work on behalf of overseas Koreans – who will return on the basis of a pleasing photograph to meet potential spouses –and also on the behalf of business-men who have little time for social matters.

to pass on the family name – little more than nine months later.

urban South Korea, old customs survive in the countryside. There, after a wake, and a shaman ritual to ensure the soul's safe passage to the other world, the funeral bier is taken to a hill-side, where the body is buried. Grave sites are chosen with care, for from here the dead will continue to influence the living as an ancestor.

At lunar new year, *seollal*, and during the harvest festival, *chuseok*, it seems that the entire urban population rushes to escape to the countryside. These are the traditional times for tending ancestral graves and visiting family elders, and it is at these times that Koreans, both young and old, return to their roots. ❏

The final journey

Koreans traditionally retire when they reach 60, and this, the *hwangap* birthday, is a time for great celebration. It marks the completion of one life cycle, based on the Chinese astrological system of 12 earthly animals and 10 heavenly characters. The celebrant sits enthroned on cushions, surrounded by tables piled high with fruit, rice cakes, cookies, and candies, receiving respectful kowtows from children and grandchildren.

When Koreans die, they hope to do so at home. Although cremation is encouraged in

---

FAR LEFT: a Korean wedding. **LEFT:** the world's most symbolic flag. **ABOVE:** Koreans traditionally retire at 60. **RIGHT:** KFEM environmentalists.

ENVIRONMENTAL CONCERNS

One of the most radical moves in recent years has been the formation of the Korean Federation for Environmental Movement (KFEM), which brought together several smaller green pressure groups. KFEM has organized boycotts of polluting industries, opposed nuclear expansion, joined forces with Greenpeace to halt whaling, and generally raised the profile of environmental issues in South Korea.

The bad old days when the *jaebeol (see page 56)* could do what they wanted in pursuit of profit, riding roughshod over environmental considerations, have been called into question, as a new generation has demanded change.

BUSINESS CULTURE

Both national etiquette and the intricate make-up
of the country's major conglomerates played a key
part in South Korea's economic miracle

South Korea's economic growth since the dark days of the 1950s has been nothing short of miraculous. To understand the modern nation, it is essential to examine this "economic miracle," and its central character, the businessman, although a significant number of Korean women have also excelled in this field. Much of the national confidence that has freed Koreans from a sense of regional inferiority is due to the success of the country's export machine, which has turned it into one of Asia's economic powerhouses. South Korea was a nation of farmers a little more than a generation ago, but now, because of its economic success, over two-thirds of the population count themselves as part of the urbanized middle class.

The role of the *jaebeol*

The backbone of this success has been the *jaebeol* business conglomerates, and the industrial chiefs who run them: the top 30 companies account for over 50 percent of GNP – and over 70 percent of exports. They may have espoused Confucian ideals and regarded their employees as "family," yet they exerted tight control over their businesses, typically by means of a complicated series of cross-shareholdings, and ran up huge debts. Backed by the government, the *jaebeol* were the main vehicle for astonishing economic growth; in one generation per capita GDP grew from US$100 to US$6,000, and by the middle of the 1990s had passed the US$10,000 mark.

Although the economy slumped sharply during the Asian financial crisis of 1997–8, the recession forced a long-overdue restructuring and gradual opening of the economy. Consequently South Korea was by far the quickest

of the Asian "tigers" to recover and, by 2006, per capita GDP reached US$18,000. Though reform slowed in the final years of the Kim Dae-jung administration, under his successor, Roh Moo-hyun, economic success and, later, reform pulled the once-closed doors of the Hermit Kingdom off their hinges. South Korea also appears to have emerged relatively unscathed from the global downturn of 2008–9.

The first industrial barons were masters of all they surveyed, but these days many of the new generation of chairmen educated overseas tend to be more open to advice. Nonetheless, old habits of nepotism persist, and senior executives or "advisers," who may well wield more power than MDs of subsidiaries of the *jaebeol*, are often schoolfriends or army colleagues of the chairman. Many of these advisers are major figures in their own right. They tend to work in

> In South Korea, the namecard is to be treated with respect. It should be received with decorum and read, not taken casually and slipped into the pocket. Give your own (bilingual) card to the most senior person first.

the chairman's office or secretariat, or are the heads of "think-tanks." This is usually a euphe-

tionship there and then on the basis of a poor impression. Such a setback may be caused by an innocent "mistake" such as arriving unannounced, or failing to produce a namecard.

Foreigners should have a go-between, such as a consultant or mutual acquaintance. Bringing a lawyer implies lack of trust, so bring an interpreter instead. Just because an executive speaks English, do not assume everything is understood. Korean language teaching is not geared towards conversation. One of the great sources of misunderstanding is the Korean use of the word "yes." It may often mean "I heard you" rather than "I agree with you," and sometimes it

mism for the planning and coordination office (*gijosil*), the chairman's office (*hwoejangsil*), or even the secretaries' office (*biseosil*). These offices are charged with collecting and processing information useful to the business, functioning as a group intelligence agency.

Business etiquette

Foreign executives approaching these key conglomerate offices should seek some guidance on etiquette. The initial meeting is the most important and is taken seriously by Korean executives, who might decide to end the rela-

can even mean "I don't understand what you're saying but keep talking." Foreigners are advised to speak non-colloquial English slowly and clearly, and to pause occasionally (yet discreetly) to make sure they are being understood.

Koreans are warm, but at the same time they are very formal. Informality only exists between close friends. Never use first names unless invited to do so. Be prepared for questions about your age, marital status, and religion.

Ironically, the final piece of advice is that, after brushing up on etiquette, you should be your natural self. Koreans are more familiar with the outside world than vice versa. They expect to meet a courteous foreigner, not a mock-Korean. ❏

LEFT: the business district of Busan. **ABOVE:** Korean businessmen.

RELIGION

South Korea is a country of diverse spiritual traditions and philosophies, where major belief systems have become established alongside regional folk religions

There are five strands of religious practice in South Korea today: folk religion; Buddhism; Confucianism; Christianity; and various new syncretic religious traditions which have grown up since the end of the 19th century. It is hard to calculate the numbers of adherents in the different traditions because the understanding of self-identity varies from tradition to tradition. For example, people might only call themselves Christian if they were baptized or registered members of a church, whereas a person might identify him or herself as a Buddhist if their mother went to a particular temple. Likewise, attitudes toward worship vary greatly. Christians would probably feel that frequent attendance was a sign of faith, whereas Buddhists would take a more relaxed attitude toward formal worship, and believers in the folk tradition would view participation in certain important annual festivals as being sufficient.

Even given these difficulties in defining the numerical size of the religious traditions, about one-third of the population of South Korea would identify themselves as Buddhist, one quarter as Christian, and the remainder adhere to Confucianism, traditional practices, and the syncretic traditions in various combinations, or have no clear religious identity.

Folk religion

The indigenous religious traditions of Korea have no name apart from "shamanism." Yet this is not a name for the folk religion, but rather a description of it, and an inaccurate one at that. The folk religious traditions of Korea

LEFT: a monk at Bulguk-sa temple, Gyeongju.
RIGHT: guardian deity, Bulguk-sa Temple.

never became a formal religious tradition with ritual buildings, formalized rituals, recognized scriptures, and an organized clerical leadership. Korean folk religion has remained a noninstitutional, customary series of practices, the received traditions of the nation. How can you name it? Like any folk tradition, it just *is*.

There are two principal threads within the folk strand of Korean religious life; one is focused on village and household rituals, the other on the practices of the shaman, or *mudang* in Korean. These shamanistic practices are the most colorful, vibrant features of Korean folk religion. The shaman is an intercessor, a person who has been selected by spirits to have a special relationship with a particular spirit or group of spirits. Because of this power, the shaman is thought to be able to cure disease by finding the spirit causing the illness, to bring blessing and prosperity on a family or person, and to be able to see that the souls of the dead are successfully escorted into the next world. During the *gut* or shamanistic ritual, the shaman's special spirit is believed to descend into her body and to speak through her mouth.

Korean shamans are predominantly women. Whatever their sex, when they perform a *gut* the clothing of the opposite sex is worn. The *gut* are lively and noisy because of the drums

the *mudang* who remains a shaman for life.

Other Korean folk customs range from indigenous, non-Confucian ancestral practices – both shamanistic and non-shamanistic – to simple acts of tossing a stone onto a pile of stones, called a *seonghwangdang*, when crossing a mountain pass as an offering to *Sansin*.

The principal shamanistic shrine in Seoul, the *Guksadang*, stands on the western slope of Muaksan just to the east of the Independence Arch, by the Dongnimmun station on the Number 3 underground line. The *Guksadang* is surrounded by a cluster of buildings which proclaim themselves to be Buddhist temples, but which in real-

and percussion instruments accompanying the actions of the shaman. These features of Korean shamanism point to a link with the practices of the most ancient inhabitants of Siberia, the Paleo-Siberian tribes of the far northeastern corner of the Asiatic landmass.

In contrast to these colorful rituals, village ceremonies are more restrained. At certain key points in the cycle of the lunar calendar, for example the first or 15th day of the first lunar month, one or more adult male members of a village will be chosen to offer up a sacrifice at the village shrine to *Sansin*, the mountain god, or to the spirits of the founding ancestors of the village. These rituals are short and the leaders are selected for a brief period of time only, unlike

ity are shrines dedicated to syncretized Buddhist and shamanistic practices. Ascending the hill past these shrines leads to the *Guksadang* itself and a strange pockmarked rock which is the center for its own cult.

Buddhism

Buddhism is a missionary religion from India which spread from China into Korea some time during the 4th century, eventually becoming the state religion of all three of the ancient kingdoms of Korea – Goguryeo, Baekje, and Silla. By the time it reached the Korean peninsula, Buddhism had altered from its earlier form in India, absorbing various elements of the local folk traditions of the countries into which it had spread.

By the 7th century Buddhism was well established, as evidenced by the many great temples which had been erected throughout the peninsula, the numbers of monks who went to China and India to study, and the important role which Korean monks played in the spread and development of Buddhism in Japan.

> Joseon scholars, in their continued support of Confucianism, classified Buddhist monks as social outcasts, along with prostitutes, peddlers, and butchers.

By the end of the Silla period in the early 10th century, Buddhism had effectively taken on its current form. Monastic Buddhism is predominantly of the meditative *Seon* school (better known by the Japanese term *Zen*), whereas popular Buddhism, the Buddhism practiced by the laity, belongs predominantly to the Pure Land traditions. The all-encompassing doctrinal *Dienai* school (*Jeondae* in Korean) remained important for a few more centuries, but the meditation and Pure Land schools came to form the core of Buddhist practice in Korea. The *Seon* school is based on the idea that suffering is caused by attachment to things of this world, and that release from suffering can only come through the abrupt realization of the illusionary nature of all things. Methods of meditation and monastic life are meant to bring the monk or nun into a state of sudden enlightenment. The Pure Land doctrines, in contrast, teach that there is a great Buddha, *Amita*, who is the ruler of the Western Paradise or Pure Land and who desires the salvation of all people. The teaching of this school has a kind of Lutheran "by faith alone" aspect, as it is believed that anyone who truly and faithfully repeats the name of Amita 10 times will be brought to live in the Pure Land. The figure most closely associated with Amita is *Gwaneum* (Chinese *Guanyin*, Japanese *Gannon*), or Goddess of Mercy.

Buddhism during the Goryeo period (918–1392) flourished, existing in a complementary state of harmony with Confucianism. However, by the end of the 14th century, as Buddhism

had been associated with the Mongol overlords of Korea and as recent developments in Confucianism made Buddhism seem superstitious, the neo-Confucian Joseon dynasty (1392–1910) suppressed Buddhism, and on two occasions attempted to eradicate it altogether. By the end of the 19th century the religion was only a shadow of itself during the heyday of the Goryeo era.

With the demise of the Joseon dynasty, and the annexation of Korea by Japan, Buddhism's fortunes changed dramatically. The modernization of Buddhism is due to the work of both more traditionalist monks, and modernizers

UPDATING BUDDHISM

Consciously or unconsciously, the modernizers of Korean Buddhism looked to the rapidly growing Protestant Christian community in the country both for inspiration and as a competitor. Many features of contemporary Korean Buddhism reflect Protestant practice, such as the emphasis on lay groups, institutional outreach in the form of schools, universities, print and broadcast media, as well as popular liturgical practices that use Buddhist words to the tunes of well-known Christian hymns.

The modernization of Buddhism has effectively allowed its return to an important position on the Korean religious scene.

LEFT: a shaman goes into a trance during the *gut* ritual. **RIGHT:** around one in four Koreans follow the Buddhist religion.

who looked to the laity as the core of the Buddhist community.

Although temples were banned from the cities during the Joseon dynasty, all major South Korean cities now contain numerous temples. In Seoul, the most important is the Jogye-sa temple, head temple of the *Jogyejong*, the largest – by far – of the Buddhist denominations. It is the most untypical of all Korean Buddhist temples, because the structure was originally the central shrine for a provincial syncretic sect which was brought to Seoul in 1935 and reassembled on the present site. Nonetheless, it provides the visitor with a good introduc-

tion to Buddhist ritual activity. Other temples worth seeking out are the Haein-sa temple west of Daegu, housing the 80,000 printing blocks of the entire Buddhist canon, the Tongdo-sa temple north of Busan, housing a relic of the Buddha in its central pagoda, and the Bulguk-sa temple just outside the ancient capital of Silla, Gyeongju, with the associated Seokguram grotto overlooking the East Sea, housing one of the finest Buddhist statues in East Asia.

When visiting a Buddhist temple, certain buildings and structures stand out. The *iljumun* using two large tree trunks as pillars is topped by a tiled roof and displays a placard enscribed with the name of the temple and the mountain on which it is located. This gate marks the

outer perimeter of the temple grounds. Further along, the *Sacheonwangmun*, or Gate of the Four Heavenly Kings, guardians of the four cardinal points of the universe, marks the entrance into

> *Although some shrines are actual buildings, it's not uncommon to find local shrines that are no more than a large stone in front of a tree in the midst of a grove of trees.*

the inner area of the temple. Beyond this will be a *beopdang*, or lecture hall. Passing under or by this hall will lead into the main court of the temple with pagodas containing the cremated remains of eminent monks. In front will be the *daeungjeon*, the principal shrine dedicated to the Buddha. Nearby a *myeongbujeon*, or hall of judgment, will contain statues of the 10 kings of hell. Behind this main complex, often to the left and rear of the *daeungjeon*, is the *sansingak*, containing a portrait of the Mountain God seated under a pine tree, with a tiger nearby.

Confucianism

Confucianism is not a religion as such, but a system of sociopolitical philosophy which has absorbed an extensive ritual system derived from the practices of the Zhou dynasty of ancient China (1111–429 BC). Confucius (Kongfuzi; Gongja in Korean, 551–479 BC), the first and greatest philosopher of East Asia, developed a political philosophy which was revolutionary in its day, arguing that the ruler of a state should appoint ministers and officials on the basis of merit alone. Confucius saw that society was composed of five sets of relationships – ruler/ruled, parent/child, husband/wife, older/younger sibling, friend/friend – which were hierarchical and characterized by benevolent actions from above and loyalty from below. These relationships imply a high degree of mutual responsibility, which explains why languages like Korean have so many ways of indicating social distance or closeness. Confucius felt that the outward expression of filial love was symbolized by the performance of ancestral rituals.

The conduct of these rites, listening to the stately music of the day, and the study of classical philosophical literature, all led to moral cultivation. Confucius implied, and subsequent Confucian thinkers stated, that human nature was good in essence and only needed cultivation (education) to refine and develop itself.

With the establishment of the Han dynasty in the 2nd century BC, Confucianism became the state ideology. The bureaucracy was grounded in Confucian political thought, schools grew up to train the next generation of scholarly bureaucrats, and an exam system was instituted to admit people on merit. The pattern of Confucian government was set for the next two millennia.

In the 4th century, when the Korean kingdoms were absorbing substantial amounts of Chinese civilization, a process called Sinization, Buddhism and Confucianism were accepted as here and now. The rise of neo-Confucianism, a philosophy with a strong interest in issues such as the origin and nature of the universe, created a clash with Buddhism, which came to be viewed as superstitious. The Joseon scholars set about creating a model Confucian society, suppressing all aberrant tendencies, heterodox thoughts and superstitions.

With the Manchu conquest of China in the 17th century, the Korean Confucian élite felt that Korea was the last bastion of orthodox East Asian civilization. This led to attempts to suppress the Catholic Church from the late 18th century.

Today, Confucianism does not have the formal

part of a cultural package. As Confucianism spread beyond China, its influence on other nations was threefold – political, cultural, and social. Political influences were concerned with on the structure and conduct of government, whereas the cultural influences were focused on education, the keeping of historical records, and the use of a writing system. These were the primary influences of Confucianism on Korea until the late 14th century. Until then, Buddhism and Confucianism complemented each other. Buddhism dealt with religious matters and the afterlife, Confucianism dealt with the

---

LEFT: Seokguram grotto, Gyeongju. **ABOVE:** procession during a Confucian rites ceremony.

CONFUCIAN RITUALS

Twice-yearly rituals are offered to Confucius and his chief disciples at the Munmyo Shrine in the grounds of the Sungkyunkwan University. Throughout the country, every large town will have its *hyanggyo*, the regional Confucian school in traditional times, in the grounds of which will be a shrine dedicated to Confucius and his principal followers. In a similar vein, there are many local Confucian academies called *seowon* where there are shrines commemorating the founding scholar and his chief followers. These regional shrines are ubiquitous and are the main visible signs of Confucianism's historic influence on the Korean nation, and, as such, are afforded great respect.

support of the state, but its social influence is evident. Hierarchical family and social relationships, social distance, and respect for elders, parents, and teachers are all symbolic of this influence. Christian churches have conformed to the national Confucian culture by instituting memorial rituals for deceased parents and relatives.

The ritual imprint of Confucianism can be seen in the remaining shrines and altars. Just west of the Gyeongbok Palace, the Sajikdan (altar) in the Sajik Park embraces altars to the spirits of grain and harvest. Ancestral ceremonies for the royal family are still held at the grand Jongmyo shrine on Jongno street.

this act as undermining the moral foundations of the nation as the ritual was the outward symbol of filial respect to the ancestors. The aristocratic Catholics hid themselves among the oppressed and outcast social groups where Christianity spread rapidly, as it offered an explanation for their suffering in this life and hope for the next. As this movement seemed to present a moral and political threat, the persecution was severe. Thousands of people died, including French missionaries. When the persecution stopped in the last quarter of the century, the church developed a ghetto mentality and retreated from the world for the better part of a century.

Christianity

In many ways the history of Roman Catholic and Protestant Christianity in Korea is different from surrounding countries in that both forms of Christianity were self-evangelized. The origins of the Catholic Church date to 1784 when a young Korean aristocrat who'd been baptized in Beijing returned and began to evangelize among friends and relatives. Within 10 years, by the time of the arrival of the first priest and missionary from China, there was a Christian community of about 2,000 people. From the 1790s, a persecution of the Church began which was to last for more than 70 years and was over the issue of the refusal of Christians to perform the *jesa*, or ancestral ritual, as it was idolatrous. The élite saw

From the end of the 19th century, Protestantism (primarily North American Presbyterianism and Methodism) spread rapidly throughout the peninsula, beginning with the self-dissemination of the Korean translation of the New Testament (using the Korean alphabet) from Manchuria. Before missionaries arrived in Korea, there were small Christian communities already formed in parts of northern Korea. By 1910, 1 percent of the population claimed adherence to a Protestant group. Early mission work involved the establishment of hospitals, schools, and universities, a work which appealed to Koreans who looked to rebuild their nation intellectually and spiritually. During the era of Japanese colonial occupation (1910–45), a substantial number of Korean independence leaders were Christian. As with the Catholic church in an earlier period, many Koreans died as a result of their opposition to idolatrous worship at Japanese *Sinto* shrines. Even more people were subsequently martyred under the communists, and this has given a politically conservative cast to many Protestants.

During the generation of rapid development from the 1960s onward, Catholics and Protestants alike were in the forefront of movements for democracy, social equality, workers' rights, and equality for women. Of a total Christian population of over 13 million (out of a national population of 48.6 million), there are over 5 million Catholics, over 2 million Methodists, and over 6 million Presbyterians.

Christian monuments are, for the Catholics, martyr shrines. Myeongdong Cathedral is built on the site of the home of the first Korean martyr, Kim Bom-woo. Next to the Hapjeong station on the Number 2 underground line is the Jeoldusan Martyrs' Church and Museum, located on the site of the main execution grounds for Catholics in the Seoul area. There are three other sites outside the walls of the old city. The oldest extant Protestant church in Seoul is the Jeongdong Methodist Church, behind the Deoksu Palace. Other major points of interest in Seoul are Sogang, Yonsei, and Ewha women's universities, which are respectively Catholic, Methodist/Presbyterian, and Methodist in foundation. The modernistic Yonsei chapel is worth a visit. There is also a small Orthodox Christian community from a Russian foundation dating back to the late 19th century.

New religions

At the end of the 19th century, various new syncretic religious movements emerged which combined elements of the folk religion with other traditions. The best known of these movements is the Donghak (Cheondogyo, Religion of the Heavenly Way). Its founder, Choe Jewoo (1824–64), had a shamanistic-type experience of the Ruler of Heaven who gave him a formula to cure disease. He was executed for being a crypto-Catholic. Subsequently his group became a major political movement at the end of the 19th century and a force in the Independence Move-

ment against Japan in the early 20th century.

Another important new religious movement is the Holy Spirit Association for the Unification of World Christianity, or simply the Unification Church (Tongilgyo). Founded in Seoul right after the Korean War by Sun Myung Moon (hence the nickname, Moonies), this movement came to prominence in the late 1950s and 1960s, not least for the media coverage granted to its mass wedding ceremonies. Its doctrines concern the Lord of the Second Advent, a mysterious figure who is to complete the unfinished work of salvation started by Jesus Christ. This movement has not proved highly successful in South

Korea, but has been extraordinarily successful in spreading throughout many other parts of the world, although not without some controversy, mainly centering on sex and financial scandals.

Islam

In addition to these groups, there is a small South Korean Muslim community, numbering around 30,000, which descends from Koreans living in Manchuria in the late 19th century who had converted to Islam. This community has been augmented by Koreans who worked in the Middle East in the 1970s or later and had converted to Islam while there. There is a large mosque in Seoul in the Itaewon area, and mosques in several other cities. ❏

LEFT: Catholic nuns. **RIGHT:** Jeongjadong Catholic Cathedral, Suwon. Churches are part of the South Korean landscape, in both urban and rural settings.

SOUTH KOREA'S VIBRANT FESTIVALS

For short-term visitors to South Korea, there's no better way to appreciate the country's true character than to witness one of the many colorful festivals

Spring and fall are lively seasons in Korea, where almost every weekend there is a festival going on somewhere in the country. Some, such as the Andong International Mask Festival, are large affairs that attract people from all over South Korea. Others, such as the Tea Festival in Boseong, are local celebrations that you might come across while traveling the countryside. Visiting a festival is a great opportunity to see just how downright sociable Koreans can be. Despite all the pushing and shoving, and those stony Confucian faces encountered in the city, Koreans can party with the best of them. While attending a festival, it's likely you'll be offered a sip of *soju* from some grandfather's bottle, or maybe a brightly dressed *ajumma* will ask you to sit and enjoy a plate of *gimbap*.

Local flavor

Activities at Korean festivals revolve around a theme, usually a product or a cultural activity for which the region is famous. Ginseng, gimchi, mud baths, mushrooms, and Korean liquors all have a weekend set aside to celebrate their attributes. But, invariably, you'll also be treated to folk performances – the noisy farmer bands, the softer sounds of *pansori* (traditional song), the local mask dance, and probably some fascinating ceremonies performed by shamans to ensure the community's prosperity. If at all possible, schedule a day for a festival while visiting South Korea.

ABOVE: brightly colored lanterns fill the courtyard of a mountain temple during the week-long celebration of Buddha's birthday (April/May), Korea's most important Buddhist festival.

ABOVE: *neol ttwigi*, at the spring Dano festival, is South Korea's version of the seesaw.

ABOVE: a shaman in action at the Dano festival.

RIGHT: the Boseong Tea Festival in Jeollanam-do showcases every aspect of the tea industry, and the numerous varieties of Korean tea.

LEFT: the colorful Andong mask festival takes place in late September or early October.

18

BELOW: during the Buddha's birthday celebrations, sometimes referred to as the Lotus Lantern Festival, the capital is lit up with colorful lanterns and illuminated displays.

KOREAN KITE FIGHTING

In South Korea, kites *(yeon)* aren't just for children. Indeed, you're more likely to find an accountant or college professor holding a kite string than a bright-eyed waif. It's been that way for centuries, as soldiers and the upper class used fighting kites to hone their battle strategies.

The objective of Korean kite fighting is to maneuver your kite so it cuts your opponent's kite string, sending their kite floating ignobly to earth. Strings are made of silk, with ceramic filings (or even finely crushed diamonds) along their length – making them deadly when rubbed against an opponent's string. The kite itself is rectangular, with a hole in the middle of the sail, whose size affects the speed at which the kite can be flown. And the reels, with four to eight spokes, allow the kite flier to release or reel in long lengths of line amazingly fast.

A favorite location for kite flying is the Hangang Citizen's Park in Seoul. Go on a windy Sunday, and you'll see members of the Seoul Kite Club engaged in good-natured combat, or discussing strategies and admiring each other's kites. The International Kite Festival is held here in the first month of the Lunar Year.

ABOVE: Gwangju's Gimchi Festival. Foreigners are encouraged to try their luck at making the ubiquitous Korean staple.

RIGHT: at many festivals, village bands from the surrounding region compete to see which is the most colorful and noisy.

SPORT AND LEISURE

From martial arts and traditional street games to modern Western sports, Koreans enjoy a wide range of competitive and recreational activities

S ports and pastimes are immensely popular in South Korea, and the hosting of the 1988 Olympic Games and the 2002 soccer World Cup tournament *(see panel, opposite)* has underlined that enthusiasm. Yet South Koreans also keep alive the traditions of the martial arts and sports such as kite flying and archery.

The Olympic legacy

South Korea first participated in the Olympic Games under her own national flag in 1948 in London. These days, athletes train at an indoor 77,000-sq-meter (18-acre) camp at Taenung on the eastern outskirts of Seoul. Sports facilities at Taenung include an indoor pool, shooting range, and gymnasia for wrestling, boxing, and weightlifting. All kinds of sports events take place at the Olympic Sports Complex in Jamsil which was built for the 1988 Seoul Olympics. The stadium here has a seating capacity of 100,000 and there are world-class facilities for a wide range of sports.

Western sports

Baseball: There has been a professional baseball league in South Korea since the early 1980s, with the major teams sponsored by large corporations. Professional games attract large crowds.

Golf: Increasingly popular in Korea, golf is no longer the exclusive preserve of rich businessmen. Courses are operated on a membership basis, although guests are welcome. Green fees aren't cheap – although they are considerably cheaper than those in Japan. Most courses are in the environs of Seoul, and all of them are 18-holed. South Korea occupies an important leg on the annual Asian Circuit, with substantial prize money on offer.

Horse-racing: There are three race tracks in South Korea; the best of these is right next to Seoul Grand Park in Gwacheon (subway line 4, Seoul Racecourse Park Station). This track is run by the Korea Racing Association, which is affiliated to the Ministry of Agriculture and Forestry. Races are held on Saturdays and Sundays. The horses are imported mainly from Japan and the United States and none is privately owned.

Skiing: There are a number of ski resorts in South Korea, with accommodations, ski lifts, restaurants, and coffee shops. Most of the resorts are in Gangwon and Gyeonggi provinces. The best-known resort is Muju, which has hosted numerous international events. Snow machines extend the ski season from December to March.

Soccer: South Korea has long been established as one of Asia's leading international soccer teams, and has put in an appearance at most of the recent World Cup tournaments. With the co-hosting of the World Cup in 2002 and the success of the national team in that year, the sport has become more popular than ever. South Korea participated in the 2006 World Cup finals in Germany but was eliminated at the group stage, and both North and South qualified for the 2010 finals.

Outdoor pursuits

Hiking and mountaineering: Walking in the hills is a popular pastime for young and old alike. Hills and mountains cover nearly 70 percent of the peninsula, and the 17 National Parks are crisscrossed with a great network of trails.

Hunting and fishing: Hunting on Jeju-do and a few other areas is only for those with an official license. Hunting equipment, rifles, and dogs are rented. Game animals include the male ring-necked pheasant, quail, turtledove, wild boar, hare, and river and roe deer. The sport attracts thousands of Japanese tourists to South Korea during the season, which generally lasts from the beginning of November to the end of February. Fishing is a leisure activity enjoyed along rivers, lakes, reservoirs, and the coasts. Fishing gear is sold everywhere.

Martial arts

Taekwondo, literally the way of combat kicking and punching, is a martial art exercise that has been developing in Korea for more than 2,000 years. It focuses the combined strengths of body, mind, and spirit in devastating fist and foot blows. This empty hand-fighting technique was learned from China during the Tang dynasty and has been developed since the Three Kingdoms Period (post AD 650).

The World Taekwondo Federation (WTF) has a membership of more than 180 nations. A separate organization, the World Taekwondo Headquarters (Kukkiwon), which supports the WTF, has a *taekwondo* practice gym in the southern outskirts of Seoul. Regular exhibitions are staged for tourists.

LEFT: baseball is an American export that has become popular in South Korea. **RIGHT:** *taekwondo* dates back over two millennia.

Yusul ("soft art"), another martial art, was introduced from China to the Korea Royal court in 1150, but declined in popularity by the 17th century. It was a characteristically passive defense which consisted of throwing, choking, or blocking an aggressor. *Yusul* was taught to the Japanese, who called it judo, and was later reintroduced to Korea during the Japanese Occupation when it was restyled and called *yudo*. It is now a compulsory martial art for Korean policemen.

Ssireum – Korean wrestling – was introduced by the Mongol invaders during the Goryeo Period. Once a form of self-defense, *ssireum*

THE 2002 WORLD CUP

In 2002, for the first time, the Fifa World Cup came to South Korea, as joint host with Japan. While the honor of holding the final went to Yokohama, Seoul was awarded the privilege of kicking off the tournament as the venue for the first match in its stunning hi-tech stadium. Nine other Korean cities – Incheon, Suwon, Daejeon, Daegu, Gwangju, Jeonju, Ulsan, Busan, and Seogwipo – were selected to host various matches. With over a million spectators attending the matches, and many more watching on TV sets across the world via satellite, staging the World Cup constituted a spectacular promotion for South Korea. And the home team did superbly well to reach the semi-finals.

today is a folk sport for students and villagers. Contestants hold each other around the back and wrap a cloth strip around their opponent's thigh; they then try to throw each other to the ground using a range of leg, hand, and body maneuvers. *Ssireum* matches are held during *Dano* and *Chuseok* (spring and fall festivals, respectively).

Western wrestling has taken a firm hold on Koreans, since their enthusiasm was fueled by a major victory in the 1976 Montreal Olympics (in the featherweight freestyle event) and by their success at the 1986 Asian Games, which were held in Seoul.

SWINGING AND JUMPING-SEESAW

The simple pleasures of swinging *(geune ttwigi)* and jumping-seesaw *(neol ttwigi)* are traditionally celebrated by women during the spring festival of Dano. In the game of *geune ttwigi* young girls stand on swings suspended by 6-meter (20ft) lengths of rope, and gleefully pump their way skyward. The *neol ttwigi* draws laughter as girls, on either end of a solid length of wood set on large bags stuffed with rice straw, spring each other into the air. These recreations were reputedly designed to allow the aristocratic Korean women of old to see up and over their high compound walls, as they were not allowed out of their premises during the daytime.

Korean archery

Once a means of hunting, a weapon of war, and a prerequisite for Joseon-dynasty military leaders, Korean archery survives as a recreational sport. Contests are held at various traditional sites by the Korean Archery Association. One of these ancient sites, Hwanghakjeong (Yellow Crane Pavilion), is located above Sajik Park in northwestern Seoul.

Traditional games

Nearly 70 percent of the folk games in South Korea are said to have been created and played during the winter months. Traditional games and recreation which are still the delight of Koreans today include:

Chess (*janggi*): *Janggi* is the Korean version of chess introduced from Mesopotamia through China. Men can be seen crouched over engrossing games on sidewalks, in shops, and in parks. Sixteen pieces are given per player: one general, two chariots, two cannons, two horses, two elephants, two palace guards, and five soldiers, which are represented by Chinese characters written on checkers. The object of the game is to checkmate the general.

Game of wits (*baduk*): *Baduk* (called "Go" in Japan) is a contest of wits between two players to occupy more territory (houses) on a board divided by 19 vertical and horizontal lines. Black and white button-like stones are used as markers. Once exclusively the game of high officials, *baduk* increased in public popularity after 1945. *Baduk* halls now exist in almost every town.

Cards (*hwatu*): Korean playing cards are called *hwatu*. A pack consists of 48 matchbook-sized cards, representing the 12 months of the year. A bit of gambling spices the game. These flower cards are also used for fortune-telling, and in Japan are called *hanafuda* cards.

Backgammon (*yut*): *Yut* is a form of backgammon often seen played by old men sitting in the street. Four 25cm (10in) sticks used as dice are tossed in the air, and the player moves his pawns according to the number of backs or faces that turn up on the sticks. The first player who gets all four of his pawns to a goal wins.

Kite flying (*yeon nalligi*): Kite flying has long been a favorite pastime in South Korea, both for children and adults *(see page 67)*. ❑

(see page 67)

LEFT: Korean chess *(janggi)* is a popular pastime.

Bathhouses *(Mogyoktang)*

For the uninitiated, the Korean bathhouse is quite an experience. A range of body treatments will leave you refreshed and revitalized

A visit to a Korean *mogyoktang* bathhouse offers much more than a simple wash and brush-up. Both men and women are completely free to decide their own schedule, regimen, timing, and style. There is a considerable price range, although all offer the same basic accoutrements, focusing on the essential enjoyment of a steamy, soothing soak.

The correct *mogyoktang* etiquette is to bathe before entering the communal tub, and soap and dirt should be kept out of the bathwater. Next comes a leisurely soak in the central tub, where muscles can relax and pores dilate. Then, it's back on the curb-like lip ringing the tub and time to commence some serious exfoliation scrubbing, again using a basin.

The *mogyoktang* hand towel is just the right size, doubling both as an ample washcloth and as a fig-leaf substitute – for modesty's sake – as one moves around the bathhouse. Small red washcloths are available, too – very abrasive, but effective for removing dead skin and stubborn city grit. And for the patron who doesn't savor the strain of a vigorous scrub, attendants are usually on hand to rub with cloths until the customer's skin approaches the hue of a raspy red fabric. A scrubbing session is by far the best opportunity for a

---

ABOVE: a relaxing soak in the communal tub.
RIGHT: enjoying a head massage.

shave. Steam, suds, and sweat combine to create the fleeting impression that there is no actual blade in the razor.

Nearly every ordinary Korean bathhouse offers, in addition to the central tub and showers, an extra-hot tub, a cold tank, and, in many cases, a sauna as well. These present many alternatives to the basic cycle of bathe, soak, bathe. The last step in the bathing area is usually a final rinse under the shower – hot or cold, or both.

After all that time in the baths, most patrons seem to feel it a bit abrupt simply to get dressed and leave. So, instead, they dry themselves at considerable leisure, perhaps in front of a fan, but

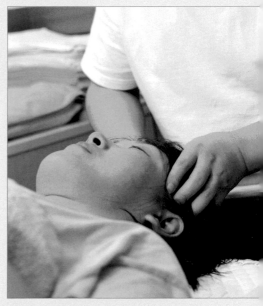

better yet, while grabbing one last catnap. Others clip their nails, read newspapers or magazines, or toy with their cell phones, or simply sit and contemplate. Men can get the same finishing touches they would in a barber shop, while ladies can relax one last time under a hair dryer. Eventually, though, everyone has to leave. Massages are available in some establishments.

Essentially, a visit to a *mogyoktang* is about far more than just getting clean; it's a social outing, somewhere to repair with friends or family as a getaway from the stresses and strains of the outside world. Most bathhouses close at around 8pm, many hours earlier than the counterpart *ofuro* in Japan, but they also open earlier as well, at approximately 5 or 6am. ❑

PERFORMING ARTS

Koreans love singing and dancing as forms of
entertainment, but these arts are also considered
a means of spiritual and political expression

olssigu! Jota! Such shouts are heard at
Korean parties, encouraging people to
dance or sing. The clickety-clack of chopsticks beaten against the edge of a table punctu-
ates the hearty, perhaps inebriated, voices. Take a
tourist bus and a microphone will be passed
around so that everyone can sing, and – though
officially illegal – passengers will stand in the
aisles and dance. And few towns lack a *norae
bang*, a "song room" where karaoke is king.

For the average Korean, singing and dancing
are an essential part of having fun. The aim is
to create something similar to what the Irish
would call a "craic," a state of heightened emotion and pleasure known in Korean as *heung* –
how you feel when the spirit moves you.

A rich tradition of music and dance

South Korea has a rich and ancient music and
dance tradition, dividing into court and folk genres. When Japan made Korea its colony, the court
music institute began to struggle for survival. It
was resurrected in 1950 as the National Center
for Korean Traditional Performing Arts. The
Center, now situated next to Seoul Arts Center,
employs 350 musicians, dancers, and researchers
to preserve traditional court music and dance.
Recently, with modernization and urbanization, much of the folk tradition has declined. To
counter this, the government passed legislation
in 1962 to encourage conservation, appointing
specific genres as Intangible Cultural Assets.
Today, folk arts contests are held annually, and

LEFT: traditional Korean dance.
RIGHT: performer at the mask dance drama, Hahoe
Folk Village.

master musicians and dancers continue to teach
and perform. Within just a few decades, traditional music and dance have been reinvented as
a symbol of Korean identity.

Court music can seem slow and motion-
less, a combination of the upright propriety
demanded by Confucian etiquette and the
apparent slowing down of many melodies over
time. However, it always remains enigmatic. To
Western ears it sounds strange, as melodic con-
tour is less important than the ornamentation
of individual tones, and because pentatonic
scales are favored over the Western diatonic system. There is no harmony, and the soft timbres
of instruments are tempered by elements of

noise – the plucking of a silk string, the sound of a plectrum hitting wood as well as the string, the rush of air on a wind instrument.

Some of the 65 traditional instruments are restricted to the two surviving court rituals, the twice-yearly Rite to Confucius *(Munmyo jeryeak)* and the annual Rite to Royal Ancestors *(Jongmyo jeryeak)*. These rituals date back to two gifts from Song China and revised in the 15th century after the founding of the Joseon dynasty. The first gift was banquet music, the second was ritual music: 428 instruments together with costumes, musicians, and dancers. All other Chinese music was soon Korean-ized, and today only two pieces are still played, the orchestral *Nagyangchun* and *Boheoja*. A suite based on a poem written by King Sejong (r. 1418–50) to celebrate the creation of the Korean alphabet, *Yomillak*, is more commonly performed in concerts.

Dances – *ilmu* – are prescribed for the two rituals, performed in rigid lines with little spatial movement. The dancers hold symbolic objects, a feathered stick and flute to represent civil paraphernalia, and a military axe and shield. A second dance category, *jongjae*, signifies court entertainments that until the 20th century had never been seen by the public. *Hwagwanmu*, the

NEW VOCAL GENRES

Beyond the confines of the traditional court music and dance, and from the 17th century onwards, the Koreans developed forms of music around three distinct vocal genres: *gagok* lyric songs, *gasa* narrative songs, and *sijo* sung poems. The literati, part middle class, part aristocracy, left many manuscripts of notations dating back to the 16th century, and today these are used by musicologists to reconstruct repertory and to determine appropriate performance practice. Most notations are for the *geomungo*, a favored six-stringed zither-type instrument with frets, which legend says was invented in Goguryeo in the 5th or 6th centuries.

flower crane dance, is the most commonly performed, followed by the oldest, a mask dance known as *Cheoyongmu*, the *Mugo* drum dance, the *Chunaengmu* nightingale dance, and a solemn ball game, *Pogurak*.

A new musical culture developed from the 17th century onwards beyond the court. This is normally associated with the emergence of a professional middle class, the *jungin*. The instrumental suite *Yeongsanhoesang* is representative of this music.

Eight sounds and eight materials

Korean instruments are by tradition divided into "eight sounds" *(pareum)*, according to the material from which they are made: skin, silk, bamboo, metal, earth, stone, gourd, and wood. Representative of the skin category is the *janggu*, an hourglass-shaped double-headed drum seen wherever Korean music is performed. Originally from China, *janggu* were present in Korea at least by the 12th century, made with wooden or pottery bodies and skins of ox or horse. Played solo, two sticks are used; played for accompaniment, one stick and the hand punctuate phrases. The *gayageum* is the most popular instrument in the silk category. This is a 12-stringed zither plucked with the fingers. Legend tells how this was invented in the 6th century by U Reuk in Gaya: King

stalk of bamboo that split into two at night and fused as a single trunk during the day. When it fused, storms abated and the sea was calm. King Sinmun was instructed to make a flute from the bamboo, and it is said that peace reigned throughout the Silla kingdom whenever the instrument was played.

Other Korean instruments derive from Chinese models but, over time, have become closely associated with the peninsula. The oboe, the *piri*, with a large double reed, produces a plaintive sound that is said to attract the spirits whenever played in shaman rituals. Bronze bell and stone chime sets, *pyeonjong* and

Gasil saw a Chinese zither and commented that, since Korean and Chinese were different languages, Koreans should have their own instruments.

Typifying the bamboo category is the long bamboo flute, the *daegeum*. This has a sympathetic resonator that adds a buzz to pitched tones, and it is prominent in both court and folk music. Again, a legend tells of its invention. A mountain was observed floating in the East Sea late in the 7th century. On it there was a

pyeongyeong, long since consigned to history in China, still dominate Korean ritual orchestras. And the *haegeum* fiddle, originally transported via China from Central Asia, is the only instrument considered to be made from all eight materials, with silk strings, a gourd resonator, a bamboo neck, leather on the bow, and so on.

Masks, dance, and acrobatics

The various Korean masked dance dramas (*tal-chum*) each offer a similar set of vignettes, portraying the foibles and misadventures of a group of apostate Buddhist monks, a lecherous old man with a concubine, a stupid aristocrat outsmarted by his servant, a charlatan shaman, and dangerous tigers that gobble up unsuspecting children.

LEFT: classical Korean music features an array of stringed instruments including the *gayageum*, a 12-stringed zither. **ABOVE:** Korean drums. **RIGHT:** early 20th-century zither musician.

As actors, participants encourage the audience to laugh at themselves; as dancers, they jump, leap, and squat to the rhythmic pounding of a small percussion group. The most famous masked dance is from the village of Hahoe, where unpainted wooden masks are used. The Bongsan and Yangju versions are more frequently performed, using grotesque and brightly painted papier-mâché masks. Masked dances once functioned as a way for commoners to release their frustrations about landowners and the clergy.

Early visitors to the peninsula often encountered bands of Koreans playing drums and gongs in the fields or marching from house to house through villages. Percussion bands, known as *pungmul*, can be traced back many centuries. A 3rd-century Chinese source, Chen Suo's *Sanguo zhi*, describes how Koreans in the southwest sang and danced to rhythmic music at times of celebration. Bands were commonly used to purify village wells and to protect homes from the unwelcome attention of troublesome goblins. They now play for entertainment, performing at Seoul's *Nori madang*, at festivals, and in inter-village championships. Four styles are distinguished: the coastal *yeongnam* from the southeast, the urban *gyeonggi*

CHILD PRODIGY YOO YE EUN

In a country where children are routinely dragooned into artistic and musical extracurricular activities, Yoo Ye Eun stands out. Born blind in 2002, she has wowed audiences in Korea and beyond with her amazing talents at the keyboard. She has been playing the piano since the age of three, and can play a tune after listening to it only once. Yoo has performed live in front of Singapore's prime minister Lee Hsien Loong. Despite the inevitable comparisons with Wolfgang Amadeus Mozart, who displayed a similarly precocious talent, Yoo has apparently been little affected by her sudden fame and continues to practice hard every day.

near Seoul, and *jwado* and *udo* from the southwest, the former fast and acrobatic, the latter slower but featuring intricate, contrapuntal rhythms.

In rural Korea, egalitarianism and communal activities meant that an abundance of folk songs – *minyo* – accompanied work, entertainment and the rituals surrounding death. Three folk-song styles are distinguished. *Namdo minyo*, from the southwest, are based on a sorrowful tritonic mode; *Gyeonggi minyo*, from the centre, are more joyful and lyrical; *Seodo minyo*, once common in the northwest but now only found around Seoul, feature nasal resonance and much vibrato. From the late 19th century, a second, more popular and professional, folk-song style began to flourish, giving rise to Korea's most famous folk song, *Arirang*. Eight folk-song genres are now preserved with government support as Intangible Cultural Assets. Two folk dances are also Assets – *Seungmu* and *Salpuri*. In the first, the dancer wears a hooded robe with extended sleeves, finding enlightenment as she beats a single drum. *Salpuri* developed from shaman dances in the early 1930s. It is a dance of exorcism in which the dancer, using a long white scarf as her only prop, strives to free her spirit from trouble and anguish.

Very often, Korean folk arts have both amateur/local and professional/urban forms. In contrast

In the 1970s, the Korean genre of masked dances was appropriated by students, who used it to poke fun at South Korea's politicians.

and tells how a blind man's daughter sacrifices herself so his sight can be restored; *Heungboga* critiques the Confucian system in which the oldest son inherits everything, describing an evil older brother and his generous younger brother; *Sugungga* offers a twist on the story of the wily rabbit and the slow turtle; *Jeokbyeokga* is based on the story of a Chinese battle.

to folk songs, the most developed vocal genre is the professional storytelling-through-song tradition, *pansori*. Performed by a lone singer accompanied by a drummer, *pansori* is of epic proportions: a performance can last five or more hours. The singer, holding just a fan and a handkerchief, tells one of five stories through a mixture of singing, narration, and basic dramatic action. The stories are well known: *Chunhyangga* is a Cinderella story in which the daughter of an entertainer falls for an aristocratic Prince Charming; *Simcheongga* is about filial piety,

LEFT: masks and performers of the Bongsan Dalchum dance at the Andong Mask Festival. **ABOVE:** the farmers' dance celebrates a good harvest.

From the 1920s onwards, operatic troupes, *changgeukdan*, toured the countryside performing staged versions of *pansori*. They met an earlier form of itinerant traveling troupe, *namsadang*, who since the early Joseon dynasty had been setting up in marketplaces to perform music, dance, and acrobatics. In 1978, a new urban equivalent appeared. This was *samullori*, a four-man percussion band playing updated pieces sequencing rhythms from each of the old *pungmul* styles. *Samullori* sit where old percussion bands marched and danced. *Samullori* have proved remarkably popular, and several dozen professional teams now work in Seoul. *Samullori* has revitalized the old, and percussion performances today range from student groups to a massed band of 1,100 that played at the opening ceremony for the 1993 Daejeon Expo. This last, in the words of one drummer, was indeed a "Big bang *Samullori*," and earned a mention in the *Guinness Book of World Records*.

Today, though, the majority of music heard on Korean radio and TV is Western in orientation. South Korea has orchestras, opera, and ballet companies of international standard, and many Korean musicians are active in Europe and America, including the singer Sumi Jo, the violinist Kyungwha Chung, and the conductor Myunghoon Chung. For *Samullori*, this pro-vides opportunity for fusion, most notably with the jazz group Red Sun.

Ppongjjak and pop

Repeat *"ppongjjak"* a few times, and it becomes onomatopoeia for the foxtrot rhythm that underpins a standard song style, *yuhaengga*. This, often arranged in purely instrumental versions, is the music of preference of many older Koreans. It remains popular fare in cafés, taxis, and long-distance buses.

This particular style arrived from Japan in the 1920s, and the best-remembered songs are also among the oldest, such as the "Adoration of Death," set to a Russian melody and released in 1926. The first such popular song was *"hemangga"*/"Song of Aspiration," probably written in 1923 by an unknown composer.

Speeded up in the 1960s, *ppongjjak* took on elements of rock 'n' roll, with lyrics telling of love and desertion. Lee Mi-ja and Patti Kim Hye-ja are two singers from the era who remain popular in South Korea today.

By the 1970s, students had taken American acoustic folk guitars and created their own style, *tong* guitar. From here, a song movement associated with campaigns for democracy grew, led by Kim Mingi. Kim was duly imprisoned during Chun Doo-hwan's presidency. Through the 1980s, the government continued to censor lyrics, creating a uniformity of style. The style was common to most Asian ballad traditions, and in Korea it was promoted by the likes of Cho Yong Pil and Lee Sun-hee. The lack of copyright control – South Korea only became a signatory to international conventions in 1985 – meant that cover versions of songs were common.

Pop music changed dramatically in the early 1990s, when Seo Taiji burst onto Korean TV screens singing rap. Musicians jumped on the bandwagon, assimilating any foreign style they liked the sound of, and the rapid innovation helped the local recording industry to grow. Into the second decade of the 21st century, Korean pop music ("K-pop") is distinguished by a predilection for bubblegum pop, although R&B, dance, and hip-hop are also very popular.

Developing a social conscience

In recent years, democracy has allowed the arts to become a medium for social commentary. In 1992 the ballad singer Lee Sun-hee released

FASHION

When Kang Seung-Hyun (aka Hyoni Kang) won the Supermodel of the World contest in 2008, it sent a certain frisson through the fashion industry as she was the first Asian model to do so. But in South Korea the general reaction was: What took you so long? The country's rag trade has been driven to global prominence by various factors. Many young Koreans have spread their wings to study design overseas, and set up their own businesses, notably Jean Yu and Christina Kim. An increasingly prosperous nation has had more money to spend, creating a demand for home-grown styles. And what better promotion than stunning models such as Hyoni Kang strutting down the catwalk?

an album dedicated to the tragedy of "comfort women" – women forced into sexual slavery by the Japanese military. Three years later, Seo Taiji celebrated the lifting of government censorship with the song *Gyosil idea* ("Education Idea"), criticizing in blunt terms the economic management of the Kim Young-sam administration. Im Chintaek updated *pansori* with settings of Kim Chiha's satirical *Ojeok* ("Five Enemies") and *Ttong bada* ("Sea of Shit").

Movie directors have also moved away from re-creations of history to social commentary. An early example was the 1981 movie *Eodumui Jasikdeul* ("Children of Darkness"). More

blockbuster *Shiri* (1998) by Kang Jae-Kyu; and *JSA* (*Joint Security Area*) by Park Chan-wook (director of the better-known *Oldboy*), which shed light on the division of the Korean peninsula into South and North. In the 2006 movie *Host*, director Bong Joon-ho explores social and environmental issues, including the dumping of toxic materials into the Han River by the US.

Aware of the heritage, but often questioning the past and criticizing the present, contemporary performance arts now reflect both diversity and maturity; Korean yet international, they are surely well worth exploring. ❏

recently, the director Im Kwontaek returned to *pansori*, but criticized the lifestyles and practices it represented, in *Seopyeonje* (1993). A year later, in *Taebaeksanmaek* ("Taebaek Range of Mountains"), he reassessed the brutal repression of left-wing sympathizers that occurred before the Korean War.

The trend has continued, notably with *Kkonnip* ("A Petal"), a 1996 movie by Jung Sun Woo that looks through the eyes of a child at the Gwangju massacre of 1980; the 1999 movie by Pak Kwangsu, *Ijaesu ui nan* (*The Uprising*); the-

LEFT: Busan fashion show. **ABOVE:** an open-air folk music performance in Seoul.
RIGHT: breakdancing "B-Boys."

LIVE PERFORMANCES

Music fans can have their fill in Seoul. Korean preference in Western classical music tends to the tried and true – Beethoven, Brahms, Tchaikovsky – and opera. South Korea produces some talented musicians, such as concert violinists Chung Kyung-Wha and Kim Young-Uk. Concert-goers will pay high prices to hear these artists or touring foreign performers, but tend to neglect other local talent – with the exception of Korean pop singers (such as boy band Dong Bang Shin Gi), who are extremely popular among young people. Traditional Korean folk music is performed at many venues, too. *For a list of major venues and what's on magazines, see page 292.*

ARTS AND CRAFTS

It is possible to trace the development of the Korea's religious traditions and dynastic history by viewing its rich legacy of treasures

From Joseon-dynasty folk paintings and images of Buddhist deities to intricate temple bells and the breathtaking crowns of Silla, from regional pottery to regal riches, diversity and uniqueness are the words that spring readily to mind when exploring the world of Korean arts and crafts. Whether it's the graceful work of porcelain designers or elaborate jewelry recovered from burial mounds, there is always something surprising to be found in this surprising country.

Ceramics

Throughout South Korea, antique shops and museum stores offer visitors original and replica pots. To enjoy the diversity of Korea's ancient and contemporary ceramics, it is important to know a little about the centuries of potters' work and patrons' taste that formed the distinctive ceramic style of South Korea.

In the first millennium, when the regions of the Korean peninsula were ruled separately and each had a very distinctive local culture, potters produced vessels of hard, dark stoneware for ceremonies and for burials. Many of these have been excavated in modern times, showing that the kingdoms of Silla, Baekje, and Goguryeo all turned out high-fired stonewares in great numbers. Judging from the decorations carved on the sides of some large pots, they were used during ceremonies that connected humans with the heavens or an afterlife. A striking feature of early Korean pots is their shape, typically a high splayed circular stand, divided into rows

or bands of linear perforated patterns, and rising to a bowl or cup shape. Some of these high stands with punched-out holes are of imposing dimensions, reaching 50 or 60cm (2ft) in height, but most are smaller, suggesting that their use was widespread at all social levels.

After Buddhism spread throughout Korea between the 4th and 6th centuries AD, believers adopted the custom of cremating the dead. This created a need for urns to contain ashes, still greyish in tone, but smaller and rounder in shape.

Around AD 1000, Korean potters began to produce work in an entirely new style. Inspired by the graceful and attractive pots from south China, they began making green-

LEFT: *Gwanseum-bosal with Willow Branch*, painted with mineral colors on silk by Sogubang, a 14th-century Goryeo artist. **RIGHT:** contemporary ceramics.

glazed ceramics of their own, establishing large kilns to supply fine vessels for the court. These green-glazed wares of the Goryeo dynasty were produced for aristocratic clients during an era of elegant living. Ships were loaded with bowls, jugs, wine cups, vases, and even roof-tiles made in the southern kilns, to supply eager clients at the palaces and temples of the capital hundreds of kilometers away in the north of the country.

Today, the ruins of the kilns at Sadangni and Yuchonni are an eloquent testimony to the sophisticated tastes and impressive organization of the ceramic industry in the Goryeo dynasty.

Far from the capital, potters in the coastal areas turned out thousands of bowls, wine cups, teapots, incense burners, garden stools, roof tiles, pillows, boxes, bottles, and many other items. These craftsmen were among the lowest ranks in society; their profession was handed down from father to son, their payment poor, and their work anonymous. These days, unblemished Goryeo pieces command astronomical prices in antique shops and auction rooms, but their makers gained little benefit from producing them.

Known to Koreans as *cheongja* or greenglazed ceramics, these sought-after pieces take their Western name from a character in a French play. Celadon, a humble shepherd, wore a cloak of a subtle and unforgettable green color. Somehow, the name of celadon has passed into use among art-lovers, long after the play has been forgotten.

Anonymous potters of the 12th century even introduced a stunning innovation known as *sanggam* or inlay decoration, adding sparkling mica and iron-rich clays to the decoration of their pots to produce a unique style. After throwing the vessel on a wheel, the potter let the clay dry for a while before using a bamboo knife to cut designs on the leather-hard surface. The indented pattern was then filled with creamy liquid containing tiny particles of mica. When the excess was wiped off and the

piece was glazed and fired in a kiln, sparkling white pictures appeared. By a similar process, black patterns could be produced, using an infill rich in iron compounds. The potters in the Goryeo period also took pleasure in mak-

> For Koreans, Goryeo-period green ceramics are an emblem of national pride. Their lustrous color and marvelous shapes were admired even by the haughty Chinese.

ing art imitate nature by molding and carving their vessels to resemble fruits, flowers, and even human figures. Melons, vines, pumpkins, and bamboo shoots were all reproduced in green-glazed stoneware, for the pleasure of a luxury-loving aristocracy. Fine green-glazed ceramics were used to serve food and wine at court and in the residences of the nobility. In Buddhist temples too, delicate green incense burners and water sprinklers played their part in the services and devotions. Ingenious potters carved delicate veins to make leaves more lifelike. They fashioned spouts and handles in teapots to look like the sections of a stem of bamboo or the tendrils of a vine.

A new type of pottery came into vogue in the early years of the Joseon dynasty. Known

The Joseon dynasty (1392–1910) was, like the Goryeo, an important consumer of ceramics at court. The Royal Kitchens ordered tableware

> *Painted Korean porcelains are quite austere in taste, often featuring a single design feature, such as a blossoming spray, fish, a dragon, or a grapevine, set against the plain white pot.*

and ceremonial vessels to be produced at its kilns. Most prestigious of all were pure white porcelains, imitating the splendid blue-and-

to Koreans as *buncheong* or powder-green ware, these ceramics are unpretentious and spontaneous. Painted, brushed, carved, inlaid, and stamped patterns were applied to bottles, bowls, and vases in plain shapes far removed from the refined and ornate designs of the Goryeo. These plain vessels appealed greatly to the Japanese taste, and since the 16th century have been treasured in Japan as tea-ceremony ceramics. The British potter Bernard Leach also admired Korean *buncheong* wares and introduced them to the West in the 20th century.

FAR LEFT: Goryeo-dynasty celadon bowl dating from *c.*1150. **LEFT:** Joseon-dynasty pottery (*c.*1500). **ABOVE** continuing an age-old tradition.

white porcelains of Ming-dynasty China. When these were first seen at court in Korea, in the early 15th century, they created a sensation, and no effort was spared in making a Korean version. Blue painted decoration was thought to be particularly beautiful, and designs of trees, birds, flowers, bamboo, and dragons are seen on surviving pieces.

Ceramic revival

Korean ceramics have experienced something of a revival over the past decade. University fine art departments train potters who work in different styles, some of them responding to the patterns of Korea's past by creating pots in the celadon, stoneware, and *buncheong* styles.

Working with stone

Koreans excel in granite sculpture, a skill perfected over the centuries in a land where the terrain is 70 percent mountainous granite and limestone. Naturally, Koreans developed a special love for stone and a skill in its use both as building material and for sculptural pieces. Huge dolmens of early times speak of the strength and dexterity of unknown Neolithic inhabitants on the peninsula. By the 4th century AD, the northernmost of the three Kingdoms, Goguryeo, was constructing monumental tombs, half the size of the Egyptian pyramids. They used dressed granite blocks that were so perfectly engineered that

the mountains. Images of Buddhist deities were also cast in bronze and iron, the early examples appearing relatively flat and linear, while the later period produced fully three-dimensional work of grace and quiet inspiration. The meditating Maitreya (in Korean, *Mireuk*) figures in the National Museum, and the Seokguram cave-grotto near Gyeongju, date from as late as the 8th century, and display a religious tenacity. The cave-grotto has many relief carvings of deities sculpted on rectangular blocks expressing the apogee of the Buddhist tradition. In addition, Seokguram contains a giant central freestanding sculpture, representing the quin-

they have survived to this day, together with the frescoes on their walls. However, the Goguryeo tombs are difficult to visit, being situated partly in an area of China that was formerly Korean territory and partly in North Korea. One can gain an understanding of ancient beliefs about death from these Korean tombs, with their wall scenes and decorative symbols on the ceilings. Hunters, musicians, and dancing girls populate the wall paintings, in scenes that seem to capture the way of life of the tomb's occupant. The ceiling frescoes, meanwhile, show stars, planets, and heavenly creatures, since they portrayed the afterlife – the realm of the spirit of the dead.

The Korean peninsula is dotted with Buddhist figures skillfully carved in the granite rocks of

tessence of Buddhism's spiritual momentum in the Far East.

Much of the work of Japan's renowned Asuka period can be attributed to Korea since it was created by Koreans and then exported, or else made in Japan by Korean immigrant artists.

Paper

One of the oldest crafts in Korea is papermaking, which is thought to date back around 1,600 years. *Hanji* is made from the bark of the mulberry tree, whose fibers are especially long, resilient, and shiny. These qualities make *hanji* especially durable, and it can last for centuries without losing its luster or smoothness. It was even used to make furniture. *See page 251.*

Heavenly bells

Some of the most intricate, melodious, and beautiful temple bells in the world were created by Korean artisans. The earliest dated one was cast in AD 725 and now hangs at Sangwon-sa in the Odaesan National Park area. The most famous is the "divine bell," or the Emille Bell (cast in AD 771), now kept in a special pavilion at the entrance to the Gyeongju National Museum. It is said that the sonorous notes of this 3.6 meter- (12ft)-high bell could be heard 64km (40 miles) away on a clear day. The sound chamber at the top took the form of a dragon, but the most spectacular decoration consisted of two pairs of Buddhist angels or devas, holding censers of incense and floating on lotus pods amid wisps of vegetation. Gossamer-thin garments swirl heavenward, taking the place of actual wings.

These bells, which played a major role in ritual and worship, are major works of bronze sculpture inspired by Buddhism at its peak.

Silla relics

By the early 6th century, most of the Korean peninsula had adopted Buddhism. The kingdom of Silla, however, in the remote and mountainous southeastern region, was still ruled by shaman kings. This belief was coupled with the custom of cairn-type tomb burial in which shaman royalty went to their graves in full religious regalia. This made the Silla capital, Gyeongju, one of the world's most spectacular archeological sites. Hundreds of tombs are yet to be explored in this city which has already become a veritable outdoor museum.

Breathtaking crowns fashioned for the king to wear in the afterlife were among the treasures buried in Gyeongju's mounded graves. Their fascination lies not only in the use of precious materials, but also in their intricate design. So far, 10 slightly different "gold crowns of Silla" have been brought to light. Alongside the crowns, other royal possessions have been discovered, such as golden girdles, ornate belts, elaborate earrings, silver and gold goblets, necklaces, bracelets, finger rings, and ceramics. One intriguing crown was unearthed in 1973 at the excavation of Tomb No. 155 in the heart of Gyeongju city. When viewing the crown, one first sees its outer circle of beaten

FAR LEFT: Goryeo artifacts dot the countryside. LEFT: paper-making. RIGHT: king's crown from the Silla dynasty.

gold with jagged wave designs representing the watery nether world. An inner golden cap fits closely to the head. Fifty-eight jade tiger claws hang from the crown. In the shaman religion, the tiger is associated principally with three things: a strong power to destroy evil forces, human fertility, and male virility. These curved pieces carved from jade formed a major part of the symbolism when the gold crowns were worn. They were suspended loosely on thin, twisted gold wires, while several hundred tiny golden spangles, suggesting golden raindrops, were affixed onto the crown with more thin gold wires. When the shaman king, who embodied the power of the sun as

well as other forms of nature's energy, moved his head even slightly, he created a dazzling sight and vibrating sounds. Pendants of thick golden leaf-shaped droplets hung on each side of the crown. The key to understanding the meaning behind all this regal magnificence lies in the three upright pieces attached to the circular head-band at the base of the crown. These are in three symbolic forms: deer antlers, trees, and pairs of wings, all carrying shamanistic associations. The antlers symbolized reindeer, whose fleetness the shaman king acquired by wearing their horns. Birds and trees both play important parts in shaman ritual, bearing spirits from one world to the next.

After the excavations in 1973, Tomb No. 155, The Magical Flying Horse Tomb, was restored to its original state. Half of it is now supported by a steel framework, and a glass wall has been erected across the mid-section, so that tourists can enter to look at the exact position in which the crown, sword, girdle, pottery, and many other objects were buried.

Another fascinating discovery was in a large box at the head of the shaman ruler's tomb. Here, an actual royal horse had been offered in sacrifice, indicating the traditional importance of horse riding to these people, former nomads of northwest Asia. A special horse belonging to this shaman king was believed to be a flying horse. This creature could levitate just as a pow-

erful shaman could. When the horse was killed, his saddle flaps made of laminated birch bark, sewn together with deer leather trimmings, were buried in the grave along with other horse trappings and valuable treasures. Six of these saddle flaps have been found and they are as amazing as the golden crowns.

Goryeo devotional art

Before an exhibition in Japan in 1978, Koreans knew little about the survival of exquisite devotional paintings, made to hang in Buddhist temples. These beautiful Buddhist works of art, painted around 1200–1350, were

FOLK PAINTING SYMBOLS

The major symbols used in Korean folk paintings are:
Four Sacred Animals of Good Luck: turtle, dragon, unicorn, and phoenix.
Ten Symbols of Longevity: deer, crane, turtle, rocks, clouds, sun, water, bamboo, pine, fungus of immortality (bullocho).
Auspicious Ideograms: bok (good fortune), su (longevity), nyeong (peace), and gang (health).
Fertility Symbols: pomegranate, jumping carp, 100 babies, and "Buddha's hand citron."
Special Guardians: tiger (front gate or front door), dragon (gate or roof), haetae (fire or kitchen), rooster (front door), and dog (storage door).

Four Noble Gentlemen: orchid, chrysanthemum, bamboo, and plum.
Three Friends of Winter: pine, plum, and bamboo.
Individual Symbolic Associations: peach (longevity), pomegranate (wealth), orchid (scholar, cultural refinement), lotus (Buddhist truth, purity), bat (happiness), butterfly (love, romance), bamboo (durability), peony (noble gentleman, wealth), and plum (wisdom, hardiness or independence, beauty, loftiness).

A formal list of symbols was never compiled in writing; it was simply a part of Korean tradition passed down through works of art, familiar to everyone from itinerant painter to "drunken master."

thought to have vanished. It remains a painful topic to Koreans today, since almost all these masterworks are still in Japanese private and public collections. The paintings depict the Buddha, the goddess of mercy Gwaneum, and other divine figures, with shimmering robes of finest silk in a delicate yet precise style that reflects the artists' devout reverence for the Buddhist faith. Buddhist subjects continued to find patrons and artists throughout the following centuries, but the splendor and transcendent beauty of the Goryeo-period works have never been equalled.

Art in the Joseon dynasty

During the Joseon dynasty (1392–1910) an official "Painting Bureau" was supported by the court, and artists were commissioned to paint portraits of the aristocracy. By the 18th century some artists had begun to paint scenes of common people going about their business. These miniature master-works are treasured both as paintings and as evidence of a way of life that has now disappeared.

An entirely different approach to art is revealed in Joseon-dynasty folk paintings. They reflect the actual life, customs, and beliefs of the Korean people. Since collectors in Korea and abroad have "discovered" them, the value of such works has escalated.

One example of attractive and now valuable artwork is a kind of screen decorated with letter pictures. Artists rendered the terms for the Confucian virtues into paintings which were mounted on paneled screens in the homes of the well-to-do.

Based on the belief systems of ancient China, a number of themes appeared in the folk arts of Korea. Among the most important were the correlatives of heaven and earth, yang and yin, male and female, along with five directions (north, south, east, west, and center), five colors (black, red, white, blue, and yellow), and five material elements (water, fire, metal, wood, and earth).

Buddhism too brought a number of emblems and themes into the Korean artistic vocabulary. These include the lotus, the official religious flower, which calls to mind the beauty and purity that emerge out of the mire of human existence. After centuries of religious co-existence, the origins and meanings of the multitudes of symbolic plants, animals and figures found in Korean art can be difficult to determine. For example, the animals, of the zodiac are often depicted. They usually relate to time, and astrologers still use them to foretell suitability in marriage. The zodiac was also associated with the Chinese principles of yang and yin (in Korean, *yang* and *eum*). It read, in clockwise order: rat, ox, tiger, rabbit, dragon, snake, horse, sheep, monkey, chicken, dog, and wild boar (or pig). These astrological animals also represented the 12 points of the compass.

Folk painting created for the home was rich in symbolism, and further associations can be seen in furniture, linens, clothes, and all accessories, even hairpins. All things, including outside walls, are full of the five elements, the 10 symbols of longevity, the four directional animals, the 12 zodiacal animals, and propitious ideographs. Even the more educated citizens put some measure of faith in these emblems, partly convinced that such symbols can repel evil and attract good fortune.

The legacy of folk painting can be viewed today in South Korea's many modern art galleries, principally in Seoul, which have evolved an eclectic and thoughtful style, drawing admirers from around the world. ❑

LEFT: Joseon-dynasty painting of a *gisaeng* house.
RIGHT: iron bell detail, Bomun-sa Temple, Seongmo-do island.

TRADITIONAL KOREAN COSTUME

With its flowing lines and distinctive style, traditional dress is still worn on special occasions and holidays by Koreans of all ages

Traditional Korean clothing is usually known as *hanbok*, and consists of a two-part ensemble of short jacket with voluminous skirt for women, and a jacket with loose trousers tied at the ankles for men. Clothing in this style was worn, as long ago as AD 500, as we know from wall-paintings found in ancient tombs. Tailoring and proportions varied over time, with the Joseon period preferring a short jacket length for women along with very long, trailing skirts.

Since Koreans sat on the paper-covered floors of their houses, rather than on chairs, loose, flowing skirts and trousers were both comfortable and practical. When traveling or visiting, upper-class men would wear long coats, woven from silk or ramie and lined with fur to ward off the cold. The costume was completed by a distinctive black hat, which hid long hair tied up into a topknot. Commoners had woven straw shoes, or wooden clogs for muddy paths. Indoors, woven shoes of silk, hemp and animal hides were the norm. Children were dressed in bright colors until they reached adulthood, whereas married women wore sober, restrained colors. Farmers and laborers wore undyed workclothes, although on special occasions they would don bright and festive attire. Put simply, clothing marked the wearer's social standing.

TOP LEFT: the traditional gown and hat of a *harabeoji* (grandfather).

LEFT: guards at the Deoksugung Palace in Seoul wear long, plain robes and broad-rimmed hats as they beat time with brightly decorated drums.

RIGHT: a Confucian ceremony at Jongmyo shrine in honor of royal ancestors. Courtiers wear black silk hats and round-necked robes.

FOLK VILLAGES: A KOREAN SPECIALTY

This actor is playing the role of magistrate at the Folk Village at Suwon, a short way outside Seoul, one of many such villages scattered around South Korea. These villages provide a useful introduction to traditional Korean ways of life, as well as to the many types of clothing worn by different people at different times; actors, in appropriate costume, represent the various occupations of traditional Korean society, from laborers and weavers to schoolteachers and officials.

Magistrates ranked among the highest officials in the complex government machine of pre-modern Korea. They were drawn from the ranks of the educated classes and recruited through regular nationwide examinations that tested their knowledge of the classic Confucian texts. Magistrates were responsible for tax collection and public order in the regions under their control.

ABOVE: the bright jacket, *jeogori*, tied with an ornamental bow to the right, contrasts with the darker skirt, *chima*, in this modern version of the *hanbok*.

LEFT: dressed in a traditional stripe-sleeved silk coat, this child marks his first birthday by choosing an object that foretells his future. Money or rice suggests riches.

RIGHT: traditional *hanbok* in Joseon-Dynasty style. The upper garment is the *jeogori*, the skirt is known as *chima*.

ABOVE LEFT: working clothes. In contrast to the flowing lines of formal *hanbok*, working clothes are designed for ease of movement and comfort.

ABOVE RIGHT: the shaman is an enduring feature of Korean society. Here a shaman's assistant wears a hood bearing tri-colored *taegeuk* symbols.

FOOD AND DRINK

Hot spices and hard drinking are just part of the culinary kaleidoscope in this country that loves to wine and dine. For many, the satisfying cuisine is one of the most enjoyable aspects of a visit to South Korea

Spicy. Fiery. Earthy. Cool. Korean food is diverse and provocative. Its bold and subtle tastes, textures, and aromas are sure to elicit conversation and a variety of emotions at every meal from novices and Koreans alike.

Most foreigners associate pungent garlic and hot chili pepper with Korean cuisine. It is true that garlic-eating has been heartily appreciated by Koreans since the earliest days, but few people know – even in South Korea – that the chili pepper did not even exist in this country until the 16th century when it was first introduced by Portuguese traders.

No matter how these two ingredients may have reached Korean plates and palates, they are now used in many dishes – most liberally and notoriously in *gimchi*. For the newcomer, learning to eat this unique dish is the first step to becoming a Korean food connoisseur.

Gimchi culture

Gimchi is the dish that has made Korean food famous. Next to rice *(bap)*, it is the most important component in any Korean meal. It is not known when or how *gimchi* originated, but like curry in India, it's in Korea to stay. So institutionalized is it, that one of the country's most important annual social events is *gimjang*, or fall *gimchi*-making, an occasion marked by numerous festivals, notably in Gwangju *(see page 257)*. At *gimjang* time, women gather in groups throughout Korea to cut, wash and salt veritable mountains of cabbage and white radish. The prepared *gimchi* is stored in large earthenware crocks, then buried in the backyard to keep it from ferment-

ing during winter months. Throughout the dark and cold winter, when in times past there was little or no fresh produce available to the average citizen, these red-peppered, garlicked, and pickled vegetables were a good source of vitamin C.

In warmer seasons, a variety of vegetables such as chives, pumpkin, and eggplant are used to make more exotic types of *gimchi*. The summer heat makes it necessary to prepare a fresh batch almost every day, often in a cool, light brine. Raw seafood, such as fish, crab, and oysters, are *"gimchi*-ed" too, and indeed, in South Korea, a woman's culinary prowess is often determined first and foremost by how good her *gimchi* tastes.

LEFT: selling seaweed at Seogwipo market, Jeju-do.
RIGHT: *galbi* (beef rib barbecue).

A wide range of ingredients

Not all Korean ingredients are quite so passionate as the garlic and chili pepper. In fact, the earliest Korean dishes consisted of understated flavours. To Koreans, almost every plant and animal in their diet has a herbal or medicinal quality, and certain dishes are purposely eaten to warm or cool the head and body. Wild aster, royal fern bracken, marsh plant, day lily, aralia shoots and broad bell-flowers are just a few of the many wild and exotic plants included in the typical Korean's diet. Others, such as mugwort, shepherd's purse, and sowthistle, are also seasonally picked and eaten.

More common vegetables – such as black sesame leaves, spinach, lettuce, mung beans and soybeans – are typically grown in the backyard, but others are found only in the wild. All

> Seaweed soup made from dried seaweed (miyeokguk) *is tasty and nutritious. It is eaten mainly by new mothers for iron, to replenish blood lost during delivery.*

are collectively called *namul* when they are parboiled, then lightly seasoned with sesame oil, garlic, soy sauce, and ground and toasted sesame seeds.

Korean dishes

Soup *(guk)* is a vital part of the Korean meal. Especially popular is *doenjangguk*, a fermented soybean paste soup with shortnecked clams stirred into its broth. Also popular are a light broth boiled from dried anchovies, and vegetable soups rendered from dried spinach, sliced radish or dried seaweed *(miyeokguk)*. A seafood dish of some kind is usually included with various side dishes which are called *banchan*. This may be a dried, salted and charbroiled fish or a hearty and spicy hot seafood soup called *maeuntang*. A delicious *maeuntang* usually includes firm, white fish, vegetables, soybean curd *(dubu)*, red pepper powder, and an optional poached egg for richness.

Probably the most popular Korean entrée ordered or automatically served to foreigners is *bulgogi* (barbecued beef). Most beef-eaters are unanimous in their appreciation of this dish which is essentially strips of red beef marinated and then grilled over a charcoal brazier. Another popular meat dish is tender and marbled *galbi* short ribs which are marinated and barbecued in the same way as *bulgogi*. *Bibimbap* is a satisfying dish of boiled rice mixed with vegetables, served in an earthenware pot.

Every visitor to South Korea should sample the tempting array of snacks at the numerous street food stalls *(pojangmacha; see page 140)*; these are extremely popular throughout the country, and are usually excellent (and very cheap). Try the ubiquitous *tteokbokgi*, spicy rice paste rolls, and *twigim*, a Korean version of Japanese tempura involving seafood and vegetables deep-fried in batter. Other snacks include a

RICE

Foreigners may be surprised to find that Koreans will often eat a bowl of rice and maybe have an extra helping even though tastier side dishes remain unfinished. To Koreans, rice – not meat – is considered to be the main dish of the meal. In fact, one of the most common street greetings *"Siska hasheosseoyo?"* literally means "Have you eaten rice?" If you run out of a particular item, the tradition is that the lady of the house will bring more. When you've had enough to eat, place your chopsticks and soup spoon to the right of your bowl; do not leave them stuck in the rice or resting on any of the bowls.

variety of pancakes; *pajeon* (green onion) and *bindaetteok* (mung bean) are the most common varieties.

Dining etiquette

When Koreans sit down to a traditional meal, they relax on a clean lacquered paper floor. The meal is brought to them on a low table. Usually the food is served in a neatly arranged collection of small metal bowls. The utensils used are a pair of chopsticks and a flat soup spoon.

A dish of sliced and chilled fruit is usually served as a dessert. Depending on the season, muskmelon, strawberries, apples, pears, and

There are few proscriptions against alcohol here (for men or women), and many social reasons for imbibing. Drinking with Koreans gives foreigners a chance to penetrate Korean culture. This is partly because of the salience of drinking in the culture and partly because, like anywhere else, alcohol removes inhibitions.

History doesn't reveal exactly when the Koreans first discovered fermentation, but drinking has long been an important part of the culture. During the Silla dynasty, the king and his court are known to have relaxed at the *Poseokjeong* drinking bower outside Gyeongju. Here a spring bubbled up into an abalone-

watermelon are among the fresh and sweet selections. At major celebrations, special steamed rice cakes *(tteok)* are presented as a tasty ritual treat.

The Korean drinking tradition

Drinking alcohol is an important part of Korean culture. There are various types of establishment to choose from, including beer halls with draft and bottled beer, market wine shops, and roadside carts where passers-by can duck in for a quick drink on the way home.

LEFT: drying red peppers, an important element in Korean cuisine. **ABOVE:** a bulgogi restaurant in Seoul: the metal tube is a vent that helps prevent the pungent odors permeating into people's clothing.

shaped stone channel. The drinkers would set their cups afloat in the channel and then compete to compose poems before the cups drifted all the way round.

Later Korean dynasties continued to enjoy drinking and its associated pleasures. Probably the most popular surroundings were *gisaeng* parties. *Gisaeng* were female entertainers who played musical instruments, sang, danced, composed poetry, and practiced calligraphy to amuse the male aristocracy at palace parties. They also poured drinks, served the men food, and flirted. According to tradition, high-class *gisaeng* took lovers but weren't promiscuous. At one point in the Joseon dynasty, there were estimated to be more than 20,000 *gisaeng*.

The most famous heroine in classical Korean history was the *gisaeng* Non-gae, who lived in the late 16th century when the Japanese

> The main patrons of gisaeng *parties are Korean businessmen who pay large sums to entertain customers, and some tourists who pay even more in the hope of taking the girls back to their hotels.*

invaded Korea. Forced to entertain a victorious Japanese general, the forlorn Non-gae beguiled

public. With closer scrutiny, however, the Confucians would find that not all of the old practices have vanished. There is still the practice where a groom consumes rice wine during his wedding ceremony and at the celebration afterwards. According to an old custom, the guests may hang the groom upside down and beat him on the soles of his feet if the alcohol runs out.

At memorial services for ancestors, filial Koreans still customarily set a bowl of wine among offerings on the altar. After the rites are completed, the living consume the wine, toasting the spirits and strengthening the bond between them. Funerals and wakes also involve plenty of

the man into walking with her along the steep cliffs overlooking the Nam River. While locked in embrace, she managed to lure him near the brink and forced him over the edge, sacrificing her life to kill the hated enemy conqueror.

These days, few *gisaeng* can claim to play classical instruments, compose poetry, or write with a brush. Instead, most *gisaeng* parties include a band with drums and electric guitar, with the *gisaeng* and their guests go-go dancing around the table after the meal is finished.

In Confucian cups

Conservative Confucians would be distressed to find what has happened to drinking today, especially with college co-eds drinking freely in

drinking – to help the living forget their grief.

Confucians might also be surprised to find that, although bowing while drinking has been largely forgotten, other elements of traditional etiquette still remain. The cardinal rule is that one does not drink alone or pour his own glass. Generally, in a gesture of respect and friendship, a drinker will give his cup to another politely with both hands. His companion receives the cup with both hands and holds it thus while it is filled to the brim. He may then drink. After emptying the cup, he again uses both hands to return it to the owner. Then, grasping the wine vessel with both hands, he refills the cup for the owner, returning the favor. In a group, several drinkers in succession may offer their cups to a single person, leaving an array of brimming cups before him. A person who has given up his cup cannot drink until the recipient returns it or someone else gives him his. So whoever has received a cup has an obligation to empty it and pass it on without inordinate delay.

The custom of forcing drinks on each other hardly encourages moderation. Public drunkenness carries no stigma. On the contrary, when most Koreans drink, they seem to have a responsibility to do so until they are drunk. The rise in car ownership has reduced this tendency, but Koreans remain heavy social drinkers.

The working man's brew

A popular Korean brew is *makgeolli*, a milky liquor that most rural households ferment at home from rice. Reputed to be highly nutritious, farmers found that a few cups during a long working day helped stave off hunger. *Makgeollijip*, establishments that serve *makgeolli*, vary in style and quality, but are generally comfortable, unpretentious places. The *makgeolli* is dipped out of a hug tub or vat into cheap teapots or bottles, and any old bowl may serve as a cup.

The two most important factors are the quality of the *makgeolli*, and the kinds of side dishes, *anju*, that it serves, since all drinking in South Korea inevitably involves eating. The many types of *anju* that go best with *makgeolli* range from fresh oysters, peppery octopus, dried fish, tasty squid, or cuttlefish to tofu, soups, bean pancakes, scallion pancakes, and omelets.

Another popular beverage, *soju*, is distilled from potatoes, with a quality somewhere between gin and kerosene. A high alcoholic content makes it South Korea's cheapest drink. While far from smooth, *soju* goes down well with certain foods, such as pigs' feet, barbecued pork, Korean sausage and other meat dishes. Equally potent, *dongdongju* is distilled from rice, a process that takes approximately two weeks. It is also called *buryuju* (floating alcohol) as grains of rice tend to float to the surface while it is being made.

Yet tastes are changing. Beer, popular for years, has overtaken its rivals, especially with young people. Since the mid-1970s, South Korea has been importing, in bulk, Scotch and other spirits and bottling their own brands. The resulting

Korean scotch, gin, vodka, rum and brandy are much cheaper than imported brands.

Where should the foreigner visiting Korea go drinking? To get a feeling for what remains of the traditional, the best place would be a *makgeolli-jip*. Korea also has plenty of beer halls, known as *hofs*. Try the Myeongdong district in downtown Seoul or the Sinchon and Hongdae-ap districts in the midwest of the city, popular with students (*see page 129*). If you are dining at Korean or Chinese restaurants, beer or traditional spirits may complement the meal. Restaurants usually don't serve *makgeolli*, but they will have some beer, *soju* or *jeongjong*, a Korean version of *sake*. ❑

THE *POKTANJU* CEREMONY

Late in the evening, if you hear the sound of clapping coming from a large restaurant, you can bet a *poktanju* ceremony is being performed. If you take a look inside you'll see a group of people in business suits sitting on the floor around a table clapping and cheering while one of them downs a mixture of *soju* (rice wine), beer, and whisky in a tumbler with a shot glass inside it. It begins with the host preparing a glass of *poktanju* and drinking it in a long series of swallows. He then rattles the tumbler and shot glass above his head before preparing a second glass, which he passes to the next person. It continues until the last person downs his *poktanju* and the host starts another round.

LEFT: picnic at Yongduam (Dragon Head Rock), Jeju-do.
RIGHT: *soju* is the most popular liquor in Korea.

TRADITIONAL KOREAN ARCHITECTURE

Buddhist temples, palaces and pagodas provide many of Korea's imposing architectural treasures

Traditional architecture plays an important role in South Korea. While high-rises may soar above Seoul and other cities, ancient temples, palaces and even private homes are the bricks and mortar of a proud nation that fought off foreign domination over the centuries.

Seoul has five royal palaces. The king's primary residence, Gyeongbok Palace, was a modest facility of about 390 gan (a gan, the space between two pillars, is an old unit of measurement) finished in 1395. Changdeok Palace, completed by the third Joseon king, Taejong, in 1405, and Changgyeong Palace, restored by King Gwanghaegun as his official residence in 1615, were secondary palaces to the east. To the south lie Gyeongun Palace (renamed and better known as Deoksugung) and Gyeonghui Palace. Local palaces in Suwon and Onyang accommodated the king's entourage when he traveled, and two refuge palaces were built within Namhansan Fortress to the south and on Ganghwa Island to the west.

The five palaces share a similar plan, with a government area in front of a residential area. Each has an enclosed garden. The government area functioned as the center for activity, and housed the state administration, with the imposing throne hall (*jeongjeon*) positioned in front of state buildings where officials met the king (*pyeongjeon*). The hidden royal quarters were further back, divided, according to Confucian custom, into separate sections for king and queen. The residential area proper was a set of building clusters for the queen, the crown prince, and other royalty. Gardens were designed to promote harmony, featuring lotus ponds, pavilions, and clusters of trees; the best preserved is the Secret Garden (Biwon), part of Changdeok Palace.

Palace protection

The walls to palaces were originally tapered, with large stones beneath and small stones above. No building was allowed to be taller than the wall, to ensure privacy for the royal family. Massive gates protected each palace.

In 1927, the Japanese colonial administration moved Gyeongbok Palace's main gate (Gwanghwamun) to behind the east gate and erected a concrete government building directly in front of the throne hall. The new building, in Western style, was used as the Korean Government complex after liberation and later as the National Museum. Burned down during the Korean War, Gwanghwamun was rebuilt in 1968 and moved back to its original site. As part of a 20-year project to restore the original palace, the Japanese building was demolished in 1998. In 2006, the Cultural Heritage Administration began another project to restore the tile-roofed stone gate. Under a nine-year plan, Gwanghwamun will be moved to its original site, a 2.5km (1½-mile) long fortress wall will be restored, and a plaza will be created in front of the site.

In the 1592 invasion, the king fled his palace. The people were incensed, and burnt it. The palace was reconstructed only in 1867, but on a much larger scale – 350 buildings were erected, symmetrically positioned along an axis running from the North Mountain (Bugaksan) behind to

Temple treasures

Nine late-4th century Buddhist temples are known of, including Geumgang-sa near Pyongyang, noted for its octagonal pagoda flanked by three rectangular halls. A later flowering of temple construction began in the 10th century. The main halls of temples usually have gabled roofs with single or double eaves supported by brackets, symbolic ornaments flanking the slightly curved main ridges. Often, and typically at a higher elevation to the rear, there are shrines to the mountain god and to the Taoist Big Dipper. Some of the most impressive structures are pagodas, housing relics of Buddha or

the front gate, on a site 18 times larger than the original. The new throne hall, the *Geunjeongjeon*, was built on two terraces reached by stone staircases. The tall columns are buttressed by wooden beams, and there is a double ornate canopy. Outside, ceremonial bronze incense pots are positioned at the corners, and beneath the terraces are nine pairs of stone markers, each inscribed with ranks, where officials lined up. Behind the throne hall, through a gate, is the single-storied audience hall, the *Sajeongjeon*. The only surviving residential quarters were for the queen dowager.

LEFT: old-style Korean housing in central Seoul's attractive Bukchon *hanok* neighborhood. **ABOVE:** classic Silla-era architecture at Bulguk-sa temple, Gyeongju.

others who achieved attainment. Early Goguryeo temples copied China's multi-storied wooden pagodas, but none survives intact. There are,

> The unified Silla gave Korea its most prized temple, Bulguk-sa; with the rise of esoteric Buddhism, many temples began to be built in secluded highland areas.

however, more than a thousand granite pagodas, along with some made from brick. The oldest is at Mireuk-sa, a Baekje site; originally built with nine stories; six survive. Two of the most prized are Seokgatap, the Sakyamuni Pagoda, built in three parts to the ratio of 4:3:2, and the sarira shrine Dabotap, "Pagoda of Many Treasures", both in the main courtyard of Bulguk-sa.

Bulguk-sa, built to the east of Gyeongju to protect the capital from Japanese invasion, was begun in 751, along with the nearby Seokguram grotto. Grotto caves were common in India and China, but this unique Korean example, now with the temple, and a Unesco world heritage site, was built by piling stones around a stone cliff face. A rectangular anteroom that was originally tiled leads to a rear rotunda. The rotunda ceiling is of dressed stone slabs with knuckle stones, a central stone shaped as a lotus

flower forming a canopy above the seated Buddha. Eight guardian deity sculptures protect the anteroom, clad in armour. Mythical figures, birds and heavenly guardians line the corridor to the rotunda, and surrounding the Buddha within the rotunda are bodhisattvas, gods, and the 10 Disciples. Above the structure, the roof was reinforced with two layers of granite stones covered with earth and clay topped with tiles..

Older even than Haeinsa *(see panel, below left)*, Jikjisa ranks as the senior temple of the Jogye Order of Korean Buddhism. Looking down over the valley from the side of Hwangaksan in Daehang-myeon, Gimcheon, it is regarded as one of

BUDDHIST TEMPLE OF HAEINSA

One of the most amazing temples is Haeinsa, first built more than 1,000 years ago in the Gaya Mountains. Since 1398, it has housed the Tripitaka Koreana, the entire Buddhist scriptures delicately carved onto more than 80,000 wooden printing blocks. The temple has been renovated over the centuries, but is unique in that its 14th century design was intended specifically to house the scriptures, and used ingenious techniques to ensure they would not be damaged by the elements. Incredibly, the scriptures survived a fire in the early 19th century, the Japanese occupation, and the devastation of the Korean War. Haeinsa remains an active temple for teaching and is highly revered by pilgrims.

the oldest temples in South Korea. Temple legend has it that Jikjisa was first constructed by the Goguryeo monk Ado some time in the 5th century AD, considerably before Buddhism gained widespread acceptance in Silla. The temple was almost totally destroyed during the Seven Year War in the 1590s, and a lengthy construction program stretched on until the late 17th century. Due to its antiquity and accessibility, this is a popular destination for tourists and worshippers alike.

Protecting Gyeongbok palace are fire-eating *haetae*, but access to the throne hall is guarded by four animal deities on the stone banisters to the upper terrace, the symbolism coming from the four directions: the dragon breathing flames, the powerful tiger, the positive phoenix, and the auspicious part-deer *girin*. On the lower banister there are zodiacal animals: time and space were divided into 12. Smaller figures, *japsaeng*, are perched on many palace, temple, and shrine roofs. These offered protection from fire, particularly a phallic man-like figure, a miniature of the *harubang* made from volcanic lava in Jeju Island. Dragons or waterspouts feature on endtiles. Carvings of lotus, peony and vines are common decorations for roof beams, plaster and wall painting, supplemented by the "eight treasures" taken from Buddhism, the symbol for longevity, and the "four gentlemen". Geometric patterns are everywhere in Korean architecture, symbol-

the living area *(sarangbang)* are the men's quarters, where guests are welcomed, and the raised rooms with verandahs – designed to counter

> Japanese colonists attempted to eradicate Korean heritage, including its architecture, even dismantling gardens; however Koreans resisted by building their houses in traditional style.

summer heat – are flanked with storage areas. In the center are the woman's quarters *(an bang)*, warmed by *ondol*, the characteristic

izing thunder, fusion and the radiation of divine power – the last being the swastika. One of the most important symbols is the *taeguek*, the two interlocking commas that represent cosmic creation and the interaction of opposites.

Domestic architecture

Traditional Korean houses recreate the concerns of palace architects in miniature. Walled for protection, gates are offset from the center, to avoid power being lost. Buildings are constructed around a courtyard. To the left, around

underfloor heating system. Many houses also had ancestral shrines.

Much evidence remains of a time before glass was widely available: doors functioned as windows, constructed with white paper pasted over a wooden lattice frame. Straw thatch marked poor houses, but upper-class houses had clay tiles.

One of the best places to appreciate Korean domestic architecture is the town on Andong, half way between Seoul and Gyeongyu. It is seen as the home of Confucianism, and during the Joseon dynasty many schools were set up here. Following in their wake, aristocrats built houses in the vicinity, many of which are still standing today, and – more incredibly – a number are still in the hands of relatives of the original owner. ❑

Above: wooden houses at Hahoe Folk Village.
Above: the Chinese influence is clear to see.
Right: *ondol* underfloor heating.

PLACES

A detailed guide to South Korea, with
principal sites clearly cross-referenced by
number to the maps

The various provinces of South Korea defy the logic of their official borders. This land of "10,000 peaks, 10,000 islands and 10,000 waterfalls" is a place of never-ending contrasts. After a few busy days spent in the bustle of hectic, high-rise Seoul where traditional markets compete for space with burgeoning office blocks, the time soon beckons to venture out into the many unexpected corners of this complex land.

From the beaches and volcanic landscapes of Jeju-do in the south, to the rocky mountains of Seoraksan National Park in the northeast, there is a wealth of diversity. Go on the search for the fabled plum blossoms in Gyeonggi Province, north of Seoul, then work your way down into the Chungcheong Provinces of central South Korea where the ginseng fields spread out between the ancient capitals full of treasures. Delve deep into the history of South Korea's southeastern valley region of Gyeongju with its massive burial mounds, keeper of the riches of the forgotten dead, or visit some of the 3,000 solitary islands of the southwestern Jeolla Provinces. Or, if the thought of all this activity makes you giddy, head for the relaxing beaches of the "Island of the Gods," the southern island of Jeju-do.

South Korea, the "Land of the Morning Calm," holds 5,000 years of history, art, and culture. There are fashionable shopping precincts, breathtaking scenery, and a proud and open people. Discover the ancient kingdoms of Joseon, or take a tour to the Demilitarized Zone (DMZ), now open for the first time since the civil war split the country in two half a century ago.

The ice of this "Cold War holiday destination" is slowly starting to thaw as a result of the Pyongyang 2000 summit and subsequent negotiations, leading to a gradual *rapprochement* and, in 2007, the much heralded rail journey between the two deeply divided parts of the peninsula. Tour groups from the South can now visit by boat a beautiful tract of North Korean territory on the east coast near mystical Mount Geumgang, the Diamond Mountain, an area of exquisite rugged scenery.

The time to visit is now, before the tourist hordes descend on this largely unexplored Asian nirvana. ❑

PRECEDING PAGES: festival lanterns at Beopju-sa temple; Tumuli Park at Gyeongju; a stroll through the cherry blossoms in spring. **LEFT:** Sinheung-sa temple, Seoraksan. **ABOVE LEFT:** doorway symbolism. **ABOVE RIGHT:** Hyeopjae beach, Jeju-do.

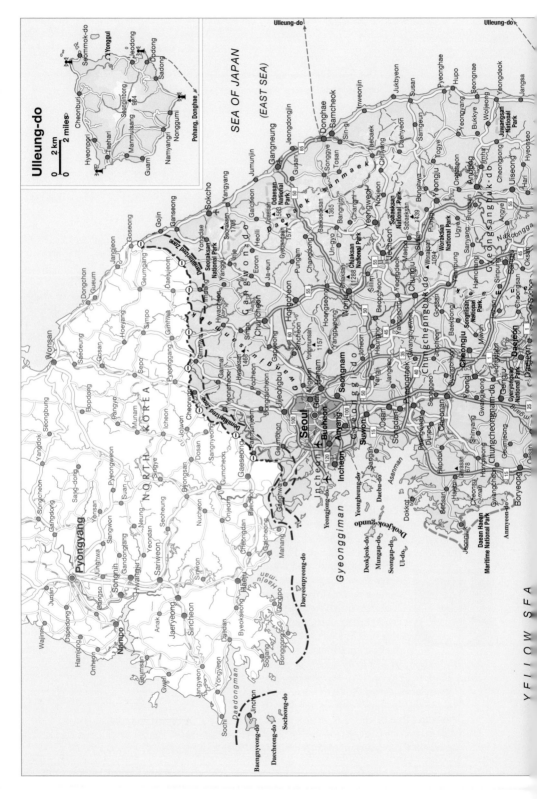

Ulleung-do

0 2 km
0 2 miles

Yonggul
Seommok-do
Cheonbu
Jeodong
Dodong
Sadong
Seonginbong
984
Mannulsang
Hyeonpori
Taehari
Namyangri
Nongguri
Pohang, Donghae
Guam

SEA OF JAPAN
(EAST SEA)

Ulleung-do

Ulleung-do

YELLOW SEA

NORTH KOREA

Pyongyang
Nampo

Seoul
Incheon
Bucheon
Anyang
Suwon

Gyeonggiman

Demilitarized Zone
Demilitarized Zone
Demilitarized Zone

Gangwon-do

Gyeonggi-do

Chungcheongbuk-do
Chungcheongnam-do
Cheongju
Daejeon

Gyeongsangbuk-do

Gangneung
Donghae
Samcheok

Seoraksan National Park
Odaesan National Park
Chiaksan National Park
Sobaeksan National Park
Woraksan National Park
Songnisan National Park
Juwangsan National Park
Gyeryongsan National Park
Daean Haean Maritime National Park

Baengnyeong-do
Daecheong-do
Socheong-do
Daeyeonpyeong-do
Jincheon
Deokjeok-sundo
Deokjeok-do
Mungap-do
Seongap-do
Ul-do
Dokkot
Yeongjong-do
Daebu-do
Asanman
Anmyeon-do
Jeongju

Nakdonggang
Hangang

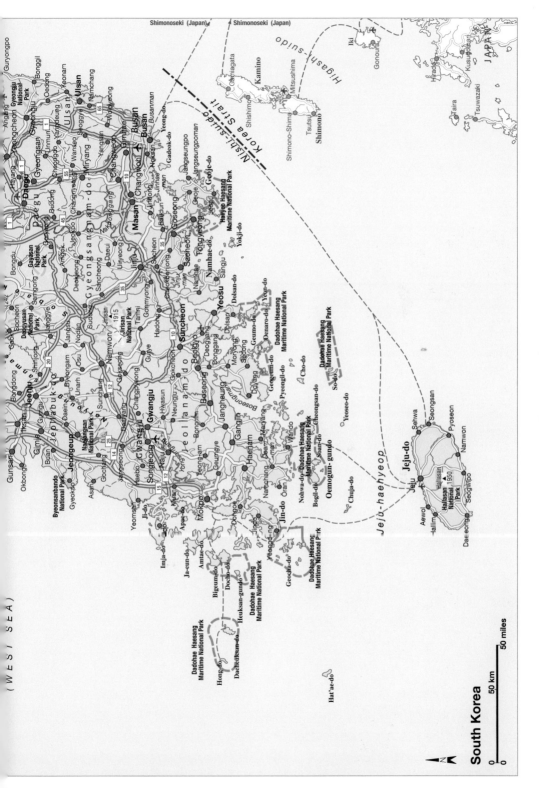

South Korea

SEOUL, GYEONGGI, AND GANGWON

South Korea's fascinating capital city offers a heady mix of history, culture, and nightlife, while the surrounding rural areas offer mountain scenery, cultural sights and the world's last Cold War frontier

A s the heart of South Korea, and the nation's capital for more than six centuries, the vast, high-tech, high-rise city of Seoul has it all: fashionable shopping areas, labyrinthine arcades, thriving markets, historic palaces, soaring office blocks, and dynamic nightlife. One of Asia's largest conurbations, with a population of well over 10 million, it is brimming with exuberance and energy.

Seoul has risen over the years from the ashes of wartime destruction and grown in international standing in these times of burgeoning globalization, even outstripping Tokyo in many respects. The city's clamor and congestion are proof of the country's economic achievements; its peace and grandeur remind the outside world of the tenacity of Korean culture in this great capital where past meets future head on. There is much to see, including the historic Deoksugung Palace, a variety of Buddhist temples, the bustling modern center of Myeong-dong, and the buzzing nightlife of Itaewon and Hongdae. For those seeking peace and quiet, Citizen's Park is perfect for picnics, watersports, and the national pastime of kite flying.

The city is bordered by eight mountains, and the hilly countryside that extends to the north, south and east is marked by the royal tombs and ancient castles of Gyeonggi Province, and its capital Suwon. Day-trip options include the Korean Folk Village near Suwon, and Bukhansan National Park, just short drive from downtown Seoul. Panmunjeom, on the border with North Korea, makes for a different kind of day trip – a fascinating opportunity to

visit the world's last remaining relic of the Cold War. Further afield, you can mix sightseeing with skiing, hiking, and climbing in Gangwon Province, where you'll find some of the peninsula's most breathtaking scenery at Seoraksan National Park. ❏

LEFT: Bongeun-sa temple dates back over 1,000 years. **TOP:** out and about in Itaewon. **ABOVE LEFT:** changing of the guard ceremony, Deoksu Palace. **ABOVE RIGHT:** masks in Insa-dong.

| 0 | 200 m |
| 0 | 200 yds |

Gansong Museum

Sungkyunkwan
University **J**

Dongsomunno

Songbukno

BIWON
(SECRET GARDEN) **I**

Hyehwa **M**

SEONGBUK-GU

Hansung University

Botanical
Garden

National
Science
Museum

Seoul National
University Dental
College

MARRONNIER
PARK

Changgyeonggungno

Daehangno

ngdeokgung
ace of
trious Virtue) **H**

Seoul National University
Medical College

Changsin **M**

Sungin
Post Office

Changgyeonggung
Nakseonjae **K**
Honghwamun

Changsin
Sijang

ongjeon

Myeongjeongmun

Ihwajang
Museum

Yeongnyeongjeon
Jongmyo
(Royal Ancestral Shrine) **L**
Jeongjeon

Wonnam
Post Office

Yulgongno

Jung-ang
Church

Wangsanno

Bokum
Church

Yulgongno

Dongmyo **M**

Olympic
Park

JONGNO-GU
Jongno 3-ga

Changgyeonggungno

Daehangno

Dongdaemun
Church

Dongdaemun **M**

Dasanno

Seoul Sports
Complex

Jongno 3-ga **M**

Cho-dong
Church

JONGMYO
PLAZA

Jongno 3-ga

Jongno 5-ga **M**

Jongno

Dongdaemun
(Great East Gate)

Dongshin
Church

M Dongdaemun

Seun
Arcade

Gwangjang
Sijang

Dongdaemun Sijang **R**
(Great East Gate Market)

Dongdaemun
Chain Store

Cheonggye
Arcade

nggyecheon Stream **E**
nggyecheonno

Cheonggyecheonno

Bangsan
Sijang

Pyeonghwa
Sijang

Shin Pyeonghwa
Sijang

Deong
Pyeonghwa
Sijang

Cheong
Pyeonghwa
Sijang

Daerim
Arcade

Citizen
Hall

Donghwa
Arcade

Cheonggyecheonno

Euljiro 3-ga

Euljiro 4-ga **M**

Euljiro

Hwanghakdong
Flea Market **S**

M
o 3-ga

Euljiro
Underground Arcade

Sampung
Arcade

Jungbu
Sijang

Hullyonwongil

Hongingmunno

Dongdaemun
Stadium

Heungindong
Post Office

Mareunnaegil

Dongdaemun
Stadium **M**

Dongdaemun
Stadium **M**

Wangshimnigil

New Korea
Wedding Hall

Shinseong
Arcade

Jung-gu
Office

Baegogaegil

Mareunnaegil

JUNG-GU

Toegyero

Gwanghuimun

Gwanghuimun
Church

Chungmuro
egyero **M**

Jinyang
Arcade

Haengbok
Wedding Hall

Baptist
Church

Gyeongdong
Church

Jangchungdangil

Jungang
versity Hospital

Samsung Jeil
Hospital

Korea
House

Jangchungdan
Church

Shindang-dong
Catholic
Church

Cheonggu **M**

Namsangol
(Folk Village)

Dongguk
University

Samyeongdaesa

Dongguk
University **M**

JANGCHUNG
PARK

Jangchung
Gymnasium

Seong-dong
Church

Dongho

Dasanno

Na
msangongwon

Yi Jun

1st Namsan
Tunnel

JANGCHUNGDAN

PARK

Namsangongwongil

2nd Namsan Tunnel

Itaewon

Yaksu **M**

SEOUL

Seoul is the heart of South Korea – a mixture of chic shopping districts, traditional markets, historic palaces, towering office buildings, crowded streets, and pulsating nightlife

An old Korean saying advises: "If you have a horse, send it to Jeju Island; if you have a son, send him to Seoul." Jeju Island is the choice for horses because the grass is green and lush. Seoul is swarming with thousands of students attending its numerous universities and colleges, and the city hosts the head offices of the country's major enterprises – commercial, financial, and governmental. Therefore sending a son to Seoul gives him the best opportunities. So many people, both sons and daughters, have responded to Seoul's pull that the city is now home to one-fifth of the country's population. Its residents number around 10.5 million, and it has been the nation's capital for over 600 years.

Rising from the ashes

South Korea's capital has emerged from the ruins of its wartime desolation and is now rushing into the mainstream of international activity; depending on whom you speak with, Seoul is Asia's most international city, surpassing even Tokyo. South Koreans have long been determined to improve the homeland and to gain international recognition while retaining much of the traditions and values of the old days.

Seoul's noise and congestion are living proof of the country's economic achievements; its calm and grandeur

attest to the strength of Korean culture. As you walk around the city you will feel the push to the future and the pull of the past. And you'll find that the city just grows on you, as do the people. So many people speak English that one barely has time to pull out the tourist map before someone has stopped at your side, asking (in better or worse English) if they might help. Even people who don't speak your language will go out of their way, sometimes acting out monologues in sign language or taking you by the hand

Main attractions

N SEOUL TOWER
DEOKSU PALACE
NATIONAL PALACE MUSEUM
  (GYEONGBOK PALACE)
CHANGDEOK PALACE
BIWON (SECRET GARDEN)
GANSONG MUSEUM
JONGMYO TEMPLE
INSADONG
JOGYE-SA TEMPLE
MYEONGDONG
NAMDAEMUN MARKET
GYEONGDONG MEDICINE MARKET
ITAEWON
NATIONAL MUSEUM OF KOREA
SAMSUNG MUSEUM
  OF ART LEEUM
YONGSAN ELECTRONICS MARKET

LEFT: Deoksu Palace guard.
RIGHT: evening shopping in Myeongdong.

*Office workers in
Seoul's downtown
business district, with
the Jongno Tower in
the background.*

to where you need to be. And while it never hurts to be careful, polite, and respectful, most Koreans are quite proud of their country and are excited that you're taking time to explore it. It's safer traveling here than in many places in the West, and the rewards are considerable.

THE CITY CENTER

Topographically, the center of Seoul is wooded **Namsan** (South Mountain), a 243-meter (800ft) hill topped by the **N Seoul Tower** (Mon–Thur and Sun 10am–11pm, Fri–Sat 10am–midnight; charge), which extends your viewing platform upward another 237 meters (777ft). This is a great place to get your bearings, with sweeping views across the downtown area to the conically shaped **Bugaksan** (North Peak Mountain), and in the opposite direction to the Han River and beyond.

Take the cable car up from the northwestern side of the hill, and walk back down to the city along peaceful forest paths – a singular contrast with the endless tower blocks of the *Bladerunner*-esque city below.

On the northern slope of Namsan is Korea House, one of Seoul's best Korean restaurants *(see page 288)*. Several traditional buildings here lie in a lovely wooded setting. There is also a performance theater, and nearby is the **Namsangol Hanok Village**, showing how life in Seoul used to be lived.

The old walled city once sprawled between Namsan and Bugaksan; the 16km (10-mile) encircling wall made of earth and dressed stone is gone, but a few crumbling stretches on Bugaksan and Namsan, and other restored patches, have survived. Nine gates once pierced this wall. Five still stand, and the two largest – **Namdaemun** (Great South Gate) and **Dongdaemun** (Great East Gate) – are regal presences in the midst of the modern city's swirl, and reminders of the capital as it was once laid out. In 2006, however, Namdaemun was badly damaged by fire *(see page 45)* and is currently undergoing restoration.

City Hall Plaza

The true hub of the city is further north, amid the office blocks and

traffic-choked thoroughfares of the downtown area. At the epicenter of it all is the **City Hall Plaza ®**, the fountain square bounded on the north by City Hall, on thc south by the Plaza Hotel, on the east by the entrance to **Euljiro** (one of the main east–west streets), and on the west by Deoksu Palace. The plaza is a link between the old and the new Seoul. Running under the plaza are two subway lines. In 2005, traffic was largely banished from City Hall Plaza which was made into a green area and restored to pedestrians. If traffic allows, you can stand in the middle of the north–south street, **Taepyeongno**, and look south to Namdaemun and north to **Gwanghwamun** (Gate of Transformation by Light), the reconstructed gate in front of the Gyeongbok Palace.

The **Gwanghwamun intersection ©**, the next crossing north of City Hall Plaza, is another major city-center hub. It is dominated by a looming statue of Yi Sun-sin, Korea's great 16th-century naval hero. From here, Taepyongno runs south, **Sejongno** north, **Shinmunno** west, and **Jongno** east – the

streets change name as they cross. To add to the confusion, the Gwanghwamun intersection is not directly in front of the Gwanghwamun gate for which it is named – that's another long block north of here.

Deoksu Palace

For a more modern exploratory opener, begin your tour of Seoul at the central and historical **Deoksugung ©** (Tue–Sun 9am–9pm; charge), the Palace of Virtuous Longevity, whose gate faces City Hall Plaza. Deoksu is not the oldest of the surviving palaces – it was built as a villa toward the end of the 15th century – but it is important for its role at the unhappy end of the Joseon dynasty. King Gojong, who was forced to abdicate in favor of his son Sunjong in 1907, lived in retirement and died here in 1919 after having seen his country annexed by the Japanese in 1910 and his family's dynasty snuffed out after 500 years.

Among the most conspicuous structures on the palace grounds, regularly open to the public, is a statue of Sejong, the great 15th-century

On the northeast corner of Gwanghwamun intersection sits South Korea's largest book store. On any given day, the Kyobo Bookstore (daily 9.30am–10pm) is full of book-hungry Koreans checking out the latest publications from Korean and Western authors.

BELOW: Deoksu palace guards.

TIP

One of your first stops in South Korea should be the Korean National Tourism Organization's excellent Information Center (open daily 9am–6pm, Nov–Feb closes at 5pm) on Cheonggyecheonno Street. To get here, take subway line 1 to Jonggak Station, or Line 2 to Euljiro 1-ga Station.

king who commissioned scholars to develop a distinctive Korean writing system, different from the traditional Chinese characters, and who officially promulgated it in 1446. There's also a royal audience hall and two startlingly European-style stone buildings, with Ionic and Corinthian columns, designed in 1909. The palace grounds offer a welcome relief from the city's hustle and bustle, especially in the fall when its aisle of ginkgo trees is aflame in gold.

Visitors to Deoksu Palace are often surprised to find themselves in the middle of odd-looking, spear-carrying soldiers marching to the beat of huge drums and elongated bugles. This is the ceremony of the **Changing of the Palace Gate Guards** (daily 10.30am, 2pm, 3.30pm), performed much as it was when kings and queens lived and ruled behind palace walls more than 100 years ago. The colorful costumes and serious (sometimes scowling) faces remind tourists that this is not just a simple show. It's Korean heritage we're lucky enough to be viewing, and it should be appreciated with dignity.

Cheonggyecheonno

Leading east from the Gwanghwamun intersection, Cheonggyecheonno was for many years a rather unlovely street with a notably decrepit overpass, until in 2005 a large urban renewal project was completed with the restoration of the new **Cheonggyecheon stream** Ⓔ. The broad paved walkways and little hopping stones make for nice daytime strolls, and at night the area is lit with colored lamps. The stream, once completely buried beneath the concrete streets, has now become one of Seoul's biggest attractions and is a prime place for a leisurely stroll – as well as being popular with amorous couples. It was built among significant controversy from groups opposed to wasting money for a beautification project when so many social issues remained unsolved, as well as local area businesses who worried that rising real-estate costs would push them out. Nevertheless, it became one of then mayor, current South Korean President Lee Myung-bak's signature achievements; some believe it helped propel him to the presidency.

BELOW:
Cheonggyecheon stream.

The exact **geographical center of the old city** can be definitely placed, but in the name of progress it's now almost impossible to find. Just off Insa-dong, an area east of Gwanghwamun known for its art galleries, art supply stores, and antique dealers, there used to be a square granite marker enclosed by short octagonal pillars. That square of granite marked the geographical center of the old walled city. Typically enough, this particular piece of Joseon-dynasty history was ignored: neither the stone itself nor any signboard proclaimed what this spot was. This remnant of history was carted off during construction in the mid-1980s, and a new office block stands in its place. Just by this spot, marked by a plaque, stands the former house of a Joseon-dynasty prince, where leaders of the 1919 independence uprising planned their protest against the Japanese rulers.

Gyeongbok Palace

To the north of the Gwanghwamun Intersection is the governmental heart of the old walled city, **Gyeongbokgung** ⓕ (Wed–Mon Mar–Oct 9am–6pm, Nov–Feb 9am–5pm, Sat–Sun until 7pm; charge), the Palace of Shining Happiness, Taejo's residence and seat of power. He and his successors used it until 1592 when it was burned during warfare with Japan.

If you inquire more closely, you will discover that Gyeongbok's throne hall, the **Geunjeongjeon** (Hall of Government by Restraint), rebuilt in 1867, was the very center of Taejo's governmental heart. Here the king sat to receive ministers ranged in orderly ranks before him, made judgments, and issued proclamations. The hall faces south down Sejongno and commands an unobstructed view through Gwanghwamun to Namdaemun.

In 1926, Japanese colonial rulers built a mammoth colonial Capitol Building between the front gate and the throne hall. This was an obvious symbolic severance of the link between the Korean people (the gate) and the royal family (the throne hall). In 1998, finally fed up with this affront, the city tore down the building in celebration of Korea's 50th year of independence from Japan. The **National Palace Museum of Korea**

Striking modern sculpture enlivens the park at the Cheonggyecheon stream.

BELOW: Gyeongbok Palace.

Hand-colored manuscript from the Royal Joseon household, National Palace Museum.

BELOW: Changdeok Palace detail.

(Tue–Sun 9am–6pm, Sat–Sun until 7pm; charge) opened in 2005 inside the Gyeongbok Palace area, with a collection of over 40,000 pieces of Joseon-dynasty royal treasures taken from the Royal Museum in Deoksu Palace, and from Changdeok and Gyeongbok palaces and the Royal Ancestral Shrine.

Also inside the palace grounds stands the **National Folk Museum of Korea** (same days and hours as Gyeongbok Palace; charge), which houses artifacts of everyday use and dioramas showing how they were used. Flanking the palace gate are two stone *haetae*, mythical animals from Korean lore, which have witnessed Seoul's evolution ever since they were carved and placed here in the 15th century to guard the old palace from fire.

When the weather is fine, lines of schoolchildren stream through the gate of the palace. They scatter around the grounds where, with paintbrush and palette in hand, and canvas on easel, they work intently to capture the color of the flowers and leaves, and the charm of interior vistas once seen only by royalty and their attendants.

A favorite subject is **Gyeonghoeru** (the Hall of Happy Meetings), a two-story banquet hall that was built in 1412, burned down in 1592, and rebuilt in 1867 when the ruling regent had the entire palace renovated for his son, King Gojong. The hall extends over one end of a spacious square pond. Swans glide over the water and, in winter, skaters glide over the pond's frozen surface.

East to Changdeok Palace

Between Gyeongbok and Changdeok palaces is one of the city's largest surviving areas of traditional Korean housing (*hanbok*). The neighborhoods of **Bukchan-dong** and **Samcheong-dong** are full of small winding streets lined with old wooden houses and a plentiful supply of teahouses and cafés. It's a refreshing change from the unrelenting modernity of much of the city. There are some great places to stay around here; *see page 281.*

Abutting these characterful streets to the east is **Changdeokgung** , the Palace of Illustrious Virtue (English tours 3 times daily, otherwise group tours every 15 and 45 mins 9am–5pm; closed Mon; charge). One of Seoul's most famous sights, Changdeokgung is well worth braving the crowds for. Originally built in 1405 as a detached palace, it burned down in 1592, was rebuilt in 1609, and used since then as the official residence of various Joseon kings, including the last one, Sunjong, until his death in 1926.

The best preserved of Seoul's palaces, Changdeokgung has a throne room hall surrounded by long drafty corridors leading past reception rooms furnished with heavy upholstered European chairs and sofas. In the private living quarters, however, the furnishings are typical of those of traditional Korea: low, slatted beds, lacquered chests and tables. **Nakseonjae**, a small complex of buildings within Changdeok's grounds, is still the residence of descendants of the royal family: ensconced there are an elderly aunt

of Sunjong; the wife of the last crown prince, Sunjong's son (who never ruled); her son; and his wife. In the formal back gardens of Nakseonjae, with a series of stepped granite-faced tiers planted with azaleas, it is possible to feel totally isolated from the sounds of modern Seoul.

From within a small raised octagonal pavilion at the top of this garden, you can perhaps imagine the royal family sitting here, gazing out over the curved roofs of the palace buildings and the arabesque walls encircling them. Under leafy treetops that stretch towards Namsan in the distance, you can hear court whispers and imagine the turbulence and intrigues of Korea's late Joseon dynasty.

Biwon, the Secret Garden

Behind Changdeok lies the extensive acreage of **Biwon ❶** (entrance through Changdeok Palace, with same opening days and hours; guided tours), the Secret Garden, so-called because it was formerly a private park for the resident royal family. In wooded and hilly terrain, footpaths meander past ponds and pavilions and over small bridges.

The most picturesque of these sites is **Bandoji** (Peninsula Pond), shaped like the outline of the Korean Peninsula. From its shore extending out over the water stands a small, exquisite, fan-shaped pavilion from which Injo, the 16th king, could cast a line for a bit of quiet fishing. Biwon and portions of Changdeok Palace may be visited by joining one of several daily guided tours at the Biwon entrance. The Nakseonjae complex is open to the public twice a year for royal ceremonies.

Munmyo Shrine

Twice a year, during the second and eighth lunar months, people gather at the **Munmyo Shrine** in the grounds of **Sungkyunkwan University ❶** (daily 9am–6pm; free) to the northeast of Biwon, to honor his spirit. Sungkyunkwan University is a modern transformation of the old Sungkyunkwan, a national institute sponsored by the Joseon Court. It was here that Korea's best scholars pursued the Confucius Classics and instructed those who aspired to pass government examina-

BELOW: Biwon, Seoul's Secret Garden.

The teachings of Confucius, the great sage, exert considerable influence on Korean society.

BELOW: Confucian dancers at Munmyo Shrine.
RIGHT: Confucian ceremony at Jongmyo, the Royal Ancestral Shrine.

tions to receive official appointments. The Hangnyeong, the rules which govern students' lives at Sungkyunkwan University, state: "Any student guilty of violating human obligations (prince and minister, father and son, husband and wife, brothers or friends), of faulty deportment, or of damaging his body or his reputation, will be denounced, with drumbeats, by the other students. Extreme cases may be reported to the Ministry of Rites and barred from academic circles for life." After all, the aim of the school was *sung*, "to perfect human nature," and *kyun*, "to build a good society." This is the dual purpose of a good Confucian education.

The Gansong Museum

Around 1km (2/3 mile) to the northeast of Sungkyunkwan University, the **Gansong Museum** (open two weeks in May and two weeks in October; free; tel: 02-762-0442 for opening times and dates) contains some of Korea's most priceless treasures, purchased at great expense by the museum's founder, Jeon Hyeongpil. A wealthy businessman, he realized that the only way to

prevent the purchase (often at prices well below what the art was worth) by foreign collectors was to purchase art himself. Jeon Hyeongpil is considered a hero by many for his effort to ensure that these priceless antiquities remained in Korea. The museum is packed for its spring and fall openings and lines often stretch around the block as people wait for a chance to view the treasures.

Changgyeong Palace

One block east from Changdeokgung lies **Changgyeonggung** Ⓚ (Wed–Mon 9am–6pm, Nov–Feb until 5pm; charge), another palace with its extensive grounds now open to the public – the largest public park in Seoul, and a very pleasant place to wander around. The palace dates back to the early 15th century. In 1907 the Japanese turned it into a leisure park, complete with a zoo and botanical garden; the latter is still in place.

Jongmyo, Confucian hub

From Changgyeong take the footbridge across busy Yulgongno to reach

Jongmyo ❶ (Wed–Fri, Mon 9am–5pm, Sat–Sun 9am–6pm, Nov–Feb closes at 4.30pm; charge), the Royal Ancestral Shrine, which along with Changdeok Palace was designated as a Unesco World Heritage Site in 1996. This walled complex includes two long pillared buildings housing, according to Confucian requirement, ancestral tablets listing the names and accomplishments of the 27 Joseon kings and their queens. Jongmyo is open to the public and is a favorite strolling ground for young couples. Once a year on the first Sunday in May, a traditional ceremony honoring the spirits of kings and queens is held here. Ancient court music, not otherwise heard, rings eerily over flagstones and beyond cedar pillars. Confucian celebrants pay appropriate respects and offer proper foods and wine to each of the enshrined spirits in a ritual lasting six hours.

The teachings of the great sage Confucius (Gongja), who lived in China about 2,500 years ago, became more deeply rooted in Korea than in their native land, especially during the Joseon dynasty, when they formed the basis of government and code of behavior in Korean society. Many aspects of Confucianism live on in Korean society, such as the emphasis placed on education, respect for one's elders, and ancestral worship.

Tea, art, and antiques in Insadong

A short distance west of Jongmyo is **Insadong ⓜ**, one of the city's tourist hotspots. A time-honored location for antiques dealers, there are a huge number of small specialist shops selling fine Goryeo celadon, Silla pottery, and Joseon-era furniture, along with numerous art galleries, art supply stores, teahouses, restaurants, and a few bookshops.

Although some of the antiques stores face the street, others lurk in back alleys snuggled between tiny restaurants, teahouses, junk dealers, and music stores. Some vendors spread their wares on blankets on the ground. It's a real bargain hunter's wonderland, but be cautious (as anywhere) with prices for items – especially antiques – that seem too inexpensive to be true. Hanji paper

For much of the Joseon and Japanese periods, Insadong was the neighborhood of choice for wealthy Seoulites. Many of the area's famous antique shops trace their origins back to the late 19th and early 20th centuries, when their antecedents catered to the city's moneyed elite.

BELOW: Insadong antiques.

Seoul Teahouses

Congestion is a problem in Seoul, both in- and outdoors. Try sitting in a *dabang* (tearoom), for instance. Although there are thousands of *dabang* of various sizes in the city, finding a seat in a busy one will be the first hurdle. *Dabang* are popular throughout South Korea for their convenience as meeting places for colleagues, family, and friends. Each *dabang* tends to specialize in a certain clientele – university students or businessmen, for example – largely in response to the kind of music the tearoom offers. A *jeontong chatjip* is a traditional tearoom, with a wide variety of teas and an esoteric serving procedure. Herbs are steeped in earthenware pots over a low-burning coal briquette for an hour or two until an essence is thus extracted. Many places also sell a large range of pastries and are also good for a quick breakfast.

items, from cards to wrapping paper to dolls, are high-quality.

At weekends, the streets of Insadong take on a festive atmosphere, as Koreans and foreigners (the area is a favorite with the expat community) crowd the streets and shops. With its network of tiny side alleys and its main flowing avenue filled with shoppers, Insadong is something of a flashback to an older, smaller city.

The area is a great place for walking. Don't be afraid to wander past gated doors and tiny stores before discovering that the street has ended abruptly. Small shops display snakes embalmed in *soju* (good for a man's stamina, so they say, as with ginseng root), and behind stone walls you can hear businessmen singing their hearts out to entertain each other in expensive salons.

Insadong is also well known for its traditional (*jeontong chatjip*) and not-so-traditional (*dabang*) teahouses, where bell jars of dried herbs line the shelves. Ginseng is the most popular, but various other home-made brews are also served. These include aromatic ginger tea (*saenggangcha*) made with

BELOW: street
art, Insadong.
RIGHT: Tapgol Park.

boiled and strained ginger root and raw sugar; porridges such as *jatjuk*, made of pine nuts, water, rice flour, and salt or sugar to taste; and *kkae-juk*, toasted black sesame seeds, water, rice flour and salt or sugar. *Mogwacha* (quince) *daechucha* (jujube), *yujacha* (lemon), and *maesilcha* (plum) are a few Korean teas that taste quite sweet but are still refreshing.

Tapgol Park

At the southern end of Insadong is **Tapgol Park** (daily 6am–8pm; free), also known as Pagoda Park after the Joseon pagoda situated in its center. This became Korea's first Western-style public park when it opened in 1913. Tapgol is famous for its role in the events of March 1919, when the declaration of Korean independence, in defiance of oppressive Japanese rule, took place here (*see page 35*). The wall surrounding the park features scenes depicting the dramatic events of the March 1 Movement, and a bronze cast displays the Declaration itself. Every year on March 1, a ceremony takes place to commemorate those who died

in the ensuing Japanese crackdown on the nationalist movement.

Jogye-sa Temple

The Confucian Joseon court tried hard to extinguish the spirit of the Buddha throughout the country, but it failed miserably. Buddhist temples abound. City temples, though, are hardly places of quiet retreat. **Jogye-sa Temple** Ⓞ (open daily, 24 hours), just across Ujeonggungno from Insadong, was founded in 1910 and is the headquarters of the official sect of Buddhism in South Korea. As the country's center of Buddhism, it hums with activity, and on the occasion of Buddha's birthday, on the 8th day of the 4th lunar month, it becomes the hub of Buddhist festivities in South Korea.

On this day, in common with all Buddhist temples in the country, the courtyard in front of Jogye-sa's main hall is strung with parallel strands of wires on support poles. As dusk falls, worshippers come to the temple to buy a paper lantern and candle. The names of all the members of the worshipper's family are written on a tag dangling from the bottom of the lantern. The worshipper fixes the candle into the lantern, lights it, hangs the lantern on one of the wires, then bows and murmurs a prayer when finished. Row after row of flickering candle flames illuminate the courtyard as darkness deepens. If in some stray gust of wind a lantern catches fire and burns, everyone stands aghast and mute at this stroke of ill fortune – an evil omen for the year to come. Meanwhile, within the main hall, devotees light incense on the altar before the Buddha's golden image, bow to the floor three times in reverence, and offer prayers.

Every part of the temple is thronged with people. Anyone may buy and hang a lantern; and many non-Buddhist foreign residents do so. Some even march in the lantern parade that winds through downtown Seoul – an elaborate affair with floats and bands. It is a good way to try to ensure good luck for a year.

Myeongdong

Many people think Seoul's real center today is modern **Myeongdong**, an area of narrow alleys that starts a 10-minute walk southeast from City Hall Plaza directly across from Lotte Department Store. Myeongdong's main thoroughfare, a one-way street, is lined on both sides with swanky shops that sell chic clothes and accessories, and it ends at the top of a low hill before **Myeongdong Cathedral** Ⓟ (daily 9am–9pm). This grand center of Catholicism used to be one of the largest buildings in the city decades ago. Now large hotels and office buildings dwarf it, but it still remains a landmark. In recent years it has become a rallying point for anti-government demonstrators.

Not only has the Catholic faith attracted politically active converts through its human rights stance, but also many protesters, ranging from the homeless to radical students, who have sought refuge within its hallowed grounds. Even as late as the 1990s, the pungent smell of tear gas from demonstrations often lingered over the area around the cathedral.

Myeongdong is the liveliest part of downtown Seoul in the evening.

BELOW: shopping in Myeongdong.

Hangeul, the Korean script

King Sejong's legacy to Korea was the development of a writing system that would eventually bring mass literacy to the nation's people

A mong Korea's long procession of royalty, King Sejong (r. 1418–50) is pre-eminent. In Korea, it is impossible to forget him, since his portrait appears on the 10,000-won note, and everywhere you look you see his most famous invention – Hangeul, the Korean alphabet.

King Sejong felt morally obligated to improve the lot of his subjects. Since the majority were farmers, he first concentrated on improving agricultural production. Scholars were sent out to survey farming techniques, bringing back innovative ideas that were then applied to plots within the palace grounds. After years of experimentation, the treatise "Straight Talk on Farming" was published and regional officials disseminated the new farming technologies to the peasants, such as the rain gage and sundial.

The king and his scholars then turned their attention to producing a book on Korea's indigenous medicines, resulting in the publication of "The Classified Collection of Medical Prescriptions." A true Renaissance man, Sejong also composed Confucian music with instruments that gave ritual performances at the Korean court a distinctive sound.

His greatest legacy, however, was the development of Hangeul. For centuries, Korea had been using a modified version of Chinese script, made up of thousands of ideograms that required years of study to master. In Korea, only the *yangban* had the time, money (tutors were expensive), or inclination to learn it. Consequently, only 10 percent of the population was literate.

The task King Sejong set his scholars was formidable – create a system of writing that would better represent the Korean language and be simple enough for a peasant to learn. The result was quite remarkable. Discarding ideograms, the scholars developed a phonetic alphabet that used 28 symbols (only 24 are used today). Instead of spending years trying to memorize thousands of symbols, Hangeul could be learned in a matter of weeks, if not days. This made literacy accessible to nearly every Korean.

Unfortunately, it wasn't that simple. Although there were books published in Hangeul, the *yangban* refused to use an alphabet that they felt was suitable for women and farmers, but not true scholars. It was not until the 20th century that Hangeul was widely accepted.

Today, Hangeul is a source of considerable pride to all Koreans. It is all the more remarkable when you consider that an alphabet developed over 550 years ago is perfect for the computer age – while the Chinese (and Japanese) struggle to fit ideograms onto a keyboard, the 24 letters of Hangeul fit very nicely. ❑

ABOVE: the Korean script empowered the masses.
LEFT: statue of King Sejong, Renaissance man.

Myeongdong's alleyways come alive in the evening when they are crowded with after-work strollers window-shopping – "eye-shopping" in Korean – past the fancy displays of shoes and handbags, tailor-made suits and custom-made shirts, dresses in the latest designs, handcrafted modern jewelry, and cosmetics. Traditional confections such as rock candy, Korean taffy, and candied yams make a great snack, though standard offerings like chocolate, cotton candy, and ice cream are just as popular. These streets are also lined with restaurants. But these are only the surface attractions of Myeongdong. The district was famous during the Park Chung-hee era for its tiny hideaway drinking houses that used to serve cheap liquor up until curfew time. These have largely been replaced by fashionable coffee shops packed with young Koreans.

Namsan, City Hall Plaza, Gwanghwamun, Myeongdong: perhaps the visitor should think of Seoul as having more than one center: it's certainly a city big and old enough for more than one special center of interest. Understand the collective meaning and you start to understand Seoul's soul.

Seoul's traditional markets

Any foreign visitor to Seoul should venture into a proper market; if not one of the neighborhood markets, then certainly into one or both of the great central markets downtown. Take one of the hundreds of neighborhood markets and multiply it by 50, and you have **Namdaemun Sijang Q** (Great South Gate Market, located east of the gate itself). The shops and stalls are open from 10am until sunset, though it's said that the real bargains are bought after midnight on weekends.

Remember to barter for any purchase – if you don't, you will end up paying way too much. The stalls selling watches, jewelry, kitchenware, and bric-a-brac are everywhere, with clothing outlets occupying most of the shop space. There are also numerous street food stalls, serving a tempting array of seafood snacks (*for more on Korean street food, see pages 140–1*).

Triple the size of Namdaemun and you have **Dongdaemun Sijang R** (Great East Gate Market), a large area that stretches south of Jongno 5-ga and 6-ga. Feast your eyes on the silk market here (which operates similar hours to Namdaemun) – stall after stall of brilliantly colored silk and synthetic brocades, a truly dazzling display. The history of this market goes back to the 14th century and the roots of the Joseon dynasty.

In more recent years, many refugees from North Korea escaping the communist regime there rebuilt their lives by taking jobs at the market. In addition to silks they sell bedding, kitchenware, handicrafts, and sports goods.

At either market you can find almost anything you want, and, perhaps, many things you'd rather not find. On weekends the crowds are so intense, you have simply got to move with the flow to survive. Hawkers shout out bargains, and the louder the better, since bargain hunters gravitate to a noisy

Herbal medicine at Dongdaemun market.

BELOW:
Hwanghakdong
Flea Market

BELOW:
Namdaemun
Market. **RIGHT:**
arcade-style games
are popular.

crowd like a shark to spots of blood. This is also a good place to sit down to a *sundae*, stuffed intestine, or that most pungent of Korean delicacies, *beondegi* (silkworm larvae). Really, you haven't experienced Seoul until you have spent some time at Namdaemun or Dongdaemun markets.

Further to the east, in Dongdaemun stadium (subway lines 2, 4, and 5), is the sprawling **Hwanghakdong Flea Market ⑨**, officially known as Dongdaemun Pungmul (all-trades) market (daily 8am–6.30pm). If you're looking for a life-size statue of an American Indian, reproduction antique furniture, used ice skates, or an old TV, you stand a good chance of finding it here. For the truly bizarre, there is the snake salesman with microphone in hand. He dips his free hand into a bag and brings out a handful of snakes, tossing them into a plastic tub. A few turtles are added for good measure. Somehow he manages to sell this writhing basket of reptiles to one of the middle-aged men crowding around. While the salesman sets up another sale, his assistants boil the basket of turtles and snakes,

and quickly bottle them in *soju*. Minutes later, the lucky customer leaves with a big smile, knowing that it will be a long time before he will be suffering from virility problems. Prescription medications have cut into this once-booming impotence remedy trade, but it still exists even today.

Continuing into the sprawling eastern suburbs is the equally unusual **Gyeongdong Oriental Medicine Market** (daily 8am–6.30pm except 1st and 3rd Sunday of each month; subway line 1; Jegidong Station). This is a great place to buy fresh ginseng, or dozens of other odd-looking roots and fungi that are said to be good for a myriad ailments. There are also a few dealers of dog meat, which is considered a "health food" (think men's stamina) in the Orient.

A little more conventional is the **Janganpyeong Antiques Market** (daily 10am–8pm except 1st and 3rd Sunday of each month; subway line 5; Janganpyeong Station). Dozens of small shops are located in several two-story buildings. Most of the dealers here do not handle top-of-

the-line antiques (you need to go to Insadong for those), but since there are regulations concerning the export of valued Korean antiquities anyway, Janghanpyeong is the perfect place to find a funky piece to decorate your living room. How about a large wooden bowl that was once used to clean rice? Or a handmade wooden plow? Or a Korean ceramic pillow makes a great conversation piece.

Be aware that trafficking in certain items, especially antiques and animal products such as turtle shell or ivory, may well be illegal.

Labyrinthine arcades

More convenient and popular than traditional markets these days are the numerous department stores such as Lotte and Shinsegae on Namdaemunno. South of the river are the Lotte World (*see page 135*), New Core, Grace, Galleria, Hyundai, and Hanyang department stores. Also south of the river in Apgujeongdong is the informally named "Rodeo Drive," a street of up-market international and local fashion houses.

There are seemingly never-ending streets of shops built underground, along Jongno and Euljiro, and smaller and pricier arcades underneath the **Westin Chosun**, **Lotte**, and **Plaza hotels**. Above ground there is the **Nagwon Arcade ❶** (Mon–Sat 9am–8pm) at Jongno 2-ga, and a four-block arcade running north-south from Jongno 3-ga to Toegyero 3-ga.

The Sogong Arcade runs from under the corner of the Plaza Hotel, turns left at the Westin Chosun Hotel and continues alongside Lotte department store to the edge of Myeongdong; the **Hoehyeon Arcade ⓤ** (daily; shop hours are generally 10am–8 or 9pm) starts in front of the Central Post Office and runs up to Toegyero; and other mini-arcades exist where pedestrian underpasses allow room for a few stores. These arcades offer clothes, jewelry, cosmetics, cameras and other electronics, and souvenir items including reproductions of antique porcelain – some convincing, others less so.

Above ground, specialized shops tend to run along together in a row. Barbells, volleyballs, and various other

South Korea is Asia's most Christian country after the Philippines.

BELOW: Korean medicine utilizes all kinds of ingredients. These *scolopendra* centipedes are used to treat arthritis.

Market Life

By day, the main markets of Seoul are the place to go for a real taste of the city. You can buy almost anything you could think of, from herbal medicines to jewelry and furniture. The multi-story hives of shops are connected by alleyways or walkways. The stores open 10am–8pm, while most markets are open from 6am. Sit in one of the restaurants and watch the bustle of Korean life as streetside money-changers, purses clutched to chests, exchange notes in illegal transactions.

In the evening, another aspect of market life unfolds: the *suljip* or drinking house. A *suljip* is neither bar, cocktail lounge, nor beer hall. Here the market workers gather for a few after-work snacks and beer and *soju* liquor, which soon leads to loud singing, accompanied by the fervent banging of metal chopsticks against the tables.

Seoul

sporting paraphernalia can be found at any one of the half-dozen stores under the shadow of Seoul Stadium (an apt location) at Euljiro 7-ga. Buddhist rosaries hang at the shops near the entrance to Jogye-sa; brightly painted dog houses line Toegyero 4-ga and 5-ga.

Need hub caps and car seat covers? Go to the street connecting Cheong-gyecheon 5-ga with Euljiro 5-ga. Men's tailored suits? Visit Namdaemunno north of Euljiro, in an area called Gwanggyo. When the urge to shop begins to pall, simply head for the restored Cheonggyechon stream (*see page 118*).

OUTER SEOUL

Away from the downtown area, Seoul sprawls for many kilometers, its thoroughfares and high-rises extending south to the Han River and beyond. With the exception of lively Itaewon, most of these outer zones lie well off the tourist trail, although many have become shopping and entertainment hubs that rival those of the city center.

Although some suburbs are less easy to get to than Itaewon (one or two subway transfers may be needed), they offer opportunities you won't find in the center of Seoul. The thing to do is to make a day of it, and check out several places of interest – there is no better way to get to know modern Korea than by exploring the fringes of the capital.

Sinchon district

Seoul has several entertainment centers that appeal to the young, but one of the most popular and interesting is **Hongdae ❶** *(see panel, below)*, which caters to students from four nearby universities. The streets in this district, **Sinchon**, have such a profusion of restaurants, bars (some with live entertainment), games arcades, clothing stores, and coffee shops that young people from all over Seoul come here. The liveliest area of all is just to the west of Hongik University.

If you are planning on getting married, **Wedding Street ❷** (shops: daily 10am–8pm; subway line 2 to Ewha Womans University, exit 4 or 5) might be the place for you. Rows of shops display wedding gowns in their windows

BELOW: the bright lights of Itaewon.

Seoul Nightlife

Itaewon is the main area for foreigners' nighttime partying, especially since the government allowed the entertainment centers to remain open until the wee small hours. In the city center, Myeongdong is lively at any time, and is full of bars. Gangnam – and particularly Apgujeong – south of the river, is also known for its nightlife.

But nothing can compare with the action on offer in **Hongdae**, part of the Sinchon district in the west of the city, particularly for the teens to early-thirties set. On a Friday or Saturday night the subway station is so packed that people move by force of the crowd alone. Hundreds of tiny bars, discos, nightclubs, and restaurants mean there's something for everyone, and live clubs or bars are popular. Tango and salsa clubs are on the rise, too.

Nightlife in the south has grown up to match the daytime opportunities. It is not uncommon for young Seoulites to head out to Shinsa for an evening of tango at one of the salons there, or to follow a day of shopping in Gangnam with a night of drinking there too. Fusion spots that mix flavors and become their own are just as much a part of Seoul's character.

Coffee shops, a legacy of the American presence, are everywhere in Seoul.

hoping to entice well-heeled 20-year-olds. Weddings are a serious business in Korea – a wedding gown, make-up, and hairstyle (all these services are offered at the wedding shops) will set Daddy back thousands of dollars. Then there is the wedding hall, the dinner for all the guests, a photographer, and wedding gifts (from the parents); a Korean wedding runs into the tens of thousands of dollars.

Itaewon

Itaewon ❸ (accessible via subway line 6 to Itaewon Station) is an urban area that runs down from the southern flank of Namsan and eastward from the fenced edge of Yongsan Garrison, the site of the headquarters of the 8th US Army and the huge War Memorial. The main thoroughfare that bisects the army base into north-south posts similarly bisects Itaewon into an uphill-Namsan side and a downhill side toward the Han River.

For years, that flank of Namsan has been one of the main housing areas for Westerners as the Korea Housing Corporation, a government agency, built and maintained Western-style houses there. That idea is perpetuated, but for-eigners, not all of them Western, now occupy multi-story apartment build-ings higher up the mountain – a loca-tion that gives them a sweeping view of the Han River and mountain ridges south of the city.

Buddhist monks kept a free hostel for travelers near here for some 500 years. Today, you could walk for sev-eral blocks and hear not a lone word of Korean; instead, you'll hear English, French, Spanish, Indonesian, Japa-nese, and Afrikaans. The main street is lined with American fast-food and coffee chains; the Grand Hyatt Hotel's mirrored façade overlooks the city; and the twin minarets of the onion-domed mosque lie below, from which resounds the muezzin's call to prayer.

Centuries back, Itaewon was used as a stopover point for visitors to the cap-ital. Then, during the Japanese Occu-pation, Japanese troops were housed here. These soldiers were replaced after the Korean War with Ameri-can soldiers stationed at the adjacent Yongsan base, and Korean merchants moved into the thoroughfare to cater to the troops' needs. The future of the large US base in the centre of Seoul has been a matter of discussion for many years. Korea and the US agreed to relocate Yongsan US military base to Pyeongtaek, south Gyeonggi Prov-ince, in July 2004. The two countries agreed in February 2007 to complete the relocation by 2012.

National Museum and War Memorial

In the south of Itaewon, close to the Han River, is the **National Museum of Korea ❹** (Tue, Thur and Fri 9am–6pm, Wed and Sat 9am–9pm, Sun 9am–7pm; charge; subway line 1 and 4 to Ichon Station, exit 2), which has the finest (and largest) collection of Korean art and antiquities in the world. The col-lection includes over 100,000 items from ancient times through the Joseon Dynasty period. These include Baekje

BELOW: the War Memorial of Korea.

tiles, Silla pottery, gilt Buddhas, Goryeo celadons, and Joseon calligraphy and paintings.

Just to the east of the centre of Itaewon, the **Samsung Museum of Art LEEUM** ❺ (daily 10.30am to 6pm; charge) is one of Seoul's finest museums, featuring two exhibition halls and all kinds of art from ancient to contemporary. Equally impressive is the architecture itself, designed by three different architects so that each gallery has its own unique character. Visually impressive inside and out, with its landmark giant spider and the children's gallery, the museum is very close to Hangangjin Station on the subway line 6.

A short taxi ride west from Itaewon is the **War Memorial of Korea** ❻ (National Museum War Memorial of Korea; Tue–Sun 9am–6pm; free). Located on the large plaza in front of the Memorial is one of Seoul's better museums, filled with Korean War-era airplanes, tanks, and artillery pieces. Inside, displays, movies, and dioramas tell you all you need to know about the Korean War.

Yongsan Electronics Market

South Korea embraced the online revolution earlier than most, and in the early years of the 21st century is emerging as a global leader in cutting edge electronics. Gadgets and gizmos are available almost everywhere in Seoul, but the largest concentration of discount dealers is in the **Yongsan Electronics Market** ❼ (daily 10am–7pm), a short taxi ride to the southwest of the War Memorial. Housed in three multistory buildings and spreading out to a few smaller arcades, the market draws Koreans in their thousands to try out the latest computers, computer games, cellphones and cameras. Virtually anything electronic can be found here. A lot of expats living in Korea shop here. For visitors, there are a few limitations. For one thing, English software and instructions are rare. Another problem is that South Korea runs on 220 volts, so their electronic devices are a bit inconvenient for those 110-volt countries, such as the United States. Be especially cautious if purchasing things like CF or SD cards, as many low-quality fakes masquerade as high-speed transfer

The Seoul Equestrian Park attracts hordes of bet-happy South Koreans (mostly men) on weekends from 11am to 6pm. You can watch the races in luxury from a hospitality room on the fourth floor: the English-speaking staff make placing a bet or buying a cool beer a breeze.

BELOW: cycle path by the Han River.

TIP

Deluxe taxis are black with a yellow sign on top. They are more expensive than regular taxis (though still relatively cheap), but the drivers are generally more courteous and the vehicles more comfortable.

BELOW: going shopping in Apgujeong. **RIGHT:** street food.

devices when in reality they are simply normal or even older products that have been repackaged with better labels. If you plan on bargaining, it is best to check the price at several different locations first and go online, then return to a place that seems particularly promising. If it's too cheap to be true, it probably is.

Tennis, golf, and city picnics

While hiking may be the most popular outdoor recreation, tennis does not lag far behind. Tennis courts can be found all over the city, and Koreans play both in the summer and winter. There are several golf clubs outside the city, but they are expensive. However, the city does offer some practice driving nets.

As part of the beautification program for the 1988 Seoul Olympics, the city cleaned up the once scruffy and disused banks of the Han River and turned them into the **Hangang Citizen's Park ⓫**, a leisure zone for the city's 10.35 million people. There are facilities for water sports, swimming pools, sports fields, and many kilometers of park area for picnicking and

kite flying. It's also possible to take 50-minute pleasure-boat cruises with C& Hangang Land (tel: 02 3271 6993; daily 11am–10.30pm; charge).

To the west of the city is the stunning **Seoul World Cup Stadium**, built for the 2002 soccer World Cup and easily reached on subway line 6 – a five-minute walk from World Cup Stadium (Sangam) Station.

Also close to the river, but far to the east, the **Walker Hill Resort ⓭** complex (subway line 5 to Gwangnaru Station, then take a taxi) is a lovely spot from which to view Seoul over a Martini. This nightlife area hosts Las Vegas-style revues (dinner shows at 5.30pm and 8pm, closed Sun; tel: 02 455 5000), gambling (in the Sheraton Walker Hill Casino), upmarket dining and events in the W Seoul Walkerhill hotel, and resort amenities.

Island in the river

The island of Yeouido was once little more than a large sandbar in the middle of the Han River. During the past few decades it has been transformed into an important corporate and gov-

ernment center. The big attraction for visitors is **Hanwha 63 City** ❿ (daily 10am–9pm, observatory until midnight), for many years Seoul's tallest building and, along with the N Seoul Tower, the city's most visible landmark. The 63-story building (hence its name) may not seem especially tall, but it towers over its surroundings on the banks of the Han River. There is a terrific observation deck, while the basement houses Seoul's best **aquarium**, and its grandest **IMAX theater**. After taking in the view from the top, and perhaps a movie, try one of the many restaurants in the building. Then take a walk along Hangang Citizen's Park to watch the kite flyers in action.

The **Noryangjin Fish Market** ⓫ (subway line 1 to Noryangjin station, then take the walkway back over the tracks) is just to the south of Yeouido island. Fresh fish on ice, live crabs, translucent squid, and fat, succulent shrimp all promise gourmet experiences; but you will have to get there in the pre-dawn hours if you want to compete with those who have come here to get supplies for their own fish stalls

in neighborhood markets. Perhaps the best feature of the fish market is the raw fish restaurants on the second floor. You can dine in relative luxury while watching all the fish market activity below.

SOUTH OF THE RIVER

Beyond the Han River, the southern suburbs of Seoul are grid-ironed into right angles, with rows upon rows of apartment blocks extending out towards the hilly margins of the city. The most desirable address is fashionable **Apgujeong** ⓬, where many of the city's affluent live and shop: on Rodeo Street (as in Los Angeles' Rodeo Drive) are the boutiques of many famous international design houses, as well as a surprisingly large number of Korean designers. The clientele here are worlds apart from the middle-aged *ajumma* (housewives) who shop across the river in the traditional markets – the women here are carrying Gucci handbags rather than baskets of cabbages.

The area is also known for its nightlife, and for those who feel in need of Western chain food, Apgujeong is home to a number of familiar establishments:

Lotte World roller coaster.

BELOW: ice-skating at Lotte World.

TIP

Just to the west of Apgujeong, the Sinsa-dong neighborhood is anchored by Garosugil (officially Dosan-daero buk 5-gil), a great place for cafés and foreign-themed restaurants. Koko Bruni is a tango-themed coffee, chocolate, and cake shop. The chocolates are named after famous Argentine Tango composers, and the delicate melt-in-your-mouth cakes, velvety lattes and espresso drinks are worth seeking out.

BELOW: open-air theater at Seoul Nori Madang.

Outback Steakhouse, Tony Roma's, and TGI Friday's, to name but a few. Yet you need not feel like you're leaving South Korea behind you: there are still numerous bars for *hof* and *soju*, as well as international bars which focus on South Asia, Italy, or Japan.

A little east of here (subway line 2; Jamsil Station), but still within Seoul's upscale neighborhoods, is the gargantuan **Lotte World** ⑬ (daily 9.30am–11pm; charge to amusement park), an all-in-one shopping mall, entertainment center, amusement park, and sports center. Two Lotte department stores anchor the mall on opposite ends of the complex. There are plenty of independent shops in the basement and adjacent building offering everything from one-of-a-kind dresses to black-market items (purchased on the US military bases and resold at a handsome profit).

One wing of the complex has a sports center complete with an Olympic-size swimming pool. In the center of it all stands a huge glass-covered amusement park – Lotte World Adventure – with a bridge leading outdoors to

an island ("Magic Island") that looks suspiciously like Disneyland's Fantasyland. There is also a large indoor **ice-skating rink**.

By way of variety, a short distance away are two areas where you can see **tombs** that date to the Baekje Kingdom (18 BC–AD 660). The tomb sites (they are large mounds of earth) have been made into attractive parks and make an enjoyable trip for hardcore history buffs.

Korean folk performances

Seeming a little incongruous among all the kitsch is the **Seoul Nori Madang** ⑭ (daily 9am–6pm; subway line 2 to Jamsil Station, exits 3 and 11), an outdoor amphitheater surrounded by a stone and mud wall – if you ignore the amusement rides it has the feel of a rural Korean village. The surroundings are perfect for the free folk performances held here.

One of the performances you may see at the Seoul Nori Madang is the Yangju Mask dance, traditionally held during Dano (a spring festival held during the 5th lunar month). The show begins with an introductory parade around the

amphitheater by the various characters dressed in full costume and dramatic masks (made of paper or gourd). It is a colorful and almost surreal sight to see a monk, a lotus leaf "spirit of heaven," a winking spirit of earth, an acupuncturist, a shaman witch, an aristocrat's concubine, a monkey, a police inspector, and 14 other characters (who play some 32 roles using 22 masks) parading around.

There is much enthusiastic audience participation during the performance. Metal bowls of *makgeolli* rice wine and *tteok* rice cakes are passed around in the audience (who sit in a broad circle around the performers), and when the various characters say something the audience agrees with, the audience calls out, "*Olchi, jalhanda!*" (or "That's right. Well said!").

Amsadong Prehistoric Settlement

A few subway stops and a short taxi ride from the Lotte World is the **Amsadong Prehistoric Settlement Site** ⓯ (Tue–Sun 9.30am–6pm, Nov–Feb until 5pm), the largest Neolithic site in South Korea. Its former resi-

dents lived mainly by hunting and fishing (the site is next to the Han River, though separated by an expressway these days), and some rudimentary farming. Numerous pit-house foundations, pottery chards, and stone tools were found during excavations that began in 1925. This quiet park, on the edge of the city, has an excellent little museum with dioramas, displays of tools, farm implements, and movies about Korea's prehistoric past (some displays are in English). On the grounds, nine pit houses have been built to give the visitor an idea of what a village in the Seoul area might have looked like some 8,000 years ago.

Korea World Trade Center

Going west from Lotte World is the **Korea World Trade Center** – the center of business for many foreign firms. Next door is Seoul's largest convention center, **COEX** ⓰ (Korea Exhibition Center), which plays host to the annual auto show, travel fair, and various other trade shows. Floor B-1 of the COEX is one of the most crowded shopping malls in South Korea; it also

Amsadong Prehistoric Park is the largest Neolithic site in the country.

BELOW: a reconstruction of the prehistoric settlement site at Amsadong.

TIP

Like anywhere,
bargaining in South
Korea should be fun,
not abusive. Most
market vendors will be
happy to reduce your
item. Ask for a discount
by saying "kkakka
juseyo."

has a multiplex movie theater and the largest **aquarium** in the country (daily 10am–8pm; charge).

Bongeun-sa

If you find yourself in the area, you might want to go to the hill just behind the COEX, where one of the city's oldest temples is found. **Bongeun-sa** (daily 4am–9pm; charge) may not look old (most of the buildings were destroyed during the Korean War, and subsequently rebuilt), but it has been around since AD 794. During the Joseon dynasty, when temples (and monks) were not permitted within the gates of the city, Bongeun was the largest and most important temple in the vicinity.

The Halmoni House of Sharing

Those wanting to take a close look at Korean wartime history should make a point of visiting the **Halmoni House of Sharing** (tours by RSVP at visits@houseofsharing.org; free, donation suggested). These courageous women have brought the issue of their sexual slavery at the hands of the Japanese

to the forefront of Korean and international politics, and despite many of them being in their eighties or nineties, they still demonstrate weekly outside the City Hall each Wednesday, demanding that the Japanese admit their wrongdoing and apologize to them. Joining a tour will be one of your most moving experiences in Seoul.

Korean theater

Seoul has an active theater scene, with a dozen small theater groups based in the city. The **Seoul Arts Center** ⑰ (subway line 3, Nambu Bus Terminal Station, then a ten-minute walk) is a modern building complex south of the Han River. Its location reflects efforts by the city authorities to move many key facilities out of the congested downtown area, and they did it in a big way when they constructed this impressive complex of arts and cultural buildings on a picturesque hillside. The Arts Center is now the primary center for the staging of Seoul opera (three performance theaters), and hosts big-name international performers and musical companies in the Seoul Concert Hall.

Adjacent to the Arts Center is **The National Center for Korean Traditional Performing Arts** ⑱, where the tradition of Korean court music and dance is kept alive. There are regular performances here on Saturday afternoons (4 or 5pm–6.20pm) that are always popular with tourists. If you do go to one of the Saturday concerts, be sure to get there early and visit the museum next door, which exhibits some odd-looking Korean musical instruments.

On special occasions the courtyard in front of the concert hall is given over to traditional Korean games. Parents join their children in a noisy mêlée of activities including the lively Korean version of the seesaw (*neol ttwigi – see panel on page 70*) which involves jumping onto the plank, a game of tossing arrows into a narrow metal vase (*tuho*), and large group games such as the ubiquitous tug-of-war (*juldarigi*). ❑

BELOW: performance at the Sejong Center for the Performing Arts. **RIGHT:** the view south from the N Seoul Tower.

STREET FOOD

Pojangmacha, or street vendors, liven up the night, inviting passers-by to stop in for a late-night bite. Cheap, hot, and delicious, some feel this is Korean food at its best

Few visitors to South Korea will stay without noticing the abundance of street food. *Pojangmacha,* as they're known in Korean, are pushcarts or makeshift restaurants which line alleyways, often around subway exits. There's something Hopper-esque about the lonesome late-night shack with one or two customers, steam and aromas rising up into the night air. Eating street food after singing at a *noraebang* or getting a bite before heading off to another nightclub is part of what makes Korea what it is.

Infinite Variety

What exactly are all these things that are offered in the street? That depends in part on where you are – items in Seoul will be somewhat different than items in Busan. But one thing that figures prominently everywhere is seafood. Dried squid comes in a variety of shapes and sizes, from whole tentacles to flattened round pancakes. Fish cakes are common, usually served in a tasty warm broth. Noodles and soups make a wonderful late-night warm-up before heading home. Sweets and breads are delicious breakfast fare. But nothing is more popular than *tteokbokki,* a dish made of rice cake (*tteok*) cooked in a fiery sauce. Koreans will walk 15 minutes in the bitter cold just to stop for good *tteokbokki* before turning in. It's often eaten from a paper cup – ask for some warm broth if you like, to wash it down.

ABOVE: diners crowd around a popular food stand, where vegetables and seafood are dipped in tempura batter and fried to a deep golden brown color.

BELOW: spooning out *tteokbokki,* a ubiquitous dish made with rice cakes and a fiery beef-based sauce.

LEFT: a chef stretches out a batch of fresh noodles until they are just the right thickness.

DRINKING *SOJU*

Perhaps most ubiquitous of all are the spots to drink *soju*, a distilled rice or potato-starch liquor. It is often served with a variety of *anju* (appetizers) ranging from beer nuts all the way to barbecued hagfish (*gom jang eo*), a kind of benthic sea eel, more palatable than it sounds.

Drinking is more than just a good time – it's an important way for Koreans to develop business and social relationships. One pours for the others; never for himself or herself. Younger members, especially women, will show respect for elders by turning their heads away to the side when taking a sip.

Unlike other Asian cultures, it is not acceptable to refill peers' and colleagues' glasses until the moment that they've drained their glass. Any sooner, you're rushing things; any later and (so Korean folk wisdom has it) you doom them to refill their own glass, which means they will never get married.

ABOVE: seafood *pajeon*, a pancake-like meal with squid and scallions.

ABOVE: silkworm pupae, *boondaegi*, are served piping hot at festivals or street corners, and are (rumor has it) very popular with schoolchildren.

RIGHT: whether fried, steamed, boiled, dried, grilled, or roasted, there's a cornucopia of street foods to be tried, and part of the fun of being here is sampling the outlandish-looking offerings.

ABOVE: no food is more Korean than gimchi, a side dish served morning, noon, and night that's made from vegetables (often cabbage) aged in a sauce of chili, dried shrimp, and even raw oyster until it is tender and pungent.

GYEONGGI PROVINCE

Extending from the suburbs of Seoul, much of Gyeonggi is densely populated. The south offers cultural sights, the north has attractive mountain scenery, while the heavily fortified border with North Korea makes for an unusual day-trip

Wrapped around the city of Seoul, Gyeonggi is South Korea's most populous, and prosperous province. However, there is a marked difference between the northern areas, where settlement has been hindered by rugged terrain and the close proximity of the North Korean border, and the areas further south and west, where Seoul's urban sprawl extends into the new cities of Gwacheon and Bundang, which were nothing more than farmers' fields 30 years ago. Tied into the Seoul subway system, Suwon and Incheon can almost be considered part of the Seoul metropolitan area.

There is a great deal to see, and all lies within a day trip from the city center. There are royal tombs, mountain fortresses, peaceful temples, and one of Korea's best folk villages, and it is still easy to get away from the urban centers and out into the countryside. Taking the tour up to Panmunjeom, on the border with North Korea, is a must for anyone interested in modern history.

Royal tombs

The **Heoninneung Royal Tombs** ❶ (Tue–Sun 9am–6.30pm, until 5.30pm Nov–Feb; charge), of the 3rd and 24th Joseon kings, lie in the southeast outskirts of Seoul in Naegokdong. There are several ways to access the area, but perhaps the best is to take bus No. 36 from the express bus terminal in Gangnam, in southern Seoul (subway line 3; Express Bus Terminal Station).

Heonneung is the location of the tombs of King Taejong (1367–1422) and Queen Wongyong (1364–1420), and **Inneung** for the tombs of King Sunjo (1790–1834) and Queen Sunwon (1789–1837). All are guarded by granite statues and fantastical animal sentries. If you are in Korea on May 8, you may want to attend a *jesa* (ancestor-worship) ceremony conducted annually at Heonin-

Main attractions

NAMHANSANSEONG FORTRESS
INCHEON
WOLMIDO DISTRICT
SUWON
HWASEONG
SEOUL GRAND PARK
KOREAN FOLK VILLAGE
ICHEON
BUKHANSAN NATIONAL PARK
GANGHWA-DO ISLAND
BOMUN-SA TEMPLE
DEMILITARIZED ZONE (DMZ)
PANMUNJEOM
THIRD TUNNEL OF AGGRESSION

LEFT: section of wall at Hwaseong Fortress, Suwon. **RIGHT:** at a traditional wedding ceremony, Korean Folk Village.

neung by Joseon-dynasty descendants.

The grounds at Heoninneung are well manicured, and the area's classical tomb settings make this a popular area for filming historical movies. A variety of crops such as melons, strawberries, eggplants, peppers, corn, and rice are cultivated in the surrounding countryside, and, during the warmer months, shady fruit stands are set up in fields so people can sit and enjoy refreshing breezes, sunshine, and fresh-from-the-earth fruit before hiking up to the tombs.

King Sunjo's tomb at Inneung.

Namhanseong Fortress

South Korea does not have many Western-style parks. Instead, on warm days families pack a lunch and head for a nearby palace, royal tomb, or temple. **Namhansanseong** ❷ (South Han Mountain Fortress; open 24 hours; free) is one such popular weekend picnic and hiking area about 30km (18 miles) southeast of Seoul proper. This grand highland redoubt – with 8km (5 miles) of stone walls – was originally built about 2,000 years ago during Korea's Goguryeo dynasty. Most of the fort's now-visible structures, however, date from the 17th and 18th centuries, when the fortress served Joseon kings of that period as a retreat from invading armies. Like Bukhansan Fortress to the north of Seoul (*see page 154*), Nam-

Gyeonggi Province

hansan is a mountain fortification surrounding a valley.

This spectacular place makes a cool escape on hot summer days, or a pleasant picnic outing on one of Korea's fine late fall days. If you have the energy, you can walk the entire length of the wall, or take a short walk alongside it looking at the remains of the buildings (and a few that have been rebuilt) within the walls. To get to Namhansanseong you can take subway line 8 to Namhansanseong Station, from where it's a short taxi ride to the fortification; or take a direct bus (80 minutes) from Dong Seoul Bus Terminal (subway line 2; Gangbyeon Station).

Incheon – Korea's transportation hub

Approximately 40km (25 miles) to the west of Seoul is the city of **Incheon** ❸. Until the 1880s, the settlement was a fishing village called Jemulpo, and for a long time was the only place in Korea that foreigners were allowed to visit. Today, it has been transformed into a booming harbor and South Korea's fourth-largest city. The number of trading ships calling at Incheon has increased with every passing year, and consequently the stretch between Seoul proper and the Port of Incheon has become the most important sea, road, and rail supply route in SouthKorea.

With the opening of the **Inchcon International Airport** (IIA) ❹ in 2001, the city became South Korea's most important hub for both shipping and air transportation. The airport sits on reclaimed tidal flats lying between two offshore islands. The construction effort was enormous, beginning back in 1992 and costing more than US$6 billion. The site replaces the aging Gimpo Airport, which is now used for domestic flights only. The two airports give Korea the best airline transportation facilities in northeast Asia. The airport currently has two runways (a third is under construction), and handles over 30 million passengers every year. By 2020 there will be four runways dealing with an anticipated 100 million passengers.

Besides the airport facilities, parks have been created (the airport is quite proud of its environmental record, though this seems a bit misplaced given the massive environmental

Map opposite

TIP

Incheon's official name is Incheon Metropolitan City. Songdo International City contains South Korea's tallest building, currently the Northeast Asia Trade tower. New buildings are in the works that will skyscrape even higher.

LEFT: Incheon International Airport. **BELOW:** enjoying the late fall sun.

WHERE

Incheon's Wolmido area is the only official Chinatown in all of South Korea, though there are other unofficial enclaves of Chinese speakers in all the major cities, including Seoul, Busan, and elsewhere.

impact of turning a large area of tidal flats and a few quiet islands into an international transportation hub), and there is an expressway connecting the airport to the Seoul urban area. Adjacent to the airport is an international business center, complete with luxury hotels and high-rise office blocks.

History in Incheon

Incheon is best known as the place where US General Douglas MacArthur directed a brilliant amphibious landing, thus turning the bitter Korean War around for southern Korea and its allies. That landing, code-named Operation Chromite, began at dawn on September 15, 1950. Historian David Rees writes in his book *Korea: The Limited War* that "the successive objectives of the operation called for the neutralization of **Wolmido**, the island controlling Incheon harbor, a landing in the city, seizure of Gimpo Airfield, and the capture of Seoul." Despite fierce objections from his subordinates, MacArthur's strategy proved to have the winning element of surprise. On D-Day, the 5th Marines poured ashore

at Incheon, and, after 12 days of hellish fighting, took that devastated capital.

Today, Radio Hill is known as **Freedom Hill** and looms over an earnest seaport bustling with international trade. Atop the hill, jaunty in sculpted khakis, you will find a 10-meter (32ft) statue of General MacArthur, gripping a pair of binoculars in his right hand.

The best way to get to Freedom Hill is to take the Seoul Subway train due west through alternating industrial suburbs and rice fields. Once you arrive at **Dongincheon Station**, take a cab or hike up to Freedom Hill above this town of steep streets and endless ocean terminals.

The ocean view from up here is overtly industrial, but the sea breezes are crisp, and besides the MacArthur statue you will find a whitewashed replica of America's Statue of Liberty. There is also a pavilion from where you may see a spectacular red fireball sun dropping through container cranes and ships' riggings into an amber ocean.

The walk down from Freedom Hill through old Incheon is a pleasant one, down cobble- and flag-stoned

BELOW: the memorial at Freedom Hill commemorates the turning point of the Korean War.

byways and stairs, past some of South Korea's most distinctive verandas and storefronts. There are several deluxe-priced hotels in Incheon, although if your budget leans towards a more authentic Korean experience, there are numerous *yeogwan* inns to choose from. The area has undergone a recent urban renewal, with new sidewalks, tourist-oriented walking tours and maps, and an amusement park popular with dating couples. Another great reason to come here is the delicious Chinese-Korean food. Spicy noodle dishes are a regional specialty.

Popular nearby diversions include seafood dining on one of the area's land-linked islands, either **Wolmido** (**Moon Tail Island**) or **Sowolmido**. Both are famous for their gourmet plates of raw fish and other delicacies from the deep.

During the summertime, various offshore islands become favored Korean resort destinations due to their natural assets. On these islands, you can tan on the white-sand beaches or wallow in lovely man-made lagoons rimmed by colorful cabanas. There

are several smaller resort hotels in this area, particularly near big **Songdo Beach** south of the city.

SUWON AND ITS SURROUNDINGS

Suwon ❺, the capital of Gyeonggi Province, is an old fortress-city 51km (31 miles) south of Seoul. Suwon's name, which means "water-source" or "water-field," derives from its location in an area which was traditionally known for its fine artesian wells.

These days, the city is renowned for its restored castle walls and its *galbi*, or barbecued short ribs. However, it's the late spring and summer strawberries *(ttalgi)* that come to most Korean minds when you mention the word Suwon. The city can be quickly and easily reached on subway line 1 from Seoul Station to its terminus at Suwon Station. Better yet, take the faster, more comfortable (and more expensive) train from Seoul to Suwon station.

Hwaseong Fortress

The main sight in Suwon is the **Hwaseong Fortress**, with its massive walls,

Taegeuk detail, *Hwaseong Fortress.* *The pattern represents* *the harmony of nature* *and is a variant of* *the Daoist yin-yang.*

LEFT: ubiquitous apartment complexes.

High-Rise Living

You can't miss them – wherever you look you see clusters of high-rise apartments. They appear to be the most impersonal and even dehumanizing of human dwellings and are a universal turn-off for Westerners. Indeed, the fact that these concrete blocks are taking over the countryside gives even the most avid apologist pause. But there is an obvious reason why construction companies can't build them fast enough – they are popular with Koreans. As Koreans so rightly point out: this is a small (and mostly mountainous) country with over 48 million people. Translated, that means these apartments make good sense. And they really aren't so bad, especially when one considers the drafty, uncomfortable country homes that many of the apartment dwellers grew up in.

The high-rise offers relatively spacious living, with hot water, an indoor toilet (which many country homes don't have), a place to park that new Hyundai, and 24-hour security. They are comfortable and modern, offering an improved lifestyle, and though they seem impersonal, the apartments are little villages, with an activity room for seniors, playgrounds and kindergartens for children, and informal clubs where housewives can socialize. So, when you see those slabs of concrete, try to look at them from a Korean's point of view.

Dragon detail on the West Sentry Post, Hwaseong Fortress.

BELOW: Hwaseong Fortress.

gates, and other historic architectural facilities which meander for 5.5km (3½ miles) around the old city proper. Construction began during the reign of King Jeongjo (1776–1800), the 22nd Joseon monarch, who established the fortress in memory of his father, Prince Sado *(see page opposite)*. The whole complex is an integral part of the city, so there are no opening or closing times or gates to enter.

Historians believe that Jeongjo wanted to move the Korean capital from Seoul to Suwon, but because of various personal and political problems he was never able to realize his ambition. He did, however, create a beautiful fortified city – complete with parapets and embrasures, floodgates, observation platforms and domes, parade grounds, command bunkers, cannon stands, and an archery range. Jeongjo's original fortress, known as the "Flower Fortress," was already in a decrepit state when it was heavily damaged by bombing during the Korean War.

In 1975 the South Korean government undertook a major restoration; the project took four years and cost several million dollars. The impressive refurbished walls (which average 9 meters/30ft, in height) and other structures still look a tad too new, but even so they are an irresistible invitation to a city stroll. One particularly lovely spot near the North Gate, Janganmun, is a strikingly landscaped reflecting pond, Yongyeon, which sits below an octagonal moon-watching pavilion called Banghwasuryujeong.

This meditative spot was commissioned by the esthetically inclined King Jeongjo when he initiated his Suwon fortress-city master plan in 1794. These days it's a gem of a place much favored by neighborhood *haraboji* (grandfathers), who sit inside its gabled cupola, lighting long-stemmed pipes, drinking sweet rice wine, and bouncing patriarchal thoughts off nearby castle walls. The whole classical effect is officially labeled "The Northern Turret."

The Hwaseong Cultural Festival, held every year in early October in Suwon, features music, theater, dance, and exhibitions, as well as memo-

rial services for King Jeongjo and his unfortunate father.

If, after a hike around the "Flower Fortress," you crave fresh strawberries and cool wine, take a bus or taxi to the Agricultural Green Belt area in Suwon's western suburbs near the modern Agricultural College of Seoul National University. There you can eat heaps of sweet grapes and blood-red strawberries at parasol-shaded tables next to the patches and vineyards from where they came, before visiting one of the other Suwon area sites.

Dragon Jewel Temple

Yongju-sa ❻ is a Buddhist temple which, like the Suwon fortress, was built by King Jeongjo in his father's memory. Yongju-sa, "The Dragon Jewel," rests in a rural, piney area about a 20-minute bus ride south of Suwon's mid-town South Gate.

Constructed in 1790 on the site of an earlier Silla-dynasty temple (dating from 856), Yongju-sa's grounds have a seven-story stone pagoda, a 1,500kg (3,300lb) Goryeo-era brass bell and, in the main hall, a superb Buddhist painting by the Joseon-genre master Danwon Kim Hongdo.

Yongju-sa is a popular place to visit at the time of the Buddha's birthday (on the 8th day of the 4th lunar month, usually in late April), when pilgrims from afar arrive here bearing candle-lit paper lanterns and say prayers for good fortune.

Tomb of the "Rice Box Prince"

In an appropriately serene setting 20-minutes' walk west of Yongju-sa are the mounded tombs, **Yungneung/ Geolleung** (Tue–Sun 9am–6.30pm, Nov–Feb until 5.30pm; charge), of King Jeongjo and his father, Prince Sado. Jeongjo posthumously awarded his father the title "King Jangjo," and father and son were laid to rest here together. Jeongjo's grandfather and Sado's father, King Yeongjo (reigned 1724–76), was convinced that his son was attempting to overthrow him, and ordered him to be locked in a rice box until death. He was initially buried in a rather inauspicious location, but when his son became king he had his father

WHERE

Even fairly remote day hikes from Seoul can be crowded, often frustratingly so, for anyone hiking to "get away from it all." Try for early morning (sunrise) or mid-week hikes for the maximum peace and quiet.

LEFT: worshipper at Yongju-sa.
BELOW: tomb protector, Yongju-sa.

Traditional food can be enjoyed alfresco at the Korean Folk Village.

reinterred in what was believed to be the best tomb site in the realm.

The location of this tomb, just outside of Suwon, is a fair distance from Seoul, especially when one considers all the hoopla that went on when the king left the safe confines of the palace grounds. Twice a year the king was required to make the journey to pay respects to his unfortunate father's spirit. Each visit took several days and thousands of people to accomplish – it even required a separate palace and the most modern (for the 18th century) of fortifications to protect it all. Thanks to that son's devotion, the fortification at Suwon really is the gem in the crown of Korea's distinguished history of fortress-building. In 1997, Hwaseong was given the acclaim it deserves when it was officially designated as a Unesco World Heritage site.

Parks, zoos, and museums

BELOW: martial arts display at a cultural festival, Hwaseong Fortress.

Nearer Seoul, set in the hills southwest of the city by the satellite city of Gwacheon, is **Seoul Grand Park** ❼ (daily 9am–7pm, Oct–Mar until 6pm).

With a zoo (which features a dolphin show; charge), botanic garden, the **Seoul Land** amusement park (daily 9.30am–6.30 to 10pm, varying with season/festivity; charge), the Seoul Horse Race Track (racing weekends 10.30am–5.30pm), and the **National Museum of Contemporary Art** (Tue–Fri 10am–6pm, to 9pm Sat–Sun, until 5pm Nov–Feb; charge), there is something for everyone. Be prepared for a lot of walking and traffic jams; less so if you go on a weekday. Plan to spend an entire day at the Grand Park; there is a lot to do here, especially if you have children. From the center of Seoul, it takes about a half-hour to get to Seoul Grand Park Station on subway line 4.

An African safari, American zoo, and Korean amusement park come improbably together at **Everland** ❽ (daily 9.30am–9pm, Sun from 9am; charge), a recreation complex on the north side of National Highway 4, 35km (22 miles) southeast of Seoul. Among its popular attractions are South Korea's only pair of pandas (a gift from China after diplomatic relations were established). Amusement parks are a favorite

with Koreans, and if you stay in South Korea for any length of time, you're sure to be asked to accompany your Korean friends to one.

Not far from Everland is the **Ho Am Art Museum** (Tue–Sun 10am–6pm; charge), one of Korea's finest private museums (owned by Samsung, as is Everland). The museum's permanent collection features early devotional art, and, remarkably, 91 of the pieces have been designated as national treasures (the oldest temples can usually claim only a few national treasures). To enter the museum grounds, you pass through a delightful traditional garden, complete with pond and bamboo stand. There are regular shuttle buses operating between Everland and the Ho Am Art Museum.

The Korean Folk Village

The **Korean Folk Village ❾** (daily 9am to at least 5pm, closing times vary; charge) is best visited as a day trip from Seoul, being located 45km (28 miles) south of the capital, close to the city of Suwon. Allow several hours to take in the 240 homes, shops, and other attractions in authentically reproduced Joseon-dynasty villages from the various regions of South Korea. In fact, many of the old buildings here are the real thing, having been transported to the Folk Village from the countryside.

There is a wide variety of ceramic and bamboo shops to visit, and you can drink rice wines in a wayside tavern, then join the staged wedding procession of a traditionally costumed bride and groom who are transported via palanquin, trailed by a colorful, whirling farmers' dance band.

Skilled silk-weavers, basket-makers, fan-makers, mulberry paper-makers, and other skilled craftspeople carry on traditional crafts that have mostly disappeared from the countryside today. Even in an entire day, you may not be able to view all the fascinating exhibits in this sprawling museum.

The overall effect is memorable, although less so at weekends when things can get overcrowded. Direct buses leave from the Suwon Railway/Subway Station every hour.

Icheon and its ceramics

The soulful pottery kilns of two of South Korea's finest potters are located approximately 70km (43 miles) southeast of Seoul near **Icheon ❿** (a short distance north of National Highway 4). Icheon has been Korea's most important center of ceramic production for over 600 years. Today, the area has 80 kilns firing pots, and there are dozens of shops and showrooms exhibiting the work of local artists.

At the **Icheon Ceramics Village**, 4km (2½ miles) northwest of Icheon at the village of Seokgwangni, it is possible to observe Goryeo celadons being created by ceramics master Yu Geunhyong, and marvel at Ahn Dongo's Joseon-dynasty whiteware as it is pulled hot from his traditional kilns. These gentlemen's fine work can be purchased on the spot or in prominent ceramic art galleries in Seoul. At the other end of the potting spectrum, you will find, here and there in the

Icheon is the centre of the country's ceramics industry.

BELOW: the Ceramics Village near Icheon.

greater Icheon area, row upon row of the ubiquitous shiny, brown, tall, and oblong *gimchi* pots. These utilitarian wares are hand-thrown and fired in humble adobe huts.

Icheon and nearby Yeoju *(see below)* are both good places to shop for ceramics, since prices here are usually lower than in Seoul. You can still expect to pay hundreds or even thousands of dollars for pieces from famous artists, though. On the other hand, an attractive Korean tea service can be purchased for less than US$50.

Though the subtleties are lost on the majority of foreigners, rice from Icheon is also highly prized, and throughout South Korea many restaurants proudly state they serve Icheon rice. Gourmands should be sure to try a bowl and see if they can detect the difference in flavor or texture.

Yeoju

On the eastern edge of Gyeonggi Province is the modern city of **Yeoju** ⓫, with three or four attractions that might entice you to linger before continuing on your way to the natural

wonders of Seoraksan National Park *(see page 178)* and the east coast.

About 3km (2 miles) northwest of the city is **Yeongneung** (Tue–Sun 9am–6pm, until 5pm Nov–Mar; charge), the tomb of Korea's renowned and beloved King Sejong (reigned 1418–50). Entering through a forest of twisted trees, you walk past the small shrine and climb the brick walkway to the edge of the tomb.

As you get closer, soldiers, scholars, and horses – life-size statues that adorn tomb sites of important officials, and were once thought to have protected and accompanied the spirit on its journey – surround the tomb. The tomb is not a massive mound of earth, like those of ancient royalty in Gyeongju, but still is appropriately sized, on a pleasant forested hill side. From the top you can enjoy an excellent view of the surrounding countryside.

If, after paying your respects to King Sejong, you still have time, you might want to visit **Silleuk-sa Temple** (daily sunrise–sunset; charge) beside the Namhangang River. Established in AD 580 by Wonhyo, a celebrated Silla monk, the temple is one of the most important in the province. It is unique in that it is located by a river rather than in the mountains, as were most temples from this period. On the other hand, its location by the river is rather pleasing, backed by hills and surrounded by a deciduous forest.

The **Mok-a Buddhist Museum** (daily 9am–6pm, Nov–Feb 9.30am–5pm; charge), located on the eastern edge of the city, is one more site which might interest the curious. It is an eclectic display of outdoor sculptures, and devotional art in an indoor museum, that will leave you wondering if you have just had a spiritual experience or witnessed one of the tackiest religious displays in South Korea. A teahouse on the grounds will give you the time to contemplate what you have seen.

As you pass through town, you will notice several pottery shops. While not as important a center for pottery

BELOW: stylized "spirit-post" guardian, Korean Folk Village.

as Icheon, Yeoju has many fine potters and a long tradition of ceramic production. As in Icheon, the prices here are likely to be more favorable than those you'll find in Seoul.

NORTH OF SEOUL

Visitors and Seoulites alike are often told that they should spend at least one late winter day in the area north of Seoul. This region is dubbed by some as the "Realm of the Immortals." If possible, try to go when plum blossoms – the year's first flowers – begin to bloom in snow-dusted forests and ravines. It is, after all, what the ancients advise: "Do as amused immortals do: whenever the boredom and frustration of a long winter indoors becomes too much for them, they put on their cape and hat, tell the attendant to saddle the donkey, and go out in the snow looking for plum blossoms."

Dobongsan, Suraksan, and Bukhansan National Park

The journey will take you on Highway 3 north of Seoul between two popular hiking mountains: **Dobongsan** and **Suraksan**. Dobongsan, the rocky, harsh mountain on the west side of the road, is said to represent the male gender, while the curved and flowing Suraksan on the east side is supposed to personify the female qualities.

Dobongsan (740 meters/2,428ft) is one of several pleasant peaks just a few miles north of downtown Seoul. The hike to the summit takes several hours. You may want to linger en route next to a clear stream, or, if you are a camera buff, photograph the many odd rock formations; or you may wish to trek along one of the winding paths leading to the picturesque Buddhist temples of Mangwol, Cheonchuk, and Hweryong.

Dobongsan lies within one of Korea's 20 national parks – **Bukhansan National Park** ⓬. Further south from Dobongsan there is a triad of granite mountains, Samgaksan (triangle peaks), which is better known as Bukhansan. The tallest of these, at 837 meters (2,746ft), is Baegundae, from whose ridges you can catch some great views of Seoul. Another peak, Insubong (812 metres/2,664ft), has a sheer granite face that many have compared to the

Those traveling in Northern Gyeonggi-do or Gangwon-do will notice what appear to be large, block-like cement bridges with narrow, fortified sides. These are anti-tank barriers. An explosive charge collapses the support, sending the massive concrete obstruction into the road, blocking the tank's path.

BELOW: King Sejong's tomb at Yeongneung.

WHERE

You can easily access Suraksan from Seoul by taking subway line 4 to its terminus at Danggogae Station, or line 7 to Suraksan Station.

better-known El Capitan in California's Yosemite National Park. Like its California counterpart, Insubong is popular with technical climbers. Bukhansan National Park is a legitimate alpine environment, even if it is surrounded by a sea of ugly concrete apartment buildings, so if you decide to do some hiking, take along plenty of drinking water and warm clothes.

Besides its abundant natural beauty, Bukhansan National Park also has historic **Bukhansanseong** (North Han Mountain Fortress), one of two major ancient fortresses in the Seoul area – the other being Namhansanseong, to the south of the capital *(see page 144)* – built to defend the royal family against attacking hordes of Manchus and Mongolians when all other defenses had failed. This historical fortress is similar in design and setting to its southern counterpart, and is located above the sprawling northeast suburbs of Seoul along the rocky high ridges of Bukhansan mountain.

Bukhansanseong was originally constructed during the early Baekje period and at various times fell into martial

disuse. Today, you can walk along most of the 8km (5 miles) of wall and see the west gate, and view what remains of the palace and warehouses within the walls. A neat village has grown alongside a stream in the crater-like center of the fortress, and meadows and small forests on its less-populated fringes are favored picnic sites.

Being so close to Seoul, this park is immensely popular for both hikers and picnickers, and the most popular trails and riverside picnicking areas tend to get quite crowded on weekends. Access from Seoul is very easy; take line 4 on the subway to Suyu Station, or to Dobongsan Station for the northern part of the park.

Goseokjeong and Sambuyeon

Traveling further north, the terrain becomes wilder, with impressive canyons and ravines. Beyond **Dongducheon**, turn at the highway into the **Soyosan Mountains** and make the short hike to **Jajaeam Temple** ⓬ (daily 9am–sunset; charge), a place famed as the testing ground for a monk's celi-

BELOW: glorious scenery at Bukhansan.

bacy. Ornately carved dragons snarl out from this quaint temple's eaves. Inside, you will find a pair of tempestuous carved dragons writhing on the ceiling. A spouting waterfall and narrow gorge with a stream complement this lovely little canyon.

An even more dramatic waterfall and river scene is located much further north in the **Sincheorwon** area. Be aware that, because there are several military checkpoints in this area close to the 38th parallel, it is recommended that foreign visitors join a tour if possible (check with the KNTO in Seoul). A massive granite boulder, **Goseokjeong** ⓮, nicknamed "The Lonely Rock," sits in the Hantangang River and invites a clamber up to its pine-studded brow. Legend says that this rock rolled in from the east coast and decided to rest at this lovely turn in the fast-flowing river. A pleasure pavilion overlooks the rock and the river's noisy rapids, and local boatmen may be hired for a ride through the narrow river canyons to the north. It is also the most popular rafting spot near Seoul. The rock is very close to the DMZ but, being in

a river valley, there are no views across the border.

Due south of the Lonely Rock – in a deep canyon and off a steep dirt road – is the little-known **Sambuyeon** ⓯ or "Dragon Waterfall." You'll probably see local villagers fishing for carp in pools above the falls. This is an appropriate pastime, because in these parts – and in oriental mythology in general – the carp and the dragon are distant and legendary relatives.

A famous story in national lore tells about a carp (regarded by Koreans as a symbol of strength and perseverance) that persistently tried to climb up this strong waterfall. On the 100th day of his attempt, this feisty carp succeeded (with the help of the gods, naturally) to scale Sambuyeon, and as a reward he was magically turned into a powerful dragon. These falls, however, are rather easy to climb (a well-trodden path runs through a stone tunnel to the right side of the falls); and, of course, there is little worry of being turned into a dragon at the top.

On your return journey to Seoul, you may want to stop off at **Sanjeonghosu**

Jajaeam, one of the most remote of South Korea's mountain temples.

BELOW: flaming fall foliage in the Soyosan Mountains.

Ganghwa-do is one of Korea's main ginseng-growing areas.

BELOW: a dolmen burial site on Ganghwa Island.

Lake , an artificial lake built by Japanese engineers during Japan's colonial occupation of Korea. This is a popular skating spot in wintertime, and for most of the year it's a splendid area for hiking (there are numerous hiking trails in the woods around the lake), boating, and relaxation. Look out for the large colorful tents which serve as dance halls.

A short detour from the main road back to the capital leads to the impressive Confucian-style burial tombs of King Sejo (1456–68), the 7th Joseon king, and his wife, Queen Yun Jeonghi. Known as **Gwangneung** ⓱ (Tue–Sun 9am–5.30pm, until 4.30pm Nov–Feb; charge), these are probably the most idyllically located tombs in the Seoul area, hidden in the midst of a beautiful forest of old trees which shade melodious, trickling streams and wide greens ideal for picnicking. The surrounding woodland is very popular with birdwatchers, being a prime habitat for Tristram's woodpeckers and other rare species.

Close by Sejo's tomb is a small temple, Bongseon-sa, with a 2.6-meter (8½ft) bell, the third largest in Korea.

Gwangneung is located 28km (17 miles) northeast of the capital and just past **Uijeongbu**, a satellite city of Seoul, with a military camp made famous in the American movie and television series M*A*S*H.

Ganghwa-do, island of refuge

Ganghwa-do ⓲, an island 50km (31 miles) northwest of Seoul across the narrow Yeomha Strait, is steeped in history. To get there, catch an express bus at Seoul's Sinchon bus terminal; the journey takes approximately 90 minutes. **Ganghwa town** ⓳ is small and easy-going, ideal for tourists to walk around its marketplaces and handicraft shops. South Korea's finest rushcraft weaving is meticulously created on the island, so in local shops you'll find numerous baskets of all kinds. You can also see fine floor mats and doorway hangings that are woven so perfectly they let summer breezes in while filtering out pesky warm-weather mosquitoes. Another kind of weaving – silkweaving – is also a specialty of this town – you can hear the sound of

machines clacking out reams of silk as you walk along Ganghwa's streets and footpaths.

Make your way to the silk factory (off the main street on the road opposite the bridge fronting the marketplace). Since visitors are no longer allowed inside for tours, take a long look instead at a **bronze bell** hanging idly inside a small slatted pavilion next to the factory. Cast during King Sukjong's reign (1674–1720), this bell used to toll at 4am to signal the opening of Ganghwa's city gates.

When French troops stormed the city in 1866 to seek revenge for the execution of several French Roman Catholic priests, they attempted to haul this 3,864kg (8,520lb) bell to their ship, but abandoned their efforts because it was just too heavy. At the top of this same road is the restored **Goryeo Palace** where King Gojong lived in retreat during his unsuccessful 29-year resistance against invading Mongol hordes in the mid-1200s.

From the Goryeo palace, take a taxi up to the neatly restored North Gate, **Bungmun**, for a view of the distant blue mountains of North Korea. On a clear day you can see for several kilometers across the Imjin estuary and into the forbidden and communist north. The most dramatic view of North Korea, however, is from **Aegibong Peak** (daily 8am–6pm). Once off-limits, except in December when church groups were able to hold Christmas services at the "Christmas Tree," a pylon decked in colored lights, the peak is now open to civilians. You have to show your ID and fill in a form at a checkpoint before you get there, a reminder that you are at the front line. It is said that this is the only place in South Korea where you can actually observe villages in the North with the naked eye.

Your next stop should be South Korea's oldest and most unusual Episcopal Church, **Gamdeok Gyohoe**. This Christian structure, built in 1900 by Bishop Charles Cort, about 10 years after his arrival in Korea, harmoniously combines Christian, Taoist, and Buddhist elements in its overall design.

The front gate of the church is decorated with a large paisleyed Taoist symbol; the church, constructed of

EAT

One of the specialties in Ganghwa-do and other outlying islands is *kalguksu*, a delicious seafood broth with noodles, clams, and vegetables. You can either eat it as is or add condiments or chili pepper for added flavor.

BELOW: Christian kitsch at Uijeongbu.

Korean Dolmen

The dolmen on Ganghwa Island are the best known in Korea, but dolmen are found throughout the country. There have been both stone tools and a few bronze items discovered in and around the dolmen, though archeologists generally associate the dolmen with the Korean Bronze Age (circa 900–400 BC).

The dolmen found in Korea are of three types. Those on Ganghwa are typical of the Northern Style (Table Style) and have large upright stones in a rough square, covered by a flat capstone. The Southern Style (found south of the Han River) has a large boulder as a capstone placed atop smaller stones. The third type of dolmen simply has a large capstone laid over the burial site.

It is intriguing that Korean dolmen are exactly like those found in Ireland, some 9,600km (6,000 miles) to the west.

Ganghwa Island is known for its production of Hwamunseok, large handwoven floor mats and baskets made of rush. On market day, about 600 pieces of Hwamunseok are sold, largely to middlemen who resell them in Seoul. The island also produces ginseng.

wood, is classically Korean in its interior and exterior architecture; a bodhi tree, an old Buddhism-related symbol, was planted in the main courtyard at the time of the church's dedication; and atop the roof is a Christian cross trimmed with fluorescent light bulbs which show visitors the way at night.

After seeing this eclectic site, catch a bus at the main terminal and head northwest of Ganghwa town to one of the most mysterious sculptures in Korea, the **Prehistoric Dolmen**. The scenery along this roadway is dominated mostly by fields of ginseng protected by low thatched lean-tos, and typical Ganghwa farmhouses and silos decorated with contemporary folk art.

This art is in the form of meticulous sheet-metal sculpture attached at the upturns of eaves and along the edge of corrugated metal roofs. Here and there you will see brilliantly painted sheet-metal cranes, lotus blossoms, airplanes, and other such symbolic and surrealistic roofcraft.

About 3km (2 miles) from town, down a dirt path behind a chicken farm, stands a primitive stone struc-

ture constructed of three large, flat boulders. Known as the **Ganghwa Jiseongmyo Dolmen**, archeologists have identified this ancient monument as a Northern-style dolmen (in Korean *goindol* – a sacred tomb or altar) which dates back to Neolithic times. Life goes on around these huge stones, as they stand undisturbed in the midst of peppers, tobacco, and ginseng.

Hidden pagoda

Further down the bus line, in Hajeommyeon, there is another old but lessvisited stone sculpture. It is a five-story pagoda, *seoktap*, that was once a part of a Goryeo temple. The temple is gone but the pagoda stands hidden in the pine forest. If you do seek out the pagoda, which is about a 2km (1-mile) walk from the main road past farmhouses, you might also wish to scale **Bongcheonsan**, the high hill that stands behind it. Hikers are promised a panoramic view of the Imjin Estuary and an opportunity to stomp around the ruins of an old stone beacon tower. This tower supported one of 696 beacon fires lit during the Joseon dynasty to relay national security mes-

BELOW: on board the Ganghwa–Seongmo ferry.

sages to Seoul. It was finally rendered obsolete when the telegraph system was introduced in 1894.

Now travel back in time to the Three Kingdoms Period. On the southern end of Ganghwado (take a bus to Onsuri from town), about 16km (10 miles) south of Ganghwa town, is one of the oldest temples in Korea, **Jeondeung-sa** ❷⓿, the "Temple of the Inherited Lamp." A Goryeo queen named Jeondeung-sa after a jade lamp presented to the temple. Formerly called Jinjong-sa, it was built in AD 381 by a famous monk named Ado. Legend has it that the wall surrounding the temple was constructed by three princes to fortify the monastery. Thus the fortress was named Samnangseong, or the "Castle of Three Flowers of Youth."

The friendly monks here may invite you to share a vegetarian meal with them or guide you to some of the remaining Tripitaka Koreana wooden blocks carved during the 13th century. It took 16 years to carve the Buddhist scriptures on these blocks, a monumental task done in hopes of preventing a consuming Mongol invasion.

On the temple grounds is an iron bell about 1.8 meters (6ft) tall. It was cast in 1097 during the Northern Sung dynasty in a typical Chinese style. Despite its foreign origin, the bell has been designated a national treasure. Before departing from Jeondeung-sa, examine the unique ornamentation of human images engraved on the eaves of Daeungjeon Hall. This particular style was popular during the mid-Joseon dynasty and is rarely seen anymore.

Dangun's Altar

About 2km (1¼ miles) southwest of Jeondeung-sa lies the small town of Sangbangni and the site of **Dangun's Altar** on nearby **Manisan**. It is an arduous climb of almost 500 meters (1,650ft) up to the summit, where one can get a sweeping view of Gang-hwa-do and touch the spot where an important Korean legend was born. Some archeologists claim Dangun's altar is no more than 400 years old, which would make it considerably younger than Dangun who, according to popular myths, descended to earth from heaven in 2333 BC.

The iron bell at Jeondeung-sa dates from the 11th century.

LEFT: the wall and an outbuilding at Jeondeung-sa.
BELOW: the Tripitaka Koreana of Jeondeung-sa temple are wooden blocks carved with Buddhist scriptures. They feature in ceremonies during Buddhist festivals – carrying them on the head represents an act of piety.

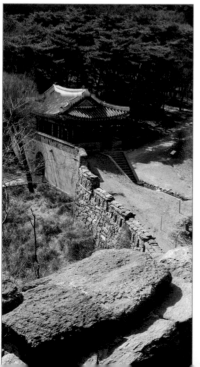

Nougat vendor on Ganghwa.

BELOW: DMZ watchtower.
RIGHT: a South Korean soldier.

Seongmo-do Island

One last significant full-day excursion is a trip to the "Eyebrow Rock" Buddha at **Bomun-sa** ㉑ on the neighboring island of **Seongmo-do**. This pilgrimage starts with a bus ride to **Uipo**, a fishing village on the West Coast. Foreigners may be asked to show their passports before taking the 10-minute ferry ride to the westward island. The bus ride from the landing on the opposite side to Bomun-sa takes approximately 45 minutes on a bumpy dirt road, but the island destination provides a serene contrast with its endless carpet of rice paddies, punctuated by many pointed church steeples.

Bomun-sa is a neatly restored 1,400-year-old temple, behind which, carved into the mountain, is a stone chamber with 22 small stone Buddhas enshrined in individual wall niches behind an altar. The Buddha statues are said to have been caught by a fisherman who dreamed he was instructed by a monk to enshrine them here. Steps lead further above this stone chamber through junipers; at the end of a steep, heart-thumping hike is the massive concave **Ma-ae Seok-buljwasang** ("Eyebrow Rock" Buddha), sculpted into the granite mountainside. He blissfully overlooks the rice fields, the pale blue Yellow Sea, the setting sun, and strangely shaped islands that dissolve into the horizon.

PANMUNJEOM AND THE DEMILITARIZED ZONE

One of the most unusual, and fascinating, experiences in South Korea involves a short journey from Seoul to the heavily fortified border with North Korea. The two countries remain technically at war, even if economic prosperity and the apparent tranquility of life in the South make the idea of hostilities breaking out inconceivable for most visitors. Yet relations have grown frosty again, with warlike proclamations from Pyongyang following the sinking of the South Korean naval vessel in 2010.

To acquaint overly optimistic tourists with this potentially volatile situation, the Korean Government and United Nations representatives have sanctioned one of the world's most unusual tourist outings. This unique visitor attrac-

tion is a day trip to **Panmunjeom** ㉒, the site of a small farming village which was obliterated during the Korean War. Panmunjeom (accessible only through an organized tour) is the historic site on Korea's 38th parallel where US and South Korean representatives of a special United Nations Military Armistice Commission have been holding periodic talks with North Korean and Chinese negotiators. Their goal: to mutually supervise a cease-fire truce that was signed here on July 27, 1953. That truce agreement formally divided Korea into North and South political sectors and put an uneasy – and still unofficial – end to the bloody Korean War.

Geographically, Panmunjeom sits in a wide valley just northwest of the broad Imjin River and about 56km (35 miles) northwest of Seoul. Cartographically, and therefore politically, it also straddles the stretch of land near the western end of Korea's Demilitarized Zone (DMZ), a demarcation line about 4km (2½ miles) wide which winds its way for 250km (150 miles) across the waist of the Korean peninsula. This truce camp is the point of official contact between North Korea and the free world. It is also a heavily mined, barricaded, and patrolled "no-man's land" only for well-armed soldiers, a few hundred farmers, and, ironically, several formerly endangered species of birds (such as the spectacular Manchurian crane). These species have flourished within the confines of the DMZ since it was declared off-limits to most of humanity in 1953.

DMZ tours

Getting to the Demilitarized Zone from Seoul is extremely easy. The tours are well advertised and run several times a day, six days a week. The most popular excursions are sponsored by the USO (tel: 795-3028/3063), but are often filled a week or two in advance. Private tour companies in Seoul offer tours with English-speaking guides and only require 24-hour advance booking, but they vary quite widely

in what they cover; make sure that the tour you book goes all the way to Panmunjeom. Many tours do not include a visit to the Third Tunnel of Aggression, which is well worth the extra time and money. *For more details of tours, see Travel Tips page 303.*

Highway to history

Your Panmunjeom-bound tour bus travels due north of Seoul on national **Highway 1** and follows wartime history through plains and valleys. Not so long ago, these peaceful surroundings were the heavily bunkered scenes of massive military advances and retreats during the Korean War and even during a Mongol invasion a few centuries ago. This area is reassuringly green and lush during the summer months, but when the winter chill sets in its beauty turns bleak and brittle. Suddenly you realize that the bleak new chain of mountains looming up ahead is North Korean territory.

"Freedom Village"

Past the checkpoints and into the DMZ is an enormous South Korean flag. This

Traveling north from Seoul there are still military checkpoints on the roads in places. In the past these could be used to look for deserters and possible infiltrators from the North. Nowadays, however, except in times of tension, these should not cause foreigners a problem.

BELOW: peering into North Korea, marked by a giant flag, from Panmunjeom.

South Korean guard in the conference room, Joint Security Area, Panmunjeom.

marks the village of **Daeseong-dong** (which means "Attaining Success Town"), a community of ex-refugees allowed to resettle in their native habitat. Called "**Freedom Village**" by the US military, Daeseongdong is about a mile from Panmunjeom. Villagers – and soldiers – have to endure propaganda blasted over from the North Korean side by loudspeakers, but for their pains they enjoy certain benefits; among them exemption from military service and taxation. In fact the residents here are extremely wealthy in comparison with other South Korean farmers. Otherwise, life generally goes on here in much the same way as it does in other parts of South Korea.

In the distance, across the dividing line in the North Korean half of the demilitarized no-man's-land, is situated another village. It boasts much bigger houses than Daeseongdong and a much bigger flag (so large, in fact, that it flops listlessly against its giant flagpole in anything less than a Force Eight gale).

The village is said to be the biggest in the world, but no-one actually appears to live there. Curiously, even the windows on the sides of the buildings appear to be nothing more than black paint. American soldiers are in the habit of calling the North Korean village "**Propaganda Village.**" However, it goes under the official name of **Gwijeongdong**.

View from the top

Once you reach the exact Panmunjeom talks site, you will be escorted around a heavily guarded sector formally known as the Joint Security Area. In the Conference Room your American military guide will explain another propaganda "war," concerning the question of who had the bigger flag.

This "battle" ended in a truce when the flags of the two sides were too large to bring into the meeting room. There is a genuine sense of absurdity about this on all sides, exacerbated by the imposed gravity of the situation. Sit back and imagine what Monty Python's Flying Circus might have to say if a skit were done here.

다리

From atop ornate Freedom House, you will have a good view of the whole village, and from **Checkpoint No 3** you have a panoramic view into North Korea itself, where you can check out billboards of propaganda and listen to loudspeakers blaring out the usual raucous banalities.

Another observation point is the **Odusan Unification Observatory** ㉓ (daily 9am–6pm, Mar and Oct–Nov 9am–5.30pm, Dec–Feb until 5pm; charge), a half-hour south of Panmunjeom at the confluence of the Han and Imjin River. There's not a lot to see from here, but it is popular with South Koreans since this is as close as they can get to the Demilitarized Zone and North Korea without joining the army.

Going underground

If things aren't bizarre enough in the DMZ, the majority of tours will also take you to the **Third Tunnel of Aggression** ㉔ situated between Panmunjeom and the Odusan Unification Observatory (guided tours only). This is a fascinating sight, so make sure you join a tour that includes it. One

of several tunnels the North Koreans dug under the Demilitarized Zone in order to sneak troops into the south, it extends almost 2km (1½ miles) into the south and is said to be capable of funneling vehicles and troops to the tune of 30,000 an hour.

Since the discovery of this and other tunnels in the 1980s, there are round-the-clock tunnel detection teams to make sure the North doesn't do any more digging underneath the DMZ.

North of the border

About 150,000 tourists make the DMZ tour from the southern side of the border every year. Since 1987, Western tourists have been able to make the Panmunjeom trip from the northern side. From Seoul this would involve flying to the northern capital, Pyongyang, via Beijing, and then a morning's drive or a longer, six-hour train journey to Gaeseong, a city near Panmunjeom. In order to avoid unpleasant confrontations, the North and South schedule their tour groups at different times. Recent tensions have resulted in some tours being cancelled. ❏

North Korean leader Kim Jong-il (the "Great General") succeeded his father Kim il-Sung as unchallenged leader of the country in 1994, at the helm of a Communist dictatorship commanding total obedience from the 23 million long-suffering people of this impoverished nation. For more information on tours to the North, see page 303.

BELOW: cycling past a propaganda poster in Pyongyang, North Korea's capital.

The North–South Divide

After a softening of positions on both sides of the Korean border, tensions have increased markedly in recent years

While it has been more than 50 years since the end of the Korean War, the hostilities are still, officially, ongoing because the two nations signed an armistice rather than a peace treaty back in 1953. The regime in Pyongyang has proved a belligerent adversary ever since, and as a result unification – still a dream for many – remains as unlikely now as it has ever been, and the DMZ is the most heavily fortified border in the world.

One of the main tactics employed by Pyongyang has been the attempted destabilization of the South. There have been efforts to encourage dissident groups, while in the 1960s, a special forces unit was dispatched in an unsuccessful attempt to assassinate the South Korean president. In the 1980s, agents first set off an explosive that killed 22 South Korean diplomats and journalists on a state visit to Burma. Then they blew up a Korean Airlines passenger jet. In the late 1990s, small North Korean submarines were routinely spotted off South Korean beaches. Then there are the infiltration tunnels dug under the DMZ, the kidnapping of Japanese to help train North Korean agents, the continued threat of nuclear weapon production and test firing missiles over the Japanese mainland. More recently, when Lee Myung-bak's hardline stance brought the detente years to a shuddering halt, Pyongyang has reacted by further aggressive acts, including the sinking of a South Korean naval ship with the loss of 46 lives (the North claims innocence, although this seems highly unlikely).

Until the late 1990s, the strategy of the South and its primary ally, the United States, was to isolate the North economically and politically – and this was successful. But the South can't take all the credit. Quirky North Korean leaders had their own policy of isolation, and their disastrous *juche* (self-reliance) economic policies have helped to drive the country to the edge of bankruptcy, making the country an oddity if not a pariah within the global community.

Since the late 1990s, however, there have been times when reconciliation seems possible, with a softening of positions on both sides of the border. Closer ties between the two nations seemed to be a very real possibility. The South came up with a "Sunshine Policy" that replaced confrontation with dialog, and instead of putting up roadblocks to the North's contacts with other countries, they encouraged them. Consequently, the North established diplomatic relations with several European and Asian countries. The long- awaited meeting of the South and North Korean presidents took place in Pyongyang in 2000. The US entered into the new spirit by agreeing to end their economic embargo, and up until a few years ago, there was some limited tourism development in the Geumgang Mountains, revered as the most beautiful place in the entire peninsula.

ABOVE: Vitit Muntarbhor, UN human rights monitor in North Korea from 2004–2010. **LEFT:** North Koreans mark the birthday of their leader. **RIGHT:** the extraordinary Mass Games, political rallies that take place in Pyongyang each year.

This thawing of tension was in part due to the effort of South Korean businessman Chung Juyung (elderly founder of the mammoth Hyundai *jaebeol*) who made some of the earliest, and most surprising, breakthroughs. Concerned that he might die before again seeing the North, Chung arranged to have 500 cows delivered to the village where he grew up. As South Koreans watched on television, Chung led a caravan of new trucks (included in the deal) packed with cows through the DMZ and on to his old village.

Visiting the North

Anyone whose visa allows them a visit to the DMZ from the Pyongyang side will see soldiers decked out in baggy, Soviet-style uniforms stand with blank faces along a roadway lined with chain-link and razor-wire-topped fencing. The soldiers and "environmental guides" along the mountain trails are there to ensure tourists follow strictly enforced rules: no spitting, no urinating, no littering, no photography (except in designated areas), no smoking, always refer to Kim Jong-il as "Great General," and definitely no political discussions or negative remarks about North Korea.

With all the rules, the fencing off of North Korean villages, and extensive propaganda elaborately carved in the canyon walls, the tour is a curiosity. As the buses pass villages, visitors will see farmers plowing with oxen and working the fields with hand tools (there are few tractors).

On the positive side, the homes and villages do look comfortable (even if there's no electricity), and the villagers look healthy and occasionally smile and wave as a bus passes. But it is sobering to think that these villages, due to their exposure to South Koreans, are probably the best in North Korea. And it's pretty obvious that the North is a desperately poor country, light years behind the South in economic development. Any reconciliation is going to require South Koreans to dig deep into their pocketbooks, and a generous supply of patience on both sides of the DMZ.

However, ambitious plans for tourism have been suspended due to the aggressive actions by the North: First a tourist was shot while apparently walking on a beach, and then American journalists Laura Ling and Euna Lee were detained and imprisoned for eight months, released only when Bill Clinton made a personal visit to Pyongyang. The sinking of a South Korean navy vessel in 2010 has seemingly sent relations back to 1980s levels of hostility. It's unclear what ambitions the North Koreans have, but peace and reunification seem as far away as ever.

For details on obtaining visas and visiting North Korea, as well as tours to Panmunjeom on the South side of the DMZ, see page 303. ❑

GANGWON PROVINCE

If you enjoy mixing sightseeing with skiing, hiking, or climbing, then visit Gangwon Province, where you'll find some of the peninsula's most impressive mountain scenery, and a rich cultural past

When a Korean is fraught with wanderlust or feels like hiking into the beauty that has inspired classical paintings, the thing to do is to head northeast to South Korea's finest collection of rivers, lakes, and mountains to the land "Where Men and Mountains Meet."

This is the great northeast province of Gangwon, where in one day a happy wanderer can bask on a lake or seaside beach, then hike through wispy mountain mists to a 15th-century Buddhist shrine scooped out of a granite cliff.

For centuries Korea has been referred to as "*samcheolli geumsugangsan*," or the land of "3,000 *li* of rivers and mountains embroidered on silk." (A *li* is about 0.4km/¼ mile.) In Gangwon, for miles in either direction from the North Han River to the Demilitarized Zone (DMZ) and the East Sea, this adage rings true. Here you will find a superb scenic tapestry delicately shaded with silken green rice terraces, swaths of amber grain, and pointilist vegetable patches winding hither and thither along cold blue rivers and craggy mountain passes.

You can begin your tour of the East Coast at several points on the East Sea (Sea of Japan), but probably the most central place to use as a pivot point for travel is **Gangneung** (*see page 171*), the major city in east Gangwon Province. This city of more than 230,000 people

is easily reached by train or bus, but the most interesting way to make the 228km (142-mile) journey from Seoul is by private car. With your own set of wheels you'll be able to not only stop and smell the flowers, but visit a number of places you wouldn't be able to reach otherwise.

THE ROAD FROM SEOUL

Route 50 (the Yeongdong Expressway) is a freeway that connects the Seoul area with Gangwon Province, the area to the northeast which, bordering

Main attractions
CHIAKSAN NATIONAL PARK
ODAESAN NATIONAL PARK
YONGPYEONG SKI RESORT
GANGNEUNG
GYEONGPODAE
SEONGYOJANG
OJUKHEON
NAKSAN TEMPLE
SEORAKSAN NATIONAL PARK
GYEJOAM HERMITAGE
JEONGDONGJIN
HWANSEONGUL CAVE
HAESINDANG

LEFT: the summit of Seoraksan. **RIGHT:** hiking is enjoyed by Koreans of all ages.

Don't feed the squirrels.

the ocean and North Korea, holds a wealth of natural gems. Route 50 is a more direct route, but there are smaller roads you can take that wind through dappled valleys, past meandering rivers and verdant green mountains rearing out of the mist.

Chiaksan National Park

Located near the city of **Wonju** (the province's largest city), **Chiaksan National Park ❶** (sunrise–sunset, hiking entry stops at 2pm; charge) is a gem that's well worth the detour. Most of the temples that once dotted the hills have gone, but the trails wind through verdant forests of pine and Korean

maple, and when the mist hangs low even the most agnostic hiker will feel that there's something genuinely spiritual about this pilgrimage.

Due to numerous accidents suffered by hikers who are unprepared for the conditions these peaks provide, access is strictly limited and the cutoff for trail entry is at 2pm. Seryeom Waterfall is a must-see, best viewed from Birobong Peak.

Though destroyed by fire and thus not original, the restored **Guryeong-sa** (Nine Dragon Temple) is a prime hiking destination. The other famed temple in Chiaksan gave this region its name. According to legend inscribed

on the bell at Sangwonsa, a man came across a pheasant (Chi, in Korean) about to be eaten by a snake. Acting swiftly, the man dispatched the snake and saved the pheasant's life, only to arrive at Sangwonsa and fall under the charms of a beautiful woman. During the night the woman revealed that she was in fact a snake and wanted to avenge the death of her husband. If the bell at Sangwonsa did not ring before sunrise, the man would die. But during the night, the bell did ring three times, and the snake woman was forced to give the man his life.

Trying to understand the miracle that had saved him, the man discovered the dead body of the pheasant next to the bell. It had rung the bell for him by using its own head, breaking its neck after the third ring. In honor of this noble bird's sacrifice the park was changed from Jeogaksan to Chiaksan, and the pheasant is, no surprise, the park's signature bird.

Pheasants are not the only wildlife here: hundreds of species can be seen, including rare plants, flowers, and birds that are difficult to see elsewhere in South Korea. Hikers will come across numerous small waterfalls, emerald pools, and moss-covered rocks that are as rewarding along the way as the view is from the peaks.

Odaesan National Park

One detour well worth making on the way to Gangneung is just beyond little Jinbu village (about 40km/25 miles west of Gangneung). This side trip carries you along paved and dirt roads to **Odaesan National Park** ❷, a charming mountain area and the location of two of South Korea's best-known temple complexes, Woljeong-sa and Sangwon-sa. The road leading to Odaesan (1,563 meters/5,128ft) is dotted with tiny secluded hermitages, Zen meditation niches and other impressive remnants of Buddhism which date from the 7th century and the Silla dynasty.

As cool, dry winds from the Mongolian steppes meet warm, moist air currents off the East Sea in this mountain region, the lush, pine-covered peaks of Odaesan are often wreathed in cool, shifting mists, giving the area a surreal, other-worldly aura. It is no wonder that

According to legend, the Buddha appears at Odaesan in the form of a small boy. When King Sejo (reigned 1455–68) came to bathe his diseased body in the mountain's healing waters, a boy came to scrub the king's back. The disease, like the boy, then mysteriously disappeared.

BELOW: low-tech footbridge in Odaesan National Park.

The Buddhist swastika symbol, as here on a temple at Woljeong-sa, represents good fortune and well-being.

BELOW: seaside village to the south of Gangneung.

early Buddhist masters chose this place as a prime meditation spot.

Woljeong-sa (daily 5am–9pm; charge), which is situated on the southern fringe of Odaesan about 8km (5 miles) off the expressway, is a sprawling temple complex distinguished by a superb nine-story octagonal pagoda and an unusual kneeling Buddha sculpture. The tiered pagoda, which rises to 15 meters (50ft), is capped with a sculpted lotus blossom and a bronze finial of intricate design; the kneeling Buddha, meanwhile, has well-weathered features and (because of an unusual cap that he's wearing) looks much like a European tin soldier. Both of these national treasures are located in front of Woljeong-sa's main hall, surrounded by a grass plot and a swastika-motif'd iron fence.

Along a riverbed road which snakes on up to the higher reaches of Odaesan, you will see occasional shrines and memorials to monks who have lived and died in this region over the centuries. One forest clearing contains tall stone stupas, most of them notably phallic in design, which are said to

contain the cremated remains *(sarira)* of famous Buddhist masters.

Even higher up, just east of Odaesan's main peak, and about 200 meters (650ft) off the road at the end of a pine-bordered pass, is **Sangwon-sa** (daily sunrise–sunset; charge), another temple established by Jajang. According to an information board there, Jajang built this temple in AD 646 during the reign of the Silla Queen Seondeok. Zodiacal images adorn its walls, and in a wooden pavilion on the grounds is a large bronze bell said to be the second largest in Korea at 1.7 meters (5½ft) – the largest is the Emille Bell at the Gyeongju National Museum *(see page 226)*. This particular Silla bell is also the oldest known example in South Korea. It was reportedly cast in AD 725 during the reign of Silla King Seondeok.

Ski Korea!

Another 12km (7 miles) south and east of the Yeongdong Expressway is a highland area with a decidedly different aura. This is the Daegwallyeong mountain region where South Korea's most modern and best-equipped ski

resort is located. In the area are several small resorts centered around a town called Hoenggye, which has produced the best skiiers in South Korea. However, insatiable skiers favor the slopes that have been developed in a place called Yongpyeong, or Dragon Valley.

The **Yongpyeong Dragon Valley Ski Resort** ❸ sprawls over 210,000 sq. meters (52 acres) and is equipped with 15 ski lifts covering 31 ski slopes. The resort also has snow-making machines, a ski school, ski rental facilities, and even lighting facilities for night-time skiing. There are long runs down the sides of the area's Gold and Silver slopes on the Barwang mountains. The longest run is down Daegwallyeong's 957-meter (3,140ft) Mt Twin Dragon, which offers advanced skiers a major headwall drop of about 50 meters (164ft) that quickly tapers off into a series of gentler slopes.

Looming over this snow complex are ski lodges, private villas, *yeogwan* inns, and a large dormitory facility in the area, which can be rented at single, double, or group rates.

A few more kilometers to the east of the turnoff to the Dragon Valley and ski country, the Yeongdong Expressway begins to narrow somewhat. Then, after negotiating the Daegwallyeong Ridge, you will begin a final, zigzagging descent to Gangneung town through the famous 99 turns of the Daegwallyeong Pass. On a clear day the view from the top of this granite cliff provides a fine first impression of Gangneung and the deep blue East Sea.

Gangneung and around

Gangneung ❹ is a sleepy, hospitable seaside town rich in traditional architecture. It has always been known as the key trading and terminal point in this part of South Korea, but has also gained local fame as the site of an annual Dano spring festival, held on the 5th day of the 5th lunar moon, usually in May. The festival takes place on the banks of a wide river that divides the town's north and south sectors. This authentic local celebration, rich

in shamanistic dancing, rituals, and general merrymaking, attracts country folk to its colorful tents, sideshows, and carnival atmosphere.

The classical Confucian academy and shrine **Hyanggyo and Daeseongjeon** (Mon–Fri 9am–5pm) is located in the northwest suburbs of the city on the grounds of the Myeongnyun middle and high schools. This hilltop structure, which was built in 1313, destroyed by fire in 1411, then rebuilt in 1413, has low, brooding rooflines and tapering colonnades typical of Goryeo-dynasty structures. Rooms on either side of this old academy's main hall are filled with boxed spirit tablets that are opened every year when Confucian *jesa* ancestral rites are performed here.

Gyeongpodae

The resort of **Gyeongpodae Beach**, just a few kilometers north of Gangneung, has long been a popular South Korean recreational spa. Offshore waters here are busy with zigzagging speedboats and sailing craft, and on shore are numerous tented seafood restaurants where you can choose

Fun and games on Gangneung beach.

BELOW: skiing on the slopes of Yongpyeong.

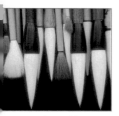

*Traditional fur
brushes used in
calligraphy.*

BELOW: a typical
east-coast fishing
village.

your lunch live from gurgling saltwater tanks. Korean tourists like to buy bundles of *miyeok* (seaweed for soup-making), dried cuttlefish, and other delicacies from vendors who ply their trade on this colorful beach.

Just inland of this beach scene, past the clutter of hotels and inns and rows of kitsch souvenir shops, is mirror-like **Gyeongpodae Lake**. This lake is dotted with islets and once had pavilions set like jewels on her shores. There, local *yangban* aristocrats met with friends to sip wine, compose poems, and watch sunsets and moonrises over the nearby Taebaek mountain range. As an old song says, from the old Gyeongpo Pavilion on the lake's northern shore "you can see the rising moon reflected in the lake, in your bowl of wine, and in your sweetheart's eyes."

If such images keep you in a romantic and classical mood, head back across the lake toward Gangneung, then detour to the northwest and cross a series of rice paddies by footpath until you reach **Seongyojang** (daily 9am–6pm, Nov–Feb until 5pm; charge). Seonggyojang has an impres-sive living compound, Confucian academy, lotus pond, and pavilion built during the 18th and 19th centuries by members of the prominent Yi Hu family clan. This complex is a perfect example of a *yangban* Joseon-dynasty living compound in South Korea. What makes it even more interesting is the fact that the Yi family still lives in the main house, just as their ancestors have for the past two centuries. Yi relatives, if you're lucky enough to talk with one, will share stories of slumber-parties in the tea pavilion and (before the parking lot and access road) having to slog through muddy rice fields to greet grandmother, reminders that this stately complex was – and still is – a family home.

This compound is picturesque in the wintertime when snow laces its curved roofs, mud and tile walls, and cozy thatched servants' quarters; and in the summertime when giant pink Indonesian lotus blossoms rise out of their shallow pond like sleepy dragons. In the fall, squirrels dance through the persimmon trees, searching for fruit to store for the winter.

Ojukheon, Black Bamboo Shrine

Another important Confucian site, just a little way north of Gangneung, is **Ojukheon** ❺ (Black Bamboo Shrine; daily 9am–6pm, Nov–Feb until 5pm; charge), birthplace of the prominent Confucian scholar-statesman-poet Yi I (1536–84). Yi I, more popularly known by his pen name Yulgok (Valley of Chestnuts), was one of a select group of neo-Confucianists who became quite powerful during the 16th century. Among positions he held were royal appointments as Korea's Minister of Personnel and War, and Rector of the National Academy.

One biographical sketch notes that Yulgok was an infant prodigy who knew Chinese script at the age of three, "and when he was seven he already composed poems in Chinese. At the age of 19, he entered the Geumgangsan Mountains and was initiated in Buddhism, but soon abandoned it for the study of the philosophy of Chu Hsi."

To honor Yulgok's example and memory, the South Korean government has in recent years revamped his birthplace site. The memorial, on the west side of the road to Yangyang and Sokcho, is a prim compound in the cheerful yellow favored by the ministry in charge of national parks and memorials. Ojukheon, which has the aura of a shrine (visitors should be properly dressed, and smoking, gum-chewing, and photography are not allowed in the vicinity of Yulgok's memorial tablet house), is a memorial not just to Yulgok but also to his mother, Sin Saimdang, who was revered during her lifetime as a fine calligrapher and artist of talent.

A collection of calligraphic scrolls by Yulgok, his mother, and other members of the Yi family are on display in a small museum at the rear of the Ojukheon compound. Also on display are several original paintings by the talented Sin Saimdang. Her precise and flowing studies of flora and fauna are superbly, artistically executed.

Before continuing northward from this site, marvel for a moment at the fine stand of black bamboo that grows luxuriantly in a garden between the museum and Yulgok's house. Then

EAT

Among the many local specialties of Gangwon is a kind of *sundae*, or sausage. Most *sundae* in Korea is made with a pork casing and often rice, noodles, and… blood. This area's version should appeal to seafood lovers: the casing is made of squid, and the filling has a variety of vegetables, rice, and seafood.

BELOW: roof detail, Gyeongpo Pavilion, on the northern shore of Gyeongpodae Lake.

Buddhist monk at Naksan-sa.

look west toward the nearby pine forests and consider these reflective lines from Yulgok's famous poem *Gosangugokga* (The Nine Songs of Mount Ko, translated by Peter H Lee):

Where shall we find the first song?
The sun lances the crown rock, and

Mist clears above the tall grass.
Lo the magic views far and near

Calling my friends I would wait
With a green goblet in the pine grove.

THE NORTHERN COAST

Proceeding north on Highway 7, the coastal road, you pass sun-lanced rocks and pine groves against the backdrop of the blue East Sea. Just above **Yangyang**, on the southern outskirts of Sokcho, you will find what was the most appealing, and impressive, religious site in this part of South Korea. This is **Naksan-sa ❻**, a Buddhist temple complex originally established by the Silla high priest Uisang in 671 during the 11th year of King Munmu's

reign. Unfortunately, in 2005 a forest fire destroyed invaluable treasures stored at the temple and large areas of the surrounding forest and buildings. Also lost was a splendid stone gate, Hongyemun, built during the time of King Sejo (reigned 1455–68), who once prayed here. Another impressive structure was a seven-story Goryeo pagoda that stood 6.2 meters (20ft) high in front of the main hall. The large bronze bell, called Beomjong, with four raised bodhisattva images, was also destroyed by the fire. The bell, 1.6 meters (5ft) tall by 1 meter (3ft) in diameter, was inscribed with poetry and calligraphy by the famous poet Kim Suon and the calligrapher Jeong Nanjong.

However, this expansive temple has now been restored to much of its previous splendor, complete with replicas of the ancient treasures including the Beomjong bell. As with many Korean temples, meals are served for monks and travelers. Hearty noodles in warm broth, *gimchi*, and rice are the likely fare. The temple is situated next to a magnificent – and very long – beach.

Dominating the area is a 15-meter

(49ft) white granite statue of Buddhism's Bodhisattva of Mercy, known in Korea as the goddess Gwanseumbosal, in China as Kwan Yin, and in India as Avalokitesvara (though Avalokitesvara is an earlier male counterpart). This particular Goddess of Mercy faces the southeast atop a 2-meter (6ft) granite pedestal and open lotus blossom.

The massive statue, the work of Busan sculptor Gwon Jonghwan, was dedicated in 1977. According to Choe Wonchol, then chief priest at Naksan-sa, an old priest appeared to him in a dream in 1972 and told him where and how to place this statue. Some six months of hard labor and 700 tonnes of granite stone were required to complete the sculpture. "From the day when the standing granite bodhisattva was solemnly dedicated, Naksan Temple went into a thousand-day prayer for national peace and security," so reads a Dedication Day story printed in *The Korea Times*.

Sokcho

From this statue, standing like an ancient beacon on this quiet and rugged coastline, continue north past Uisangdae and its tiny pink lighthouse to **Sokcho town ❼**. Sokcho is an important coastal fishing port that has long been a stop-off for travelers to seaside resorts to the north. For a time before the 2010 freeze in North–South relations, boat trips to the North were operating from here.

Two kilometers (1 mile) to the south of Sokcho and an easy taxi ride is **Daepohang**, which is worth a visit to give you a flavor of a typical Korean fishing port. On one side of a narrow lane are moored fishing boats, alongside stalls with tanks of live fish, while immediately opposite are restaurants and shops selling dried fish.

Beyond Sokcho are several quaint fishing villages, exotic inland lagoons brimming with fish and waterfowl, and broad, dune-fringed beaches. Private and government enterprise have developed several sandy areas north of Sokcho, but the all-time favorite spot for those seeking both comfort and beauty is Hwajinpo Beach, about halfway between Sokcho and the DMZ. South Korea's presidents have tradi-

Detail on the replica Beomjong bell at Naksan-sa; the original was destroyed in a fire in 2005.

BELOW: a sparse assortment of North Korean goods are usually on sale at Camp Boniface, visited at the end of the Panmunjeom DMZ tour.

North Korea: To Go or Not To Go

That is the question: While the DMZ tour is almost a must-see, the opportunity to visit the gorgeous Geumgang mountains is a powerful reason to go northwards, but also a risky one. Tensions and nuclear fears have ratcheted the rhetoric up on both sides, and, currently, visitors are not allowed across the border. Occasional boat trips from Sokcho may also be suspended. If relations improve, trips could start again. If so, they will still require significant advance planning, and items like cameras, video equipment, and even laptop computers may undergo rigid scrutiny. Make duplicates of passport info and be sure your embassy knows your plans. While in North Korea, be respectful of the rules and at no point try to confront policemen or locals on your own.

EAT

When traveling in the northeast, try some potato pancakes (gamjabuchim) with some herb tea (seorak yaksucha). For a more exotic snack, order some sliced raw squid (ojingeo hoe), often served so fresh it clings to your mouth as you eat it.

tionally maintained summer villas here.

The end of the line and as far north as you can go in southern Korea is **Daejin**, a friendly town of tiny streets with local people who might still be pleasantly surprised to see a foreigner this far off the beaten path; the town features one of the most colorful fish-markets in Korea.

THE NORTHERN ROUTE FROM SEOUL TO SEORAK-SANG

Though Route 50 (see page 167) now offers a more direct path, one of the most picturesque routes in South Korea is the road from Seoul to Seorak-san and the northeast coast. It takes you north of Seoul on a zigzag course of modern highways, inland waterways, and dusty but spectacular mountain roads. This adventure by car or by bus (from Seoul's Cheongnyangni station) heads northeast on Highway 46 through wooded mountains and along and across the snake-like North Han River and its valleys.

Several river and lakeside resorts have sprung up along the highway between

BELOW:
rose cabbage, Chuncheon.

Seoul and Chuncheon. Stop and linger a day or two according to whim, but if you would like a suggestion of where to stay, consider **Namiseom** ❽, an island in the middle of the Han River near a quaint highland town called Gapyeong. This is about an hour's drive north of Seoul, followed by a 10-minute ferry ride to Namiseom. There you can rent a small house or cabin and revert to nature, becoming one with the cooing cuckoos, falling chestnuts, and pungent pines. Wake up early to see the rising sun burn morning mists out of the little valleys which surround Gapyeong.

About 20km (12 miles) further north (a journey you can make by leisurely ferry from Namiseom if you have the time), you'll round a hill and descend into **Chuncheon** ❾ (pop. 250,000). This is Gangwon's largest city and a convenient resort for Seoulites who like to get away from it all for a day or week, to enjoy some of the country's finest lake country. Freshwater fishing, swimming, sailing, and water-skiing are readily available at several colorful resort piers which encircle **Chuncheon Lake** and other sky-blue waterways in the surrounding area. It was made famous by the Korean drama "Winter Sonata," and you'll see placards and posters pasted everywhere.

In Chuncheon, where violet, yellow, and green ornamental cabbages adorn a series of quaint mini-parks, you can follow your nose in a number of watery and earthy directions. Some people choose to ferry-hop around Chuncheon through picturesque river gorges to riverside villages, sandy beaches, waterfalls (the Gugok Falls near Namiseom are a favorite), and jade-green pools that have never been reached by car or train. Others continue north to Hwacheon and the peacefully remote **Paroho Lake** north of the Samyeong Mountains.

Probably the most popular local tour is a visit to the nearby Soyang Dam and its attendant **Lake Soyang**. On the north side of this concrete

monument of engineering and hydro-electricity, you will find a colorful boat docking area, the **Soyang Pavilion**. Here, a road-weary traveler can leave land and embark on a tour of South Korea's most splendid inland waterway. Lake Soyang is hyperbolically, but understandably, called by some Korean travel writers "the largest lake in the Orient made by man." From this pavilion you can proceed for many cool kilometers on a gliding cruise toward the Seorak Mountains and the north-eastern coast.

Cheongpyeong-sa

A popular side trip on Lake Soyang involves a brief (15-minute) cruise by open-air launch to **Cheongpyeong-sa** ❿ (daily 9am–sunset; charge). There, an ancient Buddhist temple sits about a 20-minute hike and 2.5km (1½ miles) above a sleepy floating dock and restaurant just north of Soyang Pavilion. This lofty Buddhist retreat provides a simple escape from the asphalt and beeping, fume-spewing buses below. Paths lead from the temple up to the peak of Mt Obongsan.

A well-kept trail to Cheongpyeong-sa rises steeply and steadily along a tinkling, rocky stream to a lovely waterfall and piney crags. All this comes alive at dawn and at sunset with the amazing harmony of sutras being chanted by resident devotees of the Lord Buddha. There is a small fee to enter this Buddhist center of desirelessness and non-attachment, and on the back of the entrance ticket you'll find this short story, in Hangeul: "This temple originated 1,600 years ago. A Chinese princess of the Tang period visited here to rid herself of a snake. She brought three bars of gold for the expense of rebuilding this temple, in the hope of losing the snake. At this time the gate of the temple was struck by lightning in the midst of a severe storm. The snake vanished, so the gate was renamed 'Transforming Gate' from this incident."

This deliberately perplexing tale only adds to Cheongpyeong-sa's mys-

tique. Art historian Jon Covell theorizes that this story about the princess and a snake indicates shamanist influences creeping into Buddhism. Another theory asserts that the temple was the refuge-headquarters of a tantric, or erotic, Buddhist cult. Whatever its origins, you will find your visit to Cheongpyeong-sa deeply rewarding, if only to see its fine outer wall murals which include, among other themes, an unusual Gwanseum holding a willow branch, a finely executed Oxherding Series and a well-focused tiger panel.

End of the line

Meanwhile, back on Lake Soyang, you can travel back to Soyang Pavilion near the massive dam, then catch one of many regular commuter specials (these are covered boats with a breezy after-deck) for the hour and 20 minutes, glide to a rural docking point just south of isolated **Yanggu** ⓫ town. The surrounding mountains, which are ablaze with amber and roseate trees in the crisp fall months, are reflected in the calm waters of the lake, and are reminiscent of parts of New Zealand

The clear waters of Chuncheon Lake attract bathers, sailors, water-skiers, and fishermen.

BELOW: paper lanterns mark the Buddha's birthday at Cheongpyeong-sa.

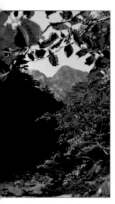

Seoraksan is famous for its fiery fall colors.

or the American Northwest. At the Yanggu dock you can transfer to a bus or taxi and proceed through the hills to reach the sleepy town itself.

Yanggu, which lies in a pleasant valley a few kilometers south of the DMZ, has several *yeogwan*, restaurants, and all the other amenities normally available in small-town South Korea. From this point, regular buses go the short distance to Inje, which is the gateway town to the spectacular mountains of Seoraksan National Park *(see below)*.

SEORAKSAN NATIONAL PARK

Seoraksan, the "Snow Peak Mountain," is now more formally known as **Seoraksan National Park ⑫** (daily; charge). In fact, it is not a lone mountaintop, but rather a series of peaks in the mid-section of the spectacular Baekdudaegan or "Great White Range," South Korea's most prominent geographical region. This panoramic backbone of South Korea's northeast province of **Gangwon** is a tourist destination which lives up to its public relations hype. The Seoraksan area is a true mountain wonderland, and

after a visit you'll understand why early Zen (or Seon) Buddhist monks chose this region to sit and strive to become one with the universe. Despite the crowds this park attracts, it is possible to enjoy some solitude within this jewel in the crown of South Korea's extensive National Park system – just avoid visiting at weekends and during school holidays.

The most popular section of the park is **Outer Seorak** (Oeseorak). This region is east of the mountain divide, closest to the East Sea and furthest from the interior of the peninsula (hence "Outer Seorak"). Visitors to the park usually end up staying in the heart of Outer Seorak, at the resort village of Seorakdong. According to park literature, up to 26,000 people can be housed within the park (it seems like more on holidays), and 90 percent are in Seorakdong. **Inner Seorak** (Naeseorak), the western section of the park, has the advantage of fewer visitors, and the disadvantage of having fewer attractions.

There are several ways to get to the area from Seoul. The quickest is on a domestic flight to **Sokcho** (40 min-

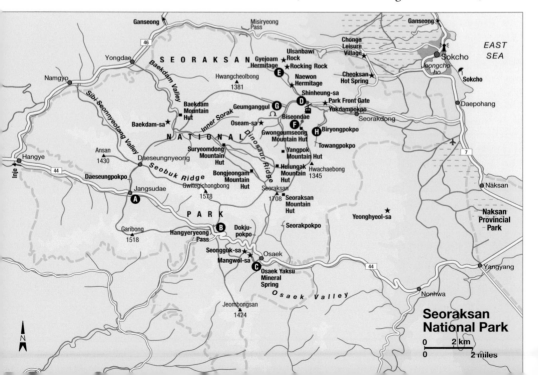

Seoraksan National Park

0   2 km

0   2 miles

utes), then by bus or taxi to **Seorakdong** (another 20 minutes). You can also take a train or bus to the terminal fishing town of Sokcho.

Korean old-timers, in less of a hurry to get to this place, prefer to enter Seoraksan slowly, from the country's scenic interior (as outlined in the preceding section on the Lake Country), and drift into the area's magic on paved, winding roads that meander through the wilds of Inner Seorak.

Mountain roads

Inje, the renowned "Gateway to Inner Seorak," is a good place to begin a tour of the area. Even in Inje town you'll have to decide which of two scenic ways you want to take to the Seorak range.

The more straightforward Southern Route winds its way through Inner Seorak, before climbing the **Hangyeryeong Pass** and passing through the southern fringes of Outer Seorak to emerge at lovely **Yangyang** town by the East Sea. The route is gently meandering, enabling you to take in the gorgeous sights in comfort. The Northern Route twists through **Misiryeong**

Pass, before descending into Sokcho on the East Sea. Most people prefer the Southern Route, both for the comfort and scenery. If, on the other hand, you prefer "roughing it," head north.

En route you will encounter, at Jangsudae, numerous nature trails (abloom in the spring and ablaze in the fall), veil-like waterfalls, red-bellied frogs, quiet creeks, and, at Osaek Yaksu, mineral springs famed for their therapeutic properties *(see p.180)*. Some travelers like to pause at **Jangsudae** Ⓐ and hike up to the **Daeseung** waterfalls (it takes just over an hour), then upward to **Baekdam-sa** (plan on taking the better part of the day for this excursion), a charming Buddhist temple smack in the interior of Inner Seorak. Ex-President Chun and his wife spent a year here over 1989–90 "repenting" for the sins of his 1980–87 dictatorship. Both hikes are spiritually healing after bustling Seoul, but be prepared with warm clothes, good walking gear, food, and drink, especially if camping overnight.

Further east at the top of the **Hangyeryeong Pass** Ⓑ, you can begin yet another trek: this one climbs all the way

The Seorakdong resort complex in the Seoraksan National Park is one of the finest places in South Korea for leisurely hiking and alfresco meals. Nature trails here accommodate everyone – from the languid wanderer to the rock-climbing fanatic.

BELOW: hiking is a national obsession in South Korea.

to the top of Mt Seorak (also known as Daecheongbong), the highest peak in the area and the third-highest mountain in South Korea at 1,708 meters (5,604ft). You can navigate onward and enter the Seorakdong resort complex by its back door. However, be warned that the steep zigzagging path can be slippery and dangerous during the winter months.

A recuperative soak in the **Osaek Yaksu** Ⓒ (mineral springs) at the far east end of the Hangyeryeong Pass road is well worth stopping for (there are several hot spring baths in the hotels, as well as a few public baths). If you're feeling fit, though, you may want to rush on down to sea level to a grand seafood meal at Yangyang, Naksan or Sokcho. Appetite thus satisfied, and braced by cool breezes off the East Sea, you are now ready to tackle mountainous Outer Seorak.

Sinheung-sa

A large, detailed sign on the roadside offers a few suggestions as you take an easy stroll up the main fir-lined path to **Sinheung-sa** Ⓓ (daily 24 hours;

charge). This ancient Zen (Seon) temple, originally built near its present location in AD 652, when it was called Hyangseong-sa, or the "Temple of Zen Buddhism," was destroyed by a forest fire in 707. It was rebuilt in 710, burned again in 1645, and rebuilt a third time at its present location in 1648.

"If the signboard date at Sinheung-sa is correct," writes Zen and oriental art authority Dr Jon Carter Covell, "then Sinheung-sa is the oldest Zen temple in the world. Nothing in China or in Japan is of this age, not by many centuries."

Just before you reach the actual temple compound, you'll pass (on the right side of the cobble path) a neatly kept and fenced-in cemetery full of unusual bell-shaped tombstones, erected to honor former illustrious Zen monks who spent much time meditating in this area. In the temple itself, which sits on a bluff with a superb view of the surrounding mountains, you'll pass through lattice doors carved and painted with a floral motif. You'll then come eye-to-eye with a standard Amit's Buddha flanked by Gwanseum and Daiseiji bodhisattvas. On a more

light-hearted note, you'll also be confronted by "the two crazy idiots of the 7th century," Hansan and Seupdeuk (known in China as Han Shan and Shih Te), who grace the temple's north wall. These absurd, grimacing, "crazy" fellows are often found in such spiritual surroundings, where they temper our overly serious lives by laughing at the absurdity of existence.

Sinheung-sa offers more such fantasy, drawing on combinations of shaman, Taoist, and Buddhist imagery. Consider the creatures which are half-tiger, half-leopard, and the writhing dragons, cranes, and bats all brilliantly painted on the ceiling. Or the drawing on the main hall's rear wall that shows a Zen patriarch offering his severed arm to a higher-ranking Zen master.

On the spiritual path

Next, proceed up this spiritual path to the **Gyejoam Hermitage ❺** (daily sunrise–sunset), about 3km (2 miles) up, along a singing streambed. Gyejo Hermitage, a subsidiary of the mother Sinheung Temple, is partially built into a granite cave at the base of Ulsan-bawi, a spectacular granite formation that dominates this part of the Seorak area. Some say that the rock, which the hermitage is located in, resembles a *moktak*, a hollow wood block that monks rhythmically beat while chanting. Legend says that because of this, it takes a monk only five years to complete his studies rather than the ordinary 10 years.

Like much of Seorak, and like the famous Geumgangsan Mountains across the DMZ in North Korea, Ulsan-bawi's face is rich with anthropomorphic images. Indeed, about halfway up the Gyejo Hermitage, an enterprising fellow with a high-powered telescope sells lingering peeks at one particularly erotic formation at Ulsan-bawi's mid-section.

Fronting the Gyejo Hermitage and Ulsan-bawi is another geological curiosity that has become a major attraction over the years. This is the famed **Rocking Rock**, a massive boulder that rocks back and forth in its secure place

when given a solid nudge. Being photographed in front of this tipsy ball of granite is a tourist's must. If you enjoyed your ramble to the Rocking Rock, then you're ready for a more challenging trek, this time on the southern trail, to Geumganggul (cave) above Biseondae.

Flying Fairy Peak

The hike to **Biseondae** (Flying Fairy Peak) **❻**, a vertical rock that juts heavenward at the entrance to a breathtaking gorge, is easy enough. At every turn you'll find yourself gawking at the beauty of chill pools and waterfalls. In the fall, fire-red maples and golden ginkgos are the seasonal attraction. "In Canada you'd have to do a lot of bushwhacking to see country like this," commented a visitor from Vancouver. Vendors sell cooling bowls of *makgeolli* rice wine and *meorujeup*, a beverage made from the berries of a local plant related to the grape. It is best to avoid weekends if possible when the trails become very crowded.

From this restful camp at the base of Biseondae, devoted Buddhist pilgrims head up a smaller path to **Geumgang-**

The cable car to the top of Biseondae (Flying Fairy Peak).

BELOW: on top of Biseondae.

Phallic totems at Haesindang.

BELOW: portrait of the mountain spirit and his messenger, the tiger.

gul Cave , which is located near the top of Biseondae and requires serious effort to attain. After negotiating 649 stairs to reach this charming cave-shrine, your heart will be pounding, but the extraordinary view from the top (as well as a halfway point promontory) will be your earthly reward. Inside the cave is a small Buddha surrounded by burning candles, incense and food offerings. Artifacts found in the cave indicate monks have been seeking meditative isolation in this cave for centuries.

Meanwhile, back at the Seorakdong base camp, other hikers opt to take the waterfall trail, and visit Yukdam and Biryong, and Towangseong waterfalls. **Biryong** (Flying Dragon Waterfall) ⬤ is located halfway between the two, at the top of a lovely gorge beneath the 1,345-meter (4,412ft) Hwachaebong. A suspension bridge across the narrow gorge and stream leads to the Flying Dragon. Local legend says that a troublesome dragon once lived beneath the waterfall but was sent flying to the heavens after the villagers sacrificed a maiden.

South from Gangneung

Heading south from Gangneung you'll find stunning coastline and a series of spectacular beaches. Not the least of these is lovely **Jeongdongjin**, a scalloped-out beach with soft sand. The town is tiny, and with the beach it also claims South Korea's closest-to-the-sea train station. The truly beach-motivated can literally step off the train in swimsuit and towel. Look towards the hills and you'll see a full-size cruise ship that's perched atop the mountain as if a tsunami placed it there. Part of the maritime museum, this eyesore/landmark is certainly one you will not overlook. This town does not offer much in the way of motels, so plan your visit accordingly. One could easily make this a day trip from Gangneung, or make it a stop in a journey that will continue further southward.

Samcheok ⓭, the furthest you can go in Gangwon-do without crossing into Gyeongsangbuk-do, is known for several interesting attractions. The first is its beach, a beautiful white sand spot which, like all the beaches along this part of the coastline, very popular in

Mountain Spirits

Mountain spirits are a remnant of Korea's shamanistic past, when rivers, trees, and mountains were believed to have spirits, or spirits residing in them. Since mountains are so dominant on the Korean peninsula, the Mountain Spirit became one of the most important spirits. Many older Koreans, particularly in rural areas, maintain a deep respect for, if not a deep-seated belief in, the Mountain Spirit. The Dano Festival originated in ceremonies once held in villages across Korea to pay homage to the Mountain Spirit.

Most Buddhist temples feature a small shrine to the Mountain Spirit (and Recluse) sitting behind the main temple on a little hill. Look inside and you'll see a brightly colored painting of a bearded, white-haired old man with a mountain tiger, his companion and messenger, at his side.

the summertime for swimming and sunbathing. Unlike Haeundae Beach in Busan, however, here you'll have peace and quiet if you look for it.

Also in this area is a large grotto, **Hwanseongul Cave** (daily 8am–7pm, Nov–Feb 8.30am–5pm; charge), where you can meander on walkways down and through a vast subterranean landscape of rock, limestone formations, caverns, and pools.

One of the largest caves in all of Asia, Hwanseon Donggul is a remarkable testament to the craftsmanship of the hand of time. Several unique species of insects and fish inhabit the blackness; as with anywhere, be mindful of posted signs and respect the natural beauty.

Haesindang: "Penis Park"

Craftsmanship of an entirely different sort lies in the curious park of **Haesindang** ⑭, affectionately named the Penis Park because of the hundreds of intricately carved penis totems that have been, ahem, "erected" around the shoreline in homage to a young maiden who drowned on the rocks there. It's a curious spot, located about 20km (12 miles) south of Samcheok, with beautiful coastline, a small museum with surprisingly modern holographic dioramas, and some kid-friendly hands-on exhibits about local flora and fauna.

The park is not at all graphic, and for anyone with a sense of humor it's quite funny: most of the carvings look more like Buddhas than a body part. Some are laughing uproariously, others thoughtful, others sad.

The shrine to the maiden is perched on a pine studded ledge. The lovely damsel was out near the shoreline and got swept into the ocean, whereupon suddenly the fish catch plummeted. The villagers were unclear as to why this maiden was so angry that she had cursed the fishing grounds, but then one day a man relieved himself in full view of the waves and to everyone's surprise, the fishing went well that day. Deciding the young girl was furious at having died a virgin without ever having seen a penis, the villagers decided to placate her by offering her glimpses anytime. Presumably, the fishing in these parts is most excellent. ❏

The small port town of Donghae, north of Samcheok, along with Pohang and Busan, offers ferry services to Ulleung-do, the largest South Korean-owned island on the East Sea. Further out is Dok-do, a disputed island legally owned by Japan. "Remember Dokdo!" is a common South Korean rallying cry.

LEFT: Hwanseongul cave. **BELOW:** the bizarre hilltop cruise ship at Jeongdongjin.

HIKING AND NATIONAL PARKS

South Koreans love the great outdoors, and their country offers plentiful opportunities to lace up the boots and seek out hidden temples and resorts amid ever-changing mountain scenery

Considering they live in a country covered by mountains, it is not surprising that South Koreans love to hike. The most enthusiastic are to be found in these pristine uplands every weekend. It is a modern manifestation of a venerable tradition: for thousands of years, the Korean mountains have sheltered temples and hermits, providing a respite to pilgrims weary of everyday life.

As Koreans tend to be of a sociable disposition, they often hike with their friends, and many people belong to climbing clubs. Whether you are a hardcore hiker taking on the big mountains or a lightweight who goes for the gentler trails, it is considered important to look the part. This means donning huge hiking boots and pulling heavy wool socks over pants. Decked out in full kit, South Korean hikers look ready to take on the Matterhorn, even if they're just going for a stroll to a scenic viewpoint half an hour's stroll from the car park.

Thanks to the this almost religious dedication to hiking, camping, and enjoyment of the great outdoors in general, the government has made far-sighted investments in wilderness areas such as Outer Seorak, where they've created a superb mountain resort. Of the 20 national parks across the country, Seoraksan and Hallasan (on Jeju-do), Odaesan and Jirisan are also popular. If you avoid weekends, however, you can still find solitude in the forests and majestic mountains.

LEFT: a park ranger at Seoraksan.

ABOVE: hiking to Mt Hallasan, Jeju-do. It is possible to ascend to the top of the mountain (South Korea's loftiest peak, at 1,950 metres / 6,398 ft) and back in one day, although be prepared for rapidly changing weather conditions.

ABOVE: taking in the view from the summit of Mt Jirisan (1,915 meters / 6,282ft) – the highest point in mainland South Korea.

LEFT: many of the country's most attractive hiking areas are also home to Buddhist temples, such as here at Sinheung-sa in Seoraksan National Park.

BELOW LEFT: hiking the Jeju Olle trail ("olle" means path). This 200km (125-mile) network of pilgrimage trails across the south of Jeju-do was inspired by the Santiago de Compostela *camino* in Spain.

RIGHT: signpost for hikers in Taejongdae, an area of dramatic cliffs southeast of Busan.

MINIMIZE YOUR IMPACT

As you enjoy these stunning mountain ranges please be respectful of these national parks and others who use them. Pick up your trash and even others' if you've got the room. Observe the signs and walk only on the pathways. Some Koreans will merrily duck under the clearly posted "No Passage" or "Do Not Enter" ropes to snap a picture at the rocks of a waterfall, unconcerned that their foot traffic damages the fragile plants and animals that call this area home. Trash left out attracts wildlife and may cause harm should it be ingested. Many signs are erected specifically to prevent accidents: a slip or fall in these remote spots could be life-threatening. Take care and use your common sense at all times.

RIGHT: wildlife at Odaesan National Park includes wild boar, roe deer and red squirrels.

RIGHT: wild flowers by the roadside, a common sight in South Korea.

RIGHT: scarlet maple leaves at Seoraksan in late October.

CHUNGCHEONG AND GYEONGSANG PROVINCES

The provinces that make up central and south-eastern South Korea are rich in natural assets, including lush forests, beautiful beaches, and secluded mountain valleys far from the beaten track

Something of a backwater for tourists, and foreign tourists in particular, the central areas of South Korea deserve at least a few days of your time. With a wealth of hidden shrines, national parks and white-sand beaches, there is a great deal to see, and it's possible to discover secluded forests and small villages that offer glimpses of a quieter and simpler world. If your tastes lean toward hiking through mountain valleys and seeking out ancient temples and shrines, the central provinces of Chungcheongnam and Chungcheongnambuk, and the southeastern crescent of Gyeongsang, will not disappoint.

Highlights include the Onyang Hot Spring and the famous Gosu Cave in Danyang. There is also the stunning HQ of Korean Buddhists, Guinsa Temple, and the awe-inspiringly massive Beopju-sa Buddha, a glittering 33-meter-(100ft) gold statue on the slopes of Songnisan in the Sobaek mountains.

Sublime coasts and National Parks

South Korea's convoluted west coast has been carved by the shallow waters of the Yellow Sea and is dotted with peninsulas and myriad small islands, with sandy beaches and fragrant pine forests. The protected waters of the Taean Haean Maritime National park along the Chungcheongnam coastal area, are home to a string of beaches such as Mullipo and Cheollipo, and the seaside resort of Daecheon with its impressive stretch of sand.

Inland, the national parks of Sobaeksan and Woraksan are home to majestic mountains and hidden Buddhist temples. The heavily forested Woraksan, bordering beautiful Chungju Lake, can be less crowded than some of South Korea's other parks, a peaceful retreat for those who appreciate solitude away from the city's throng. ❏

PRECEDING PAGES: pine trees in the mist, Songnisan National Park. **LEFT:** the 27-meter (88ft) Buddha at Beopju-sa. **TOP:** Buso Mountain Park near Buyeo. **ABOVE LEFT:** Daechon Beach. **ABOVE RIGHT:** lily fields near Cheongju.

CHUNGCHEONG PROVINCES

Country roads, vineyards, ginseng fields draped in black; hot springs, beaches, and shrines; National Parks and ancient capitals – central South Korea is full of surprises waiting to be discovered

Many tourists get only a fleeting glance at the Chungcheong Provinces (Chungcheongnam to the west, Chungcheongbuk to the east) as they speed through on buses and trains heading for Gyeongju or Busan. It's their loss: this central part of the country has dozens of historical sights, temples, and an attractive coastline. Landlocked Chungcheongbuk, to the east, is an area of forested hills and small villages, a quiet, rarely visited rural oasis that offers glimpses of a disappearing way of life.

CHUNGCHEONGNAM-DO

To reach Chungcheongnam from the capital, head south on Highway 1, the Seoul-Busan Expressway (also called the Gyeongbu Expressway), then veer west and southwest on Highway 21 into the lush, terraced valleys and rolling hills of the province. First, you might consider stopping off at the **Independence Hall of Korea ❶** (Mar–Oct Tue–Sun 9.30am–6pm, Nov–Feb until 5pm, admission ends 1 hour earlier; charge) near to the town of Cheonan. This is much more than a "Hall" – it's a full-scale museum (one of the largest in the country, in fact), with several gargantuan sculptures, a half-dozen museum buildings, and a plaza that could hold

thousands of people. It takes half a day to fully appreciate this monument to South Korea's determination, though English signs are few.

The complex was completed in 1987, and no expense has been spared in developing displays containing historical artifacts, life-size recreations of Korea resistance fighters, and even reproductions of torture scenes that are sure to give nightmares to the squeamish. After a visit here, you'll understand some reasons for the historical frictions between Korea and Japan.

Main attractions
INDEPENDENCE HALL OF KOREA
ONYANG FOLK MUSEUM
ONYANG HOT SPRING
DAECHEON BEACH
BORYEONG MUD FESTIVAL
BUYEO NATIONAL MUSEUM
GYERYONGSAN NATIONAL PARK
EUNJIN MIREUK BUDDHA
DAEJEON
BEOPJU-SA BUDDHA
GOSU CAVE
SOBAEKSAN AND WORAKSAN
   NATIONAL PARKS
GUINSA TEMPLE

LEFT: Chungcheong is South Korea's major ginseng-growing area. **RIGHT:** grisly display at the Independence Hall of Korea showing Japanese soldiers executing Korean activists.

Chungcheong Provinces

YELLOW

SEA

0   20 km
0   20 miles

Onyang

Travelers en route from Seoul to the west coast may find **Onyang ❷**, some 18km (11 miles) west of Cheonan on Highway 21, to be a refreshing stop along the way. Well-established attractions here include the **Hyeonchungsa Shrine** (9am–6pm, Nov–Feb until 5pm; charge), dedicated to Korea's great 16th-century naval hero, Admiral Yi Sun-sin. The **Onyang Folk Museum** (daily 9am–6pm, Nov–Mar until 5pm; charge) in **Gwongokdong** claims to have the best all-round collection of Korean folk art in the world. The privately owned museum houses over 7,000 traditional Korean folk articles, although this represents only a portion of the vast collection Kim Wondae has accumulated over the past two decades. Three diorama display halls depict the life and traditions of Koreans with authentic household articles, work utensils, and religious, recreational, and scholastic items.

Onyang's **hot spring** feeds soothing mineral waters to several hotels and public baths in the area. If you have not experienced a Korean public bath, take your time to immerse yourself into the almost unbearably hot tub, then hop into the invigorating cold tub. Do this a few times, and you'll be ready for anything. Primed after a stimulating hot bath, a pilgrimage to Admiral Yi's shrine, and insights into Korean culture, head westward to the coast, Mallipo Beach, and South Korea's largest arboretum.

West coast attractions

Korea's convoluted west coast, cut by the shallow waters of the Yellow Sea, is dotted with myriad peninsulas and small islands, and bordered by sandy beaches overlooking quiet pine glens. Along this coast, village fishermen and seasonal beachgoers regulate their activities according to tidal changes, because the tide differential is so extreme. In certain areas at low tide, the Yellow Sea exposes vast mud flats a long distance offshore, owing to the huge tidal range on this coast, second only to the Bay of Fundy in Nova Scotia.

Taean Haean Maritime National Park ❸ extends north–south for some 70km (45 miles) along the Chungcheongnam coast, its protected waters punctuated by a string of popular beaches such as Mallipo and Cheollipo. There is a rich variety of marine life here, although controlled fishing is permitted, and the area is well known for its seafood. The 80-hectare (200-acre) sanctuary at Cheollipo protects more than 7,000 varieties of plants.

The **Cheollipo Arboretum** (not open to the public for conservation reasons; some admissions allowed if reserved two weeks in advance; tel: 041-672-9310) was founded by Ferris Miller, a naturalized Korean originally from Pennsylvania, who lived in Korea for over five decades. Some of the plants in Miller's arboretum are indigenous, while others were imported from around the world. There are, for example, two varieties of magnolia indigenous to Korea at Cheollipo, and 180 varieties from elsewhere (the entire magnolia family consists of

A spa at the Onyang hot springs.

BELOW: wrestling at the Onyang Cultural Festival.

Lycoris flowers at Cheollipo arboretum.

some 800 varieties). Hollies have been hybridized at the arboretum, and there are presently 450 hollies there. Among the many botanical wonders flourishing in Miller's arboretum are rare species such as the *Glyptostrobus lineatus,* a conifer from southern China, and *Magnolia biondii* from north-central China. The arboretum was donated to the country when Mr Miller died in August 2002, and it is now being managed by a group of specialists.

Daecheon

Veteran Westerners in South Korea have long favored **Daecheon Beach ➍** as a summer seaside resort. This attractive stretch of sand, about 14km (9 miles) from Daecheon town (also known as Boryeong), can be reached by bus, train, or car from Seoul. As you near Daecheon town, fields of yellow barley, the staple added to rice or boiled into a drink, cut bright yellow swaths across the summer rice terraces. Daecheon is in the middle of a lush agricultural area, but it is also well known in South Korea for its coal mines in the surrounding hills, contributing the base fuel from

which *yeontan*, or charcoal heating briquettes, are made.

Daecheon Beach is unofficially divided into two sectors: a northern stretch called "KB," or the "Korean Beach," and a southern stretch called the "Foreigners' Beach." This was originally a Christian missionaries' resort, and many Daecheon homes are still occupied by missionaries or their descendants, by members of Seoul's diplomatic and banking corps, and more recently by wealthy Korean business and government leaders.

The Korean Beach, where busy discos and wine houses co-exist with sleepy fishermen's huts, is a non-stop party scene during the peak summer season, while the well-manicured Foreigners' Beach maintains a quieter residential dignity. Choose whichever spot suits your style.

If getting down and "dirty" doesn't scare you, check out the **Boryeong Mud Festival**, held each July through early August. Giant truckloads of soft, slippery mud (actually a kind of clay used in beauty products) are deposited on the beach here and thousands

BELOW: on the beach at Daecheon.
RIGHT: Boryeong Mud Festival.

of people, young and old, don bikinis and swimwear and partake in the fun. Don't forget to bring a change of clothes for the trip back to Seoul.

Buyeo

About a half-hour's drive from the coast is the town of **Buyeo ❺**, famous throughout South Korea for its relics from the Baekje kingdom (18 BC to AD 660). At Jeongnim-sa, a Baekje temple site in the center of town, is a seated stone Buddha and a five-story stone pagoda, one of three remaining from the Three Kingdoms Period (57 BC to AD 918). Other precious relics are displayed in the **Buyeo National Museum** (daily 9am–6pm, Sat–Sun 9am–7pm; charge). Prehistoric stoneware vessels, shamanistic instruments, gilt-bronze and stone Buddhist statues, gold and jade ornaments, and other treasures attest to the development and excellence of Baekje artists and craftsmen. The museum building is something of a curiosity in that it was designed by a South Korean architect along traditional Baekje lines, which were then adapted by the Japanese.

The Baekje legacy extends itself beyond the museum. Along the serene Geumgang River at **Baengmagang** (White Horse River), remnants of the grandeur and the fateful fall of the Baekje kingdom of some 1,300 years ago are preserved. Picnic on the flat rock (Nanseok, Warm Rock) on the riverbank at Saja, just as the Baekje kings used to. On the opposite side of the river is the picturesque **Nakhwaam** (Rock of the Falling Flowers) bluff with a pavilion on its brow. Tradition says that the Tang dynasty general Su Tingfang lured a protective dragon out of the river with a white horse's head, and thus was able to cross the river and conquer Buyeo.

Out of loyalty to their king and to preserve their dignity, court women jumped to their deaths from Nakhwaam into the river. As recorded in some Korean epics, they looked like falling blossoms as their colorful *chimajeogori* dresses billowed in their deadly flight.

Gongju and nearby sights

Travel another half-hour to the northeast to reach **Gongju ❻**. The city was

TIP

Buyeo's royal tombs are similar to Gyeongju's: soft mounds of earth that contain a treasure trove of artifacts dating to the Baekje era. Visit the Buyeo Royal Museum to learn about the history or go to the tombs themselves, where the rolling grass-covered hills and woods are especially picturesque.

LEFT: Baekje incense burner, Buyeo. **BELOW:** stone Buddhist statue at Buyeo.

TIP

Gyeryongsan National Park is named after its eponymous mountain: Gyeryongsan, which in Korean means "chicken dragon mountain." The 64 sq km (25 sq miles) include wildlife such as wild boar, striped squirrels and hedgehogs. (No chicken dragons, however, unless you've had too many sips of soju while hiking the trail.)

established in AD 475, and was once the capital of the Baekje Kingdom until it was moved south to Buyeo. In Gongju, a **National Museum** (Tue–Sun 9am–6pm, Sat–Sun 9am–7pm; charge) was dedicated in 1972 to house relics found around town. Almost half of the 6,800 display items were excavated from the King Muryeong (reigned 501–523) tomb. As you browse past Muryeong's gold crown ornaments, his exquisitely engraved bronze mirror, and other Baekje articles, remember that it was this same craftsmanship which was taught to the Japanese by emigrant Baekje artisans.

After visiting the museum, you may want to see where many of the items originally came from – the **Tomb of King Muryeong** (daily 9am–6pm; charge). The tomb was accidentally discovered in 1971 during a construction project, before which it had been undisturbed for 14 centuries. The 3,000 items pulled from the tomb have offered valuable insights into 6th-century Korean life. A model at the site illustrates the technique used in the construction. The tomb is a five-minute taxi or bus ride

(Gongju Intercity bus terminal) west of the city. Close by is another set of tombs, the **Songsanni Burial Mounds** (daily 9am–6pm; charge). Not far from downtown Gongju is an earthen (from the Baekje Period) and stone (from a 17th-century reconstruction) fortification, **Gongsanseong** (daily 9am–6pm; charge), lying beside the Geumgang River and surrounded by woods. To get there, you can catch a city bus at the Gongju Intercity bus terminal.

From Gongju, head southeast to **Gyeryongsan National Park ❼**, a beautiful area popular with hikers as well as with those taking time out for deeper reflection. Long considered a propitious site, Gyeryongsan is home to several minor religious sects. In the 14th century a spot here was selected for the capital city and construction began before it was decided that Seoul would make a better site. Further west you can visit the Expo Science Park at Daedok, featuring a funfair and some permanent exhibitions from the Daejeon Expo held here in 1993.

These two sites are worth at least a day on their own if you have the time.

BELOW: pagoda, Buso Mountain Park. **BELOW RIGHT:** the Eunjin Mireuk at Gwanchok-sa.

Then you could return to Gongju and head 50km (31 miles) southwest, traveling deeper into Baekje history to Buyeo on the curving Highway 23. Along the way, pause at the **Gap-sa temple** (daily 8am–6pm; charge), one of South Korea's oldest temples, on the edge of Gyeryongsan National Park.

The Eunjin Mireuk

Head southeast from Buyeo, or south from Gongju, to the town of Nonsan; a short distance south of here is **Gwan-chok-sa**, Temple of the Candlelights (daily 8am–6pm; charge), with one of the most impressive Buddhas in South Korea. As you scale the stone steps on the Banya hillside to the temple, all the superlative descriptions you've ever heard regarding the 1,000-year-old **Eunjin Mireuk** – the largest standing stone Buddha in South Korea – stir you with anticipation. Your curiosity is piqued when, at the top of a flight of stairs, your first glance at the Eunjin Mireuk is through the window of the temple (if the temple doors are open). All you can see of the "Buddha of the Future" is its face, its eyes peering back at you through

the holy sanctum. The "Standing Stone Gwanseum Maitreya" is awesome in its totality. Its disproportionate massiveness, crown, large hands, and extended earlobes all suggest a higher evolved spiritual being. Its face, however, which is occasionally scrubbed clean, has flat features and almond-shaped eyes (not unlike the Koreans) and sculpted toes, all of which lend tangible human qualities.

Science City – Daejeon

With a population of 1.5 million, **Daejeon** ❽ (240km/150 miles south of Seoul) is South Korea's fifth-largest city and the largest in the Chungcheong provinces. The city sits (more or less) in the middle of the country, and if you're traveling south from Seoul, you're sure to be going through Daejeon at some point. As Korean cities go, it's pleasant enough, but there really isn't much here to entice visitors to linger – although it is surrounded by beautiful mountains and lakes. In fact, historically, Daejeon wasn't much. Not until the railway came through in 1905, with later branches towards Mokpo, did this unassuming spot begin to prosper.

The Eunjin Mireuk, South Korea's largest stone Buddha.

BELOW: Daejeon Science Park.

Daejeon on the Map

Daejeon's name originally translated as "Large Field" and until the railway came through, few outsiders had reason to visit what is now South Korea's fifth-largest city.

The year 1905 brought the Gyeongbu railway line, which connected the cities of Seoul and Busan, and instantly placed Daejeon on the map. Stores, restaurants, and hotels were soon catering to Seoul- and Busan-bound travelers. This convenient location in one of the country's relatively scarce inland plains, made the city an ideal transport hub, and numerous other railway lines soon branched off from the new city. These days Daejeon has a population of around 1.5 million and, home to some 200 research institutes, has become the hub of South Korea's burgeoning hi-tech industries.

The major city attraction is the **Expo Science Park** (daily 10am–5.30pm; charge) on the northern edge of town. In 1993 this was the site of the Daejeon Expo. Since then, it has been reinvented as a science theme park with the 13 major pavilions housing a variety of themed attractions (space exploration, recycling, and automobiles, to name a few) with displays emphasizing technology and the future.

In keeping with the futuristic theme, pavilions come in imaginative shapes, sizes, and colors. A monorail, cable cars, and a tram shuttle people between the pavilions, performance centers, the Expo Theatre, and restaurants. The park complements a couple of top-notch science and technology universities, and a nearby science research center that has made Daejeon South Korea's principal city for science and technology. The city's profile was further boosted when it was selected as one of the venues for the 2002 soccer World Cup.

Ginseng country

The hills and valleys south of Daejeon are ginseng country. Ginseng fields are easy to spot – they're usually on a hillside or rocky slope and (unromantically) covered by black sheets of plastic to protect the shade-loving plants. The little city of **Geumsan** ❾ is smack in the middle of ginseng country, and is home to the largest and most active **ginseng market** in South Korea (likely the largest in the world). It is possible to buy ginseng along with a bewildering assortment of herbs, roots, fungi, dried lizards and toads, scorpions, and who knows what else at the many oriental medicine shops along the main thoroughfare and the side streets leading off it. But if you want to go when the place is really hopping, go on the 2nd, 7th, 12th, 17th, 22nd, and 27th day of each month. These are market days in Geumsan, and farmers from throughout the province bring in fresh ginseng, and a variety of vegetables and fruits to sell to busloads of elderly tourists who come for the best selection and prices in the country.

CHUNGCHEONGBUK PROVINCE

Chungcheongbuk is the sole landlocked province in South Korea, and mostly mountainous, with the Sobaek range lying to the east and the Noryeong range to the north. The region offers much breathtaking scenery and many manmade delights such as the ancient temple of Beopju-sa and the Buddhist headquarters of Guinsa.

Cheongju

Cheongju ❿ is the gateway to the natural attractions of Chungcheongbuk Province. First you may want to stop and rummage around a few museums to get some historical background for your visit. The **Cheongju National Museum** (9am–6pm, Sat–Sun 9am–7pm; charge) has three rooms which display the museum's permanent collection on the prehistoric period, the Three Kingdoms Period, and a variety of historical art.

Cheongju prides itself on being the first place where movable metal printing type was used (in 1377, well before

BELOW: the ginseng harvest near Geumsan.

Gutenberg printed his famous Bible), even if the technology did not take hold within Korea at that time. The **Cheongju Early Printing Museum** (Tue–Sun except major holidays 9am–6pm, until 5pm Nov–Feb; charge) displays artifacts and histories of Korea's early dabbling with printing presses.

A 30-minute drive into the mountains northeast of Cheongju will take you to **Sangdang sanseong**, a mountain fortress that has a long, if muddied, history. It was first built during the Baekje Period, then renovated during the Silla and Joseon eras. Four gates and most of the wall still stand, and it has been made into a mountain park that is popular with locals.

Songnisan National Park mountain retreat

Of these three parks, **Songnisan National Park ⑪**, a mountain retreat an hour and a half from Cheongju, is the most popular. A visit here is superb any time of the year, but is most favored by discriminating Korean weekenders in the fall when its trees are brilliantly aflame with color. Oaks, maples, and ginkgos try to outdo each other in their autumnal radiance. As one romantically minded Korean travel writer once wrote of Songnisan: "The tender green for spring, abundance of forests for summer, yellow leaves for autumn, and snow for winter all deserve appreciation."

Indeed, since ancient times, Songnisan has been a preferred resort area and, appropriately, the word *songni* means "escape from the vulgar." To achieve this Songni escape, travel from Seoul to Daejeon by train, then transfer via bus or car through Okcheon to the Songni area. Alternatively, you can also travel directly by car or bus from Seoul via **Cheongju City**. It is about a three-hour car journey one way. After passing through Cheongju City and beginning an ascent to idyllic Songni, you will enter the steep Malttijae Pass which serves as an unwinding transition from harsh urbanity to comforting nature at its freshest.

The most distinguished tree in Korea

Just beyond a glassy reservoir, on your final approach to the **Songni highlands** and **Songni village**, your local guide will no doubt point out the most distinguished tree in South Korea. This is an old pine on the left side of the road called the Jeongipine Pine, so named because the Joseon-dynasty King Sejo (reigned 1455–68) granted this hoary fellow the official bureaucratic title of Jeongipum, a rank equivalent to that of a cabinet minister. Legend and even history note that this humble tree was granted that distinction because it lifted its boughs in respect one day as King Sejo and a royal entourage passed by. The pine's loyalty and politeness was duly rewarded by the flattered king.

Just beyond this ministerial pine is the final approach to **Songnidong**, a mountain village famous for the semi-wild tree mushrooms cultivated in the surrounding area and sold at roadside stands. Seoulites try to arrive in Songni village at lunchtime, when they can enjoy a fabled Songni mushroom lunch featuring as many as six different

Cheongju Early Printing Museum.

BELOW: the South Korean flag.

TIP

Songnisan National
Park contains one of
Korea's largest
Buddhas, housed at
Beopju-sa. The Buddha
is 33 meters high and is
made of brass. Though
large and awe-inspiring,
it is not ancient by any
means: it was finished
in 1989.

mushroom dishes served with a dizzying array of side dishes, *gimchi*, and rice. Be sure to buy a take-away bag of these tender air-dried fungi.

Beopju-sa and the biggest Buddha

After this mushroom-fest, proceed uphill to Songnisan's biggest attraction, **Beopju-sa** ⓬ (daily 6am–6pm; charge), a large temple complex dominated by a massive Mireuk Buddha of the Future, appropriately fashioned from modern poured cement. This 27-meter (88ft) image, completed in 1964, is often identified by tour guides as "the biggest Buddha in Korea."

This sprawling temple complex was first built at the base of Mount Songni in the 6th century, shortly after Buddhism had been carried into Korea from China. Records note that work began in 553, during the 14th year in the reign of the Silla king Jinheung. The original founder and spiritual master was the high priest Uisin, who had returned home from esoteric studies in India. Uisin contributed several Buddhist scriptural books to Beopju-sa's first library.

Author-historian Han Gihyung, a former assistant editor of the *Korea Journal*, writes that this temple, "one of Korea's oldest," was reportedly "renovated during the reigns of Kings Seongdeok and Hyegong (702–780)." This fact can be confirmed by observing the ancient stone buildings of the temple surviving to date.

According to Han, the monarchs of not only the Silla dynasty but also the Goryeo and Joseon dynasties protected the temple. In the 6th year (1101) of King Sukjong's reign (in the Goryeo era), the king gathered 30,000 priests from all over the country to pray for the health of ailing Royal Priest Uicheon. In the Joseon era, King Sejo (1455–68) presented the temple with large tracts of paddy fields, grains, and slaves. Kings Injo (1623–49), Cheoljong (1849–63), and Gojong (1864–1906) all had the temple renovated. Remnants of this favored temple's days of spiritual grandeur can be found in every section of the compound.

Consider the famed Cheolhwak, a massive iron rice pot which was cast in 720, during the reign of Silla King

BELOW: Beopju-sa.

Seongdeok, when some 3,000 priests were living and eating here. This grand mass facility is 1.2 meters (4ft) high, 2.7 meters (9ft) in diameter, and 10.8 meters (35ft) in circumference. These days you'll find perhaps only 2 percent of that previous number of gray-robed, sutra-chanting monks, so the pot no longer has its utilitarian purpose.

Eight Image Hall

Perhaps the most celebrated historical treasure at Beopju-sa is the **Palsangjeon**, or **Eight Image Hall**, which rises in symmetrical splendor above the complex's roomy main courtyard. As Han notes: "This five-story building, presumably reconstructed during the second year of King Injo's reign (1624) in the Joseon era, is a rare architectural work for Buddhism not only in Korea but also in China, and can be compared with a similar five-story pagoda at Nara, Japan."

Other Beopju-sa curiosities include a large deva lantern surrounded with relief bodhisattvas, a second stone lantern supported by two carved lions, and, outside the temple, a large "ablu-

tion trough" carved in the shape of a lotus and where a sacred bath would be taken to remove ones sins.

To the left side of the main entrance you'll also find a huge boulder that has come to life with a serene Buddha sculpted into a wide and flat facade. If such manmade art boggles your mind, head for natural beauty in the surrounding hills that are laced with excellent hiking trails.

A view of the Beopju-sa complex from one of Songnisan's upper ridges is just reward for the huffing and puffing it takes to get up there.

Ginseng and chicken soup.

Gosu Cave

Another natural wonder well worth visiting is **Gosu Cave** ⓭, one of South Korea's most famous caverns, located in Danyang, the farthest east county in all of Chungcheon. This beautiful cave is open year-round, and in addition to being a nice way to escape the summer humidity and heat, it has stunning limestone formations and beautiful underground pools. The more striking formations have been

BELOW: rock carving at Beopju-sa.

Sobaeksan National Park is one of the most attractive in the country.

BELOW: Cheontae Buddhist festival at Guinsa.

named after resemblances to animals, birds, and people. Only about a quarter of the cave is open to the public, due to active measures taken to protect and preserve this unique part of Chungcheon's natural heritage. However, over 1.5km (1 mile) are accessible, with walkways and passages and (rather dim) lighting. As in any cave, things can be a bit claustrophobic, so be prepared for narrow squeezes and possible muddiness.

Sobaeksan and Woraksan national parks

Also in Danyang are the national parks **Sobaeksan** and **Woraksan**, offering pristine hiking opportunities in truly majestic mountains. Mt Shinseongbong is among the most famous, and has been a popular hiking destination for centuries. Among the numerous flora and fauna these mountains support are Korean mountain goats. Sightings are not common, but those with keen eyes or a powerful set of binoculars can catch glimpses of the animals on cliff sides or ravines. These goats are well adapted to living

in these highlands, eating azaleas and even moss or lichen when necessary.

Guinsa ❶ is a large temple complex in the mountains of Sobaeksan, and is the primary residence of monks following Cheontae scriptures. Some 10,000 monks can be accommodated, and the sprawling complex is quite different in feel to most Korean temples. In 1945, the Cheontae Buddhist sect had almost entirely died out, but found a new lease of life under the guidance of one Sangwol Wongak. He is also credited with reviving Guinsa, making it simultaneously one of South Korea's youngest temples yet with one of the oldest traditions. In 1966 the complex was destroyed by fire, so the buildings you see today are less than half a century old. The ostentatious architecture is quite distinct from anything else in South Korea.

As with many Korean temples, simple meals are served in Guinsa, and guests and visitors are allowed to partake. The kitchen is only open at specific times; respect posted signs, and be aware that this is not a restaurant – you must clean up after yourself. ❑

Ginseng

The legendary root is ubiquitous, its alleged life-enhancing properties celebrated throughout Korea and much of the rest of Asia

Among the herbs in Korea, the "cure-all wonder," panax ginseng, referred to as *insam* in Korean, is by far the most popular. As far back as the 3rd millennium BC in China, herbal potions and poultices were used to maintain and restore the internal eum-yang (ie the negative-positive, base-acid, female-male) forces to proper balance by stimulating or repressing either aspect. Ginseng, which grew wild in ravines and forests of Korea and Manchuria, apparently bursts with yang energy. It became a vital ingredient used in a vast range of medications prescribed in the first Chinese pharmacopoeia.

If consumed regularly in small doses, scientists claim the root will help stimulate the central nervous system. Larger doses, however, depress the nervous system by buffering out physical and chemical stress, and by promoting cell production that counteracts anemia and hypertension. Ginseng thus reportedly increases physical and mental efficiency, and enhances gastrointestinal functions. It is widely believed in Korea that the regular use of ginseng will extend one's life.

South Korea's main ginseng-growing area is in the central region, south of Daejeon around the small city of Geumsan, where the air is filled with the aroma of the root being processed, and there is a very active market attracting buyers from all over Asia.

The growth and maturation cycle of Korean ginseng takes one to six years depending on the intended use of the root. In mid-May, the plant flowers. Seeds of the strongest, most mature, five-year-old plants are selected in mid-July and planted in late October. After harvest, the roots are washed, peeled, steamed, and dried. They are then produced in two grades: white *(baek)* and red *(hong)*. Around 60 percent of the best ginseng is selected for the red variety which is further processed to preserve the potency of its chemical components. The root takes so many minerals from the soil, that once the fields have been harvested the land will not be planted with ginseng again for at least 10 to 15 years.

Valued more highly than gold in ancient times, Korean ginseng today is still a costly commodity, often eaten in very popular *samgyetang* (ginseng chicken soup). Perhaps to placate Western consumers, ginseng comes conveniently packaged in modern products.

For internal rejuvenation there are pills, capsules, extracts, jellies, teas, soft drinks, jams, candies, chewing gums, and, ironically, even cigarettes. For cosmetic needs, there is a wide range of ginseng body creams and shampoos.

At the Geumsan Ginseng Festival (mid-September) you can dig up your own ginseng, have a bowl of *samgyetang*, and have an oriental medicine doctor carry out an analysis of your health – maybe even stick a few pins in you! ❏

ABOVE: signage at the Geumsan ginseng market.
RIGHT: ginseng root on sale at Geumsan, the center of the ginseng trade.

SOUTH KOREA'S MOUNTAIN TEMPLES

While the urban centers have their attractions, a visit to Korea would be incomplete without experiencing the peace of these rustic hideaways

South Korea's largest and most historic Buddhist temples are found in mountain valleys far removed from the hectic urban centers. Many of South Korea's artistic treasures are to be found within the temple grounds, often inside the prominent pagodas which were deemed too public for robbers to steal. The greatest treasure may be the beauty of the temples and their pristine natural setting. These mountain shrines and their grounds have become the centerpieces of South Korea's well-developed system of Provincial and National Parks, from Jirisan in the south to Seoraksan in the north.

It is not happenstance that the temples are located in beautiful mountain locations. For most of the staunchly Confucian Joseon dynasty (1392–1910) Buddhist temples, and even monks, were banned from entering the cities; the mountains were their refuge. Today, these temples in the hills provide visitors with a quiet opportunity to calm, refresh, and renew their spiritual side.

Visiting the Temples

The temples, along with their surrounding mountain trails, are popular weekend destinations for both Korean and foreign tourists alike. If you choose to visit one of the temples, make a full day of it. Take time to explore the main temple complex and to appreciate the charm and delicate details of the many buildings. On the doors of the Main Hall, colorful demons repel evil, and lotus flowers promise the hope of nirvana. Inside, look up and you're likely to see dragons and cranes softly suspended from the rafters. And finally, visit the small shrine on a hillside behind the main buildings and pay homage to the Mountain Spirit and Recluse.

ABOVE: the mountain spirit. To the rear of almost every mountain temple are shrines to the Mountain Spirit and The Hermit, both remnants of a shamanistic past.

ABOVE: Maisan Temple is famous for its delicate, sometimes outrageous, stone pagodas built over several decades by a local hermit.

RIGHT: whether nestled in a remote mountain valley or just off a busy street, temples offer a peaceful escape from today's stresses and worries.

BELOW: South Korea's monks and nuns spend a good deal of the summer and winter months in meditative retreat. Fall and spring are for travel and personal reflection.

THE FOUR TEMPLE GUARDIANS

The Four Heavenly Guardians stand watch at the entrance to almost every Buddhist temple throughout Korea. In the larger temples, the Guardians are gigantic wooden or concrete statues housed in the temple's second gate. At smaller temples, Guardians are painted on the wooden doors of the temple gate.

The Guardian of the North stands with a pagoda, a reliquary for the ashes of monks, as this is the direction of death. The Guardian of the South controls the weather with his lute, and the Guardian of the West carries a sword that is able to multiply whenever needed. Finally, the Guardian of the East holds a dragon to ensure good fortune.

First-time visitors are often taken aback by the ferocity of the Guardians. They stand with sword, dragon or lute in hand; wide-eyed and with ferocious grins. Underfoot a bizarre little gremlin winces in anguish. But don't worry, their ferocity isn't directed at visitors with a pure heart; they're there to protect the temple against evil from the four directions of the compass, standing ever vigilant against devils and demons trying to gain entrance to the temple grounds.

BELOW: stone pagoda at Yongjang-sa temple site on Namsan near Gyeongju.

RIGHT: giant Buddha. Size matters, at least when it comes to Buddhas. The larger and more ornate statues are a symbol of the devotion of their creators.

GYEONGSANGBUK PROVINCE

Gyeongsangbuk Province has the most varied cultural landscape in Korea. Apart from the magnifcent tombs at Gyeongju, there are traditional folk villages, white-sand beaches and thoroughly modern cities

This eastern section of South Korea has some of its most compelling cultural sights. The royal tombs at Gyeongju and the traditional folk villages are major draws, while Jikji-sa is a stunningly beautiful mountain temple. The countryside is attractive. with the coastline marked by some lovely beaches. Far offshore in the deep waters of the East Sea is the extraordinarily beautiful island of Ulleung-do.

DAEGU

The logical starting point for a dip through South Korea's southern crescent area is the large city of **Daegu** ❶, capital of Gyeongsangbuk Province. South Korea's third-largest city is a major industrial center, and lies at the heart of a rich agricultural region famous for its apples – which are renowned throughout Asia. At first glance Daegu may appear to be either a half-hearted attempt at a city or an overgrown village, but a closer inspection reveals it to be a uniquely Korean compromise between urban and rural extremes: it is big enough to offer good hotels, restaurants and 21st-century entertainment, yet small enough to retain a relaxed ambience that is lost in Seoul or Busan.

Few of Daegu's buildings are so imposing as to obstruct the view of the surrounding mountains, and due to the presence of enlightened city-center planning, pedestrians rather than cars dominate the central streets.

Daegu's origins can be traced to an earthwork fortress from the prehistoric Samhan era. The fortress was originally constructed of several artificial hills in the middle of the broad plain that is now largely filled by Daegu. Presumably these hills supported a Korean variant of the motte-and-bailey forts once common in Europe. Late in the 14th century, at the end of the Mongol occupation and the beginning of the

Main attractions
DAEGU MEDICINE ALLEY
JIKJI-SA
ANDONG FOLK MUSEUM AND
  FOLK VILLAGE
DOSAN SEOWAN
  CONFUCIAN ACADEMY
HAHOE FOLK VILLAGE
HAHOE MASK MUSEUM
BUSEOK-SA
KING MUNMU'S TOMB
ULLEUNG-DO
GYEONGJU
TUMULI PARK
ANAPJI POND
GYEONGJU NATIONAL MUSEUM
NAMSAN
BULGUK-SA
SEOKGURAM GROTTO

LEFT: roof detail on a Daegu temple.
RIGHT: healing herbs on Medicine Alley.

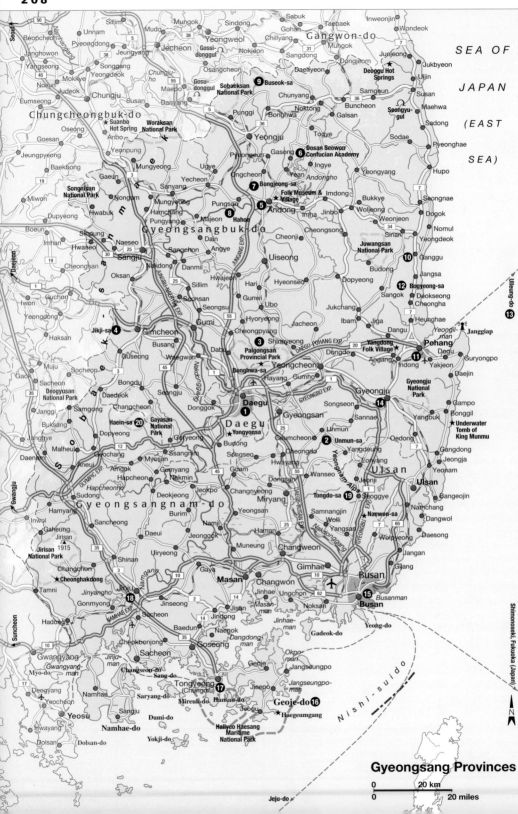

Joseon dynasty, the fort was enlarged and stones were added to its existing earthworks. In 1596, during the Imjin War, the fort was again enlarged to its present circumference of 1,300 meters (4,265ft) and height of 4 meters (13ft). The fort is now a city park, called **Dalseong** (daily 5am–10pm, Nov–Feb closes at 7pm; free), complete with a small zoo. The entrance to Dalseong is a favorite meeting place for the city's senior citizens, who lounge amicably along its cobblestone walkway, traditionally sartorial in their pastel silks.

West Gate Market (*seomun sijang*), one of the largest and oldest in the country, is just a short walk away, across Dongsan Hospital. The narrow alleys of the market are lined with cauldrons of noodle soup billowing steam, and mobile vendors with carts devoted exclusively to specialized merchandise like sewing needles and arcane mousetraps. Clustered networks of permanent stalls deal in even more mundane necessities.

Medicine Alley

Yakjeon Golmok, "**Medicine Alley**," is one of Daegu's most notable sights, a center for wholesale purveyors of traditional medicines. A stimulating barrage of scents oozes out of buckets and boxes of prepared pharmacopoeia and wafts up from magical herbs drying on woven mats under the sun. The blend of aromas shifts gradually as one wanders down this pungent street. Indeed, mere inhalations will probably relieve you of any afflictions of the nasal passages or even the soul. Should this prove ineffective, there are several licensed herbalists who will willingly prescribe healing brews.

Daegu has its own brand of nightlife that, if lacking the polish of posher establishments in Seoul, is well endowed with enthusiasm. Most after-hours partying in Daegu is centralized in several blocks near the "old station" at the center of town. Standing with your back to the station, expensive "businessmen's entertainments" are to

your right; on your left are rock 'n' roll clubs and wine stalls. Adjacent to the latter is one of the city's larger markets. At night the two merge in a spirited confusion of side alley vendors, eclectic shopfronts, blasting nightclub bands, and throngs of revelers intent on entertaining themselves.

Start your Daegu evening with a sidewalk snack of steamed crab, or, if you dare, raw sea cucumbers. Continue with dinner in a smoky bulgogi house or in an inexpensive but elegant Western-styled restaurant, then move out to explore the many raucous bars.

Sights outside Daegu

The most significant (and attractive) temple within easy reach of Daegu is **Haein-sa**, an hour or so away by bus. As this lies just over the provincial border, it is dealt with in the Gyeongsangnam-do chapter (see page 242). For those seeking something rather more remote, **Unmun-sa ❷** (daily 8am–8pm; charge) is set deep in the backwoods southeast of Daegu, at the northern end of the Yeongnam mountains. The town of **Unmun** consists of a gas station, a few

Daegu has developed rapidly and is now South Korea's third-largest city.

BELOW: Unmun-sa, deep in the Korean countryside.

TIP

There is a modern subway system in Daegu, but for most visitors the major city sites are near the railway station, or a short taxi ride away.

inns and restaurants, along with a few dozen farmhouses, including some handsome examples of traditional folk architecture. The path to the temple follows a rambling stream through a pine forest. Set in an open field, Unmun-sa is a sanctuary for a community of Buddhist nuns, who go about their work and worship unperturbed by occasional visitors who drift through to see the many fine paintings adorning the temple walls. The surrounding mountains harbor several small hermitages.

The favorite destination for Daeguites with a free afternoon is **Palgongsan Provincial Park ❸**, only a few minutes, drive north of the city. The attractions here are the gentle mountains and clear mountain streams, as well as the numerous restaurants along the roads. In season, apples, grapes, and fresh vegetables are sold from roadside stands.

During the Silla Dynasty, Palgon Mountain was one of five sacred mountains, and numerous temples were built and pilgrimages were made to make offerings to Buddha and the Mountain Spirit. There are still several temples in the mountains and val-

leys of this park. The largest is **Dong-hwa-sa** (daily 7am–sunrise; charge), a center for practicing Zen (called Seon in Korean), with several hermitages located in the mountains. The temple has recently expanded, and a giant granite Buddha was added in the hope that it would speed up the reunification of North and South Korea. Koreans come to make an offering and pray for peace at the foot of the Buddha.

High above Donghwa-sa, and reached by trail from the temple, is **Gatbawi**, a 1,000-year-old Buddha carved from mountain stone and serenely looking out over the mountains and valleys from his lofty viewpoint. Being a curing Buddha, Gatbawi is thought to have special medicinal powers, and believers come to pray for the health of their family and friends. It is commonly believed that Gatbawi will answer at least one of your prayers. Just below Gatbawi are shrines to the Mountain Spirit (Palgongsan is also an important mountain in shamanism) and Dragon. Directly across from the shrine is a cafeteria serving free vegetarian meals. Gatbawi is open 24

BELOW:
Palgongsan, mountain air on Daegu's doorstep.

hours, and you will find people praying at almost any hour, but if you go late bring a flashlight. There are stone stairs leading up the mountain (a short, but steep, climb), but no lights.

NORTH AND WEST FROM DAEGU

Jikji-sa Temple

Exquisite **Jikji-sa** ❹ (daily sunrise–sunset; charge), easily reached from Daegu via Gimcheon (about 1½ hours to the north), is a gem of a temple, repainted in an entrancing blend of blue, magenta, and gold. Figures and landscapes embellish virtually every external wall space, and Jikji-sa's shrines are populated with a bewildering array of finely carved statues. The combination of giant pine and maple trees, the stately temple buildings, the moss-covered lanterns, and the occasional bird will leave a memorable impression. In springtime the hills fill with tiny tree frogs, and their chorus in the evening is enchanting.

The temple's beauty has not gone unnoticed: it is one of several temples associated with Samyeong Daesa, who was both a Buddhist saint and a military hero. Samyeong was born in the town of Milyang in 1544. His family was of the *yangban* class (aristocrats) and he was educated in the Confucian Classics. After losing both his parents, Samyeong left his home to wander in the mountains.

He eventually made his way to Jikji-sa where his study of Zen led to his attainment of enlightenment. He became chief priest of Jikji-sa in 1574. Soon after, he set out wandering again and met Seosan, the most prominent Korean Buddhist master of the period. According to legend, they engaged in a contest of magic. Samyeong began by arduously transforming a bowl of needles into noodles. Seosan received the bowl of noodles, promptly turned it upside down, and needles crashed to the floor. Samyeong's next feat was to stack eggs end-to-end vertically, several feet into the air. Seosan followed suit, but started from the top. Samyeong responded by turning a clear blue sky to a thunderstorm and challenged Seosan to return the torrential rain to

Golden Buddha at Jikji-sa.

BELOW: Jikji-sa has a superb mountain setting.

Outside of Andong is a seven-story brick pagoda, Chilcheung Jeontap, with Unified Silla-era (AD 668–918) relief engravings of god-generals and divas. This pagoda is thought to be the oldest and biggest pagoda in the country. You'll find it in Sinsedong along the railroad tracks.

BELOW: bus passengers, Andong. **BELOW RIGHT:** an arrow throwing pot *(tohu)* – one of several 16th-century artifacts from the time of Yi Hwang displayed at Dosan Seowon Confucian Academy.

the sky. Seosan calmly met the challenge and added his own flourish by transforming the ascending droplets into a flock of birds. Duly humbled, Samyeong asked to become a disciple of the greater master.

Several years later, the Japanese invasion began and Seosan emerged as leader of a voluntary militia of monks, which eventually grew to a force of 5,000. Seosan was too old for battle, so he appointed Samyeong as field commander. Under Samyeong's command, Korea's warrior monks earned a reputation for their fierce courage and played a major role in repulsing the Japanese.

Andong

From Daegu, **Andong** ❺ can be reached via expressway in just over an hour, or alternatively via a meandering 6-hour train ride from Seoul. The monotony of hills and grain fields and modern Saemaul cement villages is broken by sturdy, wooden houses with white rubber *gomusin* (Korean shoes with upturned toes) lined up outside lattice doors on the *maru* (wooden porch).

Andong is full of traditions lost in much of modern South Korea. Expect to see stately *harabeoji* (grandfathers) dressed in *hanbok* (traditional Korean clothes), and sporting horn-rimmed glasses and wispy beards, strolling around town. For Koreans, Andong is synonymous with *yangban*, the educated upper class of the Joseon period, since the Andong Kwon clan served in high government positions during Korea's last dynasty.

Although modern times have encroached on this provincial town with the ubiquitous concrete architecture found all over South Korea, a few *yangban* manors have managed to survive through the ages with a traditional graciousness and charm. These houses are easily recognized by their roofs of charcoal-colored tile which curve upward over thick wooden beams; beneath are white and cement-covered mud walls, windows and doors of paper and wood, a hard wooden *maru*, and weathered wood railings that surround the house. Above the front entrance, a signboard in an ancestor's finest calligraphic script proclaims

the dignity of the dwelling. Nonetheless, despite appearances, few of these venerable old dwellings are without modern comforts these days.

About 3km (2 miles) east of the city center is the **Andong Folk Museum and Folk Village** (museum: daily 9am–6pm, Nov–Feb until 5pm; charge; folk village: 24 hours; free), surrounded by traditional-style homes and outdoor displays. This little folk village is pleasantly situated, and many of the homes have been turned into restaurants that serve a local clientele (always a good sign), as well as welcoming visitors.

Gourmands will want to make sure to sample some of the local mackerel, which is broiled until crispy on the outside, succulent and buttery on the inside. Fish fans might simply not want to leave. Wash the meal down with some soju, or better yet, visit the **Andong Soju Museum** (Mon–Sat 9am–5.30pm; free) for free tastings and interesting dioramas that depict soju, its manufacture, and recent soju-related events (such as visits from European dignitaries).

The **Andong Hanji paper museum** (daily 9am–6pm; free) and factory, not far from the Hahoe Mask Museum (*pages 215–6*), offers a peek at the curious paper-making process from – literally – tree to finished paper. Mulberry bark is stripped off young saplings through multiple soakings, after which the pulp is moved to a bleaching vat where it turns white or beige. When it is ready, it is churned in giant vats to separate the individual pulp fibers. Finally screens are dipped into the pulp, drained, and dried. Watching the process is fascinating, as are the curious products that the paper is used for. In addition to the usual cardstock and wrapping, *hanji* papers are made into sculptures and even sewn together in clothes.

Dosan Seowon Confucian Academy

An epitome of Confucianism that should not be missed while in the Andong area is **Dosan Seowon Confucian Acad-**

emy ❻ (daily 9am–6pm; charge). The academy is a 28km (17-mile) inter-city bus ride north of Andong, and a 2km (1¼-mile) walk down a winding paved road that overlooks a peaceful blue lake and green rice paddies. Dosan Seowon was initiated by Yi Hwang (also known as Toegye, Dosu, and Toedo; 1501–70), one of the foremost Confucian scholars of Korea and once Chief of Confucian Studies and Affairs. The name Dosan Seowon was given to the academy in 1575 by King Seonjo. The government also later acknowledged Yi Hwang and his academy by depicting both of them on the commonly circulated 1,000-won note.

Confucianism is no longer taught at Dosan Seowon, but one can stroll through the hallowed Dosan Seodang lecture hall at the main entranceway, see the wooden plates that were used for printing lessons in the Janggyeonggak archive, and study some of Yi Hwang's relics, such as his gnarled walking cane and books of his teachings rendered in his personal calligraphy. The wooden, tiled Joseon-dynasty house behind the academy and over the ridge has been

Child wearing hanbok at the Andong Folk Museum.

BELOW: Dosan Seowon Confucian Academy.

the abode of Yi Hwang's descendants for the past 16 generations.

An older institution, and one which is still very much alive with followers, is the **Bongjeong-sa** ❼ Buddhist temple, 16km (10 miles) to the northwest of Andong city. Perhaps a more awesome sight is the 12.4-meter (40ft) **Amitaba Buddha** carved onto a mammoth boulder on the mountain at Jebiwon, 5km (3 miles) from Andong en route to Yeongju on Highway 5. This Buddha, which dates back to the Goryeo dynasty (AD 918–1392), stands on sculpted single lotus petals. Its robe and hands are carved into a massive granite boulder, and its head and hair are carved from two separate pieces of rock set into holy place. A stone pagoda sits higher on the slope among gnarled pines.

Hahoe village

A purer essence of Joseon-dynasty architecture and rural life has been maintained for the past 500 years in a hamlet called **Hahoe** ❽ (daily 9am–7pm, Nov–Feb until 6pm; charge), a half-hour bus ride southwest of Andong. During the Joseon dynasty Hahoe was celebrated for its literati and military leaders, and for a form of mask dance drama that evolved there. Today, it is appreciated for its rustic, traditional esthetics.

Hahoe is certainly off the beaten track, which has helped to keep it traditional. The Andong inter-city bus makes infrequent round-trips as far as Jungni (about 4km/2½ miles north of Hahoe). You can take a taxi or wait at a bus stop at the western fringe of town for a privately run bus to Pungsan, which is 16km (10 miles) west of Andong. Pungsan is your last glimpse of paved South Korea; the zigzagging 8km (5-mile) dirt road to Hahoe passes Jungni, cutting through grain and vegetable fields, and, finally, the bus deposits you in 16th-century Korea. Earthen thatched huts, larger *yangban* manors of wood and tile, the surrounding Sobaek Mountains, and the serpentine Nakdonggang River bending around Hahoe; this is the Korea that is warm, hearty, and strongly rooted in tradition. As you wander here, please pay attention to the "No Tresspassing" signs: this is

BELOW: the Amitaba Buddha.

a living community and people are going about their daily lives. It is a novelty to have a visitor knock on the door once; when it's 10 times daily, it's something of a nuisance.

The dirt path that wends around the hamlet is inlaid with chips of ceramic and tile. Cows are tethered in the front yard, chewing on hay. Under the tiled and thatched cave of each home is a row of fermented soybean (*doenjang*) patties drying in the sun. *Jige*, or A-frames, used for carrying heavy loads, lean against mud walls. In all its natural, raw beauty, Hahoe is perhaps the most picturesque village in South Korea. Admittedly, there are a few modernities; even the oldest house – said to be 550 years old by the local museum curator – is equipped with a refrigerator on its hard wooden *maru* and a TV antenna on its lichen-covered roof.

Across the path from the *yangban* manor is a museum that imitates Joseon architectural lines and is painted in bold Saemaul colors. This museum honors an educated 16th-century aristocrat from Hahoe, Yu Seongryong. Yu competed with Admiral Yi Sun-sin for court favors during the Japanese Hideyoshi invasions of the 1590s, and eventually became the king's prime minister. Yu's voluminous books of genealogy, personal articles and government documents are displayed in the museum. The Yu clan remains the most influential in Hahoe.

Probably the most glaring visual obstruction in Hahoe is an off-white school building. It stands out most noticeably when seen from the hilltop across the river. The school was a Saemaul Undong (New Community Movement) project. The Hahoe villagers vetoed future Saemaul developments, and, with the blessing of government officials, managed to keep their home town in thatch.

The village is quite popular with Koreans and foreigners alike, even if it is a little out of the way. When Britain's Queen Elizabeth II paid a visit to South Korea in 1999, Hahoe was the one place outside of Seoul she chose to visit. Naturally, this is quite a feather in the cap for the little village, and a museum has been set up to house the photos and other mementos from the visit. More

Ornamental mask in the mask museum at Hahoe Folk Village.

LEFT: Hahoe is perhaps the most authentic "Folk Village" in Korea.

Folk Villages

There are two types of "folk villages" in Korea. One is a commercial endeavor where the buildings have either been built or moved and a village constructed on the spot. People working in the village are experienced in traditional ways, but they are being paid (though usually not a lot), and this is not their home.

The other, more authentic, type of folk village is that which has chosen to maintain its traditional ways, limiting the construction of modern buildings, and hanging on to customs long-since forgotten in South Korea's cities. It is here that you will experience Korean rural life more or less as it has been lived for centuries.

There are only a handful of these villages that have been officially recognized (such as Hahoe), but driving through the Korean countryside you are bound to come across a considerable number of villages that appear "traditional."

The fact is that life in the countryside, for many, is not a whole lot different than how it was 50 years ago. People generally live in the same homes their grandparents did, farm the same plot of land, live the same hard-working, yet quiet, life. Yet, as elsewhere in the world, this way of life is under threat, as more and more young people leave for the hustle and bustle of the modern city.

interesting is the new **Hahoe Mask Museum** (daily 9am–6pm; charge), displaying Korean masks on the first floor, and international masks on the second floor. The museum is a popular spot for school trips – don't be surprised if you turn a corner and a few classrooms of elementary schoolchildren suddenly decide that the most interesting thing in the whole museum is you.

Hahoe is famous for its *Byeolsingut Tallori*, a mask dance drama that is part shamanistic ritual and part slapstick comedy. At weekends (May–Oct Sat–Sun 3–4pm, Mar, Apr, Nov Sun 3–4pm; free), villagers perform the dance drama in the amphitheater located near the village entryway (across from the parking lot). If you are going to Hahoe, the dance drama will make the long trip worthwhile.

The nearby river with its banks of fragrant pine trees makes a great spot for a picnic lunch or a break from walking in the hot sun. Listen to the gurgle of the water, watch warblers flit about in the branches, and try to imagine that even Seoul must have felt like this, many, many years ago.

Byeolsingut Tallori, the mask dance drama at Hahoe.

BELOW: a scarecrow in the fields outside Hahoe.

Buseok-sa

Another place that is rather inaccessible but really should be seen while in the Andong area is **Buseok-sa** ❾ (Floating Rock Temple; daily 7am–5.30pm; charge), 60km (37 miles) due north of Andong along Highway 5 and a long, bumpy road. For the serious student of ancient culture, this is one of the country's most rewarding detours. The temple was established in 676 by High Priest Uisang, who returned to Korea from China with teachings of Hwaeom Buddhism. The legend relates how Uisang's former lover reunited with him in the form of a huge granite "floating rock." She later transformed herself under the main hall, her head beneath the gilded-clay Buddha and her tail 18 meters (60ft) away under a stone lantern so she could help protect Uisang's temple. That same "floating rock" still hangs protectively and precariously outside Buseok-sa's main hall.

Despite the floating rock protectors, the temple was burned down by invaders in the early 14th century, and then reconstructed in 1376. Fortunately, it was just beyond Hideyoshi's destruc-

tive reach in the 1590s, so the famed Muryangsujeon (Eternal Life Hall) main hall has been preserved to this day. This hall is considered to be the oldest and most classical wooden structure in all of South Korea. Its Goryeo style is said to have been influenced by Greek artisans through India, and this structural theory is evidenced by the hall's main support pillars that gradually taper off at the ends.

Predating the temple by at least 50 years and complementing its Goryeo architecture is a 2.7-meter (9ft) gilded clay statue of a sitting Buddha, the only one of its kind in South Korea.

Also, Buseok-sa's Goryeo interior paintings of Buddha and the Four Kings are considered to be the oldest wall paintings in Korea outside ancient tomb art.

THE EAST COAST

The east coast of Gyeongsangbuk-do is known for two things: beaches and crabs. Beaches are scattered along the coast from Pohang north to the border. Most of them have fine white sands which, except for weekends, remain surprisingly free of crowds. Granted, these beaches don't qualify as undiscovered tropical paradises, but they do offer a chance for sunbathing, some beachcombing (glass floats from Japanese fishing boats sometimes wash ashore), and an occasional dip in the chilly waters of the East Sea. You're likely to see a busload of older Koreans, who are out for a day of sightseeing, stop to have lunch. After that, they'll crank up the radio for some impromptu dancing and singing, while a few of them will head off for a walk along the beach in their Sunday best.

Most visitors combine a trip to the beach with some fresh seafood. Raw seafood restaurants (usually referred to as *hoetjip*) are very popular with Koreans, and South Korea's best seafood is found on the east coast. Just south of the city of Yeongdeok is the fishing village of **Ganggu** ⑩, which becomes jammed with visitors on weekends. You can buy fresh crab, have it steamed and then sit at a sidewalk table, perhaps with a beer or soju accompaniment, and enjoy a Neptunian feast while watching all the action around

TIP

Taxis are relatively inexpensive even if rented by the day. Bargaining with a driver for a deal on 8 hours may save you lots of slow bus rides for the out-of-the-way destinations. Air conditioning is also a plus in summer when the humidity can reach 90 percent.

BELOW: traditional wooden houses at Hahoe Folk Village.

Industrial Pohang.

BELOW: the rocky
islet where King
Munmu is buried.

you. Koreans eat everything but the crab "lungs"; they swear that the most delicious parts of the crab are wasted by Westerners. In late summer the streets are lined with squid hung out to dry, another specialty of the coast.

Pohang, steel city

At the southern end of Gyeongsangbuk-do's coastline is **Pohang** ⓫, a seaport and resort area that since 1968 has been the jewel in South Korea's industrial crown. This is because Pohang is the location of the model Pohang Iron and Steel Company Ltd (POSCO), Korea's successful producer of industrial steel and its profitable by-products.

Situated on the rim of **Yeongil Bay** and the East Sea, POSCO is one of the world's biggest steel producers. Pohang itself is not just dominated by POSCO. It *is* POSCO. Just as **Ulsan** is "Hyundai Town" where every major firm is part of the Hyundai group, so Pohang appears a one-company town. Schools, gymnasia, and housing complexes are all part of POSCO.

Pohang is friendly, and people helpful, even if they don't speak a word

of English, but not everyone wants to head out of their way for a town that is essentially an ironworks. Those heading for Ulleung-do will want to hop on the ferry without further ado.

South of Pohang, but more easily reached from Gyeongju, is the **underwater tomb of King Munmu** (*see panel, below*).

Bogyeong-sa

In the foothills of Naeyeonsan, about 15km (9 miles) north of Pohang, is **Bogyeong-sa** ⓬ (daily 6am–6pm; charge), a temple that offers a long history and a hike to a nearby waterfall.

A Western-style *yeogwan* down the road to the right is an excellent spot to stay overnight. It offers a picturesque view of the mountains and is within drumbeat range of the Buddhist temple. If you can sleep with one ear alert for the early-morning drum-call to prayer, wait outside for the sight of a sunrise and birds leaving their nocturnal perches. The only human sounds you'll hear will be your own stirring and distant sutras being chanted by monks celebrating all life on earth.

An Underwater Tomb

The Koreans have always worried – understandably – about invasion from their neighbors to the East, so much so that when King Munmu died, he requested that his body be buried underwater and promised to return as a dragon and protect Korea from the Japanese. His son complied and buried him by a tiny island near the Gyeongju shoreline. (Take a bus from Gyeongju to Bonggil-ri, look out to sea and you can't miss the little rocky islet.) A nearby temple and pavilion offer the dragon deity a resting spot and a private subterranean entrance from the water. Whether the king returned as a dragon is debatable: history shows the Japanese invaded Korea many times. Today, the site draws beachgoers in summer and tourists year round, who walk the shore and often stop in for fish at the local restaurants.

Once sleep is washed from your eyes, stroll over to Bogyeong Temple. Just before reaching the temple proper, you will see a walled-in hermitage. Next to it is Bogyeong-sa where monks hold retreats for lay Buddhists.

According to the sign posted at Bogyeong-sa, this temple was built during the Silla dynasty when Buddhism was first introduced to Korea. At that time, priests Madeung and Beomnan returned from China with the new religion and two mirrors. One mirror had 12 facets and the other had eight. The eight-faceted mirror was given to Priest Iljo, one of their disciples, who was told that if he went eastward he would find a deep pond in **Jongnamsan** on the east coast of the Silla kingdom. If he threw the mirror into the water and filled the pond with earth and built a temple there, Buddhism would flourish.

The eight-faceted mirror is said to be buried under Bogyeong-sa's **Jeongwangjeon Hall**. Fine Buddhist paintings are hung in Jeongwangjeon and Daeungjeon, but what distinguishes this temple from most others is its backdrop of waterfalls streaking the mountains that form this lush valley. An easy hiking trail beside the temple leads to a clear pool, and further to 11 other waterfalls where you can enjoy a cool summer splash.

ULLEUNG-DO

Few foreigners venture out to this remote island, situated 268km (166 miles) northeast of Pohang, about halfway between Korea and Japan. Indeed, because of its location **Ulleung-do** ⓭ is one of South Korea's best-kept secrets, although this is changing as it is being promoted as a tourist destination by the government. It is an easy place to promote: a stunningly beautiful, verdant Eden, a perfect place to get away from it all. The island, which is the remains of an extinct volcano, rises precipitously out of the East Sea to the summit of Seonginbong at 984 meters (3,228ft), with wild forests and dramatic sea cliffs towering over rocky beaches with superb snorkeling and scuba diving (but dangerous currents) in the clear waters.

Ulleung-do was settled during the Silla dynasty, before becoming depopulated around 1400. After centu-

The Ulleung-do ferry.

BELOW: view of Ulleung-do.

TIP

Ulleung-do ferries can be delayed or canceled without notice as sea conditions change quickly. You are advised to check ferry shedules prior to your trip. Pohang, tel: (054) 242-5111; Mukho, tel: (033) 531-5891.

ries of obscurity when the island was the haunt of pirates, settlers returned in the 1880s. These days the population of 9,600 makes its living from fishing and, increasingly, from tourism. Until the late 1970s there were no roads on the island. Now the round-island road is almost complete (still very rough in spots) and, of course, there are cars and trucks. However, the air is still sea-fresh and the stars still shine brightly in the clear night skies.

Dodong and the mineral springs

Embark on a speedboat ferry in Pohang, and three hours later you'll be strolling into Dodong town on Ulleung-do's southeast coast (you can also take a ferry from Mukho, in Gangwon Province). There are many *yeogwan* in town, almost all of them without locks on the doors – attesting to Ulleung-do's reputation for being theft-free. Clapboard walls without windowpanes flimsily divide the outside from the indoors during the warm season. A few of the *yeogwan* fronting Dodong Harbor have rooftop decks where you can sip a beer at sunset and watch fishermen dock their boats. Squid are fished here in large numbers, and the squid boats with their rows and rows of lanterns and the racks of drying squid are quite a sight, very picturesque and quaintly rural, a part of island life that hasn't changed much over the centuries.

Behind the town and up a path towards the rugged mountains is **Dodong Yaksu** mineral spring park (open 24 hours; free), with a mineral water fountain that spews from a stone-carved turtle's mouth set in the mountainside. Visitors often like to splash a bit of Johnnie Walker "on the rocks" and mix it with the fresh mineral water. This water is very soft (as you'll find out when you bathe), and is also pure enough to drink straight from water pumps. Close to the spring is the **Dokdo Museum** (daily 9am–6pm; free), showcasing the history and culture of the island. A cable car leads to the summit of Manghyangbong (315 meters/1,033ft), while further up the valley is the attractively located temple of Daewon-sa.

BELOW: remote Ulleung-do is one of the most beautiful places in South Korea.

Sights around the island

Just up the coast from Dodong, **Jeo-dong** is the island's main fishing port. From here you can take a boat across to **Juk-do**, a flat-topped islet jutting out across the water to the northeast. Approach this island from the south side, then scale its steep hill side. The hike up the steps to the top may seem arduous, but the men on this island actually carry calves on their backs all the way up to this island's highland farm. The fattened, corn-fed cattle are then lifted off the island by rope onto barges and sent to Ulleung-do for beef. This Juk-do beef is renowned as the tastiest and tenderest in South Korea.

Four families who live on this small island mountaintop also grow watermelon (which some say is the sweetest in South Korea). The young, thin bamboo growing here is used for stretching out and drying squid.

Large mulberry leaves are grown here, too, for silkworm production on the mainland. Indeed, though the island is small, there is even room for a camellia forest which blooms in February. Next to the camellia forest are paulownia trees – the only tree, according to mythology, on which a phoenix will land.

About 3km (2 miles) inland from Jeodong is Ulleung-do's most famous waterfall. The 25-meter (80ft) **Bongnae** falls are truly impressive, and a pleasantly cool spot in the humid summer months to take a break, although the clumsy concrete viewing tower tends to spoil the effect.

All along Ulleung-do's coast, steep mountainsides drop straight down to a sea which is a most unusual, clear shade of blue – like liquid blue laundry bleach. Off the northeast coast is a sea grotto of unique, craggy candlestick rock formations with nesting sea birds. The northernmost rock, Gongam, has a hole through which you can take a boat.

The road from Dodong to the small settlement of **Namyangri** on the southern coast makes for a spectacular drive. Keep going to reach **Taehari**, the west-coast landing site of the first Koreans to migrate to the island over 1,000 years ago. Nearby is **Sataegam**

Traditional Ulleung-do dwelling.

BELOW: spectacular scenery on the north coast of Ulleung-do.

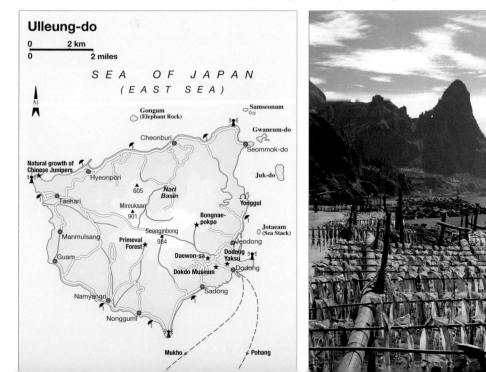

Ulleung-do

0   2 km
0   2 miles

N

SEA OF JAPAN (EAST SEA)

Gongam (Elephant Rock)
Samseonam
Cheonburi
Gwaneum-do
Seommok-do
Natural growth of Chinese Junipers
Hyeonpori
Juk-do
605
Nari Basin
Taehari
Mireuksan 901
Yonggul
Bongnae-pokpo
Seonginbong 984
Jotaeam (Sea Stack)
Manmulsang
Primeval Forest
Jeodong
Guam
Daewon-sa
Dodong Yaksu
Dokdo Museum
Dodong
Namyangri
Sadong
Nonggumi
Mukho
Pohang

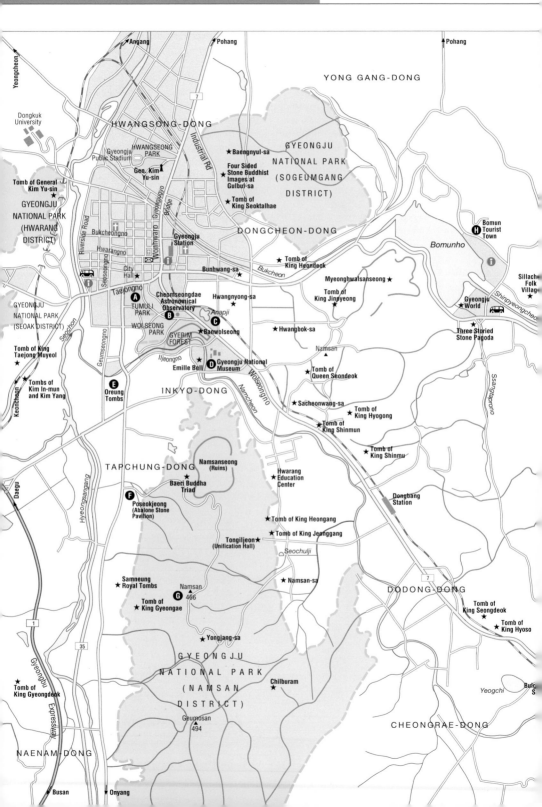

Yeongcheon

Angang

Pohang

Pohang

YONG GANG-DONG

Dongkuk University

HWANGSONG-DONG

Gyeongju Public Stadium

HWANGSEONG PARK

Gen. Kim Yu-sin

Baengnyul-sa

Four Sided Stone Buddhist Images at Gulbul-sa

GYEONGJU NATIONAL PARK (SOGEUMGANG DISTRICT)

Tomb of General Kim Yu-sin

GYEONGJU NATIONAL PARK (HWARANG DISTRICT)

Tomb of King Seoktalhae

DONGCHEON-DONG

Bomun Tourist Town

H

Bomunho

Bukcheongno

Gyeongju Station

Hwangnamno

Sillach Folk Village

Tomb of King Heondeok

Bukcheon

City Hall

Taejongno

Bunhwang-sa

Myeonghwalsanseong

Shinpyeongcheo

A

Cheomseongdae Astronomical Observatory

TUMULI PARK

B

Hwangnyong-sa

Anapji

WOLSEONG PARK

GYERIM FOREST

Banwolseong

Tomb of King Jinpyeong

Hwangbok-sa

Gyeongju World

GYEONGJU NATIONAL PARK (SEOAK DISTRICT)

Seocheon

Tomb of King Taejong Muyeol

Ijeongno

Three Storied Stone Pagoda

Emille Bell

D

Gyeongju National Museum

Namsan

Tomb of Queen Seondeok

E

Oreung Tombs

INKYO-DONG

Wolseongno

Namcheon

Sacheonwang-sa

Tombs of Kim In-mun and Kim Yang

Tomb of King Hyogong

Keoncheon

Tomb of King Shinmun

Tomb of King Shinmu

Daegu

Hyeongsangang

TAPCHUNG-DONG

Namsanseong (Ruins)

Hwarang Education Center

Dongbang Station

Baeri Buddha Triad

F

Poseokjeong (Abalone Stone Pavilion)

Tomb of King Heongang

Tomb of King Jeonggang

Tongiljeon (Unification Hall)

Seochulji

Samneung Royal Tombs

Namsan

G

466

DODONG-DONG

Namsan-sa

Tomb of King Seongdeok

Tomb of King Gyeongae

Tomb of King Hyoso

Gyeongju Expressway

1

35

Yongjang-sa

GYEONGJU NATIONAL PARK (NAMSAN DISTRICT)

Chilburam

Yeogchi

Bulg S

Tomb of King Gyeongdeok

Geumosan 494

CHEONGRAE-DONG

NAENAM-DONG

Busan

Onyang

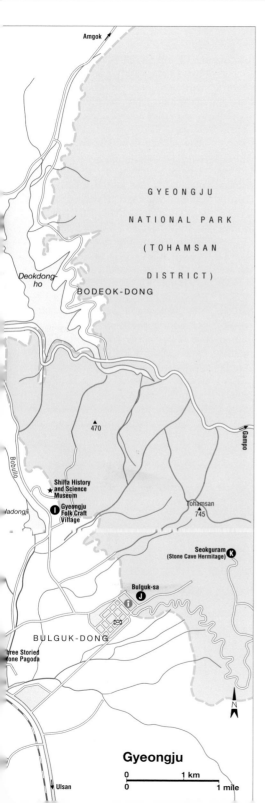

Gyeongju

0   1 km

0   1 mile

Beach, a cove with warm, calm waters that are ideal for safe swimming. On the headland to the north is a fine stand of Chinese juniper trees.

To get a memorable 360-degree view of Ulleung-do, hike up Seonginbong, the island's highest peak. Set off from Dodong at daybreak (take the path past the Mineral Park) and you'll be resting high among the clouds by mid-morning and back down just when the sun's heat turns oppressive. To circle the island, you can either hike 40km (25 miles) across valleys and along the coast (which takes three days), or take a boat trip (two hours). Either way, you'll find coves with bat caves (in Korean, *bakjwigul*) and sun-toasted beaches with cool, clear water.

GYEONGJU

It's the massive burial mounds, brown and dusted by frost in the winter, and carpeted with a dark-green nap in the summer, which punctuate any visit to **Gyeongju** ⓮. Rising here and there in populated and rural areas, they dominate all other physical realities in this riverine valley between Daegu and Busan. The mounds, memorial tombs or *neung* in Korean, represent the glory that was Silla, and the wonders contained within are now waiting to be unearthed. The area around the city is also full of interest – secluded temples, including famous Bulguk-sa, abound in the wooded hills of Namsan and Tohamsan.

Opulent shaman kings

Gyeongju was well known to Asia's ancients as Geumseong, the home of powerful and opulent shaman kings. Today, it's an easy-going resort town where rice cultivation and tourism are more important than wars of conquest. Its distinction as a one-time seat of power, however, cannot ever be forgotten. This 214-sq-km (83-sq-mile) valley is dotted with burial tombs – most from the 1st to 8th centuries but some more recent – and tired pagodas, fortress ruins, granite sculptures, palace grounds, and other remnants of the rich Three Kingdoms Period.

Gyeongju is one of the three most popular destinations in South Korea (the other two being Seoul and Jeju-do), and Koreans have an immense pride in Gyeongju and the Silla Kingdom that was able to unite the peninsula for the first time. Like the corresponding Tang Dynasty in neighboring China, the Silla period is considered the epitome of Korean art and culture. In the early Silla period, the dominant belief

The entrance to Cheonmacheong, the "Heavenly" or "Flying Horse" tomb.

BELOW: the Tumuli Park moundscape.

system was based on shamanism, that magical world inhabited by benevolent mountain spirits and malevolent demons. The huge tombs of Gyeongju and other areas on the Korean peninsula date from this period, as do magnificent golden crowns decorated with amulets. Eventually Buddhism was accepted by the royal families and spread rapidly throughout the kingdom. The religious fervor sparked by this new religion resulted in a flowering of the arts that remains unsurpassed. Much of the art was religious in nature, pagodas, statues, and magnificent temple compounds, all in praise of the Buddha.

Artifacts remaining from Silla are only a fraction of what was produced. When rebels overran Gyeongju, a wagon train several kilometers long hauled out the city's treasures. Later, in 1592, the Japanese invaded and completed the looting of Korea. What remains are those items too large to haul off, or those that were buried in tombs, lakes, and such. Nevertheless, they are impressive and prove that Gyeongju was the cradle of Korea's Golden Age.

The Silla tombs

There are several routes you can take to see Gyeongju's sites, but since **Tumuli Park Ⓐ** (park daily 9am–9pm, museum daily 9am–6pm, Nov–Feb 9am–5pm; charge) sits near the middle of the historic part of the city, it's a good place to start. This is a unique 15-hectare (37-acre) "tomb park" on the southeast side of Gyeongju with some 20 tombs of varying sizes that were originally heaped into place as early as the mid-1st century. Until 30 years ago, this restored, beautifully landscaped and lamplit complex of mounded graves was just another ordinary neighborhood in Gyeongju. When private individuals and government archeological teams began to find literally thousands of important items here, however, the area was quickly cleared of houses and was designated as a national museum and site of major historical significance. The restoration of Tumuli Park began in 1973, and the complex was officially dedicated and opened to the public in 1975.

The largest of the tombs, that of King Michu (r. 262–85), has been identified in ancient chronicles as the

"Great Tomb." However, a secondary tomb (No. 155), the so-called Cheon-machong, or "Heavenly Tomb" or "Flying Horse Tomb," is probably the best-known gravesite here. This tomb, about 50 meters (164ft) in diameter and 12.7 meters (42ft) high, was excavated in 1973, and in its collapsed wood and stone burial chambers were found numerous important treasures *(see inset, left)*.

Cheomsongdae: an ancient observatory

Across from Tumuli Park is **Cheom-seongdae ❸** (daily, Mar–Oct 8am–10pm, Nov–Feb 9am–9pm; charge). This astronomical observatory tower, one of the oldest structures in South Korea, was built during the reign of Queen Seondeok (reigned 632–47), Silla's 27th ruler.

Astronomers question just how the tower was used, but they point with interest at the following coincidences: 365 stones, the number of days in a calendar year, were used in its construction; and there are 12 rectangular base-stones, plus 12 separate levels of stones above and below a central window. Could this constructional recurrence of the number 12 imply the zodiac, or the number of months in a year? This telescope-shaped tower probably served several generations of Silla geomancers who attempted to foretell astrological fates in this historic region.

Across the road is an old hardwood forest known as the **Gyerim (Chicken) Forest**. This is the legendary birthplace of the first Kim (the most popular of the Korean family names). Legend says that a white cockerel was heard crowing under a golden box hanging from a tree branch within the forest. The king was summoned, and when he opened the box he found a beautiful infant boy. The king adopted the child and gave him the surname of Kim. This popular picnicking spot has been known as the chicken forest ever since.

Head north for a short distance to **Anapji Pond ❹** (daily, Mar–Oct 8am–10pm, Nov–Feb 9am–10pm; charge) where Silla kings and queens spent their leisure moments relaxing, writing poetry, playing games, and entertaining visiting dignitaries. This was said to have been the grandest garden in the Orient, with trees and plants brought in from throughout Asia. It lay in ruins for centuries, until 1975, when a team of archeologists began working at the site. To their surprise, hundreds of dishes, tiles, religious artifacts, and even a boat were found at the bottom of the silted pond. These items, which were discarded or accidentally dropped by royal revelers, can now be seen at the Gyeongju National Museum. Today, the pond is back, along with reproductions of three pavilions that once stood at the water's edge. While Anapji may never regain the glory of its Silla days, it remains a pleasant place to take a leisurely break while touring Gyeongju.

Gyeongju National Museum

Gyeongju is often called "Korea's Open-air Museum." The phrase is apt, because

BELOW: contemporary neo-Sillan dancers at a tourist revue.

Moss-covered Buddha image on the slopes of Namsan.

RIGHT: Hwarang Education Center.

so many of the city's treasures are outdoors where they can be seen, touched, and experienced. Yet in the **Gyeongju National Museum** Ⓓ (Tue–Sun 9am–6pm, Sat until 7pm; charge), you can see some of the finest of more than 80,000 items unearthed during recent and old-time digs in this area: metal work, paintings, earthenware, calligraphic scrolls, folk art objects, weapons, porcelains, carved jades, and gold, granite, and bronze sculptures wrought in various shamanist, Buddhist, Taoist, and Confucian motifs. Only about 10 minutes by bicycle from Anapji Pond, a visit to this world-class museum will put your tour of Gyeongju's other historic sites into perspective.

Among the museum's important pieces is the huge bronze Emille (pronounced "Em-ee-leh") Bell, The Divine Bell for the Great King Seongdeok, which is one of the world's oldest, having been cast in AD 771. It is also one of the largest, weighing 20 tonnes and measuring 3 meters (10ft) in height and 2.3 meters (7½ft) in diameter. This Buddhist bell, which originally hung

in a pavilion at nearby Bongdeok-sa Temple, is embellished with four relief devas who kneel facing each other on lotus blossom cushions. It is said that the bell's sonorous tones can be heard 64km (40 miles) away on a clear day. The bell's name, it has been written, comes from an ancient Silla term that literally means "mommy." The bell was given this name because its sound resembles the voice of a lost child crying for its mother. *For more on Gyeongju's artefacts, see pages 232–3.*

South to Namsan

The **Oreung Tombs** Ⓔ (Five Royal Tombs; daily 9am–6pm, Nov–Feb until 5pm; charge) are in a beautiful, tree-covered park setting. It is believed that these are the tombs of the first Silla king and queen, as well as the second, third, and fifth kings of Silla. While not as dramatic as Tumuli Park, this shady little corner of Gyeongju provides a welcome retreat on hot summer days.

A little further out of town on the western edge of Namsan is **Poseokjeong** Ⓕ (The Abalone Stone Pavilion; daily 9am–6pm, until 5pm

Hwarang Education Center

On the rolling, forested eastern slope of Namsan is a cluster of traditional Korean buildings housing the Hwarang Education Center. These buildings were built in 1973, but during the Silla Dynasty the best and brightest young men of the kingdom underwent mental and physical training among these same hills.

The early Hwarang (Flower Youth) have a mystique surrounding them that is analogous to knighthood in medieval Europe. The Hwarang were teenage sons from the aristocracy who were trained by Buddhist monks in the art of warfare, philosophy, history, and even dance.

Many of Silla's prominent rulers, scholars, and monks received training with the Hwarang. The five tenets that these "Flower Youth" lived by are a blend of Buddhist and Confucian thought: (1) to serve the king with loyalty, (2) to serve one's parents with filiality, (3) to practice fidelity in friendship, (4) to never retreat in battle, and (5) to refrain from wanton killing. The thought of young teenagers undergoing rigorous training and performing heroics in battle has considerable appeal for modern-day Korean youths. Stories of the Hwarang are frequently featured in television sitcoms and novels.

Perhaps the Hwarang Education Center will again produce leaders like those that once roamed the foothills of Namsan.

Nov–Feb; charge). This site received its name from the shape of a curving, stone-rimmed ditch cut in the ground next to a pleasure pavilion used by Hycongang, the 49th Silla king. This winding ditch was a large board game of sorts that involved the drinking of wine and the impromptu composition of poetry. Nearby stream water was channeled in, on which cups of wine were set afloat. A guest was challenged to compose a proper poem before his cup made a floating round of the channel. If he didn't compose a satisfactory poem, he had to drink his entire bowlful of wine and try again. According to ancient chronicles, it was great royal parlor fun. It is said that the last Silla king was indulging his pleasures at Poseokjong when the city was overrun by rebels.

Namsan

Namsan G (South Mountain) is a veritable cornucopia of history. During the Silla Dynasty, this was a sacred mountain. The sites of over 100 temples have been found on and around the mountain, and there are still a few

active ones. In addition, there are some 60 religious images carved from the mountain's granite, and 40 pagodas lying alongside the mountain trails, as well as a fair share of royal tombs along its base. It would take several days to explore all the trails and sites of this unusual mountain, but if you have only a few hours you might try hiking the trail that begins at Namsan Village and goes to the top. There, perhaps after an hour of huffing and puffing, you'll find amazing Buddhas and attendant bodhisattvas etched into sheer granite boulders and cliffs. All look east, like the Seokguram Buddha, towards the rising sun.

East of Namsan

On the east side of Namsan is **Bomun Tourist Town H** (20 minutes from Gyeongju by bus, taxi, or hotel shuttle). Alongside this attractive lake are Gyeongju's deluxe and mid-range hotels (inexpensive *yeogwan* are found in the city). The setting is pleasant enough, with a brick path alongside the lake, an 18-hole golf course (expensive), marina and clubhouse, and a

TIP

Many of the ancient sites are close to the city, and the best way to reach them is by bicycle which can be rented from sidewalk traders. Regular bus services can get you to outlying areas.

LEFT: a woodland trail on Namsan. **BELOW:** pagodas and other sacred Silla buildings are scattered around the higher reaches of Namsan.

TIP

Gyeongju is one place where it helps tremendously to have an English-speaking guide. Mr Kwon at Han Jin Hostel (tel: 010-9775-4097) offers guide services at reasonable rates, and can tailor your trip to include as much or as little as you care to see.

lake-side amusement park (tacky), but the attractions are geared more to Koreans on holiday. You'll probably want to spend most of your daylight hours visiting the historic sites or hiking the trails of Namsan. The town plays host to two annual festivals. At the end of March there is the Korean Traditional Drink and Cake Festival. Then, in every third year (the next is in 2012) in early fall, there is the Gyeongju World Culture Expo, featuring performing groups from South Korea and other countries.

Down the road from Bomun Tourist Town is the **Gyeongju Folk Craft Village ❶** (daily 9am–6.30pm, Nov–Feb until 5pm). There is a large building selling crafts made by local potters, wood carvers, and other local artisans, who live and work in the small village directly behind. Those who take the time to walk through the village can often observe artisans at work. Much of their work reproduces designs and pieces from the Silla period, an indication of the influence this culture still exerts on the Korean peninsula a millennium after its demise.

Bulguk-sa

Still furthur down the road (30 minutes by bus from Gyeongju Station) lies **Bulguk-sa ❶** (daily 7am–6pm, Nov–Mar until 5pm; charge). This sprawling temple complex about 16km (10 miles) due south of Gyeongju on the western slopes of Tohamsan is one of the oldest surviving Buddhist monasteries in Korea. First built during the reign of Silla King Beopheung (r. 514–40), Bulguk-sa, "Temple of the Buddha-land," is also Korea's most famous temple. Its renown comes not from its age or size but probably because it stands, flawlessly restored, as a splendid example of Silla-era architecture in a spectacular hillside setting lush with manicured stands of pine, plum, peach, pear, cherry, and cryptomeria trees. It also enshrines some of the country's and Korean Buddhism's most important national treasures. The historical significance of Bulguk-sa and the nearby Seokguram were recognized when they were listed as Unesco World Heritage Sites in 1995.

Wonderfully stone-crafted steps and bridges carry the visitor on an uphill

BELOW LEFT & RIGHT: Bulguk-sa is a repository for some of the country's most important treasures.

stroll to the broad granite block terraces on which this pristine temple compound stands. Almost all of the hand-painted wood structures on these terraces are of recent Joseon-dynasty construction, but most of the stone structures – large granite blocks fitted together without mortar – are original. The architect credited for this stone masterwork, Kim Dae-seong, also supervised the construction of the nearby Seokguram Grotto, an annex to Bulguk-sa and one of Buddhism's most-celebrated shrines. Architect Kim honed his design and structural skills during the reign of King Gyeongdeok, the 35th Silla king (reigned 742–65), when Bulguk-sa underwent several major modifications and restorations.

Two double-tiered stone staircases – the Seokgyemun – used to lead pilgrims and tourists up to Bulguk-sa proper. The larger, 33-stepped staircase to the right has been given two names, one for its lower flight (called Cheongungyo, the Blue Cloud Bridge), and the other for its upper flight (Baegungyo, the White Cloud Bridge). The Blue Cloud and White Cloud bridges terminate at an entrance gate called Jahamun, while the Lotus Flower and Seven-Treasure bridges climb up to a secondary entrance gate known as Anyangmum. Both are grand entryways, but these days tourists and devotees alike have to enter the temple via new stairways and gates on the left and right sides of the temple.

Premier pagodas

Pass through the small Jongnu entry pavilion to arrive at Bulguk-sa's main worship hall, Daeungjeon. This is an expansive courtyard dominated by two unusual and impressive multi-tiered Silla pagodas.

The smaller of the two pagodas, called **Seokgatap**, is 8.2 meters (27ft) high and the larger **Dabotap** is 10.4 meters (34ft) high. While Dabotap was built by Kim Daesong for his parents, legend has it that Seokgatap was built by Asadal, an esteemed artisan who came to Silla from Baekje.

Both stone pagodas (which have been restored in recent years) are considered premier examples of such Silla

Colorful guardian deity at Bulguk-sa; the temple complex is famous for the quality of its paintwork.

BELOW: with its verdant setting, Bulguk-sa is possibly South Korea's most spectacular temple.

The city of Gyeongju is quite unlike other urban areas in South Korean. Legislation passed in the 1980s has ensured that the streets retain their traditional appearance – no high-rise buildings are permitted in the city centre, and traditional hanok housing is much in evidence.

pagoda construction. Inside a niche on the left side of the Dabotap you'll spot a small growling lion sitting on a neat lotus pedestal. He's Dabotap's (the Many-Treasured Buddha's) guardian.

The smaller pagoda, Seokgatap, is not quite as quaint, but many relics of great historical and artistic value were found inside this pagoda in 1966. According to a government survey: "The relics included a *sarira* box containing gold images of Buddha and a scroll of Dharari sutras, the oldest Buddhist literature of its kind remaining in the world today.

The inscriptions engraved on the cover of the relic box say that in AD 706 King Seongdeok placed within the pagoda four *sarira* (remains of Buddha or high priests), a gold Amita figure, and a volume of sutras in memory of three deceased royal family members: King Sinmun, Queen Mother Simok, and King Hyoso."

More Bulguk-sa highlights

Other Bulguk-sa sights deserving meditative attention are the nine-pillared Museoljeon hall, the compound's oldest, largest structure; the Birojeon, which houses a Birojana Buddha found clutching his right forefinger in an overtly sexual Diamond First mudra position; and Gwaneumjeon, a hall which is home to a 10th-century wooden image of Gwanseum-bosal, the popular Bodhisattva of Mercy known to Chinese Buddhists as Kwan Yin. Most of the halls are painted in the flamboyant colors typical of Joseon dynasty buildings.

Seokguram, temple in a grotto

Seokguram Ⓚ (daily 7am–7.30pm Feb, Mar and Oct, Nov–Jan until 5pm, Apr–Sept 6.30am–6pm; charge), the Stone Cave Hermitage, is located several winding kilometers northeast of Bulguk-sa proper, and has become a major pilgrimage site for practitioners and students of Buddhism and Buddhist art. Seokguram is a grotto temple, set among pines and maples, which enshrines a white granite Sakyamuni Buddha image considered by some to be the most perfect of its kind anywhere.

BELOW: Dabotap pagoda at Bulguk-sa.

Unlike grotto temples in other parts of Asia, Seokguram was not carved out of a granite hillside or built inside an existing cave. Rather it is an artificial chapel built of large granite blocks placed on a summit. After a pleasant hike through woods you ascend a flight of stairs and enter as classical a Buddhist shrine as you would ever expect to see in the Far East.

The base of the Seokguram structure consists of a square antechamber and a round interior chamber with a graceful dome-shaped ceiling. As you enter the chapel you will first pass stone images of the Eight Generals, each representative of one of the Eight Classes of Beings. Next are the Four Deva Kings, Guardians of the Four Quarters. A pair of these directional deities cavorts on either side of the main passageway. Framed in the radiant aura of haloes, they are also depicted stomping on little demons.

Inside the main chamber is Sakyamuni, sitting in repose on a lotus dais. At his forehead is a typical protuberance, and atop his head are neatly cropped spirals of curly hair. Facing the grotto's entrance and the East Sea, the Buddha Sakyamuni sits with his right palm downward over his right leg. This is the *mudra* position referred to as "Calling of the Earth to Witness." The left palm faces up in a meditation pose. While the individual sculptures may be matched by some of those in the cave temples of China, the chapel as a whole is unequaled in the art of the Far East.

Tombs and treasures

Also high on the Gyeongju must-see list is the impressive tomb of General Kim Yu-sin, which is rimmed by carved stone zodiac figures, and the Bunhwang-sa Temple with the oldest datable pagoda in Korea.

Still craving Silla-era Buddha images? Then head for the Tap Valley on the eastern slopes of Namsan, the Buddha Valley just north of Tap Valley, the Guksa Valley east of Namsan, or the more remote Seonbang Valley. This litany of treasures grows longer and genuinely more awesome with every passing lunar year and every new discovery in Gyeongju. ❑

Seokguram grotto has an attractive woodland setting.

LEFT: festival lanterns at Dabotap pagoda.
BELOW: the Sakyamuni Buddha at Seokguram grotto.

GYEONGJU TREASURES

The rolling hills of Gyeongju are rich in ruins, with ancient burial sites giving up many fascinating relics, from jeweled headdresses to jade carvings, weapons, and gemstones

Gyeongju's Gems

Gyeongju's nickname is "The Museum without Walls" due to the abundance of ruins and remains that pepper the area. You can't walk through this town without being confronted with reminders of Silla-era majesty. But to really appreciate the riches of this astounding part of Korea's past, you need to go inside to some of the museums that display what's been found over the centuries.

Tumuli Tombs: Buried Beauty

The Tumuli tombs today are impossible to miss. These picturesque rolling hills are an icon of Gyeongju, but that wasn't always the case. A clutter of houses, shops, and stores once littered these ancient tombs, and even today there is heated controversy over how much of the current buildings are to be cleared and the area beneath them excavated.

Construction of the tombs was relatively simple: a mound of earth piled over a chamber made of stone. Much of the history of these burial sites was forgotten, so the stunning treasures contained inside these mounds were electrifying reminders of this are'as splendid past. Jeweled headdresses, sword handles, spectacular carvings of jade and gemstones, and sculptures thought to aid the royalty as they ascended into the afterlife were only some of what was found. Much like Maya and Inca cultures, Silla peoples also made sure their royalty went to heaven well prepared to be as successful in the next life as they were in their earthly one.

LEFT: fine green-glazed celadon ceramics, dating from the late 11th century, used by the Silla aristocracy.

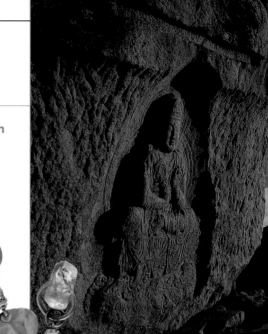

ABOVE: the Sinseonam Buddha is carved into the rock to face the rising sun. Namsan mountain, just to the south of Gyeongju, is riddled with Buddhist carvings and temple ruins.

ABOVE LEFT: golden earrings from the 5th century.

ABOVE: this Silla crown would have originally been encrusted with precious stones.

ANAPJI POND: SUBMERGED TREASURES

Though constructed by King Munmu during his Silla reign and used for years by Korean royalty, Anapji Pond was essentially an abandoned mudflat until 1974, when it was dredged with the intention of restoring it to some of its original glory. Even the archeologists' surprise, the mud contained numerous artifacts, many of them in excellent condition, which had fallen in or been discarded centuries ago. So many items were found, in fact, that the Gyeongju National Museum created a special Anapji Collection, housed in its own area. Today the pond is a treasure in its own right, especially in June, when the dazzling lotus blooms and their umbrella-like leaves cover every inch of the water's surface.

ABOVE: the striking grassy mounds of Gyeongju's tumuli park.

BELOW: roof tiles from the Silla period are adorned wirh demon images.

LEFT: a pensive Bodhisattva, dating from the mid-7th century.

RIGHT: one of the guardian figures surrounding the tomb of General Kim Yusin.

GYEONGSANGNAM PROVINCE

Visitors are drawn to Gyeongsangnam's beaches, seascapes and historical sites, which chronicle the often volatile relationship with its neighbor across the East Sea

BELOW: folk performance in Busan.

The southeastern corner of the Korean peninsula is the closest part of the country to Japan, a fact which has placed it directly in the firing line of past invasions from its powerful neighbor. This legacy continues to influence the character of the region, although there is much else besides: the energetic port city of Busan, beautiful areas of coastline, and, in the rural north, the fascinating temple of Haein-sa.

In 1592, the Japanese warlord Hideyoshi dispatched 150,000 troops in an ambitious assault on the Chinese Empire. Korea had the misfortune of being in the way – and of being loyal to China. When the Korean government refused to grant Japan free access across its frontiers, the Japanese dispensed with courtly etiquette and proceeded to fight their way through. After six years of war, they finally retreated, failing to conquer China, but – despite the heroics of Admiral Yi – thoroughly devastated Korea. Thousands of Koreans were either killed or taken to Japan as slaves. Vast tracts of farmland had been razed, and much

Admiral Yi

In 1591, Korean Admiral Yi Sun-sin was appointed fleet commander for the eastern coast of Jeolla Province. A year later the Japanese invaded and in less than a month had overrun the country. Admiral Yi quickly became the bane of the Japanese navy, which disintegrated during a series of Korean victories, climaxing in a naval rout at Hansan-do. Later in the war, the Korean navy was turned over to a rival, Won Gyun. Under Won's command the navy was decimated. Yi was hastily pardoned and asked to resume command, but his navy now had only 12 ships. Exhibiting a blend of strategic genius and gall, he led his paltry fleet in an assault of 133 Japanese ships and won, marking the turning point of the war. But less than a year later, as the Japanese were attempting to retreat, Yi was killed by a stray bullet in the last battle of the war.

of Korea's great cultural legacy was destroyed or stolen. Over four centuries have passed since this tragedy, yet all along Korea's southern coast monuments and memorials remain to keep alive the Imjin War. The dominant theme in this region, despite more recent wars and wrenching transitions, is still the Japanese invasions.

Port city of Busan

The first south-coast city to fall during the Hideyoshi invasion of 1592 was **Busan ⑮**, wedged between a range of mountains and the sea. It was then, as it is now, Korea's most important port city, and these days has a population of almost 4 million. The city is a raucous mélange of masts, loading cranes, and buildings; honking cabs, train whistles, and the throbbing air horns of passing ferries are heard; suited businessmen, deck hands, navy cadets, and fishmongers mingle. Tiny punts propelled by a single sculling oar slip through the shadows of huffing tankers. Urban gentlemen in angler outfits toy with their delicate bamboo poles, waiting patiently for nibbling minnows, while

scruffy trawler crews unload the day's catch of squid and dog sharks. Dockside fish market matrons hawk abalone, brilliant orange sea apples, deep-sea clams, and fish of all sizes, shapes, and colors. In the fall, clementine oranges and persimmons add to the mix.

Near the main nightlife district is **Yongdusan Ⓐ**, a small park made conspicuous by the imposing Busan Tower dominating the city's skyline. The park has two statues; one is a kitsch representation of a dragon, the legendary king of the sea; the other is of the patron hero of the south coast: Admiral Yi Sun-sin.

Right on the Busan waterfront is the highly animated **Jagalchi Fish Market Ⓑ** (daily 4am–10pm, except the last Tuesday of the month and major holidays), a great place to wander around, with rows of fish sellers hawking their oceanic fare. Do as the Korean tourists do – buy some fresh fish (or octopus, squid, or sea cucumber) and take it to one of the nearby seafood restaurants where they'll prepare it for you (most Koreans prefer to eat their fresh fish as sashimi – ie raw) and add some side

BELOW: looking towards Yeong-do island from Busan Tower.

Fast trains connect Busan with Seoul.

dishes and drinks. A few blocks north of the fish market, and opposite Busan railway station, is **Texas Street** , sometimes called Russian Street or, in Korean, Choryang. This shopping district has clothing and accessory stores, as well as restaurants and nightspots that cater to foreigners. As its alternative name implies, a lot of Russian sailors call in at Busan's port and this section of town. But it's not just Russians who make this one of Busan's liveliest entertainment centers; like Itaewon in Seoul, Texas Street has an international following. A large underground shopping arcade runs parallel with the main drag for those who want to burrow deeper for a bargain.

Busan is known for its strong dialect which many linguists connect to its proximity with Japan, and a variety of foods that range from the delicious to the bizarre. Slime eel, a benthic creature fished off the shores of New England, is flash frozen and served here with barbecue sauce the way Americans would eat buffalo wings. *Milmyeon* noodles, cold and served with crisp cucumber, are popular with gourmands.

BELOW: Jagalchi Fish Market.

You'll find many Japanese tourists fly in for a weekend's fun from Fukuoka, Osaka, or Tokyo. It's encouraging to think that trade and commerce are building bridges these days, rather than creating animosity. Many taxi drivers are proud of their ability to speak Japanese and English, if only enough to facilitate your getting where you need to go. While Koreans in Seoul often speak down about Busan, it's a fascinating city and there's a lot to see, do, eat, and enjoy. Locals are fiercely proud of their part of the country, in particular of the fact that Busan was the only major city never to fall to Communist rule during the Korean War. To see and do it all, you'll need to budget at least a week here, but one can see a few sights and have a flavor of Busan in just a weekend.

Getting here is easy, too: the KTX high-speed train will whisk you from Seoul to Busan in about 3 hours.

Around Geumjeongsan

Admiral Yi's staunch patriotism and military skills prevented the Imjin War from becoming a total disaster for Korea. But for the Busan and Gyeong-

sangnam Province, it was a bona fide disaster. Korea simply was not prepared for the battle-hardened samurai who took less than a month to burn and pillage their way to Seoul. At **Dongnae Fortress** (where you can still see a small portion of the old wall), defenders were faced with an overwhelming invasion force, but managed to put up a valiant resistance. When the Japanese asked the Korean Governor to surrender, he responded by saying; "It is difficult to make way for your forces, but easy to fight and die."

While the Japanese overran the fortress, the commander calmly composed a last poem for his father. **Chungyeol-sa Shrine** ❶ (daily 9am–6pm, until 5pm Nov–Feb; charge) sits on the battle site, and is dedicated to the memory of those brave soldiers who found it easier to die than allow a foreign force to occupy their land. The shrine is near a busy intersection, and offers a quiet retreat from the hassles of the city. Locals sit with friends under trees in the Korean garden while children feed goldfish in the pond. The shrine's exhibition hall displays graphic paintings of the battle, along with period uniforms.

A short taxi ride to the west of Chungyeol-sa Shrine will take you to the base of Geumjeong Mountain, and **Dongnae Hot Spring** ❸, whose waters fill the baths of several dozen hotels and *yeogwan* (making this is a good place to get rooms at reasonable rates). A few of the larger hotels have public baths open to the general public. On **Geumjeongsan** ❻ are the remains of a mountain fortress, **Geumjeongsan-seong** (daily, 24 hours; charge), built during the Joseon Dynasty. Four kilometers (2½ miles) of the original 18km (11-mile) wall remain, as do two of its four original gates, surrounded by thick forests and unusual rock formations. A cable car (daily 9am–6.30pm) runs between **Geumgang Park** (near Dongnae) and the ridge at the top of the park. The mountain is a favorite with weekenders hiking its numerous trails.

At the north end of the mountain, not far from the north gate of the fortress, is the city's most important temple, **Beomeo-sa** ❼ (daily 8.30am–5.30pm;

Beomeo-sa is known for its three gates. Walking through the second gate, you will pass by the four temple guardians, which are the ferocious protectors of the temple. The third gate, the gate of Non-Duality, symbolically suggests that, even though you are passing from the secular world into the spiritual, the two are the same.

LEFT: statue of Admiral Yi in Busan. **BELOW:** at the Russian market.

Haegeumgang sea caves.

charge), headquarters of the Dyana sect. Legend says that there is a golden well nearby in which a golden fish from Nirvana lives; in its early years (it was built in AD 678) it was known as the temple where fish from Nirvana play. It was, of course, burnt to the ground during the Japanese invasion of 1592, but the main hall that was rebuilt in 1613 still stands. The courtyards of the temple are well landscaped in traditional Korean style with trees, stone lanterns, relics, and a pagoda dating back to the Silla dynasty. There are almost a dozen hermitages spread out in the mountains around the temple.

Local beaches

Ask any Korean what Busan is famous for, and they will probably tell you the beaches. There are several to choose from. For those willing to dare the murky water of Busan harbor, **Songdo Beach** ⓗ is just a stone's throw southwest of the downtown area. Even if you prudently abstain from swimming, it offers an interesting alternative to staying in town, as there are several inns and hotels with a uniquely Busan flavor.

Considerably cleaner waters are available at three sandy beaches to the east of the city. The most popular is **Haeundae** ❶, which has good hotels and a bustling resort town. At the southern end of the beach are cliffs overlooking a rocky beach below, with the white sand beach beyond. On one of the rocks below the cliff, the Little Mermaid (*à la* Copenhagen's famous sculpture) gazes longingly out to sea. South Koreans are becoming more Western in their beach attire, though the older generation still sticks to conservative attire. Korean girls, on the other hand, will religiously diet for months before a beach trip so as to look their best in a bikini. For a view that can't be beat, head to the hills north of Haeundae where you can dine while looking out over a spectacular nightscape of illuminated skyscrapers.

Immediately to the south of downtown Busan is the island of Yeong-do, built up to the north, but covered in thick forest towards the south. **Taejongdae Park** ❶, at the southern tip, features impressive cliffs and a lighthouse dating from the late 19th century. The view over the ocean is

tremendous, and on a clear day it is just possible to make out the Japanese island of Tsushima. On the coast to the west of Busan are Masan and Jinhae, the two urban ports of the area north of Geoje-do island. **Masan** is a gritty industrial city, struggling to catch up with its status as a Free Port. **Jinhae**, smaller and more spacious, is a naval station famous for the cherry trees that swathe the city with blossoms each spring.

ALONG THE SOUTH COAST

Geoje-do ⓰ is Korea's second-largest island (after Jeju) and one of the most beautiful areas of the country. Regular jetfoils run from Busan's Coastal Ferry Terminal to Jangseungpo on the northeastern side of the island. This is a good place to get the feel of a tiny Korean coastal town.

The southern coast of Geoje-do is particularly attractive, and is easily explored by driving along the coastal highway. One of the best-known beauty spots is **Haegeumgang**, a striking camellia-covered rock outcropping undercut with anemone-infested caves. An alternative way to see this beautiful coastline is to take a tourist excursion boat from Jangseungpo or Tongyeong. Much of the area lies within the Hallyeo Haesang Maritime National Park.

It is also possible to access Geoje-do by road, via the bridge from **Tongyeong ⓱** (also known as Chungmu), a pleasant town on the Goseong peninsula. Tongyeong's small dock is always busy with ferries returning from neighboring islands, small private fishing trawlers, tourist boats, and all manner of hired craft that take people out for an afternoon of fishing or skin-diving. The marketplace begins on the dock, where catches are sold directly from piers, and continues a considerable distance into town, where local specialties such as traditional horse-hair hats, reed baskets, and, of course, all kinds of fish are available. The restaurants in town serve the usual variety of seafood.

Clams, oysters, soft-shelled crabs, and unidentifiable mollusks are thrown into everything, to the delight of those who have an appetite for submarine curiosities and to the horror of those who don't. Tongyeong has plenty of inexpensive *yeogwan* and makes a good base from which to explore Geoje-do and the other islands in the vicinity.

Across the narrow channel from Tongyeong is the island of **Mireuk-do**, linked to the town by an unusual pedestrian tunnel built by the Japanese in 1932 and originally designed for vehicles. On the north slope of a mountain that dominates the island is **Yonghwa-sa**, a tiny temple with an unusual set of appropriately diminutive altar paintings. **Gwaneum Hermitage**, a short walk away, has a lawn instead of a courtyard, and a handsome stone gate; careful landscaping manages to convey a sense of serenity, despite the incongruity of stone lanterns wired with electric lightbulbs.

To the west of Geoje-do, between Tongyeong and Yeosu and forming the western part of the Hallyeo Haesang Maritime National Park, is the **Hallye-**

Tongyeong is noted for its craftsmen who make lacquerware furniture and jewelry with mother-of-pearl inlay. The most expensive piece of furniture in a Korean home is usually an elaborate wooden and lacquerware closet.

BELOW: the rock at Haegeumgang.

Namhae suspension bridge crosses the Noryangjin Strait.

osudo waterway, sheltered from the open sea by hundreds of islands that are the ancient peaks of an inundated mountain range. Submerged valleys have become countless secluded harbors, many of them now crowded with the vibrantly painted boats of fishermen and divers.

The attractively situated town of **Yeosu** can be reached by train, bus, and ferry from Busan, and shuttles run from here to the nearby islands of Namhae-do and Odong-do, both of historic and scenic interest. (Yeosu and Odong are in fact within Jeollanam Province, but for convenience are included in this chapter.) **Odong-do** is covered with camellia and bamboo and was where bamboo arrows were made for Admiral Yi's fighting men. **Namhae-do** is linked to the mainland by a suspension bridge across the strait of Noryangjin, where Yi was killed.

Jinju and the patriotic Ju Nongae

BELOW: view of Jinju on a perfect fall day.

Buses connect Namhae, Yeosu and Sacheon to the small city of **Jinju** ⓲, one of South Korea's most enchanting

and least-visited centers. The Nam River runs through the center of the city. In early morning mists, ghostly anglers squat along the shore with the patience of statues, and elderly gentlemen in traditional dress stroll along the winding walls of **Jinju Castle** (Jinjuseong; daily 9am–6pm; charge), bringing the distant past breathtakingly close. Even the perfectly mundane concrete traffic bridge that crosses the river takes on an air of timelessness.

Jinju Castle was attacked in one of the first battles of the Imjin War. After a heroic defense by the Korean army assisted by a civilian militia, the attack was repulsed, and a planned drive into Jeolla Province was thwarted. Less than a year later, the castle was the site of an equally heroic defeat after 10 days of fierce fighting. The Japanese celebrated their victory with a banquet in **Chokseongnu** (daily 9am–6pm), a spacious pavilion within the castle. One of the Korean women brought in to provide entertainment was Ju Nongae, a *gisaeng* hostess whose patron, a Korean military official, had lost his life in the battle for Jinju. During the banquet,

Nongae lured one of the Japanese generals to the edge of the cliff between the pavilion and the Nam River. There she threw her arms around his neck and dived into the river, dragging him down with her to a patriotic and much-celebrated suicide-assassination.

Nongae's selfless courage is commemorated now, over four centuries later, in a special ritual held in July or August (according to the lunar calendar) at a small shrine built in her honor, **Nongae Shrine** (daily 9am–6pm), above the rock from which she jumped.

The walls of Jinju Castle and Chokseongnu have been tastefully reconstructed and several shrines, temples, and pavilions are preserved within the castle grounds. The most imposing structure is Chokseongnu, which is raised on stone pillars to provide a view of the Nam River below. A small gate leads to the cliff where Nongae lured the general to his (and her) death. Evidently the river was considerably deeper then or the general was a remarkably poor swimmer; or else they were killed by hitting the rocks along the shore and not by drowning. A peculiarly Korean

form of graffiti embellishes the cliff, with names (presumably of Nongae's posthumous admirers) carved into the rock. Off to one side of Chokseongnu is the shrine in Nongae's honor, which contains her portrait.

Jinju is one of few South Korean cities that have developed into urban centers without losing their individual identity or rural ambience. Wander through the narrow streets, browse in the tiny shops, visit one of the several small temples, or spend the day rowing a rented boat around **Jinyang Lake**.

NORTH OF BUSAN: HILLS AND TEMPLES

Directly north of Busan is a mountainous region known as the **Yeongnam Alps**. These gentle mountains (the name is something of a misnomer) harbor several well-known temples in peaceful highland settings. The best known of these is **Tongdo-sa** ⑲ (daily sunrise–sunset; charge), about a half an hour to the north of Busan along the expressway to Gyeongju. The road leading to the temple is a long, slow incline, sheltered by a forest whose

A portrait of Nongae, who gave her life in the cause of Korean independence, Jinju fortress.

BELOW: ceremony to commemorate those who died in the Imjin Wars against Japan.

Japan and Korea

Acrimony has characterized relations between the neighboring nations of Japan and Korea. From the Korean point of view, the Japanese have made a habit of invading their peninsula. It began with early pirate raids, then the brutal invasion at the end of the 16th century, followed by centuries of attempts to force concessions onto the Koreans, culminating in colonization from 1910 to 1945. The list of injustices heaped on Koreans during this last occupation include: repression of independence, forced labor, and sex slaves. Perhaps worst of all has been the reluctance of Japan to acknowledge and apologize (at least to the satisfaction of the Koreans) for its misdeeds. There have been overtures from both sides to end the feud. The joint hosting of the 2002 soccer World Cup was seen by many as a step toward reconciliation.

Memorial service for Jajang, the 7th-century founder of Tongdo-sa temple.

name means "pine trees dancing in the winter wind."

With a total of 65 buildings, Tong-do-sa is South Korea's largest temple. Many of the buildings are dispersed throughout the surrounding mountainside, so the temple does not appear especially big at first sight. However, virtually every major Buddhist deity is honored in a separate shrine in the central cluster of buildings, unusually liberal even for so large a temple compound. The buildings themselves comprise a variety of exceptional architecture, some left pleasantly unpainted or faded to the muted brown of weathered pine. Clustered around several courtyards, Tongdo-sa is guarded by a massive quartet of wooden divas, each rendered in vivid and intimidating detail. Inside, one fine mural depicts a boat escorting the deceased to paradise. In addition to the many fine statues housed in the shrines, an excellent collection of artwork is on display in the temple museum. Woodblock prints are available for purchase.

According to legend, Tongdo-sa was founded in 646 by a Korean religious leader named Jajang who traveled to China in search of a truth to save his nation. There he experienced a visitation by a holy being who presented him with relics of the Buddha, including his yellow robe. Jajang returned to Korea to create his temple, naming it "Tongdo," which means "salvation of the world through mastery of truth." The gifts received in his vision are preserved in a stone monument in the temple.

Haein-sa

On Gyeongsangnam-do's northern border, and just over an hour's drive west of Daegu, is one of South Korea's most famous temples. Ritual drums thunder down from the mist-wreathed **Gayasan Mountain** (daily sunrise–sunset; charge), temporarily silencing the clack of prayer knockers and ethereal chanting. The smoke of cooking fires mingles with the aroma of incense as the monks of **Haein-sa Temple** ⓴ (daily 8.30am–6pm, Nov–Feb to 5pm; charge) prepare a meal of unpolished rice, mushrooms, and mountain herbs.

Undoubtedly the most rewarding of South Korea's more accessible temples,

Haein-sa is still isolated enough to be a meditative haven; yet it is only an hour from **Daegu** by bus, and accommodations are available nearby. As with many of South Korea's mountain temples (*see page 204*), Haein-sa is set in wonderful forest; the scenery of **Gayasan National Park**, beautiful in any season, is stunning in the fall, with craggy peaks and languid streams surrounded by fiery maples and oak. As you meander, try to imagine that this priceless spot, a Unesco World Heritage Site, was to be bombed during the Korean War, and was saved only because a pilot went against direct orders, knowing this was a site the world deserved to have preserved.

Haein-sa houses the **Tripitaka Koreana**, a collection of more than 80,000 woodblocks engraved with Buddhist scriptures. This vast library was completed in 1252, during the Goryeo dynasty, after nearly two decades of labor. It was a mammoth task undertaken twice. A first set, carved as a plea to the Buddha for aid against invading Khitan tribes, was destroyed by Mongols when they took their turn at invasion. Retreating to virtually impotent exile on Ganghwa Island, King Gojong ordered the creation of a second set in hopes of inducing an avataristic intervention against the Mongols. It is difficult to assess whether the king's hopes were justified or not: the Mongols finally departed in 1382 due to the collapse of their dynasty in China.

The Tripitaka library was moved early in the Joseon dynasty, from Ganghwa Island (too near the capital for safety) to Haein-sa. The building that now protects the woodblocks was built in 1488. It was designed with an adjustable ventilation system to prevent deterioration of the blocks. A recent concrete structure with an array of modern devices to ensure a controlled environment was intended as an improved replacement; but it now sits neglected within smirking distance of the more effective old library. The temple, its repository, and the Tripitaka were designated a Unesco World Heritage Site in 1995.

One of the first statues you are likely to encounter in the temple complex is not a gilt deity but a curious self-portrait of a monk carved in wood and painted true to life. The figure sits in apparent *rigor mortis* in a glass case in Haein-sa's small museum, surrounded by displays of elaborate embroidery and remnants of the temple's past. More typical statues are to be found in the compound's numerous shrines, including an imposing 18th-century trinity in the main hall. Outstanding among the paintings inside this hall is a mural depicting scenes from the Buddha's life. In common with most of South Korea's major temples, Haein-sa has several hermitages scattered through the surrounding mountains. All are a lure to meditative exploration.

Sacks of dried wild mushrooms spill out into the streets of the local "resort" and in a few restaurants you may indulge in a fungus-eating spree in a semi-private *ondol* (floor) heated room. While most of the town's inns are adequate, there is a virtual palace located on a low hill at the western edge of town, traditionally styled with pinewood. ❏

WHERE

If you are driving, the Yeongnam Alps region is a great place for a spot of temple-hopping. Besides Tongdo-sa, there are many other temples and hermitages in the area.

BELOW: the Tripitaka Koreana library at Haein-sa.

JEOLLA AND JEJU-DO

South Korea's southwestern Jeolla Provinces are renowned for their scenery and cuisine, while the large island of Jeju-do is a captivating blend of lofty volcanic peaks and dazzling white-sand beaches

outh Korea's southwestern Jeolla Provinces (Joe-llabuk-do and Jeollanam-do) are known above all for their spectacular rural landscapes, and also encompass thousands of secluded islands. Jeollabuk-do (North Jeolla Province) with its capital Jeonju – renowned for its paper and paper products, its *bibimbap* and characterful old city centre – is also home to Horse Ears Mountain (Maisan), close to Jinan Town, Moaksan Provincial Park, and Naejangsan National Park. Jeol-lanam-do (South Jeolla Province), meanwhile, is a must-see for the ancient provincial capital of Gwangju, which

competes with Jeonju for some of the best food in South Korea. You can enjoy South Korea's center of bamboo cultivation and craftsman-ship in Damyang, north of Gwangju. Or seek out the enchanting moun-tain of Jirisan – the highest point of mainland South Korea – complete with quiet temples and some of the country's best fall foliage. And don't forget, in the southwestern corner of the peninsula lies the port city of Mokpo and the attractions of the southwestern islands.

South Korea's top spot

If the Jeolla Provinces don't take up all your time, then there is still the large island of Jeju-do, lying across the Korea strait, the country's most popular holiday destina-tion. It is not difficult to see why. The island has a benign climate, great seafood, dramatic volcanic peaks and cra-ters, and top-notch facilities including first-class hotels, golf courses, hiking trails, and sports-fishing grounds. It has been dubbed the "Bali of North Asia" and "Korea's Hawaii" and not without reason. Highlights include the extinct volcano of Mount Halla and its surrounding national park, the amazing Manjang cavern, Jeongbang waterfall, and some beautiful beaches.   ❑

PRECEDING PAGES: the stairway up Ilchulbong (Sunrise Peak), Seongsan, Jeju-do. **LEFT:** the opening ceremony of the Gwangju Gimchi Festival. **TOP:** view of Seongsan, Jeju-do. **ABOVE LEFT:** a monument to Jeju-do's famed diving women *(haenyoe)*.

JEOLLA PROVINCES

These two southwestern provinces contain some of South Korea's finest landscapes, along with more than 3,000 seldom-visited islands. It is also renowned for the best food in the country

Considered the "rice bowl of Korea," the two Jeolla Provinces are a veritable cornucopia of food, and many Korean foods (such as *bibimbap*) claim origins here in this region. In the late spring, ample rains water the fields, and the farmers can be seen bent over, planting even rows of rice. As might be expected with such a fertile agricultural region, the women from this area are considered the best of South Korea's cooks.

Many of the residents of the Jeolla Provinces feel that the area has become left behind economically, and there is probably some truth to this, considering the dynamo of development and "progress" in the north. The provinces have experienced an intense rivalry with the neighboring Gyeongsang Provinces to the east and, unfortunately for Jeolla, politicians from Gyeongsang have tended to dominate federal politics. Much of the failure to develop this region was probably intentional. Jeolla was finally able to celebrate when their favorite son, Kim Dae-jung, became the first opposition candidate to be elected to the Korean presidency in late 1997.

The conspicuous lack of heavy industry in the Jeolla Provinces does have certain advantages, however, as the region has perhaps the cleanest air and best-preserved natural environment in South Korea. A ride through the coun-

tryside reveals scenes that are only a memory in the more developed provinces. The Korean curve motif is everywhere in this pastoral scene – in the subtle curves of terraced rice paddies, the rolling curves of mountains, hills, and burial mounds, and the upcurved roofs of traditional farmhouses.

JEOLLABUK-DO (NORTH JEOLLA PROVINCE)

With a range of delights that include expansive national parks full of breathtaking scenery, the peaceful historic city

Main attractions
JEONJU
TRADITIONAL HANOK HOUSING
KOREAN PAPER INSTITUTE
JEONDONG CATHEDRAL
MAISAN PROVINCIAL PARK
MOAKSAN PROVINCIAL PARK
GWANGJU
DAMYANG BAMBOO CRAFTS
    MUSEUM
JIRISAN NATIONAL PARK
SONGGWANG-SA
MOKPO
DADOHAE HAESANG MARITIME
    NATIONAL PARK
    (TEN THOUSAND ISLANDS)
JIN-DO ISLAND

LEFT: tea plantation near Boseong.
RIGHT: Jeonju is famous for its *bibimbap*.

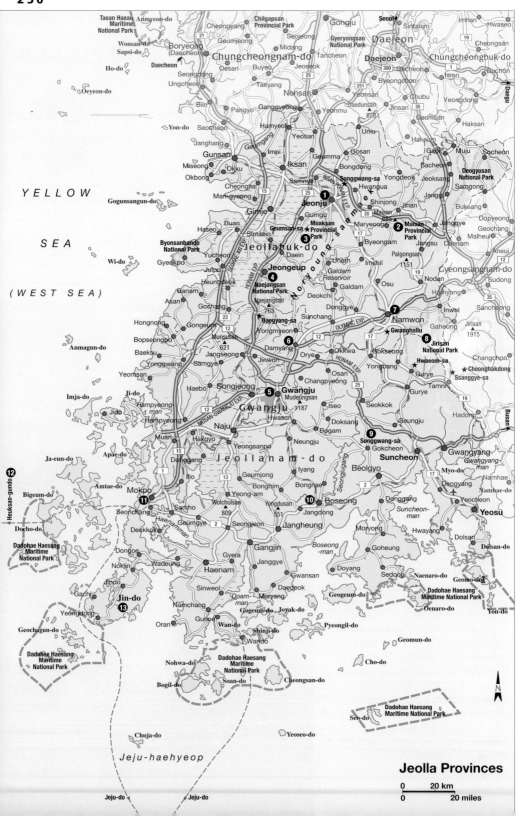

Jeolla Provinces

| 0 | 20 km |
| 0 | 20 miles |

of Jeonju, famed for its paper-making and delicious food, and the intriguing Horse Ears mountain with its two split peaks, there is so much to see and do in this scenic southwestern province.

Jeonju: papermaking and *bibimbap*

Jeonju ❶, located approximately 240km (150 miles) south of Seoul is the provincial capital of Jeollabuk-do. It is the ancestral home of the descendants of Yi Seonggye (Taejo), founder of the Joseon dynasty, and is famous throughout South Korea for its paper and paper products (such as fans and umbrellas), and for its food – particularly the delicious *bibimba*. Jeonju is also of great appeal to tourists because of the sizeable area of **traditional *hanok* housing** in the city center, built in the 1930s as a response to the Japanese-style architecture that was overtaking the country. The charming buildings are the perfect backdrop for discovering more about the city's esteemed traditions.

The best place to see traditional papermaking *(see panel below)* is at the **Korean Paper Institute** (daily 9am–5pm; free), situated in the *hanok* centre of the city. This beautiful old-style paperworks provides an illuminating introduction, with samples of Korean paper craftwork and demonstrations of how paper goes from mulberry bark to finished sheet. The **Traditional Craftwork Exhibition Hall** (Tue–Sun 10am–7pm, 6pm in winter; free), located in east of the *hanok* district, offers hands-on demonstrations of a variety of Jeonju and Korean crafts, such as paper-making, ceramics and woodcarving. Both are excellent places to look for souvenirs.

But if you ask any Korean what Jeonju is really famous for, the answer will be *bibimbap*, one of the few Korean foods to become recognized worldwide. Don't leave Jeonju without tasting this dish of rice and vegetables. The *bibimbap* often comes with the rice deliciously mixed with soy sprouts and topped with broiled and sliced meat, fern bracken, strips of boiled squid, bluebell roots, toasted sesame seeds, pine nuts, and a sunny-side-up egg. *Sanchae bibimbap* is even more exotic, using mountain roots and vegetables

Delicate fans are a traditional offshoot of Jeonju's papermaking tradition.

BELOW: handmade *hanji* paper at the Korean Paper Institute in Jeonju.

Korean Papermaking

The venerable tradition of Korean papermaking dates back around 1,600 years, and has remained largely unchanged to this day. Fibers of the *dak* (paper mulberry tree), mulberry stems and bamboo are stripped and cooked into a soft pulp, bleached and then transferred to a large wooden and cement vat. Rectangular bamboo mat screens suspended from bamboo poles are dipped in and out of these pulp-filled vats and, with rhythmic finesse, a sheet of sopping-wet paper is eventually sieved onto the bamboo screens. The various types of paper include: *unhyangji*, a coarse wrapping paper; *whaseonji* for brush painting; *jangji* used for calligraphy; *jangpanji* for ondol floors; *ttae juji*, algae paper; *jukji*, bamboo paper; *biji*, bark chip paper; and recycled paper made from various secondary papers.

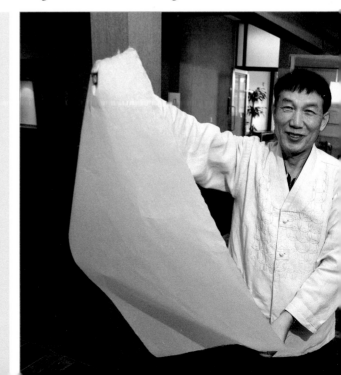

EAT

Bibimbap is found throughout South Korea, and makes a hearty, delicious meal. Another inexpensive snack popular with travelers in South Korea is *gimbap*, rice and vegetables wrapped in seaweed.

in place of the more traditional items. This savory dish is further accompanied by a bowl of beef broth and side dishes of cool seaweed and onion soup, then spiced further by at least five kinds of *gimchi*. Indeed, even at the simplest Jeonju restaurant expect to see amazing foods piled up at your table, in some cases at least as many as 20 different side dishes. When in Jeonju, don't be shy, eat!

Jeonju's other sights

Jeonju itself is quiet and peaceful, and one of the most pleasant places in South Korea in which to spend a few days. Wander through the many streets and poke into the shops, stores, and restaurants of the traditional *hanok* area of the city centre. Traditional teahouses are everywhere – stop for a cup of 5-flavor tea with pine nuts floating on top.

A notable sight is **Jeondong Cathedral**, a massive structure that ranks among the most beautiful of South Korea's many churches. It was built by the same architect who designed Seoul's Myeongdong Cathedral. The

interior is plain but pretty, with high arches and some nice stained-glass windows. Nearby, the gardens and priests' quarters are also worth a peek. Built of brick, they seem like they could be in a Washington DC or London suburb, not in southern Korea.

Gyeonggijeon Shrine (not to be confused with Gyeonggi Province) is another top stop. In addition to being picturesque, with bright colors and beautiful decoration, the shrine is famous for a portrait of one of Korea's most revered leaders, King Tae-jo Lee, the founder of the Joseon Dynasty, and the only one of a collection of five such masterpieces to survive the Japanese invasions of 1592.

Jeonju is also renowned for its small but acclaimed film festival, which highlights innovative and provocative works from Korean and international directors. In addition to hosting a variety of feature-length movies, the Jeonju Film Festival supports three "short! short! short!" feature directors with awards of up to $50,000. Held in late April, the festival is becoming a well-respected venue for new directors to

BELOW: Jeonju's hanok village is one of the most attractive urban neighborhoods in South Korea. **RIGHT:** *bibimbap* meal.

showcase their latest movies, and many artists who have gotten their first recognition here have gone on to do well at other globally known festivals, such as Cannes.

A Jeonju city bus or taxi will get you out to **Songgwang-sa** (daily 4.30am–7pm, until 6pm Nov–Feb; free; note there is another, more famous Songgwang-sa, near Suncheon; *see page 261*), a fine Buddhist temple to the northeast of the city. Located in a corner of a quaint village that produces *jangpanji* paper for *ondol* floors, Songgwang-sa offers the jaded temple seeker some of the finest mineral color murals in South Korea. Flying fairies and *mudang* (sorceresses) are painted directly on the walls and ceiling of this temple. These 150- to 200-year-old artworks were rendered in earthy and warm greens, orange, blues, and yellow. The characters posture and prance as if they were part of a modern animated movie. Carved wooden fairies, wispy as clouds, are suspended from the ceiling above three enormous gilded Maitreya Buddhas. Even the temple's main altar is splendidly wood-carved.

Maisan

The winding road on to **Maisan** ❷, Horse Ears Mountain, is properly paved these days, and points of interest crop up at almost every turn. Just five minutes outside of Jeonju, for example, you will see on your left a series of hills covered with hundreds of traditional Korean grave mounds. This is an unusually crowded pre-Christian-style cemetery. A few kilometers further, a splendid Buddha can be seen enshrined in a large granite bluff. All along this 34km (21-mile) haul eastward and over the Jinan Plateau to Jinan, farmers are out planting rice in the late spring, and, at other times, tending their plots of hay, tobacco, onions, and ginseng.

The famous Maisan "Horse Ears" are not visible until you get close to Jinan town. There, off to the right, they spring up from behind a large knoll above a meandering riverbed. From Jinan, lovely Maisan is but a 3km (2-mile) hike southward through an oak forest where mushrooms are cultivated under short logs leaning against trees.

Everything in South Korea has its divine or mythical reason for existence,

Looking down the aisle at Jeonju Catholic Cathedral.

LEFT: Jeonju's *hanok* village.
BELOW: Maisan's famous "Horse Ears" peaks.

Stone pagodas in the Tapsa Temple complex, Maisan.

BELOW: the cherry blossom comes early in the southern provinces.

and the two Maisan peaks are no exception. Legend notes that, before Maisan was created, two fairies – one male, the other female – lived there. They were enjoying their respite on earth when one day their heavenly creator called for them to make their ascent back home. He warned them to let no mortal eye witness their flight, so they carefully planned their departure for the next full moon night. This was so the moon could light their path to heaven.

The chosen night was overcast, so they decided to wait until dawn, an escape deadline decreed by their creator. As the two fairies were ascending to heaven, however, an early-rising housewife spotted them. They looked back at this eagle-eyed mortal, and were transformed into stones and fell back to earth as the two curious peaks of Maisan (moral: don't procrastinate). If you are curious as to which frozen-in-place fairy is which, the peak to the left is called *Sut Mai* (Male Horse Ear) and the one to the right is *Am Mai* (Female Horse Ear).

Once you reach **Maisan Provincial Park** (daily 9am–6pm, Nov–Feb to 5pm; charge), your expedition will

have just begun. The hike through narrow Jonghwang Pass between the two horse ears is a heart-thumping,132-step climb. Up there, near **Hwaeom Cave**, you can rest a while and enjoy a panoramic view of Jinan and environs. Continue into a small valley on the south side of the ears, veer to your right (while negotiating another 181 steps in segments) and you will come to one of the most bizarre Buddhist temples in South Korea. Built by the hermit monk Yi Gapyong, this **Tap-sa** (Pagoda Temple) religious site is a collection of stone pagodas, some of them 9 meters (30ft) high. All were built without mortar and have stood in surrealistic splendor in this narrow valley since the early part of the 20th century. Yi's architectural fantasy is reminiscent of the work of the Spanish architect Gaudí. Past these "Shaking Pagodas," the path continues through the steep mountains to temples such as Eunsu-sa, Geumdang-sa and Isanmyo Shrine, all about a 1km (²/₃ mile) walk away.

A white statue of the hermit monk Yi sits comfortably at the foot of his Maisan temple complex. He holds on

to a wooden walking staff and stares east toward the rising sun that bathes him, his narrow valley home, and his zany pagodas with an amber morning light. Several *yeogwan* on Jinan's road to Maisan offer accommodations to the weary body and soul who is not so keen to rush back to civilization.

Moaksan Provincial Park

Geumsan-sa (Gold Mountain Temple; daily 8am–7pm, Nov–Feb until 6pm; charge) on the western slope of **Moaksan Provincial Park ❸** (daily 24 hours; free), is reputedly the most beautiful temple in Jeollabuk-do. It is about 34km (21 miles) southwest of Jeonju. To visit it, take the old Highway 1 heading southwest from Jeonju toward Gwangju, and some 26km (16 miles) later, just north of Wonpyeongni, veer eastward along a side road that will lead up to Geumsan-sa.

The pathway to the temple entrance is adorned with cherry trees and Himalayan pine and a pool off to the right side of the path. This short walkway induces a meditative calm that prepares the traveler for Geumsan-sa itself.

First built in 599, Geumsan-sa was rebuilt in 766 by High Priest Jinpyo Yulsa during the Silla dynasty, and enlarged in 1079 (during the Goryeo period) by High Priest Hyedeok Wangsa. The complex was burnt during the 1592 Hideyoshi invasion, then rebuilt in 1626. Today, its main hall, Mireukjeon, stands three stories high, making Geumsan-sa the tallest temple in South Korea. This spaciousness is devoted to housing 10 cultural assets from the Silla, Baekje, and Goryeo periods. Mireukjeon, a worship hall for the god Avalokitesvara, is one of these 10 great treasures.

Inside Mireukjeon, a massive golden Maitreya (Buddha of the Future) stands 12 meters (39ft) tall, holding a red lotus blossom in its left palm. It is flanked by two crowned bodhisattvas, Daemyosang and Bophwarim. Below the statues, and behind the wooden grill, there is a stairway. One may walk down the steps to kiss the candlelit Maitreya's feet as a sign of respect and make an offering.

Next to Mircukjcon, above the left slope of the hill, is a stupa made of stone and a five-story granite pagoda where a monk's body minerals are enshrined after cremation. The pagoda's roofs are flat and subtly curved at the corners, in traditional Baekje style. The roofs to all of the temple structures, in fact, were never measured with anything but the naked human eye.

The Daejangjeon worship hall looms behind wood-carved doors that survived the 1592 Hideyoshi invasion. In the hall sits a gold-gilt Sakyamuni Buddha with a symbolic mandala around it – a rarely seen embellishment.

In the second-largest hall, the Nahanjeon Buddha sits with 500 sculptured disciples, each amazingly exhibiting different facial expressions. On the way back down the path, there is a Zelkova elm tree. Large and branching, it is renowned as a fertility tree. If someone throws a stone up the tree trunk and the stone does not drop, legend says that person will soon have a child.

At Eunsu-sa Temple, just above Tap-sa, there is an unusual building dedicated to ginseng. Ginseng is grown on the farms around Maisan. Look for freshly planted fields that have been covered with straw.

BELOW: monk at the main hall of Geumsan-sa.

The Gwangju Gimchi Festival takes place over a long weekend in late September or early October.

Naejangsan National Park

From Geumsan-sa, traverse tobacco fields along the main tributary road and rejoin the world's mainstream traffic on the Honam Expressway bound southwest for **Naejangsan National Park ❹** (daily sunrise–sunset; charge), where an entry tunnel of red maple trees reflects fiery fall colors on the faces of incoming visitors.

The journey up to Naejang (Inner Sanctum) Mountain National Park near Jeongeup is a peaceful prelude to a pilgrimage to Baegyang Temple. Up here, in maples and mist and steep mountain passes, you will find a pleasure pavilion placed esthetically onto a massive, real-life scroll painting.

Upon reaching the **Baegyang (White Sheep) Temple** you will already be properly inspired and in the mood to consider this place and its Seon, or Zen, Buddhist origins. Originally built in AD 632, Baegyang-sa was then called Baegam-sa after Mt Baegam. Son master Hwangyang Seonsa renamed it Baegyang-sa in 1574. Despite its reclusiveness, this temple befell malevolent forces, being destroyed four times by invaders. It was rebuilt a fifth time by Son master Songmanam Daejongsa in 1917. In its present form it sits like a jewel in the midst of lush mountain foliage that seems to be aflame during the late fall. An aged bodhi tree broods all on its own in the temple's main courtyard.

JEOLLANAM-DO (SOUTH JEOLLA PROVINCE)

The mountains of Jeolla's southern half eventually fragment into countless islands teeming with ports. Check out the regional capital of Gwangju and the curious coastal city of Mokpo, or head to Boseong, South Korea's largest tea plantation. The green and lovely interior is home to the national parks of Jirisan and Wolchulsan, both well worth a visit.

Gwangju

Gwangju ❺, the ancient provincial capital of Jeollanam-do, is a low-key city where at night, in many areas of the center, vehicular traffic ceases and streets become pedestrian malls busy with strolling townfolk.

Gwangju competes with Jeonju for honors such as "best food in South Korea" and "the most food served in South Korea." This is because in the past wealthy landlords established gracious food standards, and because the lush Honam Plain in Jeollanam-do has provided food for the city's gourmets. Also, the country's best *jeongjong* (barley and rice wine) and *makgeolli* (a simpler form of rice wine) are served here with an array of *anju* (drinking snacks) which make a veritable dinner out of a drink.

The best time to visit Gwangju is during one of its two popular festivals. If you have developed a taste for the pride of Korean cuisine, visit during Gwangju's **Gimchi Festival**. The festival is held over an extended weekend in late September or early October. Here you can get a taste of every gimchi imaginable, and some (such as gimchi pizza) that you never imagined. There are plenty of games and local talent performing to keep the crowds happy.

The other major festival is the **Gwangju Biennale**, which runs from September through November every even-numbered year. This is South Korea's premier exhibition for the arts, displaying works from Korea's best artists, as well as contributions from artists from more than 50 other countries.

The two-story **Gwangju National Museum** (daily 9am–6pm, Sat–Sun and holidays until 7pm, Apr–Oct Sat until 9pm; charge) was built to house Yuan-Dynasty booty that was discovered in a sunken 600-year-old Chinese ship in the Yellow Sea in 1976. This archeological find is exhibited on the first-floor gallery.

A map there illustrates the spread of Yuan-dynasty kilns throughout Eastern China down to Hong Kong, across to Korea's west coast, and on to Japan, Denega Island, and Okinawa. Among the finds are early 14th-century Luang Juan wares, including celadon vases with two rings and a peony design in relief, cups shaped like flowers, and a celadon druggist's mortar and pestle.

Upstairs on the second floor of the museum is a gallery of Jeolla Province treasures which includes Neolithic Korean relics from Daeheuksan-do, 11th- to 14th-century bronze Buddha

TIP

Gwangju witnessed a horrific event in 1980, when the South Korean military brutally crushed a student protest in the city. The protest had been directed at the leader of the recent coup d'état, Chun Doo-hwan, who had declared martial law across the country (see pages 42–3). Some people claim that over 2,000 were killed; official estimates put the number at around 200.

BELOW: the National Museum, Gwangju.

TIP

The Damyang Bamboo Festival takes place each May in the midst of the town's bamboo forest. A celebration of the versatility of the hardy plant, there are various craft-related activities, music and superb Jeolla-nam food.

bells, Joseon-dynasty scroll paintings, and white porcelain.

Mudeungsan (Peerless) Mountain hovers like a guardian over Gwangju City. A resort area has been created at its base among acacia trees and beside a whispering stream. Along Mudeung's right flank are two factory buildings that are used for tea production during the spring and autumn tea-harvesting seasons. A tea plantation previously owned by the famous early 20th-century Joseon-dynasty artist Ho Baeknyon is now cared for by Buddhist monks and sprawls next to **Mudeung's Jeungsim-sa (Pure Mind) Temple** (open daily). Perhaps it is true that tea has helped purify the minds of local monks. A monk at Jeungsim-sa explained that in Korea green leaf tea was traditionally the preferred brew of only monks and scholars. They believed this tea purified their blood and stimulated them so that they could resist sleep and study until dawn. It must work, because even today Mudeung-sa monks cultivate *chunseol* "Spring Snow" tea on slopes adjacent to their temple.

The small, tender *chunseol* leaves must be cut at a very early stage of growth and steamed and dried nine times in the early morning dew and mist (intense heat or cold spoils the delicate leaves). This is a very tedious tea-cultivation process that apparently only Buddhist monks have the patience for. The resulting tea, which smells of aromatic persimmons, is also said to aid digestion and whet the appetite.

Damyang bamboo

One of the most revered plants in South Korea is bamboo, called *daenamu* in Korean. It is splintered into chopsticks, carved into spoons, harvested for its delicious tender shoots, and immortalized in paintings and poetry.

The center of bamboo cultivation and craftsmanship in South Korea is **Damyang ❻**, north of Gwangju on the main highway. The best time to visit Damyang is on market day, which falls on days that end with the number 2 or 7. The market is held along the Gwanbangcheon stream, opposite a bright chartreuse bamboo forest. Usually, the bamboo is not cultivated

RIGHT: picking tea on a Jeolla plantation.

longer than three years, as its purpose is not for sturdy construction but specifically for gentle basket-weaving. Villagers bring these utilitarian objects down from their nearby village homes on market day, which starts at around 6am and peters out by 3pm. Straw and bamboo mats are sold near the market above the riverbank.

In the town center stands what locals claim to be the only museum devoted to bamboo. Check out the many uses made of this most utilitarian of plants in **Damyang's Bamboo Crafts Museum** (daily 9am–6pm; charge).

Namwon's legendary pavilion

Along the Olympic '88 expressway east of Damyang, in North Jeolla Province, is the ancient city of **Namwon ❼**, the birthplace of Chunhyang, heroine of Korean literature. It is not known if her birth was more than a literary event, as there is no proof of Chunhyang's existence. However, the story of her life is set in Namwon, and she has had sufficient effect on Korean life and thought for such quibbles to be immaterial.

Bamboo craftsmanship at Damyang.

"Chunhyangjeon" ("The Story of Chunhyang") is a simple, romantic tale of forbidden love and sacrifice. Mongnyong, the son of an aristocrat, falls in love with Chunhyang, the daughter of a *gisaeng* (female entertainer). The two secretly marry, and soon after, Mongnyong's father is transferred to a government post in the capital, separating the two lovers. A lecherous governor is appointed in Namwon who is determined to add Chunhyang to his roster of lovers. Remaining faithful to Mongnyong, she flatly refuses to comply with the governor's wishes. She is promptly imprisoned and beaten under the personal supervision of the enraged governor. Meanwhile, Mongnyong is appointed Royal Inspector of Jeolla Province. He soon hears of Chunhyang's maltreatment and comes to rescue her and punish the governor. The two lovers return to Seoul where they of course live happily and prosperously to a grand old age.

Chunhyang's staunch fidelity is still revered today, and her story is an essential part of South Korea's literary legacy. She is honored in Namwon with a

LEFT: bamboo at Damyang. **BELOW:** the Bamboo Crafts Museum.

Hwaeom-sa, on the slopes of Mt Jirisan.

BELOW: the entrance bridge to Songgwang-sa.

shrine as well as an annual festival held for a week or so in early May.

On the edge of Namwon is **Gwanghallu Garden** (daily 8am–8pm; charge, free entry Apr–Oct 7–8pm, Nov–Mar 6–8pm), a wonderful Korean-style park complete with ponds and streams. Gwanghallu Pavilion, where it is said the two lovers in the Namwon legend spent their evenings, is the major attraction. The huge Gwanghallu Pavilion was rebuilt in 1638 (after a fire), and is one of South Korea's four famous pavilions.

Jirisan National Park

Ask a Korean which is the most beautiful mountain, and they are likely to say Jirisan. At 1,915 meters (6,282ft), the highest point of the Sobaek Range (indeed the highest point of mainland South Korea) and sitting in the northeast of **Jirisan National Park** ❽ (daily; unlimited hours for most roads; charges for major temples), Jirisan is a stark jumble of snow-covered peaks in winter, cool and lush in summer, and brilliant with turning foliage in the fall. There are many small temples in the valleys of the mountain, and two major ones, Hwaeom-sa and Ssanggye-sa, are both easily reached from Gurye.

Hwaeom-sa (daily 7am–7.30pm; charge) was founded in the Silla dynasty. A 4.5-meter (15ft) stone lantern, the largest in South Korea, is preserved on the temple grounds. The dominant structure of the temple is the imposing, two-story Gakhwajeon ("Awakening Emperor Hall"), built in the 18th century and named in honor of the Chinese Emperor credited with funding its construction.

According to legend, **Ssanggye-sa** was founded by Priest Sambeop in 723 during the Silla Dynasty. Sambeop dreamed of becoming a disciple of the great Buddhist master of the time, Hyeneung, a patriarch of the Tsaochi sect of Chinese Zen Buddhism. Hyeneung, however, died before this dream could be realized. Sambeop found some consolation in studying transcriptions of Hyeneung's discourses that were brought to Korea. This motivated him to visit Gaiyum Temple in China, where Hyeneung's skull had been preserved. While there, Sambeop bribed a priest at the temple into giv-

Confucian Cheonghakdong

Hidden in a high valley on the eastern face of the sacred Mount Jiri, above Hadong, is Cheonghakdong, one of a few traditional villages that have been granted permission to abstain from Saemaeul Undong, the "New Community Campaign."

The colorful concrete rooftiles, ersatz chalets, paved roads, electricity, and modern plumbing that have redefined most Korean villages have not affected Cheonghakdong. "Monoleum," though, a soft, flexible linoleum in vogue in South Korea for some time, has infiltrated onto some porches and living-room floors.

The formal courtesy of Confucianism is meticulously observed in Cheonghakdong. Unmarried men still wear their hair in single long braids, and education is still conducted in the old Joseon-dynasty style: the teacher wears his horse-hair hat while lecturing on the Confucian Classics to his students (who sit cross-legged on the *ondol* floor dressed in traditional white *hanbok*).

Visitors are obliged to impose themselves on the friendly hospitality of the village residents, as no inns, hotels, or even restaurants are available in this wonderful oasis of seclusion.

Cheonghakdong is not easily accessible to visitors, and the isolation protects this timeless place from change.

ing him the revered skull. Having returned to Korea, Sambeop made his way to Jirisan where he built a shrine for his pilfered relic. This shrine gradually developed into Ssanggye Temple.

Songgwang – a Zen temple

To the south of Gurye lies the city of Suncheon, with a regular bus service to **Songgwang-sa ❾** (daily 8am–6pm, Nov–Feb until 5pm; charge), on the western edge of **Jogyesan Provincial Park**. Not to be confused with its namesake temple near Jeonju (*see page 253*), this is one of three "treasure temples" in South Korea, representing Buddha's followers: monks, nuns, and laity. It has become a center of Seon (Zen) Buddhism, and houses the International Zen Center where non-Koreans can study Buddhism in a suitably peaceful mountain setting.

Originally a small hermitage built during the Silla dynasty, Songgwang-sa was expanded in the 13th century after Bojo, a Seon Master, settled there with his followers. Destroyed during the Japanese invasion of 1592, the temple has slowly been rebuilt. Today it is a sprawling complex of buildings and courtyards nestling in a pleasant mountain valley.

A tiny, intricately carved, wooden statue of Buddha, believed to have been carried by Bojo in his travels, is preserved in the temple. The temple includes a number of architectural treasures. The oldest is the 400-year-old Guksajeon, or National Priests' Hall, which contains the portraits of prominent monks who have called Songgwang-sa home. One unique feature of Songgwang-sa is the pair of arched, covered bridges spanning a shallow stream that flows quietly in front of the temple entrance.

About 30km (18 miles) south of Songgwang-sa is **Boseong ❿**, and South Korea's major tea-growing center is just south of this small city. From atop the mountain pass, you can look down upon neatly groomed tea bushes lining the steep hillsides. Women can be seen harvesting year-round, though

spring is the best time to pick the new leaves. The tea plantations welcome visitors, and are a wonderful place to take a casual stroll among tree-lined lanes, or perhaps peek into a shed to watch workers drying and sorting the day's pickings. Afterwards, tea can be sampled in the plantation teahouses.

To the southeast of Suncheon is the town of **Yeosu**, at the western end of the picturesque Hallyeosudo Waterway (*see pages 239–40*).

Mokpo and the southwestern islands

At the southwestern extreme of the Korean peninsula is the port city of **Mokpo ⓫**, a rather drab shipping town with one or two indulgences for the visitor. Mokpo's docks abound in coarse vignettes: 2-meter (6ft) sharks for sale in a fishmonger's shop, a trawler festooned with gaudy banners, sulking ponies hitched to heavy cartloads of produce, and blubbery hogs screeching in protest as they are hauled ashore.

The major distraction of this city is the interesting view from Yudalsan, a craggy twin-peaked mountain that

Naju, a small town northeast of Mokpo, is famous for its delicious Korean "pears." The pear is actually a cross between an apple and a pear. During Chuseok (the Korean equivalent of Thanksgiving), dozens of farmers sell the Naju pear on the road between Mokpo and Gwangju.

BELOW: winter snows on Jirisan.

Mokpo New Port, a massive port complex on one of the outlying islands, will be connected by bridge to the mainland from 2011. Giant cargo ships will be able to unload with relative ease, shifting some traffic away from Busan. It remains to be seen how much the character of quiet Mokpo will change when construction is complete.

BELOW: mountain views from Yudalsan, directly above Mokpo city.

cuts right into the city center. Several kilometers of winding pathways allow visitors to walk up as far as their health or ambition permits.

Probably Mokpo's most interesting attraction is the **National Maritime Museum** (Tue–Sun 9am–6pm, Sat–Sun to 7pm; charge). The museum displays a wooden ship that had been mired in the mud of nearby tidal flats for several hundred years. Its cargo included over 30,000 pieces of Goryeo celadon, along with thousands of other trade goods. Other goods on display, many of Chinese origin, suggest that Mokpo was once a very important link in pan-Asian trade.

Land of 10,000 islands

Mokpo is the chief point of departure for some 3,000 islands, many of which make up the **Dadohae Haesang Maritime National Park**. This area is called the "Land of 10,000 islands," in fact, and at least if you aren't counting that sure looks to be true.

One of the easiest ways for the traveler to see them is from the ferry as it leaves for Jeju. Stand on the deck and for the first half of the trip you will pass through hundreds of isles. Many are quite beautiful; some are not. The largest have fishing ports and small villages, but most are essentially uninhabited. With fog rising off a glassy sea, it's one of the world's most spectacular sights to see these eerie shapes forming as the boat gets closer. Some have the silhouettes of animals or people. Others are barren, save for a lone salt-stunted pine that tops the crag like a lost lover. Beaches are infrequent but just as beautiful, strewn with millions of small stones, shells, and shorebirds. Life on the islands is centered around the ocean: harvesting fish, seaweed, kelp, clams, and anything else even remotely edible.

The two best-known islands in the national park are Heuksan-gundo and Hongdo. **Heuksan-gundo ⑫** is actually a group of 100 islands, the largest of which is Daeheuksan-do. Daeheuksan-do has several small hotels, though rooms can be difficult to find during the peak travel season of late July and August. A few of the islands of Heuksan-gundo are large enough and flat enough

to support agriculture. Stone walls, rustic homesteads, and pastoral scenes set against an ocean backdrop make these islands exquisite beauties. Legend has it that the fabled Choryeongmok Tree will summon deities when its branches are placed as an offering on a Buddhist altar. The area boasts "Eight Beautiful Sights" which must be seen when one visits here, mostly vistas from various outlooks around this gorgeous island.

Hong-do (a nature preserve with a small charge) is a rugged piece of rock to the west of Daeheuksan-do. Hong-do, the "Red Island," is named for the pink hues of its rock and is famous for the imposing, contorted rock formations and precipitous cliffs that line its coast. The best way to see this small island is by boat. There are rooms to let at the larger of the two villages. The fast ferries from Mokpo can get you there in just over two hours.

Jin-do

Less demanding is a trip south to **Jin-do** (**Jin Island**) ⑬, a large island that is only two hours' travel by ferry from Mokpo itself. The island is also connected to the mainland via Korea's longest suspension bridge, but the scenery makes the boat trip enjoyable.

Jin-do is famous for two things: a rare breed of dog and an unusual natural event. The pedigree *Jindotgae* (literally translated as Jin Island dog) has a short, nearly white coat of fur with a touch of ochre along the inner curve of its characteristic arched tail. An annual Jin-do dog show is held in the fall and billed in the English-language press as a "beauty contest."

Jin-do's other claim to fame is its impressive low tides. Twice a year (end of February and mid-June), the tides are so low that a small island nearly 3km (2 miles) offshore becomes accessible by foot. In the 1970s, a Frenchman likened it to Moses' parting of the Red Sea, and the "Moses Miracle" moniker stuck. In recent years it has become an extremely popular event, with thousands of people walking between the two islands.

The event has reached festival proportions, and become a showcase for the island's cultural traditions and enthusiastic local talent. ❑

A Jin Island dog.

BELOW: the low tide that occurs twice each year off Jin-do has become a major cultural event.

Make the Most of Mokpo

Often overlooked as tourists rush from the mainland to Jeju island is tiny Mokpo, a port city with a curious heritage perched at the southwestern corner of the peninsula, which offers plenty of tourist facilities.

One of the best views of the approximately 10,000 islands can be had by hiking up to the top of Yudalsan Peak, a large rocky hill with a temple and imposing cliffs that's only a short 10-minute walk from the KTX station.

This hike, much of it up stairs, leads past several statues and a temple, to a relatively wild area near the summit. Here you can look out (especially on a clear day) and see the scattered islands and silvery ocean spreading out below, like jigsaw pieces laid out on a mirror that have yet to be fitted together.

THE WAY OF TEA, KOREAN-STYLE

Green tea is increasingly popular worldwide, and Korean green tea is the best there is. It's finally getting the recognition it deserves worldwide

The drinking of tea *(cha)* was introduced to Korea and Japan around the 7th centuries AD by Buddhist monks from China, and over the following centuries it remained closely linked with Buddhism. However, when a new dynasty, the Joseon, took control of the peninsula in the 14th century and decided to break the power of Buddhism, the tradition was almost lost. In the 19th century the Buddhist monk Cho Ui, followed by Hyodang in the 20th century, led revivals that are only now beginning to bear fruit.

Korean Tea Today

Today, tea ceremonies are popular with housewives, while Buddhist monks and ordinary people enjoy drinking green tea in an informal manner. To enjoy the full experience, look for a *jeontong chatjip* (traditional tea house). In Seoul, the alleyways of the Insadong district offer a fine selection of these, especially in the older, more venerable spots along side alleyways. Staff will gladly show you how to prepare your tea. Koreans believe tea contains various tastes: salt, sweet, bitter, tart, peppery, in varying proportions. Ordinary tea will have lost most of its flavor after three servings, but very good tea may be used to make four or five rounds. Koreans will tell you that Chinese tea has perfume, Japanese tea has color, but Korean green tea has a deeper, richer taste than either. And it is better for you, too!

ABOVE: Korean potters copy some of the country's finest ancient pottery to create a Korean style of tea service.

RIGHT: green tea, Chinese tea, and the black tea from India or Sri Lanka are all made with leaves from the same bush, *Camellia sinensis*.

ABOVE young couples, as well as monks, frequent Korean teahouses, drinking green tea slowly in a relaxed atmosphere.

RIGHT: holding the cup in both hands, first admire the color, then inhale the fragrance, then drink and savor the aftertaste.

ABOVE: the Taepyongyang company's tea plantations at Boseong employ dozens of women during the brief tea-picking season between April and June.

THE ART OF GREEN TEA

When the freshly sprouting leaves are plucked from the tea bushes in late April or May, they are a vivid green color. To make green tea, they have to be dried before they wither; this means within a few hours of being picked. Tea bushes only grow in the far south of the Korean peninsula, on the southern slopes of Jirisan, around Boseong, and on the hills of Jeju Island off the south coast.

On the slopes of Jirisan, individual tea-makers spend hours crouched over heated cauldrons, turning and rubbing the tea by hand until it is perfectly dry. This is the finest and most expensive variety of Korean tea, although tea made industrially by such large companies as Taepyongyang can also be very good.

The first, small sprouts gathered in April give the most delicate tea, known as "Ujeon." The leaves gathered in early May yield "Sejak" and in the last weeks of May, when the taste of the leaves is beginning to grow weaker, the tea is known as "Jungjak." Menus in teahouses will often list green tea by these three categories.

BELOW: the sculptural beauty of a sunlit tea plantation.

ABOVE: the very finest green tea is slowly dried over a fire in an iron cauldron, the leaves stirred and rubbed between the tea-makers' hands.

RIGHT: finely powdered tea is whisked to a froth in warm water, in one version of the tea ceremony; more usually, green tea is brewed in a teapot and poured into small cups.

JEJU-DO

Jeju-do is South Korea's top holiday destination – and it is not difficult to see why. The island has a benign climate, beautiful beaches, wonderful seafood, spectacular volcanic peaks and craters, and superb tourist facilities including international-class hotels, golf courses, challenging hiking trails, and sports-fishing grounds. Similarities to idyllic islands further south have also played their part; *The Asian Wall Street Journal* called Jeju the "Bali of North Asia," while the Korean government has dubbed the island "Korea's Hawaii" and "The Hawaii of the Orient." More recently, the island has been referred to, appropriately, as the "Honeymoon Island."

Whichever sobriquet you choose for South Korea's biggest island, such descriptions completely debunk stereotypical visions of this country as a land of frozen mountain passes and howling Siberian winds. There are indeed several geographical similarities between Jeju-do and the Hawaiian archipelago. Jeju looks similar, with aquamarine-hued waters like those of Hawaii, and similar black lava shelves, jagged outcroppings, and steep cliffs. The most famous of these is curious Yongduam, the Dragon's Head Rock (*see page 270*).

Like its Hawaiian counterpart, Jeju has some superb beaches and warmish waters, though nothing compared to the genuine tropics. Favorite crescents of sand are located at Hyeopjae, Gwakji, and Hamdeok along Jeju's northeren shore, and at Hwasun, Jungmun, Pyoseon, and Sinyang in the south sector. Most of these resorts feature superb seafood restaurants, gaily painted tent cafés, and rentable recreational facilities. Other highlights include the breathtakingly massive Hallasan, the volcano that

Main attractions
YONGDUAM ROCK
MANJANG CAVERN
BIJARIM FOREST
ILCHULBONG PEAK
JEJU FOLK VILLAGE
MOUNT HALLASAN
SEOGWIPO
JEONGBANG FALLS
YAKCHEON-SA TEMPLE

LEFT: Yongduam rock, a favorite location for honeymooners. **RIGHT:** enjoying the scenery at Hyeopjae beach on the northwest coast.

dominates the heart of the island, and, if you visit in the springtime, brilliant rape fields that paint broad yellow splotches across the island's fertile pastureland. Jeju-do's most distinctly Hawaiian-like phenomena are man-made structures, in particular the low walls of lava-rock construction that lace the countryside. Many are almost exact replicas of lava-rock walls that wind hither and thither in rural Hawaii.

However, due to the realities of Jeju's temperate locale, once winter sets in chilly winds knife across Jeju-do and shatter all Polynesian allusions from mid-November through March.

A simple tour around the island perimeter, or a cruise along one of the two crosscut highways, are worthwhile. The pine forests, orchards, pineapple fields, mushroom caves, waterfalls, odd rock formations, and rural charms will draw you deep into Jeju-do's calm and complex beauty.

The island can be easily reached either by ferry from Busan, Mokpo, or the island of Wan-do *(see pages 276–7)*; or by regular Korean Air and Asiana

Airlines flights from the major mainland airports, and from Tokyo, Osaka, Nagoya, and Fukuoka in Japan.

Jeju's history

Until about AD 1000, Jeju, like many other remote island spots in Asia, developed in relative isolation and it wasn't until around the end of Korea's Goryeo Dynasty (918–1392) that it was influenced by off-island events. It was during the reign of Goryeo King Gojong (r. 1213–59) that Jeju received its present name. *Je* means simply "across" or "over there." *Ju* in earlier times referred to an administrative district. Therefore, Jeju is the *do*, island, in the district over there. Previously, the island was variously known as *Tammora*, *Doi*, *Tangna*, and *Tamna*, the last being the most common version in historical references.

In the 13th century, after the Goryeo kingdom had been subjugated by Mongol invaders, Jeju-do became a Mongol possession for about 100 years (from 1273–1374). Professor Sang Yongick of the Jeju National University reports that dur-

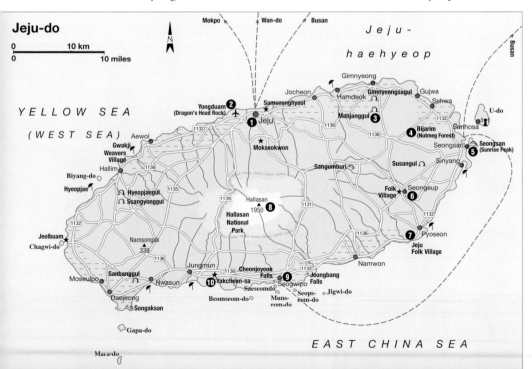

ing this time the armies of Kublai and Genghis Khan "used Jeju-do as a bridge to invade Japan." One invasion of Japan led by Kublai Khan involved 33,000 men and 900 vessels. Many of the ships were constructed of wood from Hallasan.

These Mongol conquerors permanently altered Jeju ways. The present-day dialect (unlike the language spoken on the Korean mainland) is a direct result of influence by the Mongols. Not so long ago, it was still possible to find Mongol-styled leather hats, fur clothing and fur stockings in use in the mountain areas of Jeju-do. Through the Mongols, the island became a stock-raising area, especially for horses. Also, the Mongols, along with temples and statues, brought Buddhism to Jeju. The first Westerners to visit and tell the outside world about Jeju-do (as well as the Korean mainland) were Dutch sailors who were shipwrecked at **Moseulpo** on Jeju's southwest shore on August 16, 1653. These men of the Dutch ship *Sparrow Hawk* en route from Batavia to Taiwan and then Nagasaki had ventured into fierce typhoon winds, which,

according to survivor and author Henrik Hamel, "blew so boisterously, that we could not hear one another speak, nor durst we let fly an inch of sail…"

It wasn't until 1958 that the first group of tourists descended on Jeju. Frederic Dustin was a member of that initial exploratory tour, which was led by the late Ferris Miller. Dustin quotes Miller as saying: "Over 100 people went, by boat of course since there were no commercial planes then, and the occasion was considered so important that the governor and the mayor of Jeju City met the ship. There were no hotels, so we rented all of the seven or eight inns in town, staying three nights. We also took over two bath houses, one for men and one for women, with runners to guide visitors to them through the unpaved, unlit streets."

Things have, of course, changed considerably since then. Most of the island is now crisscrossed with paved streets and highways and dotted by hotels and casinos, catering to the thousands of tourists that now make up the island's most important industry.

Dolharubang (*grandfather stones*) *are a symbol of Jeju-do.*

LEFT: Jeju-do is South Korea's number-one honeymoon destination.

Honeymoon Island

For more than 20 years, the idyllic island of Jeju-do has been *the* place for Koreans to spend their honeymoon. Its beaches, expensive hotels, and image as a tropical, exotic destination made it a perfect romantic escape. Isolated for centuries, this place of myth and magic also benefitted from its warm southern climate, subtropical greenery, and volcanic scenery. It didn't hurt, either, that it was nearly impossible for Koreans to travel outside their own country (due to inflexible passport restrictions and financial considerations). By 1990, however, the government had loosened up the rules and Korean tourists were finally allowed to travel overseas.

On the wave of a seemingly nonstop economic boom, Koreans took full advantage of their new-found freedoms, and Jeju's allure was soon eclipsed by Guam and Saipan (only a few hours away from Seoul), and even Hawaii and Thailand.

With the economic downturn of the late 1990s, though, Korea's honeymooners again returned to the island, which lies just 160km (100 miles) off the southernmost tip of the peninsula.

Who knows – with an increasing number of Japanese (and Chinese) people now visiting the island, it may become the honeymoon destination of choice for all of East Asia.

Tangerines thrive in the southerly climes of Jeju-do.

BELOW: the Manjang cavern.

Jeju City

Jeju City ❶ is comfortably the largest urban area on the island, yet is noticeably laid-back in comparison to similar-sized cities on the mainland, even though it sees many visitors from China, Japan, and the Korean mainland – as many as 4 million a year. They come not just because it is the main transportation center for Jeju Province, but also to see the city's many tourist attractions, including Dragon's Head Rock, the Samseonghyeol holes, Hallasan National Park, and the country's highest mountain (Hallasan).

About 300 meters/yds from the KAL Hotel are the abovementioned **Samseonghyeol** (daily 8am–7pm, Nov–Feb until 6pm; charge), three holes in the ground, whence emerged three male demigods, Yang, Go, and Bu. According to Jeju myths, these were the original inhabitants of the island. These male progenitors were hunters and fishermen who had the good fortune to later meet three princesses who brought with them grains, livestock, and other forms of agriculture. Yang, Go, and Bu married these princesses and thus Jeju

society was born. The births and meetings of these original Jeju ancestors are celebrated by locals on special feast days every April, October, and December.

One of the more fascinating remnants of prehistoric Jeju (and a prominent symbol of the island) are the *dolharubang*, or **grandfather stones**. These carved lava-rock statues, 52 in all, are seen in every part of Jeju-do. Anthropologists say they probably represent legendary guardians who once flanked the entrances to Jeju's largest townships. Other scholars compare them to mysterious statuary found in various locales such as some parts of the southern Korean peninsula, Tahiti, Okinawa, Fiji, and even Easter Island.

Suitable places to study these images up close are at the entrance to the **Jeju-do Folklore and Natural History Museum** (daily 8.30am–5.30pm; charge) in Jeju City or in front of **Gwandeokjeong** (a 15th-century pavilion), the oldest standing building on Jeju-do, which faces Jeju City's main square. If you find the *dolharubang* charming, miniature lava-rock reproductions are for sale at souvenir shops scattered throughout the island.

Yongduam, the **Dragon's Head Rock ❷**, is a formation by the sea in Jeju City's western suburbs near Jeju's main airport. According to local legends, this dragon descended from Hallasan and, upon reaching the sea, was petrified in place. These odd-shaped rocks are a hit with Koreans, and no Jeju honeymoon is complete unless the happy couple has their photo taken with Yongduam as a backdrop.

From Jeju City to the northeast

Unlike Hawaii, Jeju-do cannot advertise that its deep fissures and frozen lava swirls are the products of still-active volcanoes. On the other hand, it can claim the world's longest known lava tubes, the Gimnyeongsa and Manjang caverns located at Gimnyeong in the northeast of the island between Jeju City and Seongsan. The

Manjang cavern ❸ (daily 9am–6pm summer, 9am–5.30pm winter; charge), the longer of the two tubes, is a mind-boggling 13.4km (8½ miles) in length (although only 1km/²/3 mile is open to the public) with a diameter that ranges from 3 to 20 meters (10–66ft). In the summer, tourists can join lamplight tours of these caverns filled with bats, spiders, centipedes, and unusual lava formations. You are advised to dress warmly as temperatures inside the caverns stay between 10–20°C (50–68°F) throughout the year.

A short distance to the southeast of Manjgang cave is the **Bijarim** (Korean Nutmeg) **Forest ❹** (daily 9am–5pm winter, 9am–7pm summer; charge). Not related at all to the spice, these twisted, gnarled trees are stately and seem mystical, especially at dusk or when fog rolls in. In the fall, the dark green of the nutmegs contrasts sharply with the golds and reds of the Korean oaks and maples.

The east

The most easterly point on the island is marked by a small peninsula, dominated by **Ilchulbong** (Sunrise Peak), close to the pleasant small town of **Seongsan ❺**. The 182-meter (597ft) summit is a half-hour walk from the town, and the views are superb.

To the southwest, **Seongeup ❻** is an old inland village that not so long ago was the administrative center of the island. There are several old government buildings and a shrine, indicators of the village's past position. Even more interesting are the quaint homes, rock walls, and narrow alleyways which visitors are free to wander through (but don't go *in* the houses, someone still lives there!). Thankfully, the construction of concrete tower blocks has been limited in Seongeup.

On the southeast coast not far from Seongeup is a folk village with a more commercial bent, the **Jeju Folk Village ❼** (daily Oct–Mar 8.30am–5pm, Apr–July 20 and Sept until 6pm, July 21–Aug 31 until 6.30pm; charge). Like its more authentic counterpart, the Jeju Folk Village leaves you with a good sense of what the island was like before it was discovered by Japanese

If you like stone gardens (as a lot of Koreans do), don't miss the Mokseokwon, a garden with unusual displays of Jeju stones and dried tree roots. Mokseokwon is south of Jeju City, on the road to Hallasan.

BELOW: Ilchulbong (Sunrise Peak), the easternmost point of the island.

TIP

Following the Jeju Olle, a 200km (125-mile) network of trails around the south of Jeju, is a great way of experiencing the natural beauty of the island. There are currently 13 separate routes, which link up with each other; most of them are around 15 km (9 miles) long. The network was created in 2007 and was inspired by the venerable *el camino* pilgrimage route to Santiago de Compostela in northwest Spain.

jet-setters. Different areas of the Folk Village replicate village life, as it would have been a hundred years ago in the mountain, plains, and fishing villages of Jeju. Many of the buildings are authentic, and have been moved here. There is a performance area where you can watch colorful local traditions of song and dance – most of which have links to the island's shamanistic past.

Hallasan

Volcanic, cloud-wreathed **Hallasan ❽** (Mt Halla; daily; times for climbers: sunrise to sunset, but varies due to seasons and reclamation projects; check with the control office in bad weather, tel: 064-713-9950; free), at 1,950 meters (6,400ft), is the highest peak in South Korea, and a walk up to the summit is one of the highlights of a visit to the island. It dominates Jeju-do and, indeed, if there were no volcano there would be no island.

The slopes of Hallasan are included within **Hallasan National Park**, and have fauna and flora unique in South Korea. If you want to climb to the top, plan on a good half-day. There are four park entrances, each with a path up the volcano. The north and south slopes are the most strenuous hikes, while the eastern slope is the easiest.

Seogwipo and the south

Rivers and waterfall come tumbling off Hallasan. The best known are a series of waterfalls on both the east and west sides of lovely **Seogwipo Town ❾** on the south coast, a picturesque town with a wealth of bars and some great seafood restaurants. It's the main tourist resort on the island, with an idyllic setting, and there is a range of boat trips on offer, some exclusive golf courses, and fine beaches nearby. The stunning **Jeongbang Falls** (daily 8am–5.30pm; charge) right in Seogwipo town are often referred to as the only waterfall in Asia that plunges directly into the sea. Just to the east is another fall, Sojeongbang, with an observatory at the top of a cliff from which you can enjoy fine sea views.

To the west of Seogwipo, **Yakcheon-sa Temple ❿** (daily 9am–7pm; free) is a relatively new temple built in the 1990s which (according

BELOW: the Jeongbang Falls, Seogwipo.

to the temple literature) is the largest worship hall in all of Asia. This claim may be as tall (a tale) as the hall is, but largest in Asia or no, the hall is massive. The three Buddhas within stare serenely out, a white grand piano incongruously off to the side. Tiny elephant statues guard the pathway edges, ornate carvings are brightly painted, and the monks here are uniquely willing to interact with foreigners. As you enter, don't be surprised if someone approaches you and, after a piercing gaze, offers you your sickness and a recommendation of what to do to purify your soul.

Jeju's diving women

Jeju's famous diving women, the *haenyeo*, have long been a symbol of the island and its purported matriarchal culture, famed for centuries by the people of Jeju-do and Korean mainlanders alike. They are immortalized in folk songs, contemporary promotional brochures, as plaster-of-Paris sculptures, and on postcards, souvenir pennants, cups, and plates. When conditions are favorable, scores of the *haenyeo*, who range from teenagers to wrinkled grandmothers, can be seen bobbing offshore between free dives for seaweed, shellfish, and sea urchins. Fewer dives take place in winter, when the water temperature falls to around 10°C (50°F). There are several thousand women on the island still practicing the ancient tradition, and drawing in the tourists to watch the spectacle.

In times past, when the *haenyeo* would plunge into the waters clad only in loose white cotton, it was illegal for any man to set eyes upon them. Things have changed, and these days, in their slick black head-to-toe wetsuits, face masks, and snorkels, the sirens of the past look more like members of a navy team. Nevertheless, they are still the favorite target of every camera-toting tourist who visits Jeju. Do remember, though, to ask for permission before photographing the *haenyeo*, since they are often camera-shy, and some might want to be paid something for having their picture taken. ❑

One of Jeju-do's famous haenyeo *divers.*

LEFT & BELOW: Hallasan National Park.

275

TRANSPORTATION

ACCOMMODATIONS

EATING OUT

ACTIVITIES

A – Z

LANGUAGE

⚡INSIGHT GUIDES **TRAVEL TIPS**

SOUTH KOREA

T RANSPORTATION

GETTING THERE
AND GETTING AROUND

By Air

South Korea is one of East Asia's major transport hubs. **Incheon International Airport** (IIA) is 52km (31 miles) west of Seoul, and 15km (9 miles) west of Incheon (*see opposite* for more details on travel to and from the airport). For airport information, tel: 1577-2600.

South Korea is connected with the United States by Korean Air, Japan Airlines, United Airlines, and Northwest Airlines among others. Carriers routed through Seoul include Cathay Pacific, China Airlines, Malaysian Airlines, and Singapore Airlines. It is less than 13 hours from the US West Coast, 11 hours from London, 2½ hours from Tokyo, 3½ hours from Hong Kong, and 1½ hours from Beijing.

Gimpo Airport, 19km (12 miles) west of Seoul, now operates domestic flights. For airport information, tel: (02) 2660-2114.

South Korea's other international airports are at Busan (Kimhae Airport) and on Jeju Island; these operate flights to major cities in the region, mostly to/from Japan.

Following is a list of airline offices in Seoul; add the 02 prefix if dialing from outside Seoul:
Aeroflot, tel: 551-0321.
Air Canada, tel: 3788-0100 ext. 1.
Air China, tel: 774-6886.
Air France, tel: 3483-1033.
All Nippon Airways, tel: 752-5500.
Asiana Airlines, tel: 1588-8000.
Cathay Pacific, tel: 311-2800.
China Eastern Airlines, tel: 518-0330.

China Southern Airlines, tel: 775-9070.
Garuda Indonesia Airline, tel: 080-773-2092.
Japan Airlines, tel: 757-1711.
KLM Royal Dutch Airlines, tel: 774-1133.
Korean Air, tel: 1588-2001 ext. 5.
Lufthansa, tel: 3420-0400.
Malaysia Airlines, tel: 777-7761.
Northwest Airlines, tel: 732-1700.
Philippine Airlines, tel: 774-3581.
Qantas, tel: 777-6871.
Singapore Airlines, tel: 755-1226.
Thai Airways International, tel: 3707-0011.
United Airlines, tel: 757-1691.

All passengers are subject to a W27,000 airport tax (normally included in air ticket prices).

By Sea

To/From Japan

Overnight ferry services operate between Busan and the Japanese port of Shimonoseki on the western tip of Honshu (Bukwan Ferry, tel: 051-463-3161). Busan and Hakata, the port of Fukuoka, are connected by daily jetfoils (Korea Marine Express, tel: 02-730-8666) and ferries (Korea Ferry, tel: 051-466-7799).

There are also ferries to other Japanese ports like Kokura, Hatakatu, Izuhara, Osaka, and Hirosima. It is best to check the latest schedule and fare with KNTO before travel (tel: 02-1330) and then to contact individual ferry operators or a travel agency.

It is possible to purchase all-in-one train-ferry combination tickets for travel between South Korea and Japan, for instance from Seoul to Osaka via Busan.

To/From China

There are extensive ferry services from Incheon to several Chinese ports such as Dandong, Weihai, Qingdao, Tianjin, Dalian, and Yantai. They are overnight ferries and operate three times per week except for Tianjin (which operates twice a week).

Travel time is 11 hours to Dalian for the shortest (Dain Ferry, tel: 02 3218-6550) and one full day to Tianjin for the longest (Jinchon Ferry, tel: 02 515-6317).

It is advisable to check the latest schedule and fare with KNTO first before traveling (tel: 02-1330).

South Korea–China through-tickets which combine train and ferry services are also available.

Call the following companies for information on ferries traveling between South Korea and China and Japan:

Bukwan Ferry (Busan)
Tel: (051) 463-3161
Camellia Line (Busan)
Tel: (051) 466-7799
Camellia Line (Seoul)
Tel: (02) 775-2323
Dain Ferry (Seoul)
Tel: (02) 3218-6550
Dandong Ferry (Incheon)
Tel: (032) 891-3322
Korea Marine Express (Busan)
Tel: (051) 465-6111
Korea Marine Express (Seoul)
Tel: (02) 730-8666
Korea Ferry (Busan)
Tel: (051) 466-7799
Mirejet (Busan)
Tel: (051) 441-8200
Weidong Ferry (Seoul)
Tel: (02) 3271-6753

GETTING AROUND

From The Airport

Incheon

By bus

The best way out of Incheon International is currently by bus, with routes to Gimpo (the main airport for domestic flights), numerous points in downtown Seoul, Incheon City, and Gyeonggi Province. Departures coincide with the first and last flights and run regularly in between. Buses take about 50 minutes to travel between the airport and downtown Seoul. Korean Air (KAL) runs a convenient Limousine shuttle from the airport to many of the nicer Seoul and Gangnam hotels, as well as to/from Gimpo Airport.

The Incheon airport train linking Gimpo and Incheon airports runs only hourly, on the hour and it is inconvenient for people to take the subway to Gimpo and then continue on to Incheon. At peak times, such as rush hour, this train/subway option makes sense. At other times of day it is easy to take the bus. Service between Incheon Airport and Seoul Station is expected to begin in 2010, a connection that will be warmly welcomed.

The fare for the commuter train is up to W3,400 (depending on the station you exit) between Incheon and Gimpo. See www.arex.or.kr for further details.

The Limousine Bus service covers Gimpo and Seoul, with tickets priced for standard and deluxe buses at W9,000 and W14,000 respectively.

The "Seat Style Bus" (SSB or *iwaieok* in Korean) covers 14 destinations in Seoul, and is cheaper,

with fares ranging from W6,200–9,300.

Both SSBs and Limousine run to various destinations in Incheon city at costs between W3,500 and W6,500.

There are long-distance limousine services to Gyeonggi Province and as far as to Dajeon, Gwangju, and Mokpo.

By taxi

Taxis are the most expensive method of airport transfer. From Incheon to downtown Seoul costs approximately W90,000 by deluxe taxi, or W70,000 in a regular cab.

More information is available at www.airport.or.kr/eng.

Gimpo

By bus

The **KAL Limousine Bus** stops right outside 17 of Seoul's major hotels and has plenty of room for luggage, plus free water and a phone on board. There are four routes to choose from and tickets (W9,000) are available from KAL counters inside the terminal. The stops are prominently signposted, and buses leave every 15–20 minutes. Call (02) 2656-5109 for information.

As from Incheon, there are SSBs from Gimpo to Seoul.

Airport Limousine Buses go directly to the Korea City Air Terminal (KCAT) leaving every 10 to 20 minutes between 7.35am and 10.20pm. They also go to Seoul Station-City Hall, Jamsil Terminal, Seoul National University, Geumcheongu office, Gwangmyeong, and Yeongdeungpo. Tickets (W9,000) are available from the counters on the first floor of the airport. Call (02) 551-0077/8 for information.

By subway

Subway Line 5 is cheap (W900 with

transportation card/W1,000 cash) and leaves directly from the airport, but flights of stairs in the stations make this method impractical for anyone carrying heavy suitcases or using a wheelchair.

By taxi

Expect to pay about W50,000 from Gimpo to downtown Seoul for a deluxe taxi; and W35,000 if you take a regular cab. The exact fare will depend on traffic conditions and your final destination.

Domestic Travel

By Air

Several airlines, including Jeju-Air, Korean Air, and Asiana, conduct air travel within Korea. Daily flights from Gimpo Airport to Jeju-do, Busan, Gwangju, Daegu, Yeosu, Pohang, Jinju, and Ulsan are available on domestic carriers with flight times of 40–65 minutes. Flights from Seoul to Yangyang in Gangwon Province are available only on Korean Air. Visit www.airport.co.kr/eng for daily schedules. Tickets are available at major hotels and tourist and travel agencies. Security at the airport is tight; passengers and baggage are checked, and sharp items, liquids, knives, and certain other articles are withheld during the flight.

By Sea

Numerous ferries and jetfoils make regular connections between the mainland and the outlying islands. There are daily sailings between Busan and Jeju City (11½ hours); Busan and Sogwipo (15 hours); and Mokpo and Jeju City (5½ hours; 3 hours by high-speed ferry). Daily ferries operate between Pohang and Ullungdo (7½ hours).

Several routes on the south coast in the Hallyeosudo Waterway may be traveled by jetfoil from Geoje-do.

Ferry schedules change frequently and operators cancel trips at short notice if the weather gets bad, or sometimes for no apparent reason at all.

Travel arrangements should be made with travel agents and time should be allowed for last-minute changes especially if you travel during the monsoon season. The Korean National Tourism Organization (KNTO) provides information on schedules, itineraries, and fares, call (02) 1330. Giving yourself extra leeway as you plan will greatly improve your peace of mind if there are unexpected delays.

BELOW: buses connect Seoul with Incheon International Airport.

ABOVE: rail services are good.

By Rail

Three kinds of service are available in South Korea's efficient and fast inter-city train system: KTX is the high-speed bullet train with the best facilities; the super-express *Saemaul* is fast, comfortable and air-conditioned and usually has a dining car; the express *Mugunghwa* may also have a dining car and sleeper facilities, but it depends on the route. All three types of train have comfortable seats with plenty of leg room and may also have private compartments for families. If you are planning to travel on a weekend or public holiday, it's advisable to book at least two weeks in advance. For information, call 1544-7788 ext. 1. The KNTO also provides detailed information, tel: (02) 1330.

For more information about schedules and routes, browse www. korail.go.kr.

By Road

Inter-city Buses: There are four kinds of inter-city buses: the *Udeung Gosok*, which is the most comfortable and usually includes a public phone and a video; the *Gosok* express bus (cheaper long-distance); the *Jikhaeng* (first class local and direct route); and the *Wanhaeng* (round-about with frequent stops). It is advisable to buy bus tickets in advance for a reserved seat. Listed below are six main bus stations in Seoul and their major destinations:

Dong Seoul Bus Terminal: Located near the river and Gangbyeon subway station (line 2); buses run to destinations south and east of Seoul including Chuncheon, Seoraksan, Sokcho, Yangyang, Gangneung, Gwangju, and Andong. Tel: (02) 455-3161.

Gangnam Express Bus Terminal/ Central City Terminal: The main bus terminal, located south of the Han River in Banpodong, provides only express bus service to cities out of Seoul. Has its own subway station, "Express Bus Terminal," on lines 3 and 7. Tel: (02) 535-4151 for Gyeongbu Line (to Gyeongsang-do Province); tel: (02) 6282-0600 for Jeolla Line (to Jeolla-do Province).

Nambu Bus Terminal: South of the river with its own subway stop (line 3); services to Buyeo, Cheongju, Gongju, Jonju, Songnisan, Jeongju, Daejeon. Tel: (02) 521-8550 ext. 0.

Sinchon Bus Terminal: Five minutes' walk from Sinchon subway station (line 2); nonstop buses to Ganghwa-do: 5.40am–10pm; trip takes 1 hour 30 minutes. Tel: (02) 324-0611.

Sangbong Bus Terminal: Close to Sangbong subway station (line 7). Most buses are for destinations to the east of Seoul. Tel: (02) 435-2129.

Seoul Seobu Bus Terminal: In Bulgwangdong (northern Sodaemungu); service to Haengjusanseong, Uijeongbu. Tel: (02) 355-5103.

Car Rental

Foreigners should use extreme care driving in South Korea. The accident rate is one of the highest in the world and, in a legal dispute, foreigners tend to come off worse unless accompanied or supported by a local. Many road signs are only in Korean Hangeul script. Cars usually only have Korean GPS. One option is to not drive at all, but another possibility is to take on a chauffeur with your rental car, which costs around W180,000 inclusive for a ten-hour day. Hertz and Avis are represented by local companies **Kumho** (tel: 02 797-8000) and **Avis Korea** (tel: 02 1544-1600).

BELOW: a "T-Money" stored-value card for the Seoul subway.

City Transport

The majority of people living in Seoul depend on public transport to get around. The subway is efficient and foreign-user-friendly; the bus system is less adapted to non-Korean speakers but still workable, while taxis seem to swarm everywhere. Use of the T Money card system is now mandatory in Seoul subways and will likely become so in other major cities as well.

City Buses

During less hectic commuting hours, getting around on the local city bus can be interesting, quick, and cheap. The driver usually turns up his radio so everybody can listen to the local baseball game, a soap opera, or to the latest hits. Confucian ethics generally prevail on board the bus: students offer their seats to mothers toting babies and to the elderly and, out of mutual consideration, those seated relieve those standing of their schoolbooks and shopping bags. Smoking is prohibited.

Buses run frequently from 5am to around 11.45pm daily. Bus fares in Seoul are W900 for prepaid-card users and W1,100 for those paying cash. The T Money card is a convenient way to pay.

The W900 bus and subway fare applies over a given distance no matter how many times passengers transfer buses (including village buses) or subways. A surcharge of W100 is charged for every additional 5km (3 miles) beyond that given distance. (For buses, the distance surcharge only applies if you transfer.) The fare for buses linking Seoul and neighboring Gyeonggi-do is W1,700, or W1,500 for passengers using prepaid cards.

Seoul's transit system has buses in one of four colors – blue, green, red, or yellow – depending on their function. Blue buses (main line) provide services on major trunk roads between downtown Seoul and satellite cities. Green buses (branch line) service routes between subway stations and nearby residential areas and main bus lines. (These routes are often also serviced by village buses.) Red buses (wide area line) service routes between major areas (downtown, Gangnam, Yeongdeungpo, etc.) and metropolitan satellite cities (Ilsan, Bundang, Uijeongbu, etc.). Yellow buses (circular line) serve circular belt roads in the downtown and major metropolitan area.

To search for Seoul public bus routes, go to http://english.seoul.go.kr/images/SeoulBusMap.pdf.

Intra-city bus and subway fares depend on the total distance traveled. You can pay cash or purchase a transportation card that entitles you to free transfers in some cases.

In addition to the regular city buses, there are "Seat Style Buses" (jwajeok, see page 277), which follow similar routes but with fewer stops and for a somewhat higher fare. These are designed for commuter use and generally make few stops downtown.

Destinations are written on the side of the bus in Hangeul and on street signs at the bus stops. Route maps for the entire system are virtually nonexistent and change so frequently that it is impossible to keep track. The routes are mapped out on a panel inside the bus, but destinations are again written only in Hangeul. The best way to get around the matter is with directions from a hotel concierge or a business partner. Two rules of thumb: when the bus comes, run to where it stops and leap on; at the other end, get to the exit before the bus stops and jump off just as fast.

A final word of caution: beware of pickpockets on the bus and at crowded bus stops.

Subway

Roomy, inexpensive, color-coded, prominently signed in English and Hangeul, Seoul's subway system – first opened in 1974 – is the most

ABOVE: high-speed KTX train.

convenient form of public transport for visitors. There are eight lines, and the subway also hooks up with the Korean National Railway. From Seoul Railway Station, it goes to six major destinations: Cheongnyangni Railway Station and Songbuk district to the north, and to Incheon (39km/24 miles west), Suwon (41km/25 miles south), Jamsil, and Guro. One-way tickets cost a basic W900 and you must pay with the T Money card, an automated prepaid system. Trains run from 5am to midnight at three-minute intervals during rush hours, and at six-minute intervals at other times. Smoking is prohibited on platforms as well as in the cars. The following are points of interest within walking distance of each subway stop within the city walls:

City Hall (Taepyeongno): City Hall, Deoksu Place, British Embassy, major

hotels, banks, department stores, Seoul Tourist Information Center.

Jonggak (Jongno): Bosingak (city bell tower), bookstores (with foreign-language sections), Korean National Tourism Organization, Jogye-sa (Buddhist Temple), Communications Memorial Center, Seoul Immigration Office, Gyeongbok Palace, National Museum, Folk Museum, Embassies of USA, Japan, and Canada, Sejong Center for the Performing Arts, Yi Sun-sin statue at Gwanghwamun intersection.

Jongno 3-ga: Pagoda (Tapgol) Park and shopping arcade, Jongmyo (Royal Confucian Shrine), Insadong (antique shops, art galleries, etc).

Jongno 5-ga: Dongdaemun market, herb shops.

Dongdaemun: Dongdaemun (East Gate), Seoul Baseball Stadium, Hwanghakdong flea market.

Taxis

Taxis are cheap and plentiful (except late at night, when they can be hard to find). They fill in the gaps left by the bus and subway networks and provide a handy alternative when you don't feel like braving the crowds. Cabs cluster outside hotels and in ranks in busy city areas, and in Seoul may also be requested by phone (02-3431-5100, among others). Most drivers do not speak English, however, and some have a rather hazy knowledge of the geography of their home town: unless your destination is a major hotel, transport facility, or landmark, it's best to have clear instructions written in Hangeul – and, if possible, a map too.

Subtle differences in your mangling of Korean syllables can lead to problems too, so don't be impatient if it's hard to get your destination across. Though rare,

some instances of price gouging or other scams are possible. It is a good idea to ask the concierge for a price estimate prior to getting a cab.

There are two types of taxi – regular and deluxe. Cabs may be hailed to the curbside and (though techincally illegal) can be shared with other passengers bound in the same direction. Each passenger pays only for the distance he or she travels (two or more traveling together pay as one passenger). This taxi-sharing system is called hapseung, and has become less common due to stricter enforcement by authorities.

Fares for regular cabs begin at W2,400 for the first 2km (1¼ miles) with W100 for each additional 144 meters. The meter also runs on time when movement is slower than 15 kilometers per hour and W100 is charged for every 35

seconds in addition to the basic fare. Between midnight and 4am fares are automatically increased by 20 percent.

The deluxe mobeom taxis – with the black and yellow livery – cost W4,500 for the first 2km (1¼ miles) and W200 for each additional 164 meters or each 39 seconds if the speed drops below 15km per hour. Receipts and in-car phones are available and there is no late-night surcharge.

Also available are taxi vans (daehyeong taxi); their fare system is the same as mobeom taxis. They can accommodate up to eight passengers and have plenty of space for luggage. They can be requested on tel: (02) 888-2000.

US military ID holders may also use Army–Air Force Exchange taxis, which charge slightly higher rates in dollars.

A CCOMMODATIONS

HOTELS, YOUTH HOSTELS, BED AND BREAKFAST

Choosing Accommodations

Many international hotel chains have properties in South Korea, vying for business with locally run accommodations that range from five-star hotels to the most basic homestays.

The accommodations and services in South Korea's finer hotels are generally superb. As might be expected, a stay at an international hotel can be very expensive. At these up-market hotels you can expect health clubs, swimming pools, and extensive conference and business facilities. In the resort areas of Jeju-do and Gyeongju some even have indoor driving ranges, bowling alleys, tennis courts, casinos, and hot-spring baths.

Stays generally correspond to price: if you want an ultra-luxury, 5-star type experience, you'll want to choose a hotel with **$$$** as the price. Generally you'll get as good or even better facilities and service as you would in their Western counterparts. The mid-range hotels offer decent amenities and service, but rooms are simpler and there may only be one restaurant or lounge in the hotel instead of four or five.

Budget hotels cater to Korean travelers and their families. They are usually clean, and a good place to sleep if you're looking at cost rather than amenities. The rooms are likely to be small, and very basic. In the cities, some of the staff are likely to speak a reasonable amount of English, but even in the places that don't speak English staff will make efforts to communicate.

Thousands of **yeogwan** (Korean inns offering ondol-style floors) have popped up all over the countryside, where they are often the only option for the weary traveler. In the city, yeogwan cluster together, especially near transportation centers. Most are very pleasant but some can be rather dirty – the lobby is not always a good indicator of how clean the rooms are, so feel free to ask to look at a room first before you stay. Yet even the less-than-immaculate spots provide the budget traveler with an inexpensive, safe, comfortable place to sleep. You may find yourself on the upper floors, since many yeogwan also double as "love hotels," where the lower-level rooms are let by the hour. Yeogwan are a favorite of Western English teachers, and other extended travelers. Most are family-owned and operated, and unlikely to have English-speaking staff.

Many people balk at the concept of the "love hotel", where rooms can be rented by the "visit" (usually a few hours) rather than by the night; however, these hotels are often as clean as their motel counterparts, and they often have excellent in-room amenities, such as giant flat-screen televisions, DVD players and game consoles, a computer with internet service, a fridge, and so on, all for a price tag that's comparable to or often less than the similar business hotel. Stays at love hotels used to be a novelty 20 years ago, but true travelers know this can be a great way to save a few dollars while on the road.

The **hasukjip** (boarding house) has its place among students, working bachelors, and itinerants. Rooms are rented by the month, and the price includes very simple home-cooked meals. If you plan on being in Korea

Korean-style rooms

Just about every hotel in South Korea has a number of Korean-style rooms. These come with traditional ondol underfloor heating and a Korean mattress (yo) on the floor. Room rates are normally the same as a standard double room, but some hotels charge up to 50 percent extra.

for an extended stay at the same location, ask around for a goshiwon, which are tiny dorm-style rooms (some with their own bath, others shared) used by students who are cramming for exams. You must be library-style quiet in these places, but they rent for as low as W250,000 per month.

For the working foreigner, the **setbang** – a rented room in a local home – is another economical option. Except for the fact that the tenant happens to share the same roof with others, he generally has to look after himself.

A chain of **youth hostels** has been established in many of the provinces, and hostels are open to international members. The charge for one night varies but is competitive with the cheapest hotels, and offers the chance to meet fellow travelers. Reservations or further information can be obtained from the Korea Youth Hostel Association, tel: (02) 725-3031; www.kyha.or.kr/english.

The Korea Labo Corp arranges **homestays** (minbak) for foreigners with Korean families who may speak English. If you want to take part in this program, contact Labo (www.labostay.or.kr) at least two weeks in advance with details of where you want to stay, when and for how long. Rates start at W35,000 per person per night, which includes breakfast. Labo will then find a family and send you some information about them and arrange a rendezvous.

For those who would like to experience the old Korean lifestyle, a **hanok-stay** is recommended. Bukchon is the area in Seoul where traditional Korean houses are extremely well preserved and there you can find inexpensive *hanok* guesthouses: Bukchon Guesthouse, tel: (02) 743-8530; Seoul Guesthouse, tel: (02) 745-0057; Urijip Guesthouse, tel: (02) 744-0536. Easy access from Anguk station on subway line 3. Room rates are generally W35,000–70,000.

Youth Hostels

There are 63 youth hostels in South Korea which are members of the Korea Youth Hostel Association. For information and booking, call the association on (02) 725-3031; www. kyha.or.kr. The following is a small selection:
Seoul
Olympic Parktel
88-8 Bangidong, Songpagu
Tel: (02) 410-2114

ABOVE: a modern mid-range hotel in Busan.

Fax: (02) 410-2100
Gangwon-do
Seoraksan
Seorakdong, Sokcho
Tel: (033) 636-7115
Fax: (033) 636-7107
Chungcheongbuk-do
Sajo Maeul
Oncheonri, Sangmo-myeon, Chungju
Tel: (043) 846-9200
Fax: (043) 846-9107
Chungcheongnam-do
Samjung Buyeo
Gugyori, Buyeoeup, Buyeo
Tel: (041) 835-3102
Fax: (041) 835-3791

Gyeongsangbuk-do
Bulguksa
Jinhyeondong, Gyeongju
Tel: (054) 746-0826
Fax: (054) 746-7805
Gyeongsangnam-do
Namhae
Geumsongri, Samdongmyeon, Namhae
Tel: (055) 867-4848
Fax: (055) 867-4850
Jeju-do
Shinsung Resort Seogwipo YH
Seogwipo, Beophwandong, Seogwipo
Tel: (064) 739-0114
Fax: (064) 739-7552

ACCOMMODATIONS LISTINGS

SEOUL

Airport
11-21 Gonghangdong, Gangseogu
Tel: (02) 2662-1113
Fax: (02) 2663-3355
www.hotelairport.co.kr
Has 55 rooms (10 Korean-style).
Free shuttle from Kimpo airport (a few minutes' ride) Close to subway station and there is a scheduled bus to Incheon airport. Day-use available. **$$**
Central Tourist Hotel
227-1 Jangsadong, Jongnogu
Tel: (02) 2265-4121, (02) 6365-6500
Fax: (02) 2265-6139
Although the building itself is old, it is clean and in a convenient location. Right in front of the river, with a sauna. The hotel has 78

rooms (eight Korean-style).
$$
Crown
34-69 Itaewondong, Yongsangu
Tel: (02) 797-4111
Fax: (02) 796-1010
www.hotelcrown.com
Bar, sauna, and 170 rooms (13 Korean-style). A bit far from subway station (15-minute walk) but with large rooms. The interior is slightly outdated, but it remains an otherwise good hotel in a convenient location. It is close to the War Memorial/museum. **$$**
Grand Hilton
201-1 Hongeundong, Seodaemungu
Tel: (02) 3216-5656
Fax: (02) 3216-7799
www.grandhiltonseoul.com
A very swish hideaway

at the foot of Mount Baengnyonsan. 7 restaurants and bars, and an indoor pool. 20 minutes to downtown by courtesy shuttle. **$$$**
Grand Hyatt
747-7 Hannamdong, Yongsangu
Tel: (02) 797-1234
Fax: (02) 798-6953
www.grandhyattseoul.co.kr
Apart from all the joys of the "Hyatt touch" (the swimming pool overlooks city of Seoul and Han River, becomes an ice rink in winter! Dec–Feb), the Grand Hyatt is one of the nicest spots to have a nightcap or stay overnight. Many of the rooms have wall-to-wall windows that offer unparalleled views.
$$$

Grand InterContinental
521 Teheran-ro, Gangnam-gu
Tel: (02) 555-5656
Fax: (02) 559-7990

PRICE CATEGORIES
Price categories are per night for two people sharing a standard double room:
$ = under 75,000 won
$$ = 75,000–200,000 won
$$$ = over 200,000 won

ABOVE: the Lobby Lounge at the Sheraton Grande Walker Hill.

www.seoul.intercontinental.com
Business-oriented hotel in Gangnam with easy access to the COEX mall and World Trade Center. Rooms are comfortable and suites have excellent views of the city. **$$$**

Hamilton
119-25 Itaewondong, Yongsangu
Tel: (02) 794-0171
Fax: (02) 795-0457
www.hamilton.co.kr
Has 166 rooms, a nightclub and outdoor pool and sauna, both at an extra charge. 24-hour internet room for business needs. Proximity to Itaewon makes this a great location. It's clean, with friendly staff. **$$**

Seoul Garden Hotel
169-1 Dohwadong, Mapogu
Tel: (02) 717-9441
Fax: (02) 715-9441
www.seoulgarden.co.kr
Located to the west of Itaewon. Only a few mins' walk from subway stations. The airport bus departs right in front of the hotel. Close to river boat landing. Has 362 rooms (five Korean-style). Health club, sauna, and bar. **$$**

Lotte Hotel Seoul
1 Sogongdong, Junggu
Tel: (02) 771-1000
Fax: (02) 752-3758
www.lottehotel.co.kr
In the heart of the city center, and ideal for those with retail therapy on their minds. Very sophisticated interior, and service to match, the Lotte is one of Seoul's finest. **$$$**

Millennium Seoul Hilton
395 Namdaemun 5-ga, Junggu
Tel: (02) 753-7788
Fax: (02) 754-2510
www.hilton.co.kr
A mainstream conference hotel, but one that still retains an intimate and friendly atmosphere. Nicely furnished and bright rooms. Free cell phone rental for business rooms and suites. While not exactly a luxury resort hotel, it's a very good business hotel with ample luxury for those who need it. **$$$**

Novotel Ambassador Doksan
1030-1 Doksan 4-dong, Geumcheongu
Tel: (02) 838-1101
Fax: (02) 854-4799
www.ambatel.com/doksan
Health club, sauna, and bar. Not very close to downtown, but free shuttle bus to many downtown attractions make up for that. Good breakfast buffet, though not included with the room. **$$$**

Novotel Ambassador Gangnam
603 Yeoksamdong, Gangnamgu
Tel: (02) 567-1101
www.ambatel.com/gangnam
Indoor pool, bar, health club, sauna. Great business hotel with attentive staff. Close to the subway station. **$$$**

Seoul Plaza Hotel
23 Taepyeongno 2-ga, Junggu
Tel: (02) 771-2200
Fax: (02) 755-8897
www.seoulplaza.co.kr
Smart, fashionable, and excellently located for the center of the city. Good view of Deoksugung palace. Few minutes, walk from subway station. **$$$**

Ramada Seoul
112-5 Samseongdong, Gangnamgu
Tel: (02) 6202-2000
Fax: (02) 6202-2001
www.ramadaseoul.co.kr
Has a spa and sauna, and fitness club. **$$$**

Renaissance Seoul
676 Yeoksamdong, Gangnamgu
Tel: (02) 555-0501
Fax: (02) 553-8118
www.renaissance-seoul.com
A smart hotel south of the river, with the airy, spacious top-floor Club Horizon, which serves one of the best breakfasts in Seoul. Online specials can make this a competitive option, but it's a bit far from the subway for those who don't want to take a cab. **$$–$$$**

Ritz-Carlton
602 Yeoksamdong, Gangnamgu
Tel: (02) 3451-8000
Fax: (02) 3451-8188
www.ritzcarltonseoul.com
Discreet and tasteful, and head and shoulders above many of its competitors

south of the river when it comes to service and facilities. **$$$**

Sheraton Grande Walker Hill
175 Gwangjangdong, Gwangjingu
Tel: (02) 455-5000
Fax: (02) 452-6867
www.sheraton.com/walkerhill
www.sheratonwalkerhill.co.kr
A mecca for gamblers; the casino infuses the entire hotel with an aura of excitement. Offers "Supex Gimchi", pickled veggies created from its own *gimchi* research institute. Located on the ground of Shilla dynasty era's fortress, with spectacular views of the Han river. **$$$**

Grand Ambassador Seoul
186-54 Jangchungdong 2-ga, Junggu
Tel: (02) 2275-1101
Fax: (02) 2272-0773
https://grand.ambatel.com
Large hotel with over 400 rooms, a health club, indoor pool, and sauna. **$$$**

Westin Chosun
87-1 Sogongdong, Junggu
Tel: (02) 771-0500
Fax: (02) 753-6370
www.echosunhotel.com
453 immaculate rooms with in-room espresso machines. Staff are warm and breakfasts (included) are excellent. A wine hour in the lounge runs from 5–7pm. Access to subways or other city-hall area locations is excellent. **$$$**

YMCA
9 Jongno 2-ga, Jongnogu
Tel: (02) 734-6884
Fax: (02) 734-8003
Good location, 79 rooms. Inside had complete remodeling in 2006 and, although basic, it is clean and in a good location. **$**

BELOW: the Westin Chosun Hotel.

GYEONGGI PROVINCE

Incheon

Paradise Hotel Incheon
3-2 1-ga Hangdong, Junggu
Tel: (032) 762-5181
Fax: (032) 763-5281
www.paradiseincheon.co.kr
Central location by the inner harbor. Casino (for foreign guests only), sauna, nightclub, and Korean, Japanese, and Western restaurants. Has 170 rooms (20 Korean-style, they do have some *ondol* rooms, but call ahead to make sure one is available).
$$

BELOW: Castle Hotel, Suwon

Pupyong
181 Galsandong, Bupyeonggu
Tel: (032) 504-8181
Fax: (032) 504-8182
Has 31 rooms (four Korean-style), a sauna, café, and cocktail lounge. Convenient as numerous stores and restaurants are nearby. Close to subway station as well. **$$**

Ramada Songdo
812 Dongchundong, Yeonsugu
Tel: (032) 832-2000
Fax: (032) 830-2345
www.ramada-songdo.co.kr
Located next to Songdo Amusement Park. Health club, sauna, and cocktail lounge. Has 195 rooms (20 Korean-style). Number of rooms cannot be confirmed.
$$$

Suwon

Castle
Umandong, Paldalgu, Suwon

Tel: (031) 211-6666
Fax: (031) 212-8811
www.hcastle.co.kr
Business center, sauna, nightclub, and 81 rooms (two Korean-style). Next to the bus terminal. **$$**

Regency
47 Gucheondong, Baldalgu, Suwon
Tel: (031) 246-4141
Fax: (031) 243-9296
www.htregency.co.kr
Good location near (10 minutes' walk to) the south gate, with 65 rooms (four Korean-style). Friendly staff. **$$**

GANGWON PROVINCE

Gangneung

Gangneung
Ponamdong, Gangneung
Tel: (033) 641-7701
Fax: (033) 641-7712
With 74 rooms (38 Korean-style). Located between the railway station and the police station.
$$

Gyeongpo Beach
303-4 Gangmungdong, Gangneung
Tel: (033) 644-2277
Fax: (033) 644-2397
www.lekyungpobeach.co.kr
(in Korean only)
Located right on the beach to the northeast of the city, with 68 rooms (31 Korean-style). Nightclub and Western and Korean restaurants. New and modern hotel (built in 2004). Bicycle rental for guests.
$$

Sun Castle
Jumunjinri, Jumunjineup, Gangneung
Tel: (033) 661-1950
Fax: (033) 661-1958

Facilities include a tennis court. Has 52 rooms (18 Korean-style).
$$

Seoraksan National Park

Sorak Park
74-3 Seorakdong, Sokcho
Tel: (033) 636-7711
Fax: (033) 636-7732
www.hotelsorakpark.co.kr
About 1.5km (1 mile) from the park entrance, this is the region's top hotel, with 121 rooms (18 Korean-style) with private balcony overlooking mountain. Excellent facilities include casino, cocktail lounge, nightclub, sauna, and health club.
$$$

Seoraksan Tourist Hotel
151 Seorakdong
Tel: (033) 636-7101
Fax: (000) 000 7100
www.seorakhotel.com
Close to the park entrance, with an ice-skating rink and swimming pool. Has 124 rooms (36 Korean-style). Room# and facilities cannot be confirmed. But it has bright and airy rooms and wood panel exterior fits nicely with surrounding mountain scenery.
$$

Sokcho

Sokcho Royal
478-19 Jungangdong, Sokcho
Tel: (033) 631-8700
Fax: (033) 631-6758
Right on the beach, Not on the beach, but it is close to it while still easy access to bus terminal, market, and shops. About 1km (½ mile) north of the inter-city bus terminal, with 70 rooms (40 cozy Korean-style), and a nightclub.
$$

Yongpeong Dragon Valley Ski Resort

Dragon Valley Tourist Hotel
Yongsanri, Doam-myeon,
Pyeongchang
Tel: (033) 335-5757
Fax: (033) 335-0160
www.yongpyong.co.kr
Located at the center of Yongpyong with great views of the city, it has a health club, sauna, indoor golf course, ski slope, nightclub, and 195 rooms (57 Korean-style), including spacious Western-style rooms. **$$$**

PRICE CATEGORIES
Price categories are per night for two people sharing a standard double room:
$ = under 75,000 won
$$ = 75,000–200,000 won
$$$ = over 200,000 won

TRANSPORTATION

ACCOMMODATIONS

EATING OUT

ACTIVITIES

A – Z

LANGUAGE

CHUNGCHEONG PROVINCES

Cheongju

Gallery
1831 Bongmyeongdong,
Heungdeokgu, Cheongju
Tel: (043) 267-1121
Fax: (043) 263-9532
www.newgalleryhotel.com
This hotel was completely
remodeled in late 2009, but
despite the new decor it's
still very reasonably priced.
Real Korean antiques are
used to decorate the hotel's
interior, and there's a nice
cocktail lounge if you feel like
a drink or nightcap. Also has
a tea ceremony room and an
indoor driving range. **$$**

Daejeon

Chateau Grace
72-5 Yongjeondong, Donggu
Tel: (042) 639-0111
Fax: (042) 639-0077
Has 102 rooms (37
Korean-style), a sauna, and

nightclub. **$$**
Riviera Yuseong
445-5 Bongmyeongdong,
Yuoseonggu
Tel: (042) 823-2111
Fax: (042) 822-5250
www.hotelriviera.co.kr
Health club, sauna, hot-
spring baths, indoor and
outdoor pools, nightclub,
and a mix of Korean-style
and Western-style rooms.
The hotel is ideally located,
only 5 minutes' walk from
the Daejeon express bus
terminal. **$$**

Onyang

Onyang Grand Park
300-28 Oncheondong, Asan
Tel: (041) 543-9711
Fax: (041) 543-9729
www.grand-hotel.co.kr
Indoor and outdoor hot-
spring baths are what set
this hotel apart from the
others nearby. A bowling

alley is another distinction.
Sauna, swimming pool,
nightclub, and Western and
Korean restaurants. Has
151 rooms (53 Korean-
style). **$$**
Onyang Hot Spring Hotel
242-10 Oncheondong, Asan
Tel: (041) 540-1201
Fax: (041) 540-1234
www.onyanghotel.co.kr
Sauna, spring baths, fitness
center, 175 rooms. **$$**

BELOW: Onyang hot springs.

Songnisan National Park

Lake Hills Songnisan
Sanaeri, Naesongnimyeon, Boeun
Tel: (043) 542-5281
Fax: (043) 542-5198
www.lakehills.co.kr/network/tel_
songnisan/songnisan_mainl.html#
This hotel is just outside of
the national park entrance,
so it's in a prime location
for nature lovers and hikers.
Has 132 rooms (90 Korean-
style), cocktail lounge, and
outdoor pool.
$$$

GYEONGSANGBUK PROVINCE

Andong

Andong Park
324 Unheungdong, Andong
Tel: (054) 835-1501
Fax: (054) 853-5445
41 rooms (15 Korean-
style) and bar. Only a short
distance from the train
station (5 minutes' walk)
and bus terminal (10
minutes' walk). It's also
close to downtown. **$**

Daegu

Crown
330-6 Sincheon 4-dong, Donggu
Tel: (053) 755-3001
Fax: (053) 755-3367
Has 56 rooms (14 Korean-
style), a bar, and sauna.
Handy for the railway
station. **$$**
Grand
563-1 Beomeodong, Suseonggu
Tel: (053) 742-0001
Fax: (053) 742-0002
www.taegugrand.co.kr
Luxury hotel with 86
rooms (11 Korean-style),
with very tasteful decor.

It's located about 3km (2
miles) southeast of the city
center. Health club, sauna,
and nightclub. Nice buffet
restaurant is only open for
lunch or private parties, but
the classy lounge is open
from 7am to midnight. **$$$**
Hotel Inter-Burgo
300 Manchondong, Suseonggu
Tel: (053) 602-7114
Fax: (053) 953-2008
www.ibhotel.com
By the river and Mangu
Park. 133 rooms (36
Korean-style), pool, golf
range, sauna, and nightclub.

BELOW: Daegu's
Prince Hotel.

Small shopping mall and
Spanish Cultural Center
within the complex. **$$$**
Joil-jang
147-3 Duryu2-dong Dalseo-gu,
Daegu
Tel: (053)-624-4007
17 very simply furnished
rooms that will work best
for those on a tight budget.
Other similarly priced hotels
are nearby. **$**
Prince
1824-2 Daemyeong 2-dong,
Namgu
Tel: (053) 628-1001
Fax: (053) 650-5600
www.princehotel.co.kr
Located near Daegu
University. Health club,
sauna and nightclub, and
117 rooms (12 Korean-
style). Convenient location
for both business and
leisure travelers, this is also
a popular spot for university
students' parents during
graduations and school
entry, so it can be booked
solid during those times.
Reservations aren't a bad
idea at all. **$$$**

Pohang

Sun Prince Hotel
Jungang-dong 17
Tel: (054) 242-2800
Fax: (054) 242-6006
This simple hotel is a good
deal for people on a budget
and is fancier than other
motels in its class. Rooms
can be either Western or
ondol style. **$**

GYEONGJU

Bulguksa
648-1 Jinhyondong, Gyeongju
Tel: (054) 746-1911
Fax: (054) 746-1920
www.bgshotel.kr
80 Korean-style rooms. As its name implies, this hotel is located close to the Bulguk-sa temple. The rooms are simple but clean and are amply furnished with fridges and other amenities. **$**

Commodore Chosun
San 410-2 Sinpyeongdong, Gyeongju
Tel: (054) 745-7701
Fax: (054) 740-8260
www.chosunhotel.net
A luxury hotel, right on Bomun Lake; facilities include tennis courts, swimming pool, hot spring, sauna, nightclub. Has 263 rooms (37 Korean-style) and a variety of luxury-class dining options. It's a popular choice for Korean television and movie talents as well, so keep a pen handy for autographs. **$$$**

Concorde
410 Sinpyeongdong, Gyeongju
Tel: (054) 745-7000
Fax: (054) 745-7010
www.concorde.co.kr
On the shores of Bomun Lake, this luxury hotel has 307 rooms (12 Korean-style), swimming pool, sauna, and disco. **$$$**

Gyeongju Hilton
370 Sinpyeongdong, Gyeongju
Tel: (054) 745-7788
Fax: (054) 745-7799
www.kyongjuhilton.co.kr
324 rooms (13 Korean-style) that are tastefully done, with a nice lobby and a connection to the Sonje art museum nearby. Close to the convention center on the shores of Bomun Lake. Health club, tennis courts, indoor and outdoor swimming pools, and a casino. **$$$**

Gyeongju Park Tourist Hotel
170-1 Noseodong, Gyeongju
Tel: (054) 742-8804
Fax: (054) 742-8808
Good location near the bus terminal and Dumulli Park in downtown Gyeongju. **$**

Hyundai
477-2 Sinpyeongdong, Gyeongju
Tel: (054) 748-2233
Fax: (054) 748-8234
www.hyundaihotel.com
On Bomun Lake, with 331 rooms (33 Korean-style). Fully equipped luxury, with indoor and outdoor pools, health club, tennis court, and hot-spring baths. Well-appointed rooms. Along with Korean and international cuisine restaurants, there is a nice bakery for those who crave a morning croissant. **$$$**

Kolon
111-1 Madong, Gyeongju
Tel: (054) 746-9001
Fax: (054) 746-6331
www.kolonhotel.co.kr
Luxury hotel with 319 rooms (34 Korean-style), swimming pool, tennis court, indoor driving range, golf course, casino, sauna, hot-spring baths, golf course, and nightclub. Nice jogging/walking trail through their garden. **$$$**

GYEONGSANGNAM PROVINCE

Busan

Commodore
743-80 Yeongjudong, Jung-gu
Tel: (051) 466-9101
Fax: (051) 462-9101
www.commodore.co.kr
Has 314 rooms (6 Korean-style), health club, sauna, indoor pool, and nightclub. Between the railway station and downtown. Traditional Korean architecture motif is carried out nicely and gives a Korean flair for those wanting it. **$$**

Dong Bang Tourist Hotel
210-82 Oncheon 1-dong, Dongnae-gu
Tel: (051) 552-9511
Fax: (051) 552-9274
www.hoteldongbang.com
113 rooms (39 Korean-style). Sauna and hot-spring bath. Sky lounge overlooking the Nam River, with a nice buffet restaurant and coffee shop. **$$**

Haeundae Grand
651-2 Udong, Haeundae-gu
Tel: (051) 7400-5557
Fax: (051) 7400-141/3
www.grandhotel.co.kr
Located west of the city at Haeundae beach resort, with 325 rooms (38 Korean-style), fitness center, bowling alley, indoor golf range, movie center, disco. **$$$**

Hillside
743-33 Yeongju 1-dong, Junggu
Tel: (051) 464-0567
Fax: (051) 464-1214
53 rooms (28 Korean-style). Sauna. Oceanside room overlooks islands. **$**

Lotte
503-15 Bujeongdong Busanjin-gu
Tel: (051) 810-1000
Fax: (051) 810-5110
www.lottehotel.co.kr
Super-luxury hotel with 806 rooms (15 Korean-style) and a spectacular lobby. Located in the Somyon district of the city close to a lively market area, the hotel has a full range of amenities, several restaurants, and fabulous views from the top-floor bar. **$$$**

Novotel
1405-16 Jungdong, Haeundae-gu
Tel: (051) 743-1234
Fax: (051) 743-1250
www.novotelbusan.com
325 rooms. Full facilities include health club, sauna, indoor pool, tennis court, hot-spring baths, and nightclub. Situated right on the beach. **$$$**

Paradise Hotel Busan
1408-5 Jungdong, Haeundae-gu
Tel: (051) 742-2121
Fax: (051) 742-2100
http://busan.paradisehotel.co.kr
Pardise Busan and its nearby Annex are spectacular in all the ways you'd expect from a Leading Hotel of the World. There's a Shapiro in the garden for those who like art, a world-class casino, and duty-free shopping. As if that wasn't enough, Haeundae beach doesn't get any closer: step outside, you're there. **$$$**

Paragon
564-25 Goebeopdong, Sasang-gu
Tel: (051) 328-2001
Fax: (051) 328-2009
West of the city, near the airport, 5-minute walk to a subway station, this convenient hotel offers spacious Western- and Korean-style rooms, a golf shop, sauna, and nightclub/bar. **$$**

Westin Chosun
737 Woo 1-dong, Haeundae-gu
Tel: (051) 749-7000
Fax: (051) 742-1313
www.chosunbeach.co.kr
Resort hotel with 290 rooms (10 Korean-style), health club, sauna, indoor pool, and hot-spring baths. Views of Haeundae beach are superb, and the hotel opens onto the beach so sunbathers couldn't ask for a better location. **$$$**

JEOLLA PROVINCES

Gwangju

Geumsoojang Tourist Hotel
559-1 Kyelim-dong
Tel: (062) 525-2111
Fax: (062) 525-7111
www.geumsoojang.co.kr
Amply furnished hotel with Korean (ondol) or Western-style rooms, most of which have a good view of the city. It's in a convenient location too, not far from Gwangju Railway Station, and there is a coffee shop, restaurant, and bar on the premises.
$

Prado Hotel
638-1 Baekun-dong
Tel: (062) 654-9999
Fax: (062) 654-0606
The Prado Hotel is a more upmarket spot than most Gwangju hotels, offering a spa, a variety of restaurants, and a choice of very attractively furnished Korean (ondol)- or Western-style rooms. It's well located in the centre of town. The basement bar is quite lively with a variety of live music acts through the week.
$$

Mudeung Park
63-1 Jisandong, Donggu
Tel: (062) 226-0011
Fax: (062) 226-0020
www.hotelmudeungpark.co.kr
The Mudeung Park features large Western- and Korean style rooms, and a well-equipped health club, sauna, tennis court, hot-spring baths, and nightclub. The hotel also features its own bowling alley, and an amusement park.
$$

Jeollabuk-do

Jeonju Hotel Core
627-3 Nosong-dong, Jeonju
Tel: (063) 285-1100
Fax: (063) 285-5707
www.corehotel.co.kr
110 rooms in both Western- and Korean-style options. Sauna, bar, and nightclub. Walking distance to downtown and tourist attractions, and it is fairly close to Jiri Mountain, Naejang Mountain, and Byeonsan Beach, with free shuttle service provided to many areas. You've also got numerous local shops and restaurants right around the hotel.
$$

Jeonju Tourist Hotel
Daga-dong 3-ga 28, Jeonju
Tel: (063) 280-7700

Fax: (063) 283-4478
www.jjhotel.co.kr (in Korean only)
A cut above similar hotels in the same price range, the Jeonju Tourist Hotel has a nice restaurant and rooms with some stunning city views. It's a popular choice for participants in the Jeonju Film Festival, therefore advance reservations are very much recommended.
$$

JEJU-DO

Jeju Grand
263-15 Yeondong
Tel: (064) 747-5000
Fax: (064) 742-3150
www.grand.co.kr
Large resort hotel with 512 rooms (30 Korean-style), each room with a great view, and there's a casino, cocktail lounge, health club, outdoor swimming pool, nightclub, and sauna.
$$$

Cheju Oriental
1197 Samdo 2-dong

Tel: (064) 752-8222
Fax: (064) 752-9777
www.oriental.co.kr
330 rooms. There is a small casino, and rooms with either a good mountain or water view.
$$

Hyatt Regency Jeju
3039-1 Saekdaldong, Seogwipo
Tel: (064) 733-1234
Fax: (064) 732-2039
www.hyattcheju.com
Complete with casino, cocktail lounge, health club, indoor and outdoor pools, tennis court, nightclub, sauna, and 224 rooms (25 Korean-style). All rooms have balconies, either with mountain and garden view or ocean view, and a nice circular interior with a beautiful garden and ornamental carp pool. The pleasant lounge bar area makes use of seasonal ingredients for cocktails, an elegant touch.
$$$

Lotte Hotel Jeju
2812-4 Saekdaldong, Seogwipo
Tel: (064) 731-1000
Fax: (064) 738-7305
www.lottehoteljeju.com
500 rooms (45 Korean-style). Spectacular resort hotel with every conceivable luxury and all amenities. Parents will appreciate the kids' play room and children's library. Everyone will appreciate the South Pacific-themed outdoor swimming pool. **$$$**

BELOW: Prado Hotel, Gwangju.

PRICE CATEGORIES
Price categories are per night for two people sharing a standard double room:
$ = under 75,000 won
$$ = 75,000–200,000 won
$$$ = over 200,000 won

E ATING OUT

RECOMMENDED RESTAURANTS, CAFÉS, AND BARS

Where to Eat

Koreans have great pride in and an enduring love affair with their own cuisine, and of late, Korean flavors, foods, and ingredients have found a niche in Western culture as well. It's no longer hard to find Westerners who relish the heat of good *gimchi*. *Bulgogi*, *bibimbap*, and Korean-style barbecue is commonplace today. But Koreans have likewise developed a taste for Western cuisine as well, and it's not hard to find excellent international restaurants in Seoul, Busan, even remote Jeju. These restaurants cater to a younger Korean clientele, rich Korean families, and foreigners. Those on a budget need look no further than the tiny corner shop for great cheap eats, and Koreans (and increasing numbers of Westerners) love flocking to the push-cart stalls at midnight for a snack before heading home.

The best hotels have fine Western, Japanese, and Korean restaurants; though they are expensive by Korean standards. But visitors to South Korea really should try to breach the language barrier and experience Korean food. Korean restaurants, from the cheap to the pricey, offer great value and some of the finest food in all of Asia.

Those who are in the income bracket where they don't need to ask the price of a meal should contact L'Avenue (Tel: 010-8670-1604, ask for Claudia), a private restaurant/catering service on a backstreet in Itaewon. The classy one-table restaurant can be reserved for French meals worthy of royalty, celebrities, and serious gourmands.

ABOVE: eating out is one of the great pleasures of a visit to South Korea.

Most restaurants are open for lunch and dinner, often with a 3pm to 5pm hiatus in the afternoon. Restaurants with night-time entertainment usually start their live music at 8pm, and they often close after midnight.

Below are types of restaurants you are likely to encounter in Korea:

Barbecue meat restaurants *(Bulgogijip)*. Beef *(sogogi)*, pork *(doejigogi)* and short rib *(galbi)* are marinated in soy sauce, sesame oil, garlic, green onions, and toasted sesame seeds, then char-broiled.

Raw fish restaurants *(Saengson Hoejip)*. Sliced fresh raw fish is served with a soy sauce *(ganjang)* or red pepper sauce *(chojang)*. Other fish dishes include *maeun tang* (hot pepper soup of fish, soybean curd (tofu), egg, and vegetables).

Ginseng Chicken Soup restaurants *(Samgyetangjip)*. Chicken stuffed with rice, white ginseng, and dates are steamed and served hot. Deep-fried chicken is also served.

Dumpling restaurants *(Mandujip)*. Meat, vegetables, and sometimes tofu are stuffed into dumplings and steamed, fried, or boiled in a broth. Chinese-style pastries baked in the restaurant are also sold.

Noodle restaurants *(Bunsikjip)*. Noodle dishes are the specialty but so are simple rice dishes. Some of the popular dishes are *Momil guksu* – buckwheat noodles with a sweet radish sauce; *naengmyeon* – cold potato flour or buckwheat flour noodles topped with sliced meat, vegetables, a boiled egg, and a pepper relish sauce and rice; *kongguksu* – wheat noodles in fresh soya milk; *odeng guksu* – wheat noodles topped with oriental fishcake in a broth; *Ramyeon* – instant noodles in instant broth; *udong* – wide wheat noodles with onions, fried tofu, red pepper powder, and egg; *bibimbap* – rice topped with parboiled fern bracken, bluebell root, soysprouts, spinach, and a fried egg, accompanied by a warming bowl of

Drinking Notes

There are at least five kinds of *suljip* (liquor house). The common bar or pub, sometimes called a *hof*, is usually a small, simple café, which serves liquor and beer. *Anju* (hors d'oeuvres) are served in most places; they are pricey but are nevertheless customarily ordered. The cheapest liquor is *soju* (sweet potato wine). Beer *(maekju)* comes either bottled *(byeong maekju)* or on draft *(saeng maekju)*.

broth; and *japchae* – rice vermicelli stir-fried with vegetables and various meat slices.

Steamed rice restaurants

(Baekbanjip). Rice is served with a variety of *gimchi, namul* (parboiled vegetables), fish, and soup (usually made of soybean paste) – the basic Korean meal. Other simple dishes, such as *naengmyeon* and *bibimbap*, are often on the menu.

Dog-meat Soup restaurants

(Bosintangjip). *Bosinhada* means to build up one's strength. Thus dog-meat soup, *bosintang*, is considered a delicacy.

Other popular Korean dishes include: *sinseollo* – chopped vegetables, meat, quail egg, fish balls, and ginkgo nuts in a brazier; *seolleongtang* – rice in a beef and bone stew; and *bindaetteok* – the Korean bean-flour and egg pancake filled with different combinations of vegetables and meat.

Chinese Shantung restaurants are very popular. They are designated by a red or green door plaque draped with a red strip of cloth. Home-made wheat noodles with various sauces make for a slurpy meal. *Jjajangmyeon* consists of pork, seafood, and vegetable tidbits stir-fried in a sweet-sour black-bean sauce. Larger Chinese restaurants have a more varied menu.

Japanese restaurants complete with *sushi, sashimi,* and *tempura* (deep-fried battered fish and vegetables) are all over Seoul, and are even more common in the southern port of Busan. Japanese restaurants tend to be on the pricey side, but affordable sushi places are now appearing in office workers' areas of cities to serve the lunch-time crowd.

Restaurant Chains

One of the best Korean restaurant chains is the simple, no-nonsense Manbok. They've got numerous locations in Seoul and the concept is simple: Korean comfort food. Noodles, *pajeon* (scallion pancake), and *makgeolli* (a strong unfiltered rice liquor) hit the spot.

Western chains offer pretty much the same fare you'll find back home. Mexican food at TGIFs and Chili's. Steaks at all of them, with special mention to Outback Steak House. Good ribs (though some prefer Korean *galbi* restaurants) at Tony Roma's.

SEOUL

Korean – Traditional

Butumak
18-84 Euljiro 6-ga, Jung-gu
Tel: (02) 2267-2522
Daily 11am–10.30pm.
This *ssamgyeopsil* spot is popular with diners in the Dongdaemun area (East Gate) but has more than just pork-wrapped-in-lettuce-leaves: come here for *bibimbap*, noodles, and a variety of rice dishes as well. **$$**

Congee House
2-1 Myeong-dong 2-ga, Jung-gu
Tel: (02) 757-8460
Daily 7.30am–8.30pm.
If you have a hankering for Asian porridge then come to Congee House, which boasts authentic Korean-style rice stews in a variety of flavors. Octopus is quite popular. **$**

Kayarang
239-4 Itaewon 2-dong, Yongsangu
Tel: (02) 797-4000
www.kayarang.co.kr
Daily 11.30am–3pm, 5.30–10pm.
Specializes in sumptuous royal cuisine. The staff are fluent in English. **$$**

Jihwaja
National Theater, 14-67 Jangchungdong 2-ga, Jeunggu
Tel: (02) 2269-5834
www.jihwajafood.co.kr
Daily noon–3pm, 5.30–9pm.
Recognized as intangible cultural property. Famous for its recipes from the Joseon dynasty. **$$$**

Korea House
80-2 Pildong 2-ga, Jungu
Tel: (02) 2266-9101
www.koreahouse.or.kr
Daily noon–2pm, 5.30–8.40pm; one-hour traditional music and dance performances at 7 and 8.40pm (except Sunday).
Exceptional surroundings on a hillside with traditional Korean buildings, serving food formally reserved for royal families, and with entertainment. **$$$**

Lotte World
40-1 Jamsildong, Songpagu
Tel: (02) 411-2000
Most restaurants open daily 10.30am–9.30pm.
There are many restaurants in this maze of stores and entertainment centers, but try one of the traditional Korean restaurants on the third floor. **$$**

Odaegam
25-33 1-ga, Jung-gua
Tel: (02) 776-1515
www.odaegam.co.kr
Daily 11.30am–11pm.
This small franchise store specializes in fresh seafood dishes, such as seafood *pajeon* and seafood hot pots. Myeongdong's location is particularly famous. Look for the 2nd-floor restaurant that has the unmistakable blue squid on it. **$$**

Pyeongyang Myeonok
26-14 Jangchungdong 1-ga, Jung-gu
Tel: (02) 267-7784
Daily 11am–9.30pm.
This North Korean style cold-noodle and dumpling shop is unpretentious but a treat for the palate: the noodles are made from buckwheat flour and potato starch, with the production area adjoining the place where you eat. Dumplings are big and very filling, and (according to the owner) represent the North Korean version quite well. **$**

Samcheonggak
Seongbuk 2-dong, Seongbukgu
Tel: (02) 765-3700
Daily 10am–10pm.
Samcheonggak was built originally for high-ranking government officials and it was used for negotiations between South and North Koreans. It's in a quiet, wooded environment, behind the Blue House (the president's official residence) and within a large complex of traditional Korean buildings and gardens that are used as a restaurant, teahouse, function rooms, exhibition venues, and performance theaters. Asadal, the restaurant, serves fine Korean delicacies. **$$–$$$**

Seokparang
125 Hongjidong, Jongnogu
Tel: (02) 395-2500
www.seokparang.co.kr
Daily noon–3pm, 6–10pm.

Authentic Korean food in a 19th-century mansion, surrounded by beautiful gardens. **$$$**

Sokran
50-5 Daeshindong, Seodaemungu
Tel: (02) 393-4690
www.sokran.com
Daily noon–10pm.
A 350-seater restaurant with fast service and helpful staff. **$$$**

Yongsusan
118-3 Samcheongdong, Jongnogu
Tel: (02) 739-5599
www.yongsusan.co.kr
Daily noon–3pm, 5.30–10pm.
Known for its sophisticated interior and food presentation. Entertainment is visual, not only a matter of taste. There are several branches across the city – see website for details. **$$$**

Korean – Vegetarian

Pulhyanggi
726-54 Hannamdong, Yongsangu
Tel: (02) 794-8007
Daily 10am–10pm.
The best of three branches of Pulhyanggi – the others are in Jungno and Kangnam. Note that some meat and fish dishes are available as well. **$$$**

Sanchon
14 Gwanhundong, Jongnogu
Tel: (02) 735-0312
www.sanchon.com
Daily noon–10pm; entertainment from 8–9pm.
Situated on a little side street in Insadong, Sancheon restaurant serves a superb range of traditional Buddhist vegetarian dishes. Evening entertainment. **$$**

Shigolsaenghwal (aka in English: "Country Life")
16-1 Nonhyeondong, Gangnamgu
Tel: (02) 511-2402
Sun–Fri 11.30am–2.30pm, 5–8pm.
The all-you-can-eat buffet lunch (and Sunday buffet lunch and dinner) is one of the best deals in town. Uses organic ingredients. **$**

Chinese

Dongbosung
6-1 Namsamdong 2-ga, Jeunggu
Tel: (02) 754-8002
Daily 11.30am–9.30pm.

Full range of Chinese dishes, with flavors adjusted to Korean taste. **$$**

Ho Lee Chow
119-25 Itaewondong, Yongsangu
Tel: (02) 793-0802
On the second floor of the Hamilton Hotel in Itaewon, one of the expats' favorite Chinese restaurants. **$$**

French

La Petite France
135-55 Itaewondong, Yongsangu
Tel: (02) 790-3040
Mon–Fri noon–3pm, 5–11pm; weekends noon–11pm.
A taste of France on the slopes of Mount Namsan. **$$$**

Indian

Taj Mahal
132-2 Itaewondong, Yongsangu
Tel: (02) 749-0316/7
Daily noon–3.30pm, 6–10.30pm
Curries, tandoories, and all sorts of spicy fare at reasonable prices. Good lunch and dinner buffet on weekends. **$$**

International

Chalet Swiss
104-4 Itaewondong, Yongsangu
Tel: (02) 797-9664
Daily noon–11pm.
Swiss and European Continental; a favorite with diplomatic types. **$$$**

Il Ponte
Seoul Hilton Hotel, 395 Namdaemunro 5-ga, Junggu
Tel: (02) 317-3270
Daily 11.30am–2.30pm, 6–11pm.
The Hilton's fine Italian restaurant; the hotel's Seasons (French) and Cilantros (Californian) are also recommended. **$$$**

Nashville Steak House
128-9 Itaewondong, Yongsangu
Tel: (02) 798-1592
www.nashvilleclub.com
Daily 7am–2am (different floors open at different times within this).
There are plenty of hamburger joints in Seoul, but the Nashville beats them all; good steaks too, with movies downstairs and a sports bar upstairs. **$$**

Top Cloud
Jongno Tower, 33rd Fl, 1-1 Jongno

2-ga, Jung-gu. Tel: 02-2230-3000
http://www.topcloud.co.kr/
Daily, noon–2.30pm, 6–10pm.
A simple but stylish restaurant and buffet with a good steak and European/Korean mix dishes. There's a great view of Seoul as this spot is located on the top of Jungno tower. Live jazz in the evening. **$$$**

Italian

La Cantina
B1 Samsung Building, Euljiro 1-ga, Jeungga
Tel: (02) 777-2579
Mon–Sat 11.30am–2.30pm, 5.30–11pm, Sun 5.30–10pm.
Smart and friendly, with the ambience of an Italian taverna. **$$$**

Villa Sortino
124-12 Itaewon-dong
Tel: (02) 553-9000
www.sortinos-seoul.com
Mon–Sat 11.30am–2.30am (kitchen closes 10.30pm), Sun 11.30am–10.30pm.
Excellent Italian food and there is the option to have the very knowledgeable sommelier recommend a wine/entree pairing. Leave room for the delicious desserts, a house specialty. **$$$**

Wood and Brick
6 Sinmunro, 1-ga, Jongnogu
Tel: (02) 735-1160
Daily noon–10pm.
Straightforward Italian fare in downtown Seoul. There is a good bakery, too. **$$**

Japanese

Bok Chung
2-9 Myeongdong-2ka, Chung-gu
Tel: 02-774-6226
http://www.bokchung.co.kr/
11am–midnight.
Serves delicious Korean/Japanese food such as *yakiniku* and *nabe*, plus traditional Korean favorites like *bibimbap* and various kinds of noodles. Reasonable prices make it popular with Seoulites, yet it remains tourist friendly. **$$**

Namu
W Seoul-Walkerhill, 21 Gwangjang-dong
Tel: (02) 2022-0222

Daily noon–10.30pm.
Decidedly sophisticated dining with stunning views of the Han. Dishes are as artful to look at as they are delicious to taste. Those in the know will want to order a bottle of Veuve Clicquot: the Namu has an entire wall devoted to this hallowed bubbly. **$$$**

Thai

Thai Garden
737-24 Hananmdong, Yongsangu
Tel: (02) 792-8836, 792-9740
www.thaigarden.co.kr
Daily 11am–11pm.
Popular with US personnel stationed in Seoul. **$$**

My Thai
123-20 Itaewon-dong
Tel: (02) 794-8090
Daily 11am–11pm.
Simple decor but great food at this Thai-fusion spot in Itaewon. The green papaya salad is fantastic. **$–$$**

Dinner Theater (Korean)

Korea House
80-2 Pildong, Junggu
Tel: (02) 2266-9101
Mon–Sat 7–8pm, 8.50–9.50pm, Sun 8.50–9.50pm.
Presents traditional Korean dance performances. **$$$**

Samcheonggak
Seongbuk 2-dong, Seongbukgu
Tel: (02) 3676-2345
Korean traditional music, dance, and theater, from 9–9.10pm. **$$**

Sanchon
14 Gwanhundong, Jongnogu
Tel: (02) 735-0312
Daily noon–10pm. Performance 8–9pm.
Fine food all day, and a nightly Korean dance performance. **$$**

PRICE CATEGORIES

Price categories are per person for a three-course meal, or main meal and side dishes:
$ = under US$20 (W20,000)
$$ = US$20–50 (W20,000–50,000)
$$$ = over US$50 (over W50,000)

Gyeonggi and Gangwon Provinces

Gyeonggi

El Patio
Heiri Yesulmaeul 1652-540
Beopheungri Tanhyeonmyeon, Paju
Tel: (031) 942-0918
www.elpatio.co.kr
Italian menu, vegetarian food, barbecues and afternoon tea. Also has an art gallery. **$–$$**

Hakkol
Bungdong Ilsandonggu, Goyang
Tel: (031) 906-6060
www.hakkol.com
Daily noon–3am.
Live music and Italian food. **$$$**

Puffin
Jungangdong, Ansan
Tel: (031) 480-4850
Canadian-style pub restaurant, though 11pm is an early closing time. **$$**

Janggunsusang
314-5 Neungpyeongri Opomeon, Gwangju
Tel: (031) 718-1231
Seafood restaurant specializing in Maine lobster. **$$$**

Yetnal Sigolbapsang
96-8 Seongdongri
Tanhyeonmyeon, Paju
Tel: (031) 945-5957
Traditional Korean food. The restaurant is closed on national holidays. **$$**

Gangwon

Sonamujip Chodang Sundubu
Chodang-dong 354-4, Gangneung
Tel: (033) 653-4488
Gangneung's most famous tofu restaurant serves soft, fresh tofu in a variety of ways, along with Korean side dishes. It's cheap, fresh, and the quality is high. **$**

Chungcheong Provinces

Daejeon

Taepyeong Goeul Seokgalbi
Jung-gu, 413-2 Taepyeong 2-dong
Tel: (042) 524-4070
Daily 11am–10.30pm, closed at Chinese New Year and Chuseok
Famous for its pork dishes that are marinated and then served on a hot stone plate. Known as *dweji-galbi*, this is a Daejeon specialty. **$$**

Chungju

Mindeule
Dongryangmyeon Hwaam-ri 496
Tel: (043) 851-2754
Daily 11am–11pm
This place near the wharf offers Korean pancakes and other *anju* (side dishes). **$**

Gongju

Anyang Hemultang
Shingwandong 597-9
Tel: (041) 852-1818
Daily 11am–10pm
Gourmands will love this seafood hot-pot restaurant. Portions tend towards the colossal. **$$**

Gomanaru Dol Sambab
Geumsungdong 184-4
Tel: (041) 857-9999
Daily 11am–10pm
Specializes in *ssambap* – rice wrapped in lettuce. Unbeatable views of Gongsan Fortress. **$**

ABOVE: *bulgogi* beef.

Gyeongsang Provinces

Andong

Andong Yangban Bapsang
513 Sanga-dong
Tel: (054) 855-9900
The best stop for flaky Andong broiled mackerel. It's slightly outside town by the river, a short taxi ride from Andong Station. **$$**

Busan

Amisan
1434-1 Marina Center
Tel: (051) 747-0131
A popular Chinese restaurant on the 8th floor of the Marina Center. Lunch specials are quite reasonable; dinners more pricey. It's a common stop for Korean celebrities. **$$$**

Camellia
737 Woo 1-Dong, Haeundae-gu
Tel: (051) 749-7434
Daily 6.30–10am, noon–3pm, 6–10pm.
A stylish beachside buffet at Westin Busan. Pricey, but you're rewarded with excellent views of the beach and waves and whatever else happens to be there. **$$$**

Choryeong Milmyeon
Choryong-dong 363-2
Tel: (051) 462-1575
Less than a minute from Busan station, this *milmyeon* (Busan noodle) restaurant is popular with locals and tourists alike. Great noodles and *mandu* (dumplings) at unbeatable prices. **$**

Haeundae Sealand
Chungdong 957-2, Haeundae
Tel: (051) 744-4666
Daily 11am–2am.
A seafood "mall" overlooking the ocean. You can pick your fish in the first-floor market and eat them on the second floor restaurant. Or just look through menus on the second-floor restaurant and order, as it's all quite nicely prepared. **$**

Halmehjip
837-43 Beomcheon-1dong
Busanjin-gu
Tel: (051) 634-9618
Daily 8am–8pm.
Locals line up for this restaurant which specializes in a spicy octopus dish called *nakji bokkeum*. It's available all across South Korea but the Busan version has a delicious broth while other areas' versions do not. **$**

Jagalchi Fish Market
37-1 Nanpo-dong 4-ga
The best meals and best deals are in the morning, 7am, for a fresh fish breakfast at one of the many foodstalls. Many places will let you buy your own fish and they'll cook it for you. **$–$$**

Korea Art Center, 5th Floor
1502-2 Joong-dong, Haeundae-gu
Tel: (051) 742-0467
Enjoy fine wine, candlelight, and awesome views from this concrete-and-starched-tablecloth spot atop the Art Center. **$$$**

Seoul Ssamgyetang
26 Nampo-dong 2-ga, Jung-gu
Tel: (051) 246-7748
Daily 9am–11pm.
Specializing in *Ssamgyetang* (mild chicken with ginseng) since 1960. There are other items on the menu, too, but

Price Categories

Price categories are per person for a three-course meal, or main meal and side dishes:
$ = under US$20 (W20,000)
$$ = US$20–50 (W20,000–50,000)
$$$ = over US$50 (over W50,000)

ssamgyetang is what keeps people coming back. **$$**

Daegu

Madrid
300 Manchon-dong, Soosung-gu
Tel: (053) 602-7231
Daily 11am–3pm, 6–10pm.
Southern European cuisine in the Inter-Burgo hotel. Madrid serves (not surprisingly) Western and European fusion food using fresh produce from Daegu

market. **$$$**
Milano Pasta
Namil-dong 94-3
Tel: (053) 257-7401
Excellent pastas and pizzas in a cozy city-center café. **$$**

Gyeongju

LaSônjae
Culinary School of Korea,
Sinpyung-dong 375-3
Tel: (054) 771-6005
Fax: (054) 771-9991
www.culinaryschool.co.kr

While not a restaurant per se, LaSônjae offers a fascinating peek into Silla-era cooking and has classes (currently in Korean only) about how Silla ingredients promoted health and well-being. RSVP for a tour; hopefully offerings in English will be forthcoming. **$$$**
Grazie
620-467 Seonggong-dong,
2nd Floor
Tel: (054) 772-4752

Excellent pizzas and Italian specialties as well as live music at this casual restaurant. Grazie has two Gyeongju locations, both near the university. **$**
Kuro Ssambap Shikdang
106-3 Hangnam-dong
Tel: (054) 749-0600
This quirky spot specializes in Ssambap, a Korean traditional meal where morsels of meat are wrapped in various lettuce leaves. **$$**

JEOLLA PROVINCES

Gwangju

Jonggajip Seolleongtang
Seo-gu Chipyeong-dong 1261-2
Tel: (062) 374-0015
Daily 7am–11pm
Specializes in ox bone soup, a ubiquitous Korean delicacy. The broth is simmered with a variety of local ingredients and then served piping hot, along with the requisite Korean side dishes. **$**
Samhul Bullak
Seo-gu Chipyeong-dong 1230-6
Nau Building 1FL
Tel: (062) 376-3233
Daily 9am–midnight
This store's specialty is octopus grilled with beef slices – the octopi are trucked in from the coast

and kept live in holding tanks, so this is as fresh as it gets. Worth a visit for anyone interested in Korean delicacies. **$$$**
First Nepal
Dong-gu Bullo-dong 109-5
Tel: (062) 225-8771
Daily 9am–10pm
A nice break for those looking for something non-Korean, upscale without being too expensive and there's a lot to choose from on the menu. Reservations recommended. **$$**

Jeonju

Gajok Hoegwan
Wansan-gu, Jeongyong-dong 3ga
80. Tel: (063) 284-0982
Daily 11.30am–9.30pm

This is Jeonju City's officially sponsored bibimbap restaurant and as such, it's a great starting point for tasting the classic Jeonju dish. Rice served in a sizzling stone pot with a variety of veggies and meat. For many travelers, Korean food doesn't get better than this. **$$**
Gogung
Deokjin-gu, Deokjin-dong 2-ga
168-9. Tel: (063) 251-3211
Daily 11am–9pm
This traditional restaurant offers exotic Korean delicacies (such as steamed skate wing) along with standards like bulgogi and bibimbap. Set menus give diners a varied assortment at a discount price. **$$**

Hankookkwan
Deokjin-gu Geumam-dong 712-3
Tel: (063) 272-9229
Daily 11am–9pm
Hankookkwan is something of an institution, serving Jeonju-style bibimbap dishes to throngs of Chinese, Japanese, Western, and Korean diners. **$**
Sambaekjip
Wansan-gu Gosa-dong 1ga 454-1
Tel: (063) 284-2227
Daily 24hrs
Renowned for food that will cure hangovers, this humble establishment is open 24 hours. Come here for the "medicinal" Gukbap, a rice dish with accompanying side dishes, or any of the other items on the modest menu. It's all good. **$**

JEJU-DO

Dolharubang
Hyeopjae-ri 2487, Hallim-eup,
Jeju City
Tel: (064) 796-0001
Daily 9am–6pm.
This rather simple restaurant is in Jeju Hallim Park (folk tourist village). Various set menus offer excellent Korean "comfort food" such as pork bulgogi and bibimbap.
$$
Jeju Hyang
Yeon-dong 283-1, Jeju City
Tel: (064) 748-1031
Daily 11.30am–10.30pm.
Serves traditional Korean

cuisine with set menus that feature local Jeju spices, Ingredients, flavor, and style. **$$**
Mint
Seogwipo, Seongsan-eup,
Goseong-ri 127-2
Tel: (064) 731-7000
11.30am–10pm. 11am–11pm (weekend).
This modern restaurant is located within the Glass House complex on the Phoenix Island resort. It has unparalleled ocean views and serves a variety of Western and Japanese cuisine and Korean local

ingredients. Reservations required. **$$**
Cheju Dom
Yeon-dong 2326-7, Jeju City
Tel: (064) 749-7447
Daily 10am–10pm.
Serves Jeju's traditional cuisine using fresh, local ingredients such as abalone, sea urchin, and Red Snapper. Celeb friendly.
$$
Rajmahal
Yeon-dong 272-13
Tel: (064) 749-4924
Good Indian and Nepalese fare in Jeju City. Those who can reserve a window

seat will enjoy a wonderful view of the street from the second floor.
$–$$
Terrace Cafe
Hyatt Regency Jeju,
3039-1 Saekdal-dong, Seogwipo
Tel: (064) 733-1234
Fax: (064) 732-2039
Excellent dining with views of the ocean from the Terrace Cafe make a stay at the Hyatt Regency Jeju that much more enjoyable. Finer Seogwipo restaurants are hard to come by. Reservations recommended.
$$$

ACTIVITIES

THE ARTS, FESTIVALS AND EVENTS, NIGHTLIFE, SHOPPING, AND OUTDOOR ACTIVITIES

THE ARTS

Concerts

National Center for Korean Traditional Performing Arts
Tel: (02) 580-3333
Just next to Seoul Art Center, this massive airy venue is where many of the nation's finest classical musicians of different genres, including Royal Court musicians, practice and teach their art. Regular and special performances are given in its concert halls and also on the outdoor stage. Check the entertainment section of newspapers for engagements.

Sejong Center for the Performing Arts
81-3 Sejongno, Jongnogu
Tel: (02) 399-1111
The Sejong Cultural Center holds foreign and Korean classical and contemporary concerts, and dramatic performances.

Seoul Arts Center
Tel: (02) 580-1300
Located at the foot of Mount Umyeonsan in Seochodong and finished in 1993, this cultural complex is made up of a concert hall, calligraphy hall, art gallery, library, opera house, and outdoor performance areas. It is home to the National Center for Korean Traditional Performing Arts.

LG Art Center
Tel: (02) 2005-0114
Located in the heart of the business district in Gangnam, the LG Art Center hosts large-scale classical and modern dance and theatrical performances, as well as a program of concerts.

Theater

NANTA Theater
Tel: (02) 739-8288
www.nanta.co.kr
Located in the culturally rich Jeongdong area, this venue is the place to experience the non-verbal theater, NANTA, throughout the year.

Korea House
Tel: (02) 2266-9101
Situated on the slopes of Namsan off Toegyero. Korea House stages free folk dance performances at 3pm on Saturday and Sunday. Art displays decorate the rooms and Korea-related books are sold in the bookshop. A Korean restaurant overlooks an Oriental garden. *(See also Dinner Theater, page 289.)*

Space Center
Tel: (02) 763-0771
Housed in an architectural art piece near the Secret Garden of Changdeok Palace (219 Wonsodong, Jongnogu), the Space Center stages a variety of shows from classical *gayagum* (Korean zither) solos to Dixieland jazz to drama. The Center also publishes a cultural magazine called *Space*.

Other Modern Drama Theaters in Seoul

Madang Cecil Theater
192-18 Dongsungdong, Jongnogu
Tel: (02) 747-5773

Minye Theater
130-47 Dongsungdong, Jongnogu
Tel: (02) 744-0686

National Theater of Korea
San 14–67 Jangchungdong 2-ga, Junggu
Tel: (02) 2280-4114

Sanoolim Theater
327-9 Seogyodong, Mapogu
Tel: (02) 334-5915

What's On Listings

SEOUL Magazine, available from newsstands, includes monthly listings on cultural events and nightlife. Other sources of listings are the weekend editions of the two main English-language newspapers: the *Korean Herald* and the *Korean Times*. The Visit Korea website (visitkorea.or.kr) has a downloadable monthly events guide.

Hakjeon Blue
Dongsungdong, Jongnogu
Tel: (02) 763-8233

FESTIVALS AND EVENTS

Spring and Fall are the main festival seasons, but, because festivals are very profitable events, they are popping up all over the place, and you can usually find something going on at any time of the year. The Korean National Tourism Organization website (http://english.tour2korea.com) has a list of major events, and they will answer your email inquiries.

January

South Korea's favorite mountain, Hallasan on Jeju Island, is the center of attention in the midwinter Hallasan Snowflake Festival. Make a winter climb of the mountain (along with a few thousand others), take part in the snowball contest, and watch some local folk performances unique to the island. In January, mild Jeju Island is probably the best place to be in South Korea.

February

One of South Korea's two big holidays (the other is *Chuseok*) is the Lunar New Year, known as *Seollal* in South Korea (and Chinese New Year most everywhere else). Koreans dress in their *hanbok* and head for their hometown to eat, socialize, do the "deep bows" to their elders, and turn one year older. Travel is almost impossible during this holiday, so it's best just to stay put and wait for it to pass. Based on the lunar calendar, *Seollal* usually falls sometime in February.

March

South of Daegu is the small city of Cheongdo, which hosts an annual Bullfighting Festival in mid-March. There's also a bull rodeo, a traditional market, and a beauty contest for female calves.

April

The cherry blossoms bloom in early April, presenting impressive displays throughout the country. The most famous display is in the southeastern port city of Jinhae, which hosts a week of festivities right when the blossoms reach their peak.

In early April, the life of the benevolent Dr Wang In is celebrated in the southwestern town of Yeongam (Jeollanam Province). Dr Wang left Korea and settled in Japan several hundred years ago, bringing a little renaissance to Japan as he spread Korea's more advanced culture. At the festival, there is an elaborate memorial rite, some *ssireum* (Korean-style) wrestling, a few contests for intellects, and an exhibition of ancient *Asuka* culture.

May

Buddha's birthday is a national holiday when the celebrations are centered around the temples. Every temple will be decorated for the event, but the larger ones have hundreds of lanterns hanging along the roadways and in the temple grounds (they are lit in the evening), and the faithful line up for the symbolic bathing of the baby Buddha. Jogye-sa in Seoul (and some of the other large temples) has a candlelight parade along with day-long events. Buddha's birthday is based on the lunar calendar, and is usually in May.

On the first Sunday in May, the royal ancestral rites are performed at the Jongmyo Shrine in Seoul. These Confucian rites, in memory of the royal families of the Joseon dynasty, are an elaborate combination of color, ritual, and traditional music and dance. They begin early, and end by midday, but if you're in Seoul you shouldn't miss this event that preserves some of the glory and traditions of old Korea.

On the southwestern island of Jin-do, there is a semi-annual "parting of the sea" that exposes tidal lands between the mainland and an offshore island. Thousands of Koreans trudge between the two points of land. It has become something of an annual festival, with folk performances, a parade, and various contests added to the milieu. The Korean Christian community has dubbed the parting of the seas the Moses Miracle.

The Boseong Tea Festival takes place in Jeollanam-do, the country's main tea-growing area, showcasing every conceivable aspect of the Korean tea industry. Nearby, the Damyang Bamboo Festival takes place early in the month.

June

On the 5th day of the 5th lunar month (late May or early June), the Dano Festival is held in the eastern port city of Gangneung. This is a good opportunity to see traditional shamanistic performances, and mask dance dramas unique to the region.

July

The Boryeong Mud Festival takes place on Daecheon beach in mid-July and is a lot of fun. The week-long event involves mud-wrestling and muddy tug-of-war contests, but is mostly about covering yourself and your friends in mud. Very popular with expats.

The last week of July and first week of August is vacation season in South Korea. Entire companies shut down to allow their employees a week off.

August

Geumsan, the center of Korea's ginseng production, is the host of an interesting festival honoring the "elixir of life." Rows of shops sell ginseng and other medicinal herbs (along with bugs and snakes).

On the stage, there is ongoing entertainment, and hundreds of food carts ensure that you won't go hungry. There is also the opportunity to visit a ginseng field and harvest your own.

September

Gyeongju hosts a World Culture Expo that begins in September and ends in November. The Expo is held along the touristy shores of Bomun Lake and features folk performances, exhibitions, and a general carnival atmosphere. It's certainly an interesting way to kill an afternoon or two between visits to Gyeongju's historic locations.

The Harvest Moon Festival (*Chuseok*) is held on the 15th day of the 8th full moon (usually the end of September or early October). Analogous to Thanksgiving in the United States, this is a time for the

Libraries

Royal Asiatic Society (RAS)
The RAS is the Korean chapter of an international British association. Its office is in the Christian Center Building (136-46 Unjidong, Jongnogu, tel: (02) 763-9483) near Jongno 5-ga. There you'll find English translations of most books written locally about South Korea and a complete collection of their magazine, *Transactions*, which contains Korea-related articles that have been written by lecturing members since 1900. Visitors are welcome to sign up for tours conducted by the RAS and by an affiliate, the Korea Art Club.

The National Library of Korea
Banpo, Seochogu, tel: (02) 590-0542. A nice quiet environment, and a collection of 5 million volumes including foreign books and over 1,000 periodicals in foreign languages. Other facilities include free PCs and copy machines. Foreign visitors may be asked to present their ID. Open 9am–6pm, Nov–Feb closes at 5pm. Tel: (02) 535-4142.

United States Information Service
(USIS; tel: (02) 397-4368) offers a library for public viewing and study. Passport identification is needed. Library hours are 8.30am–5pm weekdays.

Unesco Library
Back issues of the *Korea Journal* and the *Courier*, as well as Korean cultural magazines, are available, the latter in English, French, and Spanish. The library is also stocked with other reference publications.

Ewha, Sogang, Yonsei, and other universities also invite foreigners to use their libraries.

Movie Theaters

Giant billboards of infernal disasters, love, and despair draw thousands of people to South Korea's commercial movie theaters. Movies undergo government censorship and are sometimes edited if too long to allow movie theaters to squeeze in a maximum number of showings. During cold months, underfloor hot-water pipes provide some warmth in the theater. Check the entertainment section of *The Korea Times* or *The Korea Herald* for current engagements.

Foreign movies are not usually dubbed, but have subtitles in Hangeul, so overseas visitors can enjoy them too. Shows usually run continuously from about 10am each day.

Located in a modern building with high-tech facilities, the Centre Culturel Français is a multi-media oasis where visitors can browse through a modern art gallery, sit and view French cultural videos, or watch a classic French movie subtitled in English. The Institute shows a variety of movies on Friday evenings and offers other cultural programs.

For further information, tel: (02) 317-8500.

family to get together, play some traditional games, and eat.

This is a three-day holiday in South Korea, and one of the big ones. Unless you are invited to someone's home to share in the festivities, this is not a great time to visit South Korea. Most shops are closed and transportation is a nightmare.

October

One of South Korea's most interesting festivals, the Andong Mask Dance Festival takes place in early October (occasionally in late September) in the city of Andong, and the nearby traditional village of Hahoe. The best dance groups in the country perform folk dance/dramas that have ancient shamanistic roots. Each year, several folk dance groups from other countries are invited to perform for the appreciative audiences.

If you like *gimchi*, you've got to pay a visit to Gwangju at the end of October. The best of the region's *gimchi*-makers display their creations inside the display hall, and vendors offer visitors dozens of varieties of *gimchis* to taste and purchase. Displays within explain the history and regional variations of this popular dish, and outside are ongoing performances to keep things interesting. There's also a *gimchi*-making contest for foreigners if you want to show off or learn how it's done.

December

Christmas is a holiday in South Korea and celebrated by a sizable Christian community. Although there are a few Christmas trees, and a Santa Claus or two (Santa Grandfather, to Korean children), there is none of the pomp and extravagant gift-giving found in the West. New Year (as opposed to Lunar New Year) is also celebrated but is low-key compared to the West.

NIGHTLIFE

Seoul's nightlife is pretty lively: from techno and hip-hop to dedicated jazz bars to hotel discos to off-the-wall electronica blast-outs.

Nightclubs and Discos

Major Western-style hotels have their own nightclubs. Drinks are heavily taxed in hotels.

Dance
Gek Cobra
Jonggak Station, subway line 1
Tel: (02) 723-3737
Nix & Nox
Ritz-Carlton, 602 Yeoksamdong, Gangnamgu
Tel: (02) 3451-8444
Nightly 6pm–3am.
JJ Mahoney's
Grand Hyatt Hotel, 747-7 Hannamdong, Yongsangu
Tel: (02) 799-8601
Sun–Wed 6pm–1am, Thur–Sat 7pm–2am.
Juliana
Hotel Elle Lui, 129 Cheongdamdong, Gangnamgu, Sinchon Station on subway line 2
Tel: (02) 514-3509
Nightly 7pm–7am.

Jazz
Chonnyondongando
Dongsungdong, Jongnogu
Tel: (02) 743-5555
daily 5pm–2am, Fri–Sat until 3am.
Janus
Cheongdamdong, Gannamgu

Tel: (02) 546-9774
Nightly 6pm–1am.
All That Jazz
Itaewondong, Yongsangu
Tel: (02) 795-5701
Nightly 6.30pm–1am.
Just Blues
Sinsadong, Gangnamgu
Tel: (02) 542-4788
Nightly 6pm–midnight.

Clubs
Hongdae-ap literally means "in front of Hongik University" in Sinchon (Hongik University on subway line 2) and refers to the area around the university, which has many popular cafés, bars, and clubs. The last Friday of each month is "Club Day," when young people pack the whole block.

Cabarets

Often located in narrow alleyways, cabarets are easy to spot: loud music, neon signs, and doormen trying to drum up trade. Dance hostesses inside expect a tip for their efforts. Patronize these *jip* with caution or with a good Korean friend, if they need be visited at all. Closing time is midnight. Salons are smarter, more exclusive cabarets.

Tea Shops

Tea shops, especially those in the side alleys of Insadong in Seoul, are wonderful for relaxation. Alhough they don't serve alcohol these are excellent places to see a slice of Korean culture that hasn't changed for centuries.

Old Tea Shop (tel: 02-722-5019) is one of the nicest, though it can be hard to find. Ask the locals for directions. Surrounded by antiques, you'll sip tea as uncaged songbirds flit about this beautifully decorated tearoom.

Bars

Seoul
Basic on the Stage
Hyehwadong, Jongnogu
Tel: (02) 766-4805/3141-6141
Daily 11am–2am.
Goshen
Cheongdamdong, Gangnamgu
Tel: (02) 515-1863
Daily 10am–5.30pm.
Hunters Tavern
158-9 Samseongdong, Gangnamgu
Tel: (02) 559-7619
Daily 5pm–2am.
Mumba
B2, Seoul Finance Building, Gwanghwamun Station, subway line 5
Tel: (02) 3783-0005

Once in a Blue Moon
Cheongdamdong, Gangnamgu
Tel: (02) 549-5490
Daily 5pm–2am, Sun until 1am.
Woodstock
1308-22 3F, Seocho 4-dong,
Seocho-gu
Tel: (02) 3482-4876
Daily 6pm–1am, Fri–Sat until 2am.

Other Provinces

Club Maktum
Haeundae Beach, Busan
Tel: (051) 742-0770
8pm–3am.
Bus
53-2 Samdeok-dong, Daegu
Tel: (053) 427-3312
Daily 24 hours.
Island Lounge
Hyatt Regency Jeju
Tel: (064) 733-1234
Daily 10am–11pm.

Gambling

Gambling for Korean citizens is
limited. Busan, Seoul, and other big
cities all have casinos for foreigners.
Here are some popular locations:
Sheraton Grande Walker Hill
Gwangjangdong, Gwangjingu, Seoul
Tel: (02) 455-5000
Paradise Incheon
3-2 Hangdong 1-ga, Junggu, Incheon
Tel: (032) 762-5181
Paradise Beach Hotel
1408-5 Jungdong, Haeundaegu,
Busan
Tel: (051) 742-2110
The Shilla Jeju
3039-3 Saekdaldong, Seogwipo
Tel: (064) 735-5114
Jeju KAL Hotel
1691-9 Yido, 1-dong, Jeju
Tel: (064) 724-2001
Wellich Chosun
Bomun Lake Resort, Gyeongju
Tel: (054) 771-2121

SHOPPING

Where to Shop in Seoul

Places to shop in Seoul include:
Antiques: Janganpyeong, Insadong,
Jungang Sijang (Central Market),
Itaewon.
Brassware: Itaewon.
Boutique goods: Myeongdong,
Idaeap.
Calligraphy paint brushes:
Insadong, Gyeonjidong.
Korean costumes: Dongdaemun
Sijang, and most other marketplaces.
Korean cushions and blankets:

ABOVE: Seoul music: DJ in a Hongdae club.

Insadong, marketplaces.
Korean herbal medicine: Jongno
5-ga, Jongno 6-ga, Gyeongdong
Sijang.
Name seals (custom-made name
seals in stylistic characters carved
of hard wood, stone): along the busy
streets.
Oriental paper: Insadong,
Gyeonjidong.
Silk Brocade: Dongdaemun Sijang
(2nd floor), Jongno 2-ga, Myeongdong
(Ko Silk Shop).
Custom-tailored men's suits: hotels,
Myeongdong.
**Sweatsuits and athletic shoes and
gear**: Itaewon, Namdaemun Sijang.
**Topaz, "smoky topaz," amethyst,
jade**: underground arcades.

Duty Free

Duty-free shopping is popular
especially among travelers from
other Asian countries, who can get
excellent prices on liquor, cigarettes
and other tobacco products,
cosmetics and perfumes, and other
brand-name goods. Lotte department
store (in both Busan and Seoul),
Paradise Hotel and Annex (Busan),
and other places throughout the
country offer duty-free services for
foreign visitors.
    You must have your passport and
your return plane ticket available at
the time of purchase. Be aware that
South Korea has high-quality fakes
(some are even sought after in their
own right!) and these may not be
allowed into your own country.

Shopping Centers

Seoul

Hyundai Department Store
456 Apgujeongdong, Gangnamgu
Tel: (02) 547-2233
www.ehyundai.com/portal/company_info/
english_main.jsp

Lotte Shopping Center
1 Sogongdong, Junggu
Tel: (02) 771-2500
Lotte World
40-1 Jamshildong, Songpeagu
Tel: (02) 411-2000
www.lotteworld.com/Global_eng/Main.asp
New Core Outlet
70-2 Jamwondong, Seochogu
Tel: (02) 530-5000
www.newcore.co.kr
Shinsegae
52-5 Chungmuro 1-ga, Junggu
Tel: (02) 1588-1234
www.shinsegae.com

Underground Arcades

At the specialty shops in underground
shopping malls don't let the price
tags deter you from bargaining.
The larger, more centrally located,
arcades include: Namdaemun Arcade,
Myeongdong Arcade, Sogong Arcade,
Hoehyeon Arcade, Euljiro Arcade,
Lotte Centre 1st Avenue Arcade.

Markets

Seoul's traditional markets run on
for block after block. Anyone who
has anything to sell is out there –
from the button merchant to the
antiques dealer to the rice cake
ajumeoni, including *jige* (A-frame)
bicycle and Kiamaster delivery
men and haggling shoppers. The
distinguishing feature of Korean
markets, however, is that shops
with the same goods tend to
group together, and even set
up their goods in the same way.
Merchants say they are not hurt
by competition caused by the
close proximity; instead, the area
becomes known for specializing
in, say, second-hand books, sinks,
or antiques. Most things can be
found at all the markets.

Regional Arts and Crafts

South Korea's unique arts and crafts and the towns that traditionally produce the best of particular products are:
Bamboo craft: Damyang
Brassware: Anseong, Gyeonggi-do
Hemp cloth: Hansan, Andong
Lacquerware: Wonju
Oriental paper: Jeonju
Pottery and porcelain: Icheon, Yeoju
Ruchecraft: Ganghwa-do City
Silk: Chuncheon, Ganghwa-do City

Bookstores

Reading material in English or European languages can be tricky to locate in Seoul, but there are several places where titles can be regularly found. The major hotels have bookstores that carry periodicals, although they are usually late in coming and are unduly expensive. For the latest issues (also at fairly high prices), try the country's biggest bookshop, the **Kyobo Bookstore** in the basement of the Kyobo Building, at 1 Chongno 1-ga. They have two further branches near Jamsil and Gangnam subway stations.
The **Youngpoon Bookstore**, on Namdaemunro by Jonggak subway station, also has a respectable foreign-language selection.
   Seoul Selection (tel: (02) 734-9565) publishes informative periodicals in English and holds cultural events. A good selection of books in foreign languages and Korean DVDs with English subtitles is for sale. You can order a drink from the little in-house café and have a read of the books on display.
   Used books and magazines can be found in Myeongdong. There are several small shops here overflowing with books and old magazines which are sold for much less than their

original cost. You can also trade in your own used paperbacks or bargain for lower prices, particularly if you purchase several books at a time.

OUTDOOR ACTIVITIES

Just about any outdoor sport can be enjoyed in South Korea, and chances are there'll be a club tailor-made for you to join. Ask your concierge or at a tourist information office.

National Parks

National Parks are the quickest and most convenient way to escape from the city. Popular parks that are a good weekend trip from Seoul include:
Bukhansan *(see page 153)*
Seoul-si, Gyeonggi Province
Tel: (02) 909-0497
Daily sunrise–sunset; charge.
Bukhansan is extremely popular, though often crowded, especially on weekends and holidays. Hikers will reward themself with stunning views of Seoul and surrounds when they reach the summit.
Chiaksan *(see page 168)*
Wonju-si, Gangwon Province
Tel: (033) 732-5231
Daily sunrise–sunset; charge.
Chiaksan's remote temples, streams and emerald pools, and stunning fall foliage make it a great escape from the city.
Seoraksan *(see page 178)*
Sokcho-si, Gangwon Province
Tel: (033) 636-7700
Daily sunrise–sunset; charge.
South Korea's most famous and most majestic park, with stunning vistas and dolomites which each seem to have their own personalities.
Odaesan *(see page 169)*
Pyeongchang-gun, Gangwon Province
Tel: (033) 332-6417

Daily sunrise–sunset; charge.
Remote enough from Seoul that you will have a quieter, more peaceful time, Odaesan is a great getaway for nature lovers. Wildlife, foliage, and colorful temples won't disappoint.
   Other key national parks you may want to visit include **Woraksan** *(see page 202)*; **Jirisan** *(see page 260)*; **Hallasan** *(see page 272)*; and **Songnisan** *(see page 199)*.
   All of the National Parks offer hiking experiences that, for the outdoor lovers, will be among the most rewarding memories of your Korean vacation. The scenery is spectacular at any time of year, and the chance to see rare wildlife, birds, and flowers is unparalleled. If your vacation offers you the chance, do take some hikes in these special, pristine, protected areas.

Outdoor Pursuits

Those wanting more than just a walk in the woods may want to try some of the more extreme sports that have become popular in South Korea these days:
River-rafting is possible from the town of Yeongwol, in the south part of Gangwon Province, about 3–4 hours' drive from Seoul. The Donggang River is especially scenic. and while the current is slower than some comparable rafting trips in the USA or elsewhere, participants may see Korean otters, a host of birds including kingfishers, and, (for those with a rod and reel) even tasty fish.
Donggan River Rafting
242 Hasong 5-ri, Yeongwol-Eup, Yeongwol-gun, Gangwon Province
Tel: (033) 370-2294
Daily, office hours 9am–6pm, Apr–Nov; trip times vary; charge.
Skiing is very popular in South Korea, especially at the Yongpyeong resort *(page 170)*. Ski trip shuttles leave from Seoul early in the morning and return by night, making this a doable day trip. For more information call (02) 3404-8102.
Diving Those in Jeju will want to take advantage of the warm waters and try diving. Your hotel may be able to offer you a discount on a diving package when you reserve your room, and they may have an operator to recommend. Those wishing to make their own arrangements can try:
Jeju Scuba Academy
Sangmo-ri 3967, Jeju Province
Tel: (064) 794-1117
Hours: 3-day advance reservation required; charge.
Jejueco (www.jejueco.com) offers diving and hiking tours.

BELOW: the popularity of baseball is a sign of American influence.

A – Z

A HANDY SUMMARY OF PRACTICAL INFORMATION, ARRANGED ALPHABETICALLY

A dmission Charges

Entry fees vary substantially. Temples are allowed to charge a small fee for use of their roads, parking, and entry. Usually this runs to around W1,500 or so. Museums often charge W9,000, sometimes more. Discounts often apply to children, students with a valid ID, and seniors. Group discounts, usually for 6 or 8 or more people, can sometimes be given if this is arranged in advance.

B udgeting for Your Trip

South Korea remains a very affordable place to visit. Thrifty travelers planning on keeping a tight budget can expect to pay less than W75,000 (US$65) for a decent, clean place to sleep. Meals per day will run around W40,000 (US$35), and other miscellaneous expenses can add another W40,000. On the other hand, the luxury traveler will find lots that's well worth the splurge: a comfortable stay in Seoul could run to W400,000 (US$350) or more, a nice meal with

a bottle of drinkable wine another W300,000 (US$260) for two. Thus, there's no easy way to calculate your budget beyond knowing what you'll be comfortable with.

Business Travelers

As well as heeding the advice given in Business Culture (see page 56) business travelers should beware of some of the pitfalls of getting around Seoul, where most major companies are located. Rush-hour traffic jams can throw well-laid schedules awry, and occasional lack of clear addresses can make finding office buildings tricky. Most taxi drivers speak only Korean, though some these days speak a smattering of English or Japanese. A well-briefed chauffeur, hired from your hotel, can save a lot of time.

C hildren

Children enjoy a special place in Korean society, and are cosseted and fussed over, especially by the older

citizens. Arriving with a family in tow means you can expect special service in restaurants, hotels, and many other public places. Note that larger babies may not fit Korean-size diapers/ nappies, while a lot of spicy Korean food may not be to Western toddlers' tastes, so plan accordingly. If your children can be persuaded to learn a few word of Hangeul, expect some bonus points.

Climate

South Korea's location on the eastern edge of the Eurasian landmass results in a continental climate, with cold winters (rather milder along the south coast and in Jeju-do) and hot, humid summers. Seoul's rather unpredictable weather is often compared to that of New York City.

From December to early March the weather is generally cold and sunny, with occasional snowfalls. Afternoon temperatures in Seoul are usually around freezing; Busan is a few degrees warmer. The cold is enhanced by the Siberian winds that whip down

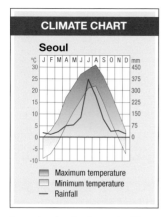

CLIMATE CHART

Seoul

- ▨ Maximum temperature
- ▢ Minimum temperature
- — Rainfall

the peninsula, often in a cycle of three consecutive cold days followed by four milder days.

A spring thaw comes in mid-April and lasts for around two months. In the early spring northwesterly gusts bring swirls of dust from the Gobi Desert and some light rain. As summer approaches, humid southerlies vie for control and the spring drizzle can become an occasional downpour, culminating in three or four weeks of heavy rains during the late July and early August monsoon season.

July and August are the hottest, most humid months, and are particularly enervating in the inland basin around Daegu, where afternoon temperatures climb into the lower 30°s centigrade (around 90°F). Daytime temperatures in Seoul are more often around 28°C (82°F). Nights are warm and muggy.

Between mid-July and the end of September occasional typhoons move north from the East China Sea to bring torrential rain and strong winds to the Korean peninsula, although these are rarely damaging as they are further to the south (Jeju-do is more at risk).

Fall arrives in early October when the air currents shift back to the crisp northerlies. The weather is normally dry and sunny.

The best months for visiting are mid-April to mid-June, and September to October just before and after the summer rains. Fall has the advantage of the wonderful displays of foliage in the Korean forests, while spring is famous for the cherry blossom.

What to Wear

Korean businessmen wear suits and ties, even in the summer. Otherwise, dress is casual. Mini-skirts and shorts are acceptable, although foreigners are advised to avoid

being too skimpily clad. An umbrella, sunglasses, and rainy-day footwear are practical accessories to pack. In the summer it is worth bringing a light sweater for mountain regions and to combat fierce air conditioning in hotels and restaurants. Bring extra-warm clothing for the chilly winters, made even colder by the considerable wind-chill factor.

Crime and Safety

Outright crime in South Korea is rare, even in Seoul. Most people will visit this country and have nothing but good stories to tell. However, that does not mean that one shouldn't take the usual precautions. Avoid walking alone late at night, and be aware that tempers in Korea are often inflamed by alcohol. It is not unheard of for South Korean men to be jealous of Westerners who are socializing with Korean women.

The best way to avoid trouble is to be polite and respectful no matter what else may be going on. If you perceive a problem arising, excuse yourself (and your guests) and choose a venue that's happy to have your patronage. Keep in mind that all Korean men are required to serve in the South Korean army; fist fights are unwise unless you are also excellent in Tae Kwon Do.

Customs Regulations

You may bring in 200 cigarettes (50 cigars or 250 grams of tobacco), one liter of liquor and two fluid ounces of perfume. Items for personal use (except goods such as vehicles, guns, and musical instruments) may be brought in duty free, but visitors must leave with these items.

Korean antiques pre-dating 1910 should be checked and appraised by the Arts and Antiques Assessment Office and a permit should be secured. For five or fewer antiques, checking may be possible at Seoul City Hall (tel: (02) 2171-2583). A limit of three kilograms of red ginseng with a sales receipt is acceptable.

D isabled Travelers

Disabled travelers will find that South Korea is not the easiest country to get around. Few concessions are made, for example, for wheelchair users, in the way of lifts or ramps. However, on the plus side, Koreans are extremely hospitable and courteous and will go out of their way to help foreigners in obvious difficulties. Depending on your level of physical mobility, plan

Electricity

220 volt outlets are standard throughout South Korea. Super deluxe and deluxe hotels also have a few 110 volt outlets. Be aware that in all but the poshest of hotels, the shape of the plug is different and you will need an appropriate adapter even if the voltage is not an issue.

ahead on what you want to do, and if possible bring along someone who can assist you.

E mbassies and Consulates

Embassies in Seoul

Note: if you are calling from outside of the Seoul area add the 02 telephone prefix.

Australia, 11th Floor, Kyobo Building, 1 Jongno 1-ga, Jongnogu. Tel: 2003-0100.

Canada, 16-1 Jeong-dong, Jung-gu. Tel: 3783-6000.

China, 54 Hyojadong, Jongno-gu. Tel: 738-1038.

France, 30 Hapdong, Seodaemun-gu. Tel: 3149-4300.

Germany, 308-5, Dongbinggodong, Yongsan-gu. Tel: 748-4114.

Ireland, 13th Fl. Leema Bldg. 146-1 Susong-dong, Jongno-gu. Tel: 774-6455.

Japan, 18-11 Junghakdong, Jongno-gu. Tel: 2170-5200.

New Zealand, 15th Floor, Kyobo Building, 1 Jongno 1-ga, Jongno-gu. Tel: 3701-7700.

Singapore, 28th Floor, Seoul Finance Center, 84 Taepyeongno 1-ga, Jung-gu. Tel: 774-2464.

United Kingdom, 40 Taepyeongno, 4 Jeongdong, Jung-gu. Tel: 3210-5500.

United States, 32 Sejongno, Jongno-gu. Tel: 397-4114.

Korean Embassies Overseas

Australia, 113 Empire Circuit, Yarralumla, ACT 2600. Tel: (02) 6270-4100.

Canada, 150 Boteler Street, Ottawa, Ontario K1N 5A6. Tel: (613) 244-5010.

China, 20 Dongfangdong Lu Chaoyang District, Beijing. Tel: (010) 8531-0700.

France, 125 rue de Grenelle, 75007 Paris. Tel: 01 47 53 01 01.

Germany, Stülerstrasse 10, 10787 Berlin. Tel: (030) 260-650.

Hong Kong (consulate general), 5/6 Floor, Far East Finance Centre, 16 Harcourt Road, Hong Kong. Tel: 2529-4141.

Japan, 1-2-5 Minami-Azabu,

Minatoku, Tokyo. Tel: (03) 3452-7611/9.
New Zealand, The 11th Floor, ASB Bank Tower, 2 Hunter Street, Wellington, New Zealand. Tel: (04) 473-9073/4.
Singapore, 47 Scotts Road, #08-00 Goldbell Towers, Singapore 228233. Tel: 6256-1188.
United Kingdom, 60 Buckingham Gate, London SW1E 6AJ. Tel: (020) 7227-5500/2.
United States, 2450 Massachusetts Avenue, NW Washington DC 20008. Tel: (202) 939-5600.

Emergencies

Police: 112
Fire and Emergency Ambulance: 119
Medical Emergency: 1339
International SOS Korea provides a **24-hour emergency service for foreigners**, acting as a link between patients and Korean hospitals for a fee. Tel: (02) 3140-1924.

Etiquette

To many Westerners, Koreans can seem rather formal, with rigid codes of behavior, but most Koreans will give you leeway as a foreigner that they would not give their peers or countrymen. You will gain respect by showing an understanding and appreciation of Korean customs; however, you'll rarely be held to Korean standards should you slip up.

Heavily influenced by Confucian ethics, the Koreans place great emphasis on respect for one's elders. Greetings, and saying thank you, are considered important. Direct physical contact, unless between close friends, is limited to a courteous handshake.

Remember to always remove your shoes before entering a Korean home, although bare feet are uncommon except on the hottest summer days.

When out for a drink or a meal with a group, be prepared to take on the role of guest, or host: Koreans will seldom pay separately, and it is Korean custom that the eldest member of the group pick up the tab (you can dine and drink scot-free by choosing friends that are safely your elders!). Talking a lot during a meal is considered impolite, as is blowing your nose at table and resting your chopsticks in the rice. Public drunkenness is quite acceptable, as long as the inebriated individual is not being aggressive or offensive.

Most of the time, no matter how ghastly your mistakes, Koreans will give you the benefit of the doubt if you are kind, polite, and sincere in your apologies.

G ay and Lesbian Travelers

Thanks in part to the liberating influence of the internet, gay South Korea is gradually coming out of its shell. *Buddy*, a gay magazine, is being sold freely, and a gay film fest (previously banned by police) takes place every year, as does the lively Queer Culture Festival. A number of bars, saunas, and night spots are thriving in Busan and Seoul, and while South Korea remains conservative on this issue, younger generations show there's hope for equality and fairness in the future.

H ealth and Medical Care

South Korea is a healthy place, although it is recommended that you take out comprehensive travel insurance before traveling. In the UK, detailed health advice for visits anywhere in the world is available from MASTA (Medical Advice for Travellers Abroad), tel: 09068 224-100 (premium rate); www.masta.org. In the US, the Center for Disease Control offers useful advice for travelers; tel: 877 FYI-TRIP; www.nc.cdc.gov.travel.

Recommended vaccinations for South Korea include hepatitis A and B, typhoid and polio, as well as tetanus and diphtheria boosters. Except for those whose itineraries include cholera-infected areas, no certificate of vaccination is required. Japanese encephalitis inoculations are recommended for those staying in rural areas in the summer months.

Medical Services

Many kinds of medicines and healthcare goods are available at local pharmacies.

Immunizations are administered at the International Clinic at Severance Hospital, which uses disposable needles, and at the Seoul Quarantine Office, located to the right of the USO compound in Galwoldong, Yongsangu.

Dentists and optometrists are generally reliable and their work is reasonably priced. Major hotels have house doctors. Most medical treatment is costly, so make sure you have adequate insurance.

The following is a list of major hospitals for foreigners in Seoul:
Asan Medical Center, tel: (02) 3010-5001/5268.
Cha General Hospital Foreign Clinic, tel: (02) 3468-3113/3127.
Cheil General Hospital, tel: (02) 2000-7062.
Gangbuk Samsung Hospital, tel: (02) 2001-1100/1101.
Samsung Medical Center, tel: (02) 3410-3300.
Seoul Foreign Clinic (Jong-no), tel: (02) 790-0075.
Seoul National University Hospital, tel: (02) 2072-2890.
Severance Hospital (International Clinic), tel: (02) 2228-5810/(02) 392-3404.
Soonchunhyang, tel: (02) 709-9158.

Drinking Water

Potable water is available in hotels. In establishments for locals, *boricha* (roasted barley boiled in water), distinguished by its light brown color, is served instead: though you will see lukewarm barley tea served, it is common for any local restaurants to serve clean drinking water, which is free of charge. Although locals rarely do so, the city of Seoul does actively promote tap water for drinking.

In Korean restaurants, you may

BELOW: gaming in a Seoul internet café.

be served another water substitute, *sungnyung*, tea boiled from browned rice gathered from the bottom of a rice pot. It is also quite safe to drink water which springs from certain mountain sites at temples in the countryside. Unboiled tap water is never advised for drinking. Bottled water can be purchased from supermarkets or convenience stores.

Internet

Most hotel business centers provide internet access, although it can be pricey. However, the internet, especially internet gaming, has caught on in a big way, and there are dozens of "PC Rooms" wherever there are young people. All you need do is walk in, mention "internet," and they'll set you up. Charges are in the range of W1,000–2,000 for the first 30 minutes, and W1,000 for each additional half hour. Free internet access is available in KNTO, banks, airports, major train stations, and some tourist information centers in busy districts.

Left Luggage

Almost all Korean train stations have coin lockers where you can leave items for less than 24 hours, though these days, true coin-operated lockers are becoming rare. It's often hard to follow the complicated directions for purchasing time; however, info booth personnel or the good Samaritan can help you complete the process. Most large stations have storage rooms where luggage can be left for the long term, usually at the rate of around W5,000 per day.

Lost Property

To recover lost possessions, including those left in cabs, contact the nearest police box (these are on every major street) or ask the hotel front desk clerk to help you do so. The Seoul Metropolitan Police Lost and Found Center is at 102 Hongikdong, Seongdonggu. Tel: 2299-1282; Fax: 2298-1282.

Maps

Maps are available at all the major train station tourist information booths. Often they are cartoon-style maps that show little regard to true scale. If you wish to have real cartography, then head to Kyobo or another large bookstore and hope that they can provide you with the map you need.

Media

South Korea has three English-language newspapers – *The Korea Herald, The Korea Times,* and *Joongang Daily*, which carry international news. The *Asian Wall Street Journal, International Herald Tribune,* and *Far Eastern Economic Review* are also circulated locally.

The most popular English-language periodicals are the *Korea Economic Weekly* and the monthly *Korea Economic Report. Time* and *Newsweek* are prominently displayed in bookstores.

Major hotels carry satellite news services like BBC and CNN, as well as channels like MTV and Star. American Forces Korean Network (AFKN) broadcasts in English in Seoul on 1530 AM, 88.5 and 102.7 FM. AFKN TV programing is carried on local TV when US military installations are located nearby; check TV channel 2, or UHF channel 30.

Money

Currency

Korean *won* comes in 1,000, 5,000, and 10,000 denomination notes and 10, 50, 100, and 500 *won* coins. Bank drafts for large amounts (normally W100,000) are available. There are also new W50,000 notes in circulation since 2009, as well as newly designed version of W1,000 and W10,000 notes which came out in 2007. In early 2010 the exchange rate was W1,130 to US$1.

Changing Money

Procuring *won* outside South Korea may be difficult. Once you have arrived, however, there are foreign exchange counters at the airport, large tourist hotels (usually less favorable rates), and major banks (some with branches in large hotels), and a few department stores (such as Lotte) in Seoul. The most viable currencies to carry in South Korea are Japanese yen and US dollars, although other major foreign currencies can also be exchanged. Remember to retain all exchange receipts for reconversion on departure from South Korea.

Credit Cards and ATMs

Credit cards are commonly used by Koreans, but may not be accepted by small shops and businesses. American Express, Visa, JCB, MasterCard, and Diners Club cards are accepted in major hotels, department stores, and restaurants, as well as tourist-oriented shops.

There are numerous ATMs dispensing cash advances on credit/debit cards. They are found at hotels, department stores, subway stations, and tourist attractions across the country, with instructions in English. Not all ATMs accept foreign cards, however, but don't let that stop you: if at first you don't succeed, go to a different bank and try, try again.

Banking in Seoul

Banks are open Mon–Fri 9.30am–4.30pm.

Korean Banks in Seoul

Bank of Korea, tel: 759-4114.
Export-Import Bank of Korea, tel: 3779-6114.
Hana Bank, tel: 1599-1111.
Kookmin Bank, tel: 1588-9999, 1644-9999.
Korea Development Bank, tel: 1588-1500, (02) 787-4000, 5000, 6000, 7000.
Korea Exchange Bank, tel: 1588-3500/1544-3000.
Standard Chartered SC Bank, tel: 1588-1599.
Shinnhan Bank, tel: 1577-8380.
Woori Bank, tel: 080-365-5000/(02) 2008-5000.

Foreign Banks in Seoul

American Express, tel: 1588-8100. (Note: There are several credit card companies (or banks) that issue American Express cards, namely Samsung, Lotte and Shinhan. 1588-8100 is the number for Lotte credit card centre. Amex does not currently have a call centre of its own in South Korea.)
American Express Bank, tel: 399-2929.
Bank of Tokyo-Mitsubishi, tel: (02) 399-6400.
Banque Nationale de Paris, tel: 317-1700.
Chase Manhattan Bank, N.A., tel: 758-5114.
Citibank, tel: 1588-7000.
HSBC, tel: 1588-1770.

Tipping

Tipping is not the norm in South Korea, and is expected only in businesses that cater primarily to Westerners. A 10 percent service charge is automatically added to major hotel room and restaurant bills (read the bill to make sure before tipping). Also it is common to see 10 percent VAT added on top of the original bill and the service charge in fancier restaurants, so it is probably a smart idea to check before tipping again. Airport baggage porters are tipped at the exit door according to a set standard. Cab drivers do not expect a tip unless they perform an extra service, although they may not return your change if it is only a small amount. Bellhops usually receive around W1,000 tip per bag.

O pening Hours

Banks: Weekdays 9.30am–4.30pm; Sat, Sun, and public holidays closed.
Department Stores: All week and some public holidays 10.30am–7.30pm.
Embassies: Weekdays 9am–5pm, usually closed one hour for lunch; Sat, Sun, and public holidays closed.
Government Offices: Weekdays Mar–Oct 9am–6pm (5pm Nov–Feb); Sat 9am–1pm; Sun and public holidays closed.
Post Offices: Weekdays 9am–6pm; Sat 9am–1pm; Sun and public holidays closed.
Private Companies: Weekdays 9am–6pm; Sat 9am–1pm; Sun and public holidays closed. More and more companies are adopting a five-day working week.

P hotography

Opportunities for photography in South Korea abound but it is important that visitors respect the privacy of their hosts. Koreans do not like ceremonies to be photographed and older Koreans don't like photos at all. Ask before you shoot. Most often, especially if you're friendly, they'll let you take whatever pics you choose.

Due to high import taxes, cameras are expensive in South Korea. Chungmuro is the best area to shop (subway lines 3 and 4).

Postal Services

Seoul's Central Post Office is just off the busy Myeongdong area, by the old Yeongnak church. The Gwanghwamun post office branch is near the corner of Taepyeongno and Jongno. Post office hours are Mon–Fri 9am–6pm, Sat 9am–1pm. Aerograms cost W400 and postcards W350. A 10-gram airmail letter to Europe, North America, or the Middle East is W580, and to southeast Asia, W520. Letters to the US and Europe take 6–8 days. You can make further enquiries at the Central Post Office (tel: 6450-1114), Gwanghwamun Post Office (tel: 3703-9011) or International Post Office (tel: (032) 743-9733, relocated to the Incheon airport since 2007).

The Korea Communications Commission, www.ekcc.go.kr, replaced

Public Holidays

January 1 New Year's Holiday.
January/February Lunar New Year *(Seollal).* Businesses closed for 3–5 working days.
March 1 Independence Movement Day *(Samiljeol).*
May 5 Children's Day *(Eorininal).*
mid-May Buddha's Birthday *(Seokga Tansinil).*
June 6 Memorial Day *(Hyeonchungil).*
July 17 Constitution Day *(Jeheonjeol).*
August 15 Liberation Day *(Gwangbokjeol).*
September *Chuseok,* harvest festival; the Korean equivalent of the American Thanksgiving festival. Takes place on the 15th day of the 8th lunar month.
October 3 National Foundation Day *(Gaecheonjeol).*
December 25 Christmas Day.

the Ministry of Information and Communication. It is directly controlled by the Presidential office, which many people view as a giant step backward away from free speech and democracy.

For a faster service, there are international courier services such as DHL (tel: 716-0001, 1588-0001), UPS (tel: 1588-6886), and Hanjin (operated by KAL tel: 1588-1612).

Public Toilets

Recent years have seen great strides made in restroom facilities. The days of the gaping, terrifying hole in the ground are gone. That's not to say restrooms are always spotless. Wise travelers will be sure to carry some anti-bacterial hand gel with them. Hand washing water is usually not hot, which, in the dead of winter, can mean

BELOW: clearly marked public toilets.

awfully cold hands. Women may want to be careful using remote restrooms late at night, as some incidents of rape or assault have been reported.

R eligious Services

There are numerous places of worship in Seoul catering to many different faiths. Details of service times are published in the Saturday edition of English-language newspapers, and your hotel concierge will also be able to provide you with information. Or you can call one of the churches with English-speaking services (unless noted):
Seoul Union Church, Sunday worship 11am. Tel: (02) 333-7393.
Seoul Church of Christ, non-denominational. Sunday Bible class 4pm, worship 5pm. Tel: (02) 2605-2309.
Seoul International Baptist Church, Sunday worship 11am. Tel: (02) 333-0662.
International Lutheran Church, Sunday worship 9am followed by brunch. Tel: (02) 794-6274.
Anglican Church, Sunday worship 9am. Tel: (02) 730-6611. Anglican Holy Communion Sundays 7am, 9am. and 11am are offered at the Missions To Seamen, Marine Center, in Busan. Tel: (051) 644-7787.
Myeongdong Cathedral, for information on daily Masses and for appointments for Catholic confession given in English, call (02) 774-3890 ext. 0.
The Seoul Central Masjid, where there are prayers in Korean, Arabic, and English. For a daily schedule call (02) 794-7307.
Lotus Lantern International Buddhist Center, ceremony Sunday 6pm. Exploring Buddhism Thursday 1.30–3pm. Tel: (02) 735-5347. For meditation programs, call (02) 735-5347.

Time Zone

Korean time is GMT +9 hours. There is no daylight saving time. When it is noon in Seoul it is 3am in London (4am during British Summer Time), and 10pm the previous day in New York (11pm from April to October).

Seoul International Zen Center, Meditation and Dharma talk, Sunday 1pm. Hwagye-sa Temple. Tel: (02) 900-4326.
Young Nak Presbyterian Church, international worship in English. Sunday 3–5pm. Tel: 011-613-5896/ (02) 2280-0228.
Myungsung Church, inter-denominational service Sunday 1.20pm. Tel: (02) 440-9004; www. msews.com.
Onnuri Church, worship and expository preaching in English. Tel: (02) 793-9686.
Somang Presbyterian Church, English service 2pm. Tel: (02) 512-9191.
Yoido Full Gospel Church, Sunday worship 9am, 11am, and 1pm with simultaneous interpretation into English, Chinese, Japanese, French, Indonesian, and other languages. Tel: (02) 783-9920.

T elephones

There are three different types of public telephone: coin phones, card phones, and credit card phones. It is also possible to make local, long-distance, and international calls direct from your hotel room, although you will pay more for the privilege. Phone cards come in denominations of W3,000, W5,000, and W10,000, and are sold at banks and convenience stores such as GS25 and 7-Eleven.

To make an international call, first dial the access code 001 (002 or 008 are also used), followed by country code, area code, and the number. International calls and collect calls can be made through the operator by dialing 00799. Dial 00794 for information on international calls.

Cell phones can be hired at Incheon Airport.

Useful Numbers

Directory Assistance (multiple enquiries at one time) tel: (080) 211-0114.
Directory Assistance (local call) tel: 114.
Directory Assistance (long distance) tel: (area code) + 114.

Tourist Information tel: 1330.
Tourist Complaint Centre tel: (02) 735-0101; fax: (02) 777-0102; email: tourcom@mail.knto.or.kr

Telephone Area Codes

Seoul 02
Busan 051
Chungcheongbuk-do 043
Chungcheongnam-do 041
Daegu 053
Daejeon 042
Gyeongsangnam-do 055
Gwangju 062
Gangwon-do 033
Gyeonggi-do 031
Gyeongsangbuk-do (Gyeongju) 054
Incheon 032
Jeju-do 064
Jeollabuk-do 063
Jeollanam-do 061
Ulsan 052

Tourist Information

A wide range of tourist information and related services is available at the KNTO head office in Seoul, which has an information counter, reservation and ticketing desk, tourism exhibition hall, book and souvenir shop, and a small theater. It also has a comprehensive library. KNTO's TIC (Tourist Information Center), 10 Dadong, Junggu, Seoul, is open daily 9am–8pm. There are also info centers at Gimpo, Gimhae, and Jeju airports that provide you with city maps, brochures, and useful information on tours, shopping, dining, and accommodations.

Tourist Information by Phone

Dial 1330 for detailed tourist info in English. Local call rates apply. If you require information for another region to the one you are dialing from, dial the appropriate area code followed by 1330. Lines are open 24 hours.

Local Tourist Offices

Seoul

KNTO Head Office, 40 Cheongyecheon-ro, Jung-gu, Seoul 100-180. Tel: (02) 7299-497~499, http://english.visitkorea.or.kr/
Gimpo Airport, tel: (02) 3707-9465
Incheon Airport, tel: (032) 743-2600-3
Incheon Ferry Terminal, tel: (032) 891-2030
Itaewon, tel: (02) 794-2490
Myeongdong, tel: (02) 757-0088
Namdaemum Market, tel: (02) 752-1913
Sinchon, tel: (02) 363-2883
Dongdaemun, tel: (02) 2236-9135
Gyeongbu Line, tel: (02) 535-4151

Honam Line, tel: (02) 6282-0808
Deoksugung, tel: (02) 756-0045

Busan
Gimhae Airport, tel: (051) 973-1100
Busan Railway Station, tel: (051) 441-6565
Busan Ferry Terminal, tel: (051) 465-3471

Jeju
Jeju International Airport, tel: (064) 742-0032
Jungmun Tourist Information, tel: (064) 738-8550

Gyeongju
Gyeongju Railway Station, tel: (054) 743-8848
Bulguksa Temple, tel: (054) 746-4747

Tourist Offices Overseas

Websites of KNTO overseas offices can be accessed through http://english. visitkorea.or.kr

North America
Los Angeles
4801 Wilshire Blvd, Suite 103, Los Angeles, CA 90010, USA
Tel: (323) 643-0280
Fax: (323) 643-0281
Email: la@kntoamerica.com
New York
Two Executive Drive, Suite 100, Fort Lee, NJ 07024, USA
Tel: (201) 585-0909
Fax: (201) 585-9041
Email: ny@kntoamerica.com
Chicago
737 North Michigan Ave, Suite 910, Chicago, IL 60611, USA
Tel: (312) 981-1717 or 800-868-7567
Fax: (312) 981-1721
Email: chicago@kntoamerica.com
Toronto
Suite 1903, 700 Bay Street, Suite 1903, Toronto, Ontario M5G IZ6, Canada
Tel: (416) 348-9056
Fax: (416) 348-9058
Email: toronto@knto.ca

Asia-Pacific
Hong Kong
Suite 4203, 42/F, Tower 1, Lippo Center, 89 Queensway, Admiralty, Hong Kong
Tel: 2523-8065; Fax: 2845-0765
Email: general@knto.com.hk
Singapore
20-01, 24 Raffles Place, Clifford Centre, Singapore 048621
Tel: 6533-0441; Fax: 6534-3427
Email: kntosp@pacific.net.sg
Thailand
15/F, Silom Complex Building, 191

Silom Road, Bangkok 10500
Tel: (02) 231-3895
Fax: (02) 231-3897
Email: kntobkk@knto-th.org
Japan
Rm 124, Sanshin Bldg 1-4-1, Yuraku
Cho, Chiyoda-ku, Tokyo 100
Tel: (03) 3580-3941
Fax: (03) 3591-4601
Email: tokyo@tour2korea.com
Australia
Level 40, Australia Square Tower, 264
George St, Sydney, NSW 2000
Tel: (02) 9252-4147
Fax: (02) 9251-2104
Email: visitkorea@knto.or.au

Europe
Germany
Basseler Str, 48, D–60329, Frankfurt
am-Main
Tel: (069) 233226
Fax: (069) 253519
Email: kntoff@euko.de
France
Tour Maine Montparnasse 33, Avenue
du Maine, BP 169, 75755 Paris 15
Tel: 01 45 38 71 23
Fax: 01 45 38 74 71
Email: knto@club-internet.fr
United Kingdom
3rd Floor, New Zealand House,
Haymarket, London SW1Y 4TE
Tel: (020) 7321-2535
Fax: (020) 7321-0876
Email: koreatb@dircon.co.uk

Websites
http://english.visitkorea.or.kr
Comprehensive, informative website
of the Korea National Tourism
Corporation.
www.visitseoul.net
Official Seoul City Tourism website.
Well-organized and detailed
information on Seoul.
www.koreaherald.co.kr
Colorful and well-organized site of *The
Korea Herald*; latest exchange rates
and breaking news stories.
www.lifeinkorea.com
Well-presented and researched site
designed for foreigners living in South
Korea.
www.koreatimes.co.kr/times.htm
The *Korea Times* homepage, featuring
great archive, and language tutorials.
http://iml.jou.ufl.edu/projects/students/Hwang/
home.htm
An excellent guide to Korean food in
all its pungent forms.
http://joongangdaily.joins.com
Joongang Daily homepage, with
useful information for foreigners.
www.adventurekorea.com
Private tour programs organized by
and for expats in South Korea.
www.eslcafe.com/jobs/korea

Provides lists of Korean companies
seeking foreign employees.
www.arirang.co.kr
English-language TV channel in Korea.
Good guide to Korean culture.
www.expat-advisory.com/homepages/asia/
eastern-asia/south-korea/seoul
http://theseoultimes.com
Homepage of the *Seoul Times*, online
English newspaper.

Tour Operators and Travel Agents

Sightseeing Tours
Panmunjeom and the DMZ: The
Korea Travel Bureau offers tours
to the Panmunjeom area, the Folk
Village, Gyeongju, Busan, and around
Seoul by day and night. Reservation
counters can be found at several
main hotels. Their offices can be
found in the Lotte Hotel in downtown
Seoul, tel: (02) 778-0150. You must
book at least one day in advance.
Cost is from W60,000–110,000.
Similar guided tours are organized by
USO (tel: 795-3028), Global Tour (tel:
776-3153) and Panmunjeom Travel
Center (tel: 771-5593).
The trip, including lunch and a US
military briefing, takes eight hours;
children under ten are not admitted.
Visitors must be smartly dressed, and
must carry a passport during the tour.
Mt Geumgang Tour: At the time of
writing, it is not possible to visit Mt.
Geumgang, North Korea.

Travel Agents
The following agencies have English-
and Japanese-speaking guides and
operate tours all over South Korea.
Freedom Travel, tel: (02) 3455-8888
Global Tour, tel: (02) 776-3153
Joy Travel, tel. (02) 776-9871
Korea Travel Bureau, tel. (02) 770
0150
Marco Polo, tel: (02) 757-2300
Minyoung Travel Services Co., tel:
(02) 752-1626
Star Travel Service, tel: (02) 569-
8114
Zenith Travel, tel: (02) 508-5781
The **Korean Tourism Association**
can be reached on tel: (02) 757-
7485. **The Korean Association of
General Travel Agents (KATA)** is on
tel: (02) 752-8692.
Two organizations in Seoul that
plan tours for resident foreigners but
also welcome outsiders are:
The Royal Asiatic Society (RAS),
Christian Building, 6/F, Room 611,
Jongno 5-ga, tel: (02) 763-9483.
**The USO (United Service
Organizations)**, 104 Galwoldong,
Yongsangu, tel: (02) 795-3028.

Travel Agents for North Korea
There are several companies offering
tours of North Korea, lasting between
three days and one week. Most will
involve flying into Pyongyang from
Beijing, although a few companies
such as Lupine Travel (www.lupinetravel.
co.uk) enter by train from northeastern
China. Many tours are timed to
coincide with the Arirang Mass Games
– the gigantic choreographed mass-
participant spectaculars in Pyongyang:
in 2010 these took place from August
through October, and other events
coincide with important anniversaries.

Koryo Tours: 27 Beisanlitun Nan
(East Courtyard), Chaoyang, Beijing
100027. Tel: (86) 10 6416 7544.www.
koryogroup.com

North Korean Tourism: www.north-
korea-travel.com. Specializes in tours for
American citizens.

Regent Holidays: Froomsgate House,
Rupert Street, Bristol BS1 2QJ. Tel:
(44) (0) 117 921 1711. www.regent-
holidays.co.uk

V isas and Passports

Visitors from most countries may
stay in South Korea for up to 90 days
without a visa if they have confirmed
out-bound tickets. Most European, and
many Asian countries have agreements
that permit citizens to stay for longer
without a visa. US citizens can stay for
30 days; Canadian citizens 6 months.
Note that any traveler holding a US,
Canadian, or Japanese visa is granted
a 15-day, visa-free stopover.

North Korea
Individual travel is not possible, and
all travel arrangements, including
your visa, are made by a travel agent
(*see above*). Recent tensions have
restricted the number of foreign
tourists allowed in to North Korea.

W omen Travelers

Women take second place to men in
Korean society, and can expect to get
served last when standing in a queue.
This can be galling, but a pithy two-
minute lecture delivered at top volume
is not going to help. Foreign women
can expect more courteous treatment.
Sexual harassment is rare, but alcohol
inflames Korean men like nothing else.

Weights and Measures

Metric.

TRANSPORTATION
ACCOMMODATIONS
EATING OUT
ACTIVITIES
A – Z
LANGUAGE

L ANGUAGE

UNDERSTANDING THE LANGUAGE

Survival Korean

The romanization of Korean Hangeul script has been revamped in recent years: the new system has dispensed with the apostrophe and the breve accent to denote different letters of the alphabet, which makes it easier to understand, and brings romanized Korean fully into the 21st-century internet age.

As with any radical language re-think, however, one of the biggest disadvantages is that most place names (including street names) in South Korea have changed. Throughout this book we have used the revised system, but some maps and street signs within South Korea have yet to absorb the new system, and a significant number of hotels and restaurants retain their old names, which can prove very confusing for the non-fluent visitor.

Basics

Hello/Good morning/Good afternoon/Good evening
Annyeonghasimnikka
Goodbye (said to somebody not departing) *Annyeonghi gyeseyo*
Goodbye (said to somebody who is also departing) *Annyeonghi gaseyo*
Can you speak English? *Yeongeo halsu isseumnikka?*
Thank you *Gamsa hamnida*
Excuse me *Sille hamnida*
I'm sorry *Mian hamnida*
You are welcome *Cheonmaneyo*
Yes *Ne*
No *Anio*
Help! *Saram sallyeo!*
My name is *Je ireumeun…imnida*
I come from *Jeoneun…eseo wasseumnida*

Revised Romanization

The following list is a summary of the changes to the romanization of Hangeul that took place in 2000:

K becomes G (Kwangju is spelled Gwangju)
T becomes D (Taegu = Daegu)
T' becomes T (T'ap-sa = Tap-sa)
P becomes B (Pusan = Busan)
P' becomes P (P'ohang = Pohang)
Sh becomes S (Shilla = Silla)
Ch becomes J (Cheju = Jeju)

Useful Words

airport *gonghang*
subway *jihacheol*
taxi *taeksi*
Seoul train station *Seoul yeok*
express bus terminal *gosok teominal*
ticket office *maepyoso*
entrance *ipgu*
exit *chulgu*
public bathhouse or private

Ch' becomes Ch (Ch'angwon = Changwon)

The rule for vowels is that where a breve accent was used on an "ŏ" or "ŭ", this is replaced by "eo" or "eu", so that Chosŏn becomes Joseon, and Ullŭng-do becomes Ulleung-do. Hyphenation remains optional; in this book we have retained the hyphen in temple and island names, eg Bulguk-sa, Jeju-do.

bathroom *mogyoktang*
restroom *hwajangsil*
restaurant *sikdang, eumsikjeom*
tea or coffee house *dabang, chatjip*
bank *eunhaeng*
hotel *hotel*
a good Korean inn *joeun yeogwan*
post office *ucheguk*
post box *uchetong*
police station *gyeongchalseo*
embassy *daesagwan*
International… *gukje…*

...**telecommunication office**
...*(jeonsin) jeonhwaguk*
dry cleaners *setakso*
public telephone *gongjung jeonhwa*
department store *baekhwajeom*
duty free shop *myeonsejeom*
marketplace *sijang*
souvenir shop *giny eompumjeom*

Glossary

ajuma **older/old woman**
ajushi **older/old man**
anma **body massage**
bulgogi **Korean-style beef barbecue**
chaebol **business conglomerate**
chatjip **tea house**
cheokkarak **chopsticks**
daejungtang **luxury sauna**
DVDbang **DVD/movie rental parlor**
goshiwon **cram-study dorm**
hanbok **traditional Korean attire**
hangeul **Korean language/ writing system**
hanji **Korean paper**
hanok **traditional Korean house**
hapseung **taxi sharing scheme**
hanji **Korean paper**
hasukchip **Korean boarding house**
jimjilbang **multi-use overnight spa, often with internet, games, sleep area**
mogyoktang **bathhouse**
noraebang **karaoke (singing) parlor**
ondol **Korean-style heated floor**
pulsang **Buddhist icons, figures**
ppishibang **PC/internet parlor**
sa **suffix for temple**
sabal **bowl**
saunatang **sauna**
shijang **market**
takgalbi **Spicy chicken dish with vegetables**
tojagi **Korean pottery, ceramics**
yeogwan **simple Korean inn**

Useful Questions and Sentences

Where is the bathroom? *hwajangshil eodi imnika?*
How far is it from here? *Yeogiseo eulmana meomnikka?*
How long does it take to go there? *Eolmana geollimnikka?*
It takes 30 minutes/1 hour *Samsipbun/hansigan geollimnida*
Please call a taxi for me *Taeksi jom bulleojuseyo*
Just a moment please *Jamkkanman gidaryeojuseyo*
Please go straight *Ttokbaro gaseyo*
Please stop here *Seweojuseyo*
What is this place called? *Yeogiga eodiimnikka?*
Hello (to get the attention of a waiter, sales clerk, etc) *Yeoboseyo*
I will have coffee (or please give me some coffee) *"Coffee" juseyo*
May I have the bill? *Gyesanseo juseyo?*
Do you have amethyst? *Jasujeong Isseumnikka?*
Please show me another one *Dareun geot jom boyeojuseyo*
How much does it cost; what is the price? *Eolma immnikka?*
It's too expensive *Neomu bissayo*
Do you understand me? *Ihae hasheosseoyo?*
Please bring me some... *...jom gattajuseyo*
...**beer** *...maekju*
...**cold drinking water** *...naengsu*
...**hot water (for bathing or drinking)** *...tteugeoun mul*
...**barley tea** *...boricha*
...**Korean food** *...hansik, hanguk eumsik*
a full-course Korean meal *hanjeongsik*
(Something, someone is) good *Josseumnida*
(Something, someone is) bad *Nappeumnida*

Korean Language Schools

Korean language courses are offered at a few institutes in Seoul in two- or three-month terms, and for which you can get student visas. Some prominent schools include:
Language Teaching Research Center 16–17 Daepyongno, 1-ga, Jongdong, Jongnogu. Tel: (02) 737-4641
Yonsei University Korean Language Institute, Taek 134, Sinchondong, Sodaemungu Tel: (02) 392-6405
Ewha Womans University Tel: (02) 3277-3183

Numbers

0	*yeong*
1	*il/hana*
2	*i/dul*
3	*sam/set*
4	*sa/net*
5	*o/daseot*
6	*yuk/yeoseot*
7	*chil/ilgop*
8	*pal/yeodeol*
9	*gu/ahop*
10	*sip/yeol*
11	*sibil*
20	*isip*
30	*samsip*
40	*sasip*
50	*osip*
60	*yuksip*
70	*chilsip*
80	*palsip*
90	*gusip*
100	*baek*
200	*ibaek*
567	*obaek-yuksip-chil*
1,000	*cheon*
2,000	*icheon*
4,075	*sacheon-chilsip-o*
10,000	*man*
13,900	*man-samcheon-gubaek*
100,000	*simman*

TRANSPORTATION
ACCOMMODATIONS
EATING OUT
ACTIVITIES
A – Z
LANGUAGE

FURTHER READING

Culture and Religion

Adams, Edward B. *Korea's Golden Age: Cultural Spirit of Silla in Gyeongju*. Seoul International Publishing House, 1991.
Breen, Michael. *The Koreans: Who They Are, What They Are, Where Their Future Lies.* St Martin's Press, 1999.
Choi, Jae Soon, et al. Hanoak: *Traditional Korean Homes*. Hollym International Corp., 1999.
Constantine, Peter & Baik, Gene. *Making Out in Korean*. Tuttle, 2003. A light-hearted look at modern Korean slang and expressions.
Covell, Alan Carter. *Folk Art and Magic: Shamanism in Korea*. Hollym Corp., 1986.
Korean Institute of Traditional Landscape Architecture, *Korean Traditional Landscape Architecture*. Hollym, 2008.
Iwatate, Marcia & Jongkeun, Lee. *Korea Style*. Tuttle, 2006. A book devoted to Korea's architecture and interior design, featuring 22 exceptional homes, studios, and public buildings ranging from vernacular to cutting-edge creations.
Kendall, Laurel. *The Life and Hard Times of a Korean Shaman: Of Tales and the Telling of Tales*. University of Hawaii Press, 1995.
Korean Buddhism. Korean Buddhist Chogye order, 1995.
Lee, Florence C. *Facts about Ginseng: The Elixir of Life*. Hollym

International Corp., 1992.
Lee, Kyonghee. *Korean Culture: Legacies and Lore*. The Korean Herald, 1995. Interesting account of traditional crafts and the people keeping them alive.
Lee, O Young. *Korea in its Creation*. Design House Publishers, 1994. Poetic writings on everyday artifacts of traditional Korean culture.
Mason, David A. *Spirit of the Mountains: Korea's San Shin and Traditions of Mountain-Worship*. Hollym International Corp., 1999.
Meijer, Maarten. *What's so good about Korea, Maarten?* Hyunam-sa, 2005. An affectionate look at Korea's culture and people by a long-term resident.
Stickler, John & Stickler, Soma Han. *Land of Morning Calm: Korean Culture Then and Now*. Shen's Books, 2003. After a brief introduction to Korea's geography and history, this handsome book spotlights one aspect of the country's culture after another.
Vegdahl Hur, Sonja & Seunghwa Hur, Ben. *Korea (CultureShock)*. Marshall Cavendish, 2006. This book is packed with practical, accurate, and enjoyable information to help you find your way and feel at home in South Korea.
Winchester, Simon. *Korea: A Walk Through the Land of Miracles*. Harper Perennial, 2005. A British writer walks the length of the country in 1988; with a postscript written in 2004.
Yoon, Seo-seok. *Festive Occasions:*

The Customs in Korea – The Spirit of Korean Cultural Roots. Ehwa Women's University Press, 2008.

Korean Food

Chang, Sun-young. *A Korean Mother's Cooking Notes*. Tuttle, 1997.
Kim, Young-hee. *Korean Cooking Made Easy*. Discovery Media, 2006.
Lee, Chun Ja, et al. *The Book of Gimchi*. Korean Overseas and Information Service, 1998.
Millon, Marc & Kim. *Flavours of Korea: With Stories and Recipes from a Korean Grandmother's Kitchen*. Trafalgar Square, 1991.
Samuels, Debora & Chung, *Taekyung. The Korean Table: From Barbecue to Bibimbap: 100 Easy-To-Prepare Recipes*. Tuttle, 2008.

History and Politics

Alexander, Bevin. *Korea: The First War we Lost*. Hippocrene Books, 1997.
Bird, Isabella. Routledge, 1985. *Korea and Her Neighbours*. Reprint of this thoroughly readable classic first published in 1897.
Choi, Sook Nyul. *The Year of Impossible Goodbyes*. Houghton Mifflin Publishing, 1992. Popular children's book (grade 6+) about the trials and tribulations of a young girl in North Korea at the end of World War II.

BELOW: Korean chess.

ABOVE: the view from the DMZ.

Cumings, Bruce. **Korea's Place in the Sun: A Modern History**. (revised). W. W. Norton & Co. Inc. 2005. Chronicle of modern Korea focusing on various aspects of the country's turbulent 20th-century history.

Duus, Peter. **The Abacus and the Sword: The Japanese Penetration of Korea 1895–1910**. University of California Press 1995.

Hamel, Hendrik. **Hamel's Journal and a Description of the Kingdom of Korea: 1653–1666**. Royal Asiatic Society, Korea Branch, 1998. First in-depth account by a European.

Haboush, JaHyun Kim (translator). **The Memories of Lady Hyegyong: The Autobiographical Writings of a Crown Princess of Eighteenth-Century Korea**. University of California Press, 1996.

Ilyon; Ha Tae Hung (translator). **Samguk Yusa: Legends and History of the Three Kingdoms of Ancient Korea**. Yonsei University Press, 1972. The first (extant) Korean history.

Kim, Elizabeth. **Ten Thousand Sorrows: The Extraordinary Journey of a Korean War orphan**. Doubleday, 2000.

Oberderfer, Don. **The Two Koreas: A Contemporary History**. Perseus Books Group, 2002. Overview of modern Korea, with regional tensions and the role of outside powers.

Oppenheim, Robert. **Kyongju Things: Assembling Place**. University of Michigan, 2008. Interesting discussion of Gyeongju as a historical and cultural center, with connections to the current modern world.

Yi, Sunshin; translated by Ha, Tae Hung. **Najung Ilgi: War Diary of Admiral Yi Sun Shin**. Yonsei University Press, 1977. Diary of Korea's naval hero of the Japanese invasion of 1597.

Yoon, Inshil Choe (translator). **Yi Junghwans's Daengniji: The Korean Classic for Choosing Settlements**. University of Sydney East Asian Series, Number 12, 1998. A classic 18th-century Korean geography.

Send Us Your Thoughts

We do our best to ensure the information in our books is as accurate and up to date as possible. The books are updated on a regular basis using local contacts, who painstakingly add, amend, and correct as required. However, some details (such as telephone numbers and opening times) are liable to change, and we are ultimately reliant on our readers to put us in the picture.

We welcome your feedback, especially your experience of using the book "on the road." Maybe we recommended a hotel that you liked (or another that you didn't), or you came across a great bar or new attraction we missed.

We will acknowledge all contributions, and we'll offer an Insight Guide to the best letters received.

Please write to us at:
**Insight Guides
PO Box 7910
London SE1 1WE**
Or email us at:
insight@apaguide.co.uk

Fiction

Carpenter, Frances. **Tales of a Korean Grandmother**. Tuttle, 1972.

Junghyo, Ahn. **Silver Stallion: A Novel in Korea**. Soho Press, 1993. A boy and his mother struggle to survive in their village occupied during the Korean war.

Lee, Chang-rae. **A Gesture Life**. Riverhead, 2000. A look at the horrors of Korean "Comfort Women."

Lee, Chang-rae. **The Surrendered**. Riverhead, 2010. The casualties of refugees of the Korean War.

O'Rourke, Kevin (translator). **Ten Korean Short Stories**. Yonsei University Press, 1981.

Watkins, Yoko Kawashima. **So Far from the Bamboo Grove**. Morrow, William, 1994. A fictional/biographical story of a Japanese girl in Korea after World War II, written for a young audience.

Zong, Insob. **Folk Tales from Korea.** Hollym International Corp., 1982.

Other Insight Guides

Over 190 titles in the acclaimed Insight Guides series cover every continent. Titles in the East Asia region include *Japan, Tokyo, China, Southern China, Beijing, Shanghai, Taiwan*, and *Hong Kong*.

Insight Fleximaps combine clear, detailed cartography with essential travel information.

The laminated finish makes the maps durable, weatherproof and easy to fold. Titles include *Seoul, Tokyo, Beijing, Shanghai*, and *Hong Kong*.

ART AND PHOTO CREDITS

4 Corners 247/T, 301
AFP/Getty 43
Alamy 82/R, 206
Emil Alfter 220
Ian Armstrong 7/MR, 270
Heather Angel 21/L
Natasha Babaian 95
Craig Brown 4/T, 60, 68, 76, 92, 145/R, 172/T, 182, 221, 241, 255, 260
Nedra Chung Collection 50
Chosun Westin 282
Corbis 44, 53, 147, 164/T, 165
Tom Coyner 152
Greg Davis 30, 104/105, 166, 274
The East West Center, Honolulu 28/L
Mary Evans 24/R
Alain Evrard 63
Michael Freeman 123, 143
Fotolia 163
From The Voyage of HMS Alceste 31
Getty Images 25/T, 52/LT
Lydia Goold Verchoyle 55/R
Andrea M Gross 2/B, 4/BL, 97, 172, 213/T
Blaine Harrington 73, 91, 89, 146, 181/T, 216/T, 241/T
Istockphoto 7/TR
Museum of Yamato Bunkakan, Nara, Japan, courtesy of A. Yoshida 80
National Museum of Korea 26
The National Museum of Korea & The Center for Korean Studies, University of Hawaii 86
Pictures Colour Library 276
Katherine Karnow 90, 94, 134/L, 158, 160/T, 269
Korea National Tourism Corporation 1, 5/T, 6/7, 7/TM, 9/T, 20, 21, 29, 62, 77, 122, 126, 136, 144, 150, 151/T, 153, 154, 155/T, 159, 171, 173, 175/T, 177, 182/T, 183/L, 193/T, 194/R , 199/T,

201/T, 202, 207, 209, 210, 218, 219, 221, 226, 230, 231/B, 238, 239, 242, 243, 258, 260/T, 261, 263/T, 266, 273/T, 283, 284/T, 286
Lee Chan-jae Collection 34, 35
Leonard Lueras 36, 157, 170, 176, 177/T, 214, 225, 271
Lyle Lawson 45
APA / Tom Le Bas 116/T, 132/T,
Samuel Moffett Collection 33, 35, 75/R
Popperphoto 39
Mi Seitelman 162L
APA / Chris Stowers 2/3, 6B/MR/ TL, 7BL/BR/ML, 8B/ML/TR, 9B/ML, 10/11, 12/13, 14/15, 16, 17B/T, 18, 19, 22, 23, 41, 46/47, 48, 49, 51, 54L/R, 55L, 56, 57, 58, 59, 61, 64, 65, 69, 70, 71, 72, 74, 75/L, 78, 79, 81, 83, 84/R, 93, 96, 99, 100/101, 102/103, 106, 107/T, 110, 111BL/BR/T, 114, 115, 116L/R, 117, 118, 119/T, 120/T, 121, 124L/R, 125/T, 127B/T, 128L/R, 129, 131L/R, 133, 134L, 135/T, 137/T, 138, 139, 142, 145L, 147T, 148/T, 149L/T, 150T, 156/T, 160L/R, 161, 162R/T, 167, 168, 169, 170T, 171T, 174/T, 178, 179, 180, 183R, 188, 189B/M/T, 190, 191, 194L/T, 195L/R, 196L/R, 197, 198, 199, 200, 201, 202/T, 203/T, 209/T, 211/T, 212L/R, 213, 215/T,216, 217, 218T, 219T, 224/T, 226/T, 227L/R, 228L/R, 229/T, 231/T, 234, 235, 236, 237L/R, 240/T, 241T, 244/245, 246, 247B, 248, 249, 251/T, 252L/R, 253L/R, 254/T, 256/T, 257, 259L/R/T, 262, 267, 269T, 270/T, 272, 273, 277, 278/T, 279, 280, 281, 287/T, 290, 291, 292, 295, 296, 297, 298, 304/T, 305, 306, 307
TIPS Images 122/T
Topfoto 25/L, 40, 42, 82/L
The US Army Archives 36, 37

Werner Forman Archive 24/L, 27, 28/R, 85

PHOTO FEATURES

66/67 **Craig Brown** 66/67,66ML/ MR, **Korea National Tourism Corporation** 66BL/BR, 67ML/TR, **AP Chris Stowers** 66TL, 67BL/TR

88/89 **Kim Chu-ho 88RM, Blaine Harrington** 88/89, **Craig Brown** BL/BR/TL, 89BM/BR/TR, **Korea National Tourism Corporation** 89BL

140/145 **All Pictures APA Chris Stowers**

184/185 **All Pictures APA Chris Stowers except Korea National Tourism Corporation** 184BR

204/205 **APA Chris Stowers** 204/205, 204TL, 205BL/BR/TR, **Korea National Tourism Corporation** 204BR, 205B/M

232/233 **Korea National Tourism Corporation** 232/233, 233ML/TR, **Topfoto** 232BL, **Werner Forman** 232BR, **Ancient Architecture Collection** 233BL, **Scala Archives** 233MB,

264/265 **Craig Brown** 264/265, **Taepyongyang (Pacific) Co** 264TL, 265TR, **APA Chris Stowers** 264BL/ BR/M, **Korea National Tourism Corporation** 265BL/BR

Map production: original cartography Colourmap Scanning Ltd

Production: Linton Donaldson

INDEX

Numbers in bold refer to principal entries

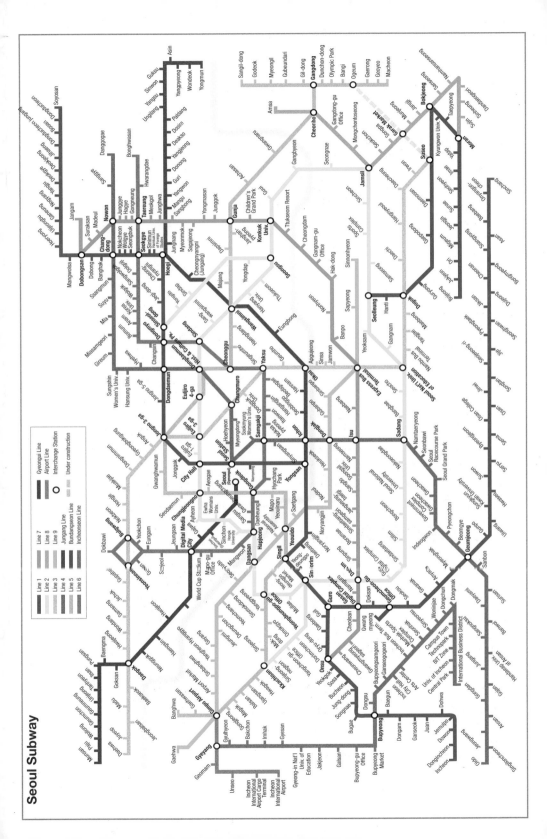

Seoul Subway